TITLE TO TERRITORY IN INTERNATIONAL LAW

Title to Territory in International Law

A Temporal Analysis

JOSHUA CASTELLINO
National University of Ireland, Galway, Republic of Ireland
and
STEVE ALLEN
Brunel University, UK

With special contribution on indigenous peoples from
Jérémie Gilbert

Maîtrise (Paris X) LLM, (Galway) Candidate, PhD, Republic of Ireland

This publication was grant-aided by the Publications Fund of The National
University of Ireland, Galway, Republic of Ireland

ASHGATE

Published by
Dartmouth Publishing Company
Ashgate Publishing Limited
Gower House
Croft Road
Aldershot
Hants GU11 3HR
England

Ashgate Publishing Company
Suite 420
101 Cherry Street
Burlington, VT 05401-4405
USA

Ashgate website: http://www.ashgate.com

British Library Cataloguing in Publication Data
Castellino, Joshua
    Title to territory in international law : a temporal
    analysis. - (Law, social change and development)
    1. Territory, National - History 2. International law
    I. Title II. Allen, Steve
    341.4'2'09

Library of Congress Control Number: 2001099631

ISBN 0 7546 2224 X

Typeset in Times by J. L. and G. A. Wheatley Design, Aldershot
Printed and bound in Great Britain by MPG Books Ltd, Bodmin, Cornwall

Contents

List of Treaties

GAOR 2625 (XXV) 1970

Geneva Convention on the Continental Shelf 1958

Genocide Convention 1950

Helsinki Final Act 1975

International Convention for the Elimination of All Forms of Racial Discrimination, 660 UNTS 195 1965

International Covenant on Civil and Political Rights 1966

International Covenant on Economic, Social and Cultural Rights, 1966

International Union of American Republics (1890)

Molotov–Ribbentrop Pact – Treaty of Non-Aggression between Germany and the Soviet Union, Secret Additional Protocol 23 August 1939 in Documents of German Foreign Policy 1918–45

Montevideo Convention on the Rights and Duties of States (1933)

OAU Assembly of Heads of State and Government 1964, res. 16(1)

Optional Protocol of the ICCPR, G.A. res. 2200A (XXI), 21 UN GAOR Supp. (No. 16) at 59, UN Doc. A/6316 (1966), 999 UNTS 302, entered into force, 23 March 1976

Organisation of American States (1948)

Pact for the Preservation of Peace 1865

Pact of Union and Defensive Alliance 1865

Panama Congress of 1826

Peace of Westphalia 1648

Peace Treaty of 1883 (Chile and Peru), *AJIL* 20(3) (1926) 614–19

Peace Treaty of 1904 between Peru and Chile, *AJIL* 21(1) [Supplement: Official Documents] (1927) 11–15

Proposed American Declaration on the Rights of Indigenous Peoples, approved by the IACHR on 26 February 1997, at its 1333rd session, 95th Regular Session, published in Annual Report of the IACHR (1996), p. 633

Spanish–Portuguese Boundary Treaty 1777

Statute of the International Court of Justice (appended to the UN Charter 1945)

Treaty of Arbitration 1890

Treaty of Confederation of February 1848

Treaty of Münster 1648

Treaty of Paris 1814

Treaty of Peace and Friendship of 1856 and 1859 (Brazil and United Provinces of the River Plate)

Treaty of Peace, Friendship, Commerce and Navigation 1832 and Additional and Explanatory Convention of 1833 (Chile and USA)

Treaty of Peace, 22 Sept. 1829, (Colombia and Peru), art. V, 16, 19 British and Foreign State Papers 1242, 1243 (1831)

Treaty of Quadruple Alliance of Chaumont 1814

Treaty of Tordesillas 1494 (Spain and Portugal)

List of Cases

Admissions case, ICJ Reports (1948) 57

Aegean Sea continental shelf (Greece *v.* Turkey) (1976–78), ICJ Reports (1976) 3

Ahmodu Tijani *v.* Secretary of State of South Nigeria [1921] 2 AC 399 (PC)

Arbitral Award of 31 July 1989 (Guinea-Bissau *v.* Senegal) (1989–91), ICJ Reports (1995)

Arbitral Award of the Swiss Federal Council of 24th March 1922 concerning boundary questions between Colombia and Venezuela, UN RIAAI 228

Arbitration of the boundary dispute between the Republics of Costa Rica & Panama provided by the Convention between Costa Rica and Panama of March 17th 1910, AJIL 8 (4) (1914) 913–41

Beagle Channel arbitration (1977) 52 ILR 11

Blackburn *v.* Attorney General [1971] 1 WLR 1037

British Guiana–Venezuela arbitration, (1899) British and Foreign State Papers, 87, pp. 1061–107

Calder *et al. v.* Attorney-General of British Columbia (1973) 34 DLR (3d) 145

Case concerning Kasikili/Sedudu Island (Botswana/Namibia) 13 December 1999 <http://www.icj-cij.org/icjwww/idocket/ibona/ibonaframe.htm>

Case concerning the continental shelf (Libyan Arab Jamahiriya/Malta) 3 June 1985, ICJ Reports (1985) 13

Case concerning the continental shelf (Tunisia/Libyan Arab Jamahiriya) 24 February 1982, ICJ Reports (1982) 37

Case concerning the frontier dispute (Burkina Faso/Republic of Mali) ICJ Reports (1986) 554

Case concerning the denunciation of the Sino-Belgium Treaty of 1865, PCIJ Series C., no. 16, vol. 1: 52

Case concerning the land and maritime boundary between Cameroon and Nigeria (Cameroon *v.* Nigeria) 15 March 1996, ICJ Reports (1998) <http://www.icj-cij.org/icjwww/idocket/icn/icnjudgment/icn_ijudgment_980611_frame.htm>

Case concerning the land, island and maritime frontier dispute (El Salvador *v.* Honduras; Nicaragua intervening) ICJ Reports (1992) 351

Case concerning sovereignty over certain frontier land (Belgium/Netherlands) 20 June 1959, ICJ Reports (1959) 209 <http://www.icj-cij.org/icjwww/idecisions/isummaries/ibnlsummary590620.htm>

Lubicon Lake Band (Bernard Ominiyak) *v.* Canada (No. 167/1974) UN Doc. A/45/ 40, vol. I , p. 1 (1990)

Maritime delimitation and territorial questions between Qatar and Bahrain (Qatar *v.* Bahrain) (1991–2001)
    <http://www.icj-cij.org/icjwww/idocket/iqb/iqbframe.htm>
Maritime delimitation between Nicaragua and Honduras in the Caribbean Sea (Nicaragua *v.* Honduras) (1999)
    <http://www.icj-cij.org/icjwww/idocket/iNH/iNHframe.htm>
Maritime delimitation in the area between Greenland and Jan Mayen (Denmark *v.* Norway) (1988–93)
    <http://www.icj-cij.org/icjwww/Icases/igjm/igjmframe.htm>
Minquiers and Ecrehos case (France *v.* UK), ICJ Reports (1953) 47
MiqMaq Tribal Society *v.* Canada (No. 205/1986) UN Doc. A/47/40, p. 213

Nationality Decrees case, PCIJ Series C., no. 16, vol. 1: 52
North Sea continental shelf (Federal Republic of Germany/Denmark) (1967–9), ICJ Reports (1969) 3
Nyali Ltd *v.* AG [1956] 1 QB 1

Oil Platforms (Islamic Republic of Iran *v.* United States of America) (1992–)
    <http://www.icj-cij.org/icjwww/idocket/iop/iopframe.htm>
Ol Le Njogo and Others *v.* AG (1913) 5 EALR 70

R. *v.* Adams, 3 October 1996 3 S.C.R.
R. *v.* The Baganda Cotton Company (1930) 4 ULR 34
R. *v.* the Earl of Crewe, ex parte Sekgome (CA) [1910] 2 KB 576
R. *v.* Côté, 3 SRC (1996) 139–98
R. *v.* Gladstone, 21 August 1996 2 S.C.R.
R. *v.* NTC Smokehouse, 21 August 1996 2 S.C.R.
R. *v.* Sparrow (1990) 70 DLR (4th) 289 (SCC)
R. *v.* Van Der Peet, 2 SCR (1996) 507
Rann of Kutch arbitration (1968) 50 ILR 407

Sara *et al. v.* Finland, Communication No. 511/1992, UN GAOR, 52nd Sess., UN Doc. CCPR/C/58/D/511/1992
Sobhuza II *v.* Miller [1926] AC 518 (PC)
Sovereignty over Pulau Litigan and Pulau Sipadan (Indonesia/Malaysia) (1998–)
    <http://www.icj-cij.org/icjwww/idocket/iinma/iinmaframe.htm>

Tee-Hit-Ton Indians *v.* United States, 348 U.S. 272 (1995)

Abbreviations

Afr.JIL	African Journal of International Law
AJIL	American Journal of International Law
APSR	American Political Science Review
APJHRL	Asia-Pacific Journal on Human Rights and the Law
AYIL	Asian Yearbook of International Law
Aus.JIL	Australian Journal of International Law
BYIL	British Yearbook of International Law
CJTL	Columbia Journal of Transnational Law
CLJ	Cambridge Law Review
ERS	Ethnic and Racial Studies
EJIL	European Journal of International Law
EPL	European Journal of Public Law
EAS	Eur-Asia Studies
FJIL	Fordham Journal of International Law
GYIL	German Yearbook of International Law
HLR	Harvard Law Review
HRQ	Human Rights Quarterly
IA	International Affairs
ICJ	International Court of Justice
ICLQ	International & Comparative Law Quarterly
ILM	International Legal Materials
ILB	Indigenous Law Bulletin
ILR	International Law Reports
Int. Aff	International Affairs
IO	International Organisation
IR	International Relations
ISIA	Irish Studies in International Affairs
JAS	Journal of African Studies
JCH	Journal of Contemporary History
JIA	Journal of International Affairs
JP	Journal of Politics
LQR	Law Quarterly Review
MJIS	Millennium Journal of International Studies
MULR	Melbourne University Law Review
NLR	New Law Review
NILR	Netherlands International Law Review

OJLS	Oxford Journal of Legal Studies
PCIJ	Permanent Court of International Justice
RIAA	Reports of International Arbitral Awards
TLJ	Turku Law Journal
TLCP	Transnational Law and Contemporary Problems
SYIL	Soviet Yearbook of International Law
Va.J.Int'l	Virginia Journal of International Law
VJTL	Vanderbildt Journal of Transnational Law
WP	World Politics
YLJ	Yale Law Journal
YJIL	Yale Journal of International Law

Introduction

One of the foundations for modern statehood is the assumption that a state consists of a defined territory. It is through this definition of fixed state territories and the subsequent allegiance between those territories and the individual or group of individuals that inhabit it that room is created for an individual within modern international law. Thus 'international society' comprises individuals and groups existing within sovereign states who are meant to gain legitimacy for their status in international law by virtue of being part of a sovereign state. Whilst this concept is being eroded to a certain extent by developments within international criminal law that seek to place onus on the individual away from the confines of his/her state, for the most part the concept of nationality remains central to personal identity within the international system. While it can be argued that notions of democratic governance are increasing (Franck 1992) even this democracy has to be expressed within the confines of an identifiable territorial state for it to gain international legitimacy. A fundamental flaw in this analysis of the growth of democracy and human rights norms lies in the denial of the right to land, which has been recognized as the first human right in the International Covenants of 1966.[1] In the context of the negotiation of those two covenants it was determined that to be able to enjoy any other political, civil, economic, social and cultural rights it was imperative first that a people had the right to determine their political destiny (see generally McGoldrick 1991, *The Human Rights Committee: Its Role in the Development of the ICCPR* (Oxford: Clarendon, 1991)). Framed positively this right nonetheless was conceived as applying to colonial peoples who were encouraged to shed the yoke of colonialism and were guaranteed international assistance in the process.[2] This right of self-determination includes not only the right of a people to determine their own fate but also to be able to exercise full control over their own natural resources.[3] What was not clarified, however, were the parameters of 'peoplehood', and although the right was interpreted in the context of colonialism, no attempts were made to delineate the nuances of such 'peoplehood'. The result was that the decolonization process that was already underway received further legal validation and new states came into being to become full participating members of

---

[1] Joint art. 1 of the International Covenant for Civil and Political Rights 1966 and International Covenant on Economic, Social and Cultural Rights 1966.

[2] As given by the 1970 Declaration, see Castellino (2000a: 34–42).

[3] Article 1(2) of the covenants states: 'All peoples may, for their own ends, freely dispose of their natural wealth and resources without prejudice to any obligations arising out of international economic co-operation, based upon the principle of mutual benefit, and international law. In no case may a people be deprived of its own means of subsistence.'

1

the United Nations system of sovereign states. However, at no point in this process was it deemed necessary to set down the parameters of the 'people' entitled to gain self-determination, since that 'people' was simplistically determined as being those that inhabited a unit that pertained to a colony during the colonization era. Thus decolonization merely privatized existing colonial entities by taking the reins of power from the colonial ruler and handing them instead to an indigenous ruler without ascertaining the consent of the people within that unit.

This definition of the sovereign state remains the foundation stone of the modern international legal system and despite the growth in respect for and recognition of other entities in international law, it still functions as the primary actor in international law and politics. In recognition of this the United Nations and international law have validated the right of states and enshrined it in art. 2(7) of the UN Charter, which states that:

> Nothing contained in the present Charter shall authorize the United Nations to intervene in matters which are essentially within the domestic jurisdiction of any state or shall require the Members to submit such matters to settlement under the present Charter; but this principle shall not prejudice the application of enforcement measures under Chapter VII.

This right to territorial sovereignty, primarily in place to prevent violation and dominance of one state by either another or an international organization, has had a salient effect on the issues being examined in this book. Despite the statement of art. 1 of the covenants mentioned above there is no international law governing the right to land; rather it is an issue that is considered to occur exclusively within the remit of a state's 'domestic jurisdiction'. While other manifestations of state sovereignty have begun to be eroded, the decision with respect to the governance and status of territory within a state is still almost exclusively the preserve of state power. Thus despite art. 1 of the human rights covenants being considered a prerequisite to the fulfilment of other human rights, the right to land as contained implicitly within that article remains outside the recourse of modern international law. Rather, a package of legal doctrines and principles can be identified within international law which seek to restrict the manner and extent to which order can be violated. The very nature of a territorial claim, being harmful to order, thus means that it is one of the implicit sacrifices made in favour of this order. This book seeks to examine two such important doctrines and principles, namely that of *uti possidetis* and the accompanying principle of *terra nullius*. While both concepts are borrowed from Roman law (Jolowicz and Nicholas 1972), the re-statement of the former at specific instances within international legal history has established it as a doctrine that continues to have resonance on international law governing territory. This doctrine has been used in numerous settings, as will be examined in the context of this book, and each restatement seems to increase its sphere of operation. One of the prime purposes of this book is thus to question that widening application by analysing its original setting, specific evolution and subsequent impact and effect on peoples and territories in international law. The principle of *terra nullius* differs from *uti possidetis* in that it is no longer considered a feasible and reasonable doctrine for all practical purposes. Initially employed to designate territory that was 'empty' and therefore free for colonization, it gradually took on racist overtones and until recently was determined to refer to territory on which people were not socially or politically organized.[4] Thus its meaning had clearly evolved to suggest that the territory in itself did not have to be empty or void of inhabitants. Rather a territory could still come within the concept of *terra nullius* if the people that inhabited it were not socially or politically organized. This subtle change from its original meaning enabled the acquisition of much land in international legal history. In addition, once this land had been acquired, boundary lines were then drawn to demarcate ownership, and via the doctrine of *uti possidetis* those boundary lines have come to be recognized as the building blocks of the international community of states and the basis on which the state right to territorial integrity, identified above, is awarded. Thus the cumulative effect of the two doctrines has been to create, within a short period of time, fixed and rigid notions within which any dialogue based on ownership of territory has to occur. To further validate this creation, international law brings into play the rule governing intertemporal law by which actions committed in a previous era are buffered from scrutiny against more modern norms and principles. Thus while the woes of colonialism are well documented the international legal system is precluded from raising legal questions about the manner in which colonialism functioned. What this book seeks to do is to examine the temporal setting against which these specific doctrines have evolved, in situations concerning the title to territory in international law. The prime assumption for this project is that if intertemporal law protects the analysis of past actions against present standards, then it is important, at the very least, to be able to analyse them against contemporary standards. With this in mind this book sets out the development of the principles highlighted here, examining the historical and cultural setting against which they were applied, reapplied and reinterpreted. In addition it suggests that this examination reveals principles of customary international law that could arguably be used to demonstrate that the rule of intertemporal law itself is a mere political handmaiden to the politics of power of the imperial states who set out on a worldwide conquest of territory. The fact that the victims of this conquest form nearly 60 per cent of the global population accentuates the need to highlight the situation and to prevent blind acceptance of past manipulations of a legal system that was created by, dominated by and imposed by imperial states upon the rest of the world. If modern trends towards the internationalization of the discourse are to be accepted then international law must begin by examining its own structures and institutions to determine their objectivity.

---

[4] *Western Sahara case*, ICJ Reports (1975) 12.

In terms of human rights law the right to land is not framed directly as one of entitlement to property, but rather as a secondary manifestation of a general right to self-determination. The notion of self-determination continues to be central to the interpretation of the right to land and in calling for self-determination proponents of the concept base their arguments on the rhetoric emanating from the 1960 and 1970 declarations that furthered the cause of decolonization.[5] However, while both these General Assembly resolutions stress the right to self-determination, they do not determine the manner or the parameters in which this process could take place. While Resolution 1541 (XV), also passed in 1960, does seek to provide substance to the issue it merely establishes that self-determination may involve any of the following three options:

a)   Constitution as a sovereign independent state
b)   Free association with an existing independent state
c)   Integration with an existing independent state.

Thus, once again, it assumes the territory of the state as being the unit that seeks this self-determination, thus setting down the challenge against Judge Dillard's later statement in the *Western Sahara* case that 'it is for the people to determine the fate of the territory and not the territory the fate of the people'.[6] If the unit that will determine its fate is accepted as the post-colonial entity then clearly it is the territory that is determining the fate of the people rather than vice versa. This determination of the fate of the demarcated territories by various post-colonial peoples led to the creation of the plethora of states that came out of the decolonization process in the UN era. Although these territories contained peoples with grave differences, they were encouraged to forge a Westphalian-type sovereign state at the altar of which their so-deemed 'narrow' differences were to be sacrificed (Deutsch and Foltz 1963). The grand idea that justified this action was that the cosmopolitan post-colonial sovereign state was ultimately to the benefit of order. However, less than 50 years later the problems of that difficult birth have begun to resurface and as a result the self-determination rhetoric, problematic at best, has begun to make a re-appearance in struggles that once more threaten peace and security. Central to these phenomena, it could be argued, is the problematic link between the peoples and the territories over which they believe they have predominance; and it is in claiming that this predominance be recognized that some of the modern so–called 'ethnic' conflicts are sown.

While the Badinter Commission looked into one such occurrence of ethnically induced conflict, it needs to be stressed that this was away from the post-colonial

---

[5] GAOR 1514 (XV) and 2625 (XXV).
[6] *Western Sahara case*, ICJ Reports (1975) 12 at 116–22 (Dis. op. of Judge H. Dillard); see also Higgins (1983).

setting discussed above. However, in applying principles that were developed in the decolonization setting; it sought to argue that the international legal responses to the breakdown of order are the same irrespective of the context in which it occurs. Indigenous peoples, also affected by the problematic interpretation of the right to territory, have also seen dispossession of their lands based on similar erroneous and often self-serving interpretations of existing legal norms. Thus this book aims to set out the principles of international law governing the title to territory and seeks to analyse them in their respective temporal contexts. The importance of the need for clarity on these issues can be seen in the growing intra-state violence wherein groups seek negotiation of rights of self-governance. With this in mind the book is divided into seven chapters to unveil the manner in which the norm of *uti possidetis* developed. While focusing on this particular doctrine it also seeks to shed some light on other related issues that pertained to the development of the doctrine, such as the principle of *terra nullius*, that of the inter-temporal rule of law, the notion of regional customary law and the method of arbitration.

1 The Doctrine of *Uti Possidetis*
Crystallization of Modern Post-Colonial Identity

'International law' has come a long way since the Spanish withdrawal from Latin America (Pastor 1992). Currently, however, the discourse still relies heavily on a number of principles that were framed in response to that specific situation. One such legal tenet that remains central to the current system is the doctrine of *uti possidetis*. This doctrine, an interdict from Roman law, was formulated during the exit of the Spanish from Latin America (Picon-Salas 1962; see also Boggs 1980: 74–94). Based on the concept of 'as you possess, so you possess', it treats the acquisition of territory as given, with no subsequent territorial adjustments allowable without prior consent of the parties (Shaw 1996). The application of this principle enabled orderly withdrawal of the Spanish from Latin America, leaving behind entities relatively secure against separatist forces and avaricious neighbours. During the era of decolonization, this norm was extensively used by the colonial powers as they withdrew from territories in Africa and Asia (Ratner 1996; Kaikobad 1983). The application of this norm today is highly problematic for a variety of reasons, the chief amongst these being the fact that it crystallized identities in nearly 80 per cent of modern states, based on grounds that are often contentious and questionable. Post-decolonization, these artificially created entities have been exhorted, in the name of coherent 'national identity',[1] to create for themselves national myths and legends in the face of 'post-modern tribalism' (Franck 1993: 3) that seeks redefinition of parameters of statehood based on concepts such as ethnicity. However, in many instances these myths and legends have not proved adequate in peacefully sustaining the post-colonial state[2] and, as a result, separatist violence is on the increase with the international legal community being reduced to bystander status while the political interests of powerful states dictate the unfolding of events.

This book examines some of the legal tenets pertinent to this process in a bid to highlight the critical moment at which the Roman law interdict of *uti possidetis* was transposed into international law and thus came to be the cornerstone for the

---

[1] For literature that examines the nature of the post-colonial state see Anderson (1993), Camilleri and Falk (1992), Connolly (1991), Constantinou (1998), Davidson (1992), Deutsche and Foltz (1963), Emerson (1960) and Grovogui (1996).

[2] For instance, witness the events leading up to the attempted secession of Biafra from Nigeria (Saxena 1978). The successful secession of Eritrea from Ethiopia is also relevant to this discussion, see Gayim (1995: 439).

maintenance of the system of sovereign states. With this objective in mind, this particular chapter is committed to revealing the theoretical aspect of the modern doctrine of *uti possidetis* and towards this end is divided into four parts. The first part sets out the origins of the doctrine of *uti possidetis* in *jus civile*, and its meaning within international law (modern *jus gentium*). This issue will be revisited in examining the finer aspects of Roman law in later chapters. The second part focuses on the manner in which this principle was extended to the decolonization process in the middle of the last century. This section provides the foundations for further analysis in the specific chapters examining the acquisition and subsequent withdrawal from territory in Africa (Chapter 4), and the treatment of these issues in an international legal forum (Chapter 5). The third part critically examines the process by which the norm was then extended to the problematic break-ups of the Soviet Union, Yugoslavia and Czechoslovakia. This section provides the basis for the modern manifestation of the doctrine as examined in the last two chapters of this book. The final part of this chapter attempts to extrapolate the limitations of the doctrine in its original aim, that is the maintenance of order, and suggests that the doctrine fails to satisfy this limited aspiration.

The Roman Law Doctrine of *Uti Possidetis*

The doctrine of *uti possidetis* basically states that 'new States will come to independence with the same boundaries they had when they were administrative units within the territory or territories of a colonial power' (Shaw 1996: 97). The norm originates from *jus civile* in Roman law where it was a basic tenet of the Roman praetor, for promotion and maintenance of order.[3] Authors such as Mazrui (1975) would see this as problematic and perhaps suggest this as further evidence of the western and Christian origins of international law. This claim cannot be totally repudiated since the development of international law was located around states emerging in post-Westphalian Europe. Traditionally, international law considers as its origin the discourse of Hugo Grotius – *De Pacis Juris Bella* – written in the sixteenth century.[4] Grotius himself did not refer to the norm of *uti possidetis*, however his tacit support for it can be gleaned from his discourse, which suggests that he considered maintenance of order a prime requirement within international law (Higgins 1990: 267–80).[5]

---

[3] In the late Republic, the praetor *urbanus* was responsible for the administration of *jus civile* and the praetor *peregrinus* held the same position with regard to *jus gentium*. See generally Muirhead (1916).

[4] For a general discussion on the influence of Grotius on international relations, see Bull *et al.* (1990).

[5] This is notwithstanding the fact that Grotius expressly recognized the right to resistance (*jus resistendi ac secessionis*) for oppressed people; see Neuberger (1986: 4).

Hedley Bull, examining notions and concepts relating to order, suggested that order in social life consists of an arrangement of life that promotes certain goals and values. He lists three primary goals of all ordered societies: security against violence, an assurance of maintenance of promises or undertakings and stable possession of things (1995: 4). From this 'order' on an international level a pattern of activity can be extrapolated that sustains 'elementary and primary goals of the society of states or the international society' (ibid.). The goals of international society could thus be stated as being:

1   The preservation of the system
2   The maintenance of the sovereignty of states
3   Peace (that is absence of war)
4   The restriction of violence (ibid.).

With this in mind the doctrine of *uti possidetis* is placed ideally as a vital tool by which these aims can be satisfied at a time when a given society is particularly vulnerable. First, it preserves the system of sovereign states by projecting the nuances of sovereignty onto the forthcoming entity, thereby legitimizing the entity itself as well as validating further the system of sovereign states. Second, by declaring an emergent entity a sovereign state bound within the sanctity of its boundaries, it internally as well as externally contributes to the maintenance of that state. Third, by doctrinally eliminating internal and external challenges towards boundaries it arguably removes one of the main factors in the break-up of peace, and by performing this function it restricts the perpetration and spread of violence. Thus if Bull's analysis of order can be accepted then the doctrine of *uti possidetis* seems an ideal tool by which orderly transition of an entity from colonization to freedom could be effected.

The doctrine of *uti possidetis*, however, traces its roots directly to the *jus civile* norm of *uti possidetis ita possidetis* which forms the basis of the modern doctrine. This norm was a possessory interdict available to the praetor, primarily to prevent the 'disturbance of the existing state of possession of immovables as between two individuals' (Moore 1944: 328, quoted in Shaw 1996: 98). Translated, it reads, 'as you possess, so you possess'. Thus according to *jus civile*, the object of the interdict was to recognize the status quo in a given situation involving immovable property such as land. It was designed to protect existing arrangements of possession without regard to its merits. Nevertheless, possession had to be acquired from the other party *nec vi, nec clam, nec precario* (without force, secrecy or permission) (see Jolowicz and Nicholas 1972: 259; Muirhead 1916: 315–39). These restrictions on the acquisition of prescriptive claims in general were developed to ensure that the *de facto* possessor exercised his or her claim to the property as of right and was thereby open to challenge by other interested parties.

This is notable since when applied to international territory, the doctrine as we shall see in succeeding chapters, reduces a situation of conflict over territory to one that could take place between two individuals. In the course of this process it treats the issue of their dispute, that is the territory, as the *de facto* as well as *de jure* legal possession of the current occupier. In fact a feature of *uti possidetis* when applied to international disputes over territory is that it does not seek to differentiate between the *de facto* and the *de jure* conferring possessor rights, albeit temporary, upon de facto possession in the event of a dispute. This feature has important ramifications for modern international law, which will be examined in depth during the course of this book. However, suffice to emphasize the crisis of the original norm at this stage: it prevented further aggravation over a particular possession by simply assuming the title of the goods belonged to its current possessor. It thereby negated the case of the aspirant to possession. This translated into an international legal situation whereby territorial disputes between sovereigns were resolved by legalizing the possession of the *de facto* occupier. Thus, the occupier was allowed to continue to exercise sovereignty over it, ostensibly dismissing the claim of the aspirant as disruptive of the peace. This was clearly a departure from the Roman law diktat since under that system rather than discuss the claim of the aspirant it merely stopped the dispute until the claim could be analysed. In this sense it could be seen as a doctrine that kept the possessory aspect of the territory in abeyance while the aspirant's claim could be examined. During this process it legitimized continued occupation by the possessor. This change in nuance of the doctrine needs to be understood against the backdrop of the need for order. As discussed earlier, the international system is inclined towards the maintenance of order – a tenet of law that reflected the Grotian vision of modern *jus gentium*. This tenet is also manifest in the crucial argument that inevitably arises in considering issues of self-determination, namely the territorial integrity versus self-determination argument that has been explored in depth by many authors (Brilmeyer 1991: 177–202, Higgins 1983, Suzuki 1976). Thus, as far as *jus civile* was concerned, the conflict between two parties over a stated possession was resolved by recourse to the praetorian interdict thus enabling the status quo to be preserved, irrespective of the legal validity of the claims in issue, whilst the issues of the overall title remained in question.

With its firm emphasis on the maintenance of order the doctrine of *uti possidetis* provided modern international law with an ideal conduit to restrict conflict and allow consolidation of the *de facto* situation following hostilities. This was convenient as it enabled a simple conclusion of peace in a given situation without redress and re-assessment of the relative merits of each side. It had the added benefit of ignoring other sources of difference, for example tribal affiliations or social cohesion, which were more cumbersome in determining the demarcation of territory. This feature is starkly visible in the review of the jurisprudence that continues to emanate from the ICJ, in Chapter 5. Hence, translated into international law, the doctrine required that peace be achieved by a simple decision to allow the aggressor continued possession of territory gained by belligerent occupation, conquest or otherwise, and for the status quo to be maintained from that point onwards. Of course in practice this would lead to a continuously available process, which would ultimately legitimize violence and occupation by force. Thus a central restriction to the doctrine was the emphasis laid on the notion of the 'critical date' (Goldie 1963) or the point at which the territorial dimensions of an entity would be considered crystallized.[6] Thus it was believed that the doctrine of *uti possidetis* when combined with the notion of a rigid critical date would ultimately yield a process that would support the preconditions necessary for order.

The first manifestation of this doctrine in international law was in the Spanish withdrawal from Latin America.[7] This process witnessed the beginning of two distinct approaches to the interpretation and application of the doctrine. *'Uti possidetis juris'* referred to a legal boundary line based on legal title, as was the rule adopted by the successor states to the Spanish Empire. *'Uti possidetis de facto'*, on the other hand, was an interpretation based on factual possession maintained by Brazil, the successor to the Portuguese colony on the continent (Shaw 1996: 100). The idea of *de facto* possession as a factor first emerged only after the war of 1801 fought by Spain and France against Portugal. It was Brazil's contention that the war abrogated the Spanish–Portuguese treaty of 1777 delimiting the relevant boundaries, and marked a reversion to the original principle of *uti possidetis* in international law that simply accepted the territorial results of war and actual possession irrespective of how this was achieved.[8] The modern interpretation of the doctrine of *uti possidetis* seems to favour the Brazilian approach of *de facto* possession over any other system.[9] The blurring of the distinction between *de facto* and *de jure* is also significant here, since if *de facto* possession is temporarily accepted in the face of a legal challenge, this itself would make the original distinction irrelevant according to the manner in which the doctrine has been used in international law. This is classically manifested in the construction of problematic boundary regimes as will be examined further in this chapter.

The Principle extended to the Decolonization Process

Having been established with relative success in preventing significant bloodbaths during the Spanish withdrawal from Latin America, the norm was sought to be reinterpreted in the modern decolonization process. The centrality of the concept of order to the international system has already been emphasized (notably by Bull 1995). With the twin experiences of the world wars, the decolonization process was always likely to take place with the need for order being paramount (see Hannum 1980 and Rigo-Sureda 1973). There was always the fear that swift withdrawal of colonial powers

---

[6] *Case concerning the frontier dispute (Burkina Faso v. Republic of Mali)*, ICJ Reports (1986) 554 at 586.

[7] For a general discussion of the Spanish withdrawal from the Americas see Picon-Salas (1962) and Pastor (1992).

[8] *Minquiers and Ecrehos case (France v. United Kingdom)*, ICJ Reports (1953) 47 at 96–7 (sep. op. of Judge Caneiro).

[9] Nevertheless there is still some ambiguity on this point, see Naldi (1987).

would lead to anarchy within the entities. As a result the international community, led by the UN and the colonial powers themselves, reinterpreted the norm of self-determination within the caveat of order. The best way to do this was determined as allowing the transition process from colonialism to independence to go ahead, with the basic requirement that external boundaries remain intransigent. This requirement was explained by reference to the doctrine of *uti possidetis*. In this sense, it was claimed that the doctrine of *uti possidetis* merely respected the *de facto* situation that existed prior to the departure of the colonial ruler. Thus lines drawn by the previous occupier (that is the colonial power) were interpreted as being sacrosanct with no alterations allowed except with the consent of the newly emerging state. Since the nature of colonialism had not allowed for grooming of non-colonial successors primed for smooth transition of power, the newly emerging entities, it was believed, remained vulnerable to vested interests who it was feared might try to seize power on the departure of the colonial ruler. These groups, normally sub-state entities, had agendas that included renegotiation of territory on the basis of historic identities that had been submerged and decimated in the face of the colonial onslaught for territory. Neighbouring states too were often interested in this renegotiation, especially when they considered that their lands had been included by the colonial ruler in the territory of the newly independent state.[10] Thus, the belief was that emerging states would need support from the international community until they could gain confidence and experience in statecraft.

In the circumstances the norm of *uti possidetis* was thus perceived as being appropriate. In its chosen guise it was seen as being capable of preventing the renegotiation of controversial boundaries. Further, in negating other claimants to the territory of the new state, it guaranteed the new ruler exclusive jurisdiction over the full extent of the physical territory deemed as being the new state. Accordingly a ruler need not exercise *de facto* or effective control over the entire territory that would be considered part of his or her state. Rather, sovereignty could be his or hers for less[11] – namely the control of the armed forces, command of government bureaucracy, the treasury and central bank, foreign aid and the support of key ethnic leaders. It is argued that this 'emperical' state (Jackson 1992), functions effectively thanks to external guarantees from the international community that recognizes it as the *de jure* sovereign of the territory without any effort made to gauge the legitimacy and physical extent of such authority. As a result it would seem that the empirical state tends to be less extensive than its territorial jurisdiction, and therefore further biurs the difference between the *de jure* and the *de facto*. This also ensured that sub-state and other state parties were effectively deterred from trying to undermine the integrity of the new state. In this climate, the newly installed *indigenous* ruler could be certain that territories bequeathed by the colonial ruler would exist as a unit,

---

[10] For example, see the irredentist claims of Somalia and Morocco in Neuberger (1986).
[11] As pointed out by Jackson (1992) in examining the nature of the state in sub-Saharan Africa.

irrespective of any claims to the contrary. The doctrine, therefore, was a recognition that in the interests of order, a 'snapshot' of the territory at the moment of independence would have to be taken as fixed, thereby ensuring that development could be pursued from that point onwards. As stated by the International Court of Justice in the *Burkina Faso–Mali* case,

> the essence of the principle lies in its primary aim of securing respect for the territorial boundaries at the moment when independence is achieved. Such territorial boundaries may be no more than delimitation between different administrative divisions or colonies all subject to the same sovereign. In that case, the application of the principle of *uti possidetis* resulted in administrative boundaries being transformed into international frontiers in the full sense of the term.[12]

Thus rather than accept a critical date relevant to the territories concerned, it was interpreted as the date on which decolonization was effected. For a deeper understanding of how this norm came to be central to the international system of sovereign states it is necessary to trace its historical development.

Modern Development of the Norm in International Law

While *jus civile* only informs the modern norm, it is interesting to note that the restrictions prevalent under that regime have not been fully evident in its interpretation within modern international law. On the contrary, it is apparent that the original application of *uti possidetis* in international law legitimizes actual possession regardless of how it was achieved. In order to facilitate protection of the status quo, the burden of proof in interdictory proceedings under *jus civile* rested with the party currently out of possession, thus providing the *de facto* possessor with an inherent advantage. Although *uti possidetis* may have the effect of resolving a particular dispute, ordinarily it was an important interim measure in contested *vindicatio* proceedings to determine title (Jolowicz and Nicholas 1972: 259–70). Therefore the interdict was not directly concerned with the rightful title to property, rather it was an interim mechanism en route to resolving such a dispute.

During the process of colonization, the international norm appeared to legitimize the actual possession of the colonial powers. However, in *jus civile*, rightful title via *de facto* possession could only be acquired by a prescriptive claim of *usucapio* established in good faith (ibid.: 151–5). It thus seems that international law has been selective in its use of Roman law in this context. Further, certain authors doubt that there is any meaningful connection between the Roman law interdict and the modern norm of *uti possidetis* at all:

---

[12] See *Case concerning the frontier dispute (Burkina Faso* v. *Republic of Mali)*, ICJ Reports 1986) 554 at 586.

> Even so 'obvious' a loan from Roman law as the use of *uti possidetis* in the Latin American
> practice since the early nineteenth century is more indicative of the differences between this
> remedy in Roman law and its application on the inter-state level than of any supposed likeness
> between these institutions.
>
> (Schwarzenberger 1957: 309)

It is readily conceded that the modern operation of the norm does not conform to the operation of the possessory interdict under *jus civile*. However, it is suggested that the link is by way of principle rather than being merely nominal in form. Indeed it could be argued that the selective adoption of the interdict into international law actually supports the contention that the modern norm is not grounded in sound legal principle but is in fact more in keeping with a political instrument to legitimate possession.[13]

Further, critics of the 'automatic borrowing'[14] of *uti possidetis* from *jus civile* have perhaps not fully appreciated the reinterpretations of *uti possidetis* within international law itself. While major alterations were made to the doctrine in the African decolonization process, fundamental changes are also apparent in the Latin American context. It is apparent that the new states of Latin America arranged their boundaries with reference to *uti possidetis* in the knowledge that such arrangements did not necessarily amount to the final determination of the question of borders.[15] The creation of an elaborate arbitration procedure, as examined in Chapter 3, can be seen as further evidence of the developing consensus concerning the problematic nature of these boundaries. While the status of boundaries established by the new states would certainly have gained external validity with the passage of time, at the initial stage it appears that the application of *uti possidetis* did not automatically lead to the creation of permanent borders for all time. This evidence suggests that the Latin American experience may have been more in keeping with the spirit of the interdict than previously supposed (Kaikobad 1983: 124; Ratner 1996: 596–600; Naldi 1987: 893). Although, it was crucial to establish and maintain the territorial integrity of these ledgling states, it appears there was some recognition that once the upheavals of independence had been negotiated, the issue of boundaries could be revisited (Shaw 1996: 141–50; Kaikobad 1983: 128). However, since it has to be admitted that the wholesale revision of boundaries was almost certainly beyond the pale of geo-strategic politics of the time and that even minor readjustments were unlikely in practice, the

---

[13] See *Beagle Channel arbitration* (1977) 52 ILR 11 at 124–5.

[14] A phrase used to express the habitual derivation of international law concepts from Roman law; see Andrews (1978: 409).

[15] Ratner (1996: 594) cites the examples of the Definitive Treaty of Peace and Friendship, 8 November 1831, Bol.–Peru, art. XVI, 19 British and Foreign State Papers 1383 at 1387–8 (1834) ('such cessions may be reciprocally made, as may be necessary for an exact and natural demarkation [*sic*]'); Treaty of Peace, 22 Sept. 1829, Colom.–Peru, art. V, 16 British and Foreign State Papers at 1242, 1243 (1831).

value of this evidence seems purely doctrinal. Thus under *jus civile*, *uti possidetis* could be understood as being essentially a provisional issue that could result in permanent consequences. However, its reinterpretation in the Latin American context signalled a paradigm shift whereby it lost its overtly provisional status, but nonetheless had yet to be labelled with the sanctity of permanence. It is submitted that many of those who doubted the doctrinal connection had not fully considered the impact of the numerous revisions of *uti possidetis* at the hands of modern international law.

The development of the doctrine of *uti possidetis* when examined temporally and combined with the principle of self-determination throws up interesting results. The first series of events meriting analysis is the Creole action in Latin America which drew on these ideas in wresting independence from the Spanish (Anderson 1993: 56–9). In this case, the use of the doctrine revealed two prime advantages: it ruled out the concept of the territory being *terra nullius*[16] since this could leave it open to newer claimants and it also prevented immediate conflict among new states of the former empire. Also significant to that process was the creation of a conflict resolution mechanism that continues to have resonance (see Chapter 6).

Although conducive to orderly Spanish withdrawal from Latin America, this doctrine encountered numerous problems when extended to the process of decolonization in the middle of the twentieth century. This was due to the nature of the boundaries erected by colonial rulers.[17] Their demarcation and restriction of each other's influence in the continent had created artificial entities continent-wide (Pakenham 1991, Shaw 1986, McEwen 1971, Lindley 1926). While this was arguably also true in Latin America, the difference in Africa and Asia was in the nature of the 'peoples' seeking emancipation (Burkeholder and Johnson 1998: 304–29). The units left behind by colonial powers had little bearing to the history or geography of the region, often placing antagonistic tribes within a common boundary (Heraclides 1991, Asiwaju 1985). Thus the dilemma faced at decolonization was either to allow renegotiation of these boundaries along less problematic lines, or to simply accept the situation created, and pursue development without the risk of fragmentation (see Herbst 1989: 673, 678–85; Kapil 1966: 656, 660). This reasoning is particularly relevant to the origins of the norm highlighted above, where the situation was resolved by a decision taken at a given point in time and considered as settled in the interests of order. Thus, in the decolonization of Africa and (to a lesser extent) Asia it was decided to choose the departure of the colonial ruler as the point or 'critical date' after which the physical dimensions of the new state would be considered crystallized. This logic was accepted by the post-independence African leadership who readily extended the

---

[16] *Western Sahara case*, ICJ Reports (1975) 12 at 83–99 (sep. op of Judge Ammoun). See also Castellino (1999c).

[17] African territory was carved up between the European colonial powers. A notable example of this process is the Berlin West Africa Conference of 1885; see Alexandrowicz (1975) and, more generally, Gifford and Louis (1971: 167–220).

doctrine of *uti possidetis* to the African continent (expressing it in the language of the Cairo Declaration in 1964 – see generally Neuberger 1986 and Mazrui 1967), and gained further support in numerous international law cases.[18] The doctrine succeeded in keeping irredentist neighbours at bay while the fledgling state was allowed the opportunity to consolidate itself. Internally, this reminded minorities without political clout that, with the option of renegotiation of boundaries ruled out, they would need to seek recompense from within the state structure. It was hoped that this would encourage minorities to participate to a greater extent within the state, rather than seek disruptive and disorderly agendas geared towards separatism and secession (Thornberry 1991).

Problematic as it was in its application in African and Asian decolonization, the doctrine of *uti possidetis* came to be perceived as conducive to the 'order' that was particularly cherished by the UN-led system of sovereign states. The next step in its development came when international order was once again threatened by separatism. The end of the Cold War and subsequent unravelling of the centrally controlled socialist bloc countries of East and Central Europe saw forces of fragmentation, controlled centrally over decades, re-ignited. In the break-up of the Soviet Union and Yugoslavia, and the Velvet Divorce between the Slovak and Czech Republics, international law took the opportunity to reiterate the importance of the norm of *uti possidetis*.

The former Republic of Yugoslavia, comprising 22 regions, had been amalgamated into six republics under Tito. These republics corresponded closely to the pre-1918 historical boundaries, but left significant minorities within each administrative republic (Stojanovic 1996: 337; Radan 1994: 183). During the break-up of Yugoslavia between 1991 and 1992, the EC Arbitration Committee stressed the importance of the doctrine of *uti possidetis*:

> it is well established that, whatever the circumstances, the right to self-determination must not involve changes to existing frontiers at the time of independence (*uti possidetis juris*) except where the States concerned agree otherwise.[19]

The workings of the Arbitration Commission are analysed in detail in Chapter 6. At this stage it is sufficient to note that in the development of *uti possidetis* this statement from the EC Arbitration Commission is interesting for two reasons. First, it seems to present evidence for the acceptance of *uti possidetis* as a doctrine of legal value, and

---

[18] Also see *Rann of Kutch arbitration* (1968) 50 ILR 407, dis. op. of Judge Bebler; Dubai–Sharjah case, ILR, vol. 91 (1981) 543; *Case concerning the frontier dispute (Burkina Faso v. Mali)*, ICJ Reports (1986) 554; *Case concerning the land, island and maritime frontier dispute (El Salvador v. Honduras)*, ICJ Reports (1992) 351; *Case concerning the territorial dispute (Libyan Arab Jamahiriya v. Chad)*, ICJ Reports (1994) 6 (sep. op. of Judge Ajibola); see also Cukwurah (1967): 102–55, 190–9.
[19] (1992) 92 ILR 168.

is stated as an additional criterion for recognition. The tone of the statement also seems to suggest that the doctrine of *uti possidetis* has been readily accepted in state practice. This arguably presents the Asian and African decolonization process as being non-controversial and also seems to purport that in the short period of time that has elapsed since those events, *uti possidetis* may have entered into customary law. What makes this particularly problematic is the conception of the emperical state (Jackson 1992: 4). If this model could be accepted without question and as a matter of course,[20] it suggests that by the mere control of certain trappings of statehood on the departure of a colonial ruler, for instance control over the monopoly of power via the armed forces, a group of persons could seize power and set about creating customary international law. This model is only plausible if two grounds are satisfied. First, that such a process occurs in a number of states at the same time and, concurrently, that the international community accepts these entities as states and recognizes their actions as part of legal state practice, thereby ultimately leading to customary international law. Both these conditions are arguably satisfied since the decolonization process saw the creation of myriad of new states within a short period of time and it would appear from the statement of the Commission above that the actions of these states have fed directly into customary international law. Were this view to be strictly accurate, it would amount to a gross devaluation of the highly respected formulation of customary international law. However, the Commission's statement seems to have attracted much criticism. While it could be maintained that the doctrine remains significant within modern international law, it arguably falls short of customary international law (Murphy 1999). Second, in view of the discussion above, with regard to the transitory nature of proceedings under *jus civile*, it reiterates the importance of the mutual consent of states to their boundaries. This requirement was clearly not presented to the new African states as it was strongly suggested that their boundaries were sacrosanct irrespective of consent. Thus the view expressed seems to find strong evidence in custom for the acceptance of *uti possidetis* as a norm of international law on the one hand, while ignoring a key aspect of the practice at the time in the formation of such dubious 'custom'.

Nonetheless, with regard to the conditions laid down by the Arbitration Commission in examining the application of the doctrine in the former Yugoslavia the stipulation was largely ignored, except between Slovenia and Croatia who had decided not to contest the borders that they inherited against each other. Thus, in its conditions for recognition of states seeking to emerge as independent entities, one of the requirements laid down was a strict following of the doctrine of *uti possidetis*. In this situation, the norm required that the previous administrative boundaries of the old federal state be maintained and given international legitimacy. There were, however, significant differences from the application of the norm in the decolonization process. First, the people of former Yugoslavia could not be considered to be under 'colonial influence'

---

[20] Many authors disagree with the model presented by Jackson, see especially Grovogui (1996).

in its narrow interpretation.[21] Second, the borders that the state fragmented along had a certain historical legitimacy (pre-1918) absent in African and Asian decolonization, which rarely respected local fault lines. However, it is important to note that the Dayton Peace Agreement 1995 which sought to address the issue of territory and boundaries in the former Yugoslavia, challenges the notion of territoriality in the context of statehood.[22] By accepting the validity of ethnicity in the process of state formation, it therefore questions the notion of territory and (thereby *uti possidetis*) by introducing ethnicity as a valid factor in addition to territory. These issues are addressed in much greater depth in analysing the workings of the Badinter Commission.

The break-up of the Soviet Union is more complicated due to several re-drawings of boundaries of the different republics by different leaders (see generally Staruschenko 1965 and Shahenn 1956). In the 1920s the Soviet Union absorbed new territories that had been independent since the First World War, including the Ukraine, Belarus, Georgia, Armenia and Azerbaijan besides smaller areas in Central Asia (Shaw 1996: 110). By 1926 the Soviet Union comprised eight republics, based on purely ethnic factors (though not to the satisfaction of all). By 1939, however, and as contemplated in the Molotov–Ribbentrop Pact, the USSR invaded and annexed the Baltic republics of Estonia, Latvia and Lithuania as well as the Romanian territory of Bessarabia, creating four new republics.[23] By the end of the Second World War, the Soviet Union had further expanded into parts of Eastern Europe. This process of expansionism was mirrored internally in Soviet moves to re-align its peoples within the new borders. Boundary changes were enforced as internal borders were rearranged, taking land away from the newer entities and amalgamating it with older republics (Forsberg 1995). In addition, there was a constant flow of people from one part of the Soviet Union to another as dictated by the vagaries of the central government. The constant movement of peoples along with the changing internal boundaries made allegiances to territory difficult to gauge.[24] At the time of the dissolution of the Soviet Union into its constituent republics, the doctrine therefore raised the spectre of similar difficulties to those faced in the transfer of power in the African continent.[25] Once more the imminent fear was that reconstitution of territories based on identity-oriented factors such as ethnicity or religion could gravely threaten order. In response emphasis was placed on order and the maintenance of newly independent states in the same shape as

---

[21] For a narrow and broad interpretation of colonial rule, see Langenhove (1954).

[22] See <http://www.state.gov/www/regions/eur/bosnia/bosagree.html>.

[23] Treaty of Non-Aggression between Germany and the Soviet Union, Secret Additional protocol 23 August 1939 in Documents of German Foreign Policy 1918–45; see also 'The Dniester Conflict: Between Irredentism and Separatism', *EAS* 45 (1993) 973.

[24] Khrushchev's gift of the Crimea from the Russian SSR to the Ukrainian SSR in 1954 and the transfer of a part of the Kazakh SSR to the Uzbek SSR in 1963 is noted by Shaw (1996: 110).

[25] For an insight into the dissolution of empires, see Leiven (1999).

when they were part of the old Soviet Union. While the initial break-up was relatively peaceful the situation today is much more fragile with the Russian state facing hostile separatist movements in Chechnya and Dagestan that threaten peace and security within the region.[26] Meanwhile, the former republics still maintain claims against each other despite the fact that the Charter for the Commonwealth of Independent States formally respects *uti possidetis* as a norm applicable within the territories of the former Soviet Union (Chase 1995: 222–39). The Agreement linking the Commonwealth of Independent States signed at Minsk on 8 December 1991 states that

> the High Contracting Parties acknowledge and respect each other's territorial integrity and the inviolability of existing borders within the Commonwealth.[27]

This is a position also strongly supported in the Alma Ata Declaration signed by 11 former republics on 21 December 1991, leading Ratner to suggest that this offers, 'important evidential support for international acceptance of the *uti possidetis*' (1996: 624). He claims further support from subsequent state practice concerning the attempted secession of Abhazia from the Republic of Georgia and the fighting between Azerbaijan and Armenia concerning the Armenian populated Nogorny-Karabakh area of Azerbaijan (see Forsberg 1995). This argument seems problematic at best, since issues of national interest largely dictate states' actions. Thus, while the Commonwealth of Independent States (CIS) endorsed the frontiers they received, they nonetheless still maintain territorial claims against each other. This makes it particularly difficult to gauge evidence concerning the CIS states' signing of the Charter since it has not been accompanied by the states relinquishing territorial claims to each other's contested territories.

The break-up of Czechoslovakia presented a very different scenario since its borders were older in pedigree. The country was initially created after the First World War when the Allies combined Bohemia and Moravia (separate units under the Holy Roman Empire) with Slovakia (part of the Austro-Hungarian Empire) and a part of Silesia and Ruthenia (Shaw 1996: 126). The border between the Czech Republic and the Slovak Republic is thus the old Moravian–Hungarian border. Nazi Germany, separating the 'protectorate' of Bohemia and Moravia from the independent state of Slovakia, also used to treat the old border as an international boundary. Thus the two republics easily dissolved their union along this historic line, without contention. The application of the doctrine of *uti possidetis* in the case of the Velvet Divorce between the Slovak and Czech republics can therefore be presented as the least problematic of modern cases. However, the settlement does not address the problem of the

---

[26] For General Assembly and Security Council resolutions on Dagestan see <http://www.un.org>.
[27] Charter of the Commonwealth of Independent States, *ILM* 31 (1992) 138.

Roma/Gypsy/Sinti nomadic peoples that exist in both of the new states (see Zoon 2001). The norm of *uti possidetis* breaks down badly when faced with any non-sedentary population, as is also the case with the continuing conflict over the Western Sahara (see Chopra 1994). In this context it would be interesting to examine the Vattelian conceptions of *terra nullius* as enunciated by Judge Ammoun in the *Western Sahara* case, to appreciate the valence ascribed to the territories on which non-sedentary peoples exist.[28]

As presented above the doctrine of *uti possidetis* has thus evolved significantly. The purpose of this book is primarily to provide a temporal setting to some of the significant events that have pointed to a need to reinterpret the doctrine. That the primary aim of the doctrine is the preservation of order remains unassailable. It is also clearly this specific incarnation of the doctrine that has made it an attractive concept with increased international legal usage. It is also interesting briefly to mention the role of *uti possidetis* in the modern separatist threats to international peace and security in Kosovo and East Timor. While in the former the boundary between what is the autonomous region of Kosovo and the state of Yugoslavia has historical validity away from colonial rule of any kind (Terrett 2000: 16–46), in the latter the boundary was clearly a Portuguese construction in the division of the island of Timor (Jolliffe 1978). To posit validity upon such a construction could arguably be seen as giving colonial rule greater legitimacy than other factors in the cohesion of identity, and subsequent grounds for recognition of entities as states. However, what perhaps provides the best support for the argument for a separate East Timor is the unquestionable oppression that the 'people' faced under Indonesian rule. Thus the argument for self-determination in East Timor could be made on the basis of self-defence in the face of a government that failed to protect the people's legitimate interests (Castellino 2000b). Thus modern separatist conflicts seem to provide support for the doctrine of *uti possidetis* in that groups seeking self-determination seem to attempt to do so along the physical limits already demarcated for them by previous events in history.[29] This arguably gives the doctrine support from non-state entities that seem to present territorially based arguments for their right to self-determination, further validating the territorially based sovereign state as the only recognizable entity within the international system of states.[30] Nonetheless this is not always the case as arguments for a greater Basque country incorporating parts of France as well as Spain (Sullivan 1988), and calls for a homeland would testify.[31]

---

[28] *Western Sahara case*, ICJ Reports (1975) 12 at 85–7 (sep. op. of Judge Ammoun).

[29] An excellent example of this phenomenon is the case of Eritrea; see Tronvoll (1999).

[30] There is also evidence to suggest that post-colonial states fully support the doctrine as can be seen in the case reviews of the ICJ in Chapter 5.

[31] This is borne out by the Spanish argument, that is the Polisario argument, in the *Western Sahara* case (1975).

Shortcomings of *Uti Possidetis*[32]

Two prime flaws of the doctrine that are examined in the course of this book are that it creates states by establishing new identities within rigid boundaries, the preservation of which are not always feasible, and, as evidenced by modern break-ups, that it transforms internal boundaries to international ones with disregard for any viable interconnection between the internal border and the forging or maintenance of national unity. This is particularly disastrous since it fails to recognize the purpose served by the boundaries in the first place. In the case of decolonization, boundaries had in many cases been drawn by colonial powers merely to restrict the influence they exercised over a territory in contrast to that of their rival to the territory, another European power (see Curzon 1907, Lindley 1926, Touval 1972, Lucas 1922). This is classically manifest in the *Western Sahara* case where one of the mechanisms used by Morocco to prove its sovereignty over the territory of the Western Sahara was by recourse to a number of treaties signed with colonial rulers indicating recognition of this alleged fact.[33] In this sense, it was a demarcation of property, the title to which was not held by any of the parties.[34] This also brings into sharp focus the issue of unequal treaties discussing titles to territory which is of particular importance since it is effectively the basis for modern territorial claims.[35]

These boundaries may have functioned well enough under colonial regimes, since the nature of the regimes on either side of the boundary was similar and there were no emotional links based on other legitimating factors between them and the territory. However, with the departure of these colonial regimes the boundaries are extremely difficult to maintain since they neglect other factors considered more important, such as ethnicity and tribal allegiances. This is as true in the case of modern break-ups such as Yugoslavia and the former Soviet Union as in the cases of decolonization since the boundaries only reflect historic realities of a few decades of government. Thus, the simple transition of a boundary from an internal/colonial one to an external international frontier presents a host of problems, which are, perhaps, central to the critique of the doctrine of *uti possidetis*. These issues are revisited in greater depth in the examination of the so-called Badinter principles in Chapter 6. In addition, there are practical impediments to the modern exercise of the doctrine in self-determination conflicts since it relies exclusively on the 'snapshot' of the territory (Goldie 1963: 1267). The ruling in the *Burkina Faso/Mali* case suggests that:

---

[32] For a critique of *uti possidetis* see Vallat (1974). See also Kapil (1966: 663–70).

[33] See *Western Sahara case*, ICJ Reports (1975) 12 at 49–57.

[34] The legality of this process was open to question even during the nineteenth century; see Alexandrowicz (1975: 51).

[35] See *Case concerning the territorial dispute (Libyan Arab Jamahiriya v. Chad)*, ICJ Reports (1994) 6.

uti possidetis applies to the new State (as a State) not with retroactive effect, but immediately and from that moment onwards. It applies to the State as it is i.e. to the photograph of the territorial situation then existing. The principle of *uti possidetis* freezes the territorial title; it stops the clock but does not put back the hands.[36]

Thus, as already elaborated, this idea of a 'critical date' is vitally important to the spatial dimensions of a territory. Shaw suggests that

the critical date as a legal concept posits that there is a certain moment at which the rights of the parties crystallise, so that acts after that date cannot alter the legal position. It is the moment which is more decisive than any other for the purpose of the formulation of the rights of the parties in question.

(Shaw 1996: 130)

However, post-colonial self-determination conflicts have revealed the absence of such spatial and temporal clarity in many boundaries. The 'critical date' is extremely hard to agree upon and fix and remains the biggest impediment to assuming a given snapshot of a territory. Thus when left open to doubts in coping with separatist forces today its application is often found to be extremely limited.

Adherence to the logic of *uti possidetis* legitimates the action of civil officers, typically situated in foreign offices in metropolitan capitals in the middle of the nineteenth and twentieth century, who have essentially shaped the identities and destinies of colonial peoples.[37] Lines drawn across a map is all that international law seems to require to cement identities, despite these lines being drawn in ignorance across rivers, lakes and mountains, as well as tribes, cultures and beliefs.[38] Newly emergent colonial people were presented with no option but to exist within boundaries drawn for them. For this purpose, principles of 'nation-building' (Deutsch 1966) were emphasized, bolstered by the idea that people were essentially similar, and that any differences between them could be easily subsumed at the altar of the sovereign state. This could, perhaps, have been a plausible alternative had the sovereign state been a creation of these societies themselves. That too, however, was imposed upon people who were suddenly supposed to realize a strong 'national' identity.

In addition, separatism from the new sovereign states was strongly discouraged in international law, which viewed this, naturally enough, as a threat to order (Brilmeyer 1991 and 1980); in national law separatists were held up as being guilty of treason for

---

[36] See *Case concerning the frontier dispute (Burkina Faso v. Republic of Mali),* ICJ Reports (1986) 554 at 568.

[37] This is supported by the norms against the use of force. Thus while in the past a state could contend a boundary by the use of armed force, this option does not exist under the charter-based system. Boundaries can thus only be changed through mutual consent. For an examination of the legal regimes in the use of force see Brownlie (1963), McCoubrey and White (1996).

[38] See the infamous speech by Salisbury as quoted in Shaw (1996: 101).

threatening to compromise principles for which their forefathers had fought bitterly to gain independence from colonial rule in the first instance.[39] This approach often created, within the confines of one state, people who gradually realized that they had little in common with each other. Sustained through the freedom struggle by the common need to oust the colonial power, their unity disappeared with the colonial enemy. Peoples, often of different ethnicity, tribe and religion, suddenly found that co-existence within new structures with inviolable boundaries often resulted in the same kind of domination as had previously existed under classical colonial rule (Jackson 1992: 1). Under colonial influence strong unrepresentative government had prevented the structure from developing along ethnic, linguistic or religious fault lines by imposition of a centrally administered external rule. However, with that force gone and power usually handed over to one set of people as against another, these differences began to resurface with problematic consequences. The root of the problem is, perhaps, that post-colonial peoples often found themselves within the boundaries of a given sovereign state with only two things in common. First, that they had been under the same colonial ruler, and second, that they existed on a territory deemed by that ruler to be a unit which would be frozen after their departure. This forthright and rigid preference by the colonial ruler for territoriality over other differences is perhaps what is most problematic about the application of the doctrine of *uti possidetis*. This approach, dictated by fear of the threat to order, causes international law to give precedence to order in the short term over the notion of equity which is so central to the norm of self-determination.[40] Not only has this often constituted defeat for 'order' in the longer term – so precious to the international community – but it has also negated 'development' that the ICJ refers to as being essential to Africa.[41]

Further reflection of this is manifest in the opinions of authors who suggest that *uti possidetis* is an 'indefinite and illusory concept with an uncertain meaning' (Fisher 1933: 403; see also Waldock 1948). A similar statement was made by a tribunal in the *Beagle Channel* case which seemed unclear as to the precise status of the norm in international law, accepting it as 'possibly, at least at first, a political tenet rather than a true rule of law'.[42] Today it can be considered as being on a more formalistic legal footing, although since its application has varied in different circumstances its precise

---

[39] For example, art. 3(3) of the Charter of the Organization of African Unity provides that all Member States pledge themselves to respect the borders existing on their achievement of national independence. This commitment was restated by resolution 16(1) of the OAU Assembly of Heads of State and Government in 1964, where the principle of *uti possidetis* was expressly reaffirmed; see Naldi (1987: 898).

[40] The chamber in the *Burkina Faso/Mali* case (ICJ Reports (1986) 554 at 633) stated that it would be quite unjust to have recourse to equity in order to modify an established boundary, as quoted by Shaw (1996: 96).

[41] Any economic development in Rwanda and Burundi has been seriously compromised by the problematic nature of identity in the region; see generally Kolodziej (2000).

[42] Beagle Channel arbitration (1977) 52 ILR 11.

substantive content remains suspect. One of the questions we are left with in modern international legal literature is whether the re-statement of the doctrine by the Badinter Commission has given this norm of political aspirations any more legal valence and whether it has entered state practice as a norm of customary international law. The nature of the development of such norms would seem to indicate that such a bold statement would be premature. However, with the re-statement of the doctrine, it appears to be taking on a legal valence of markedly different proportions to the norm as apparent in *jus civile*, as will be demonstrated during the course of this book.

Conclusions

The question of whether *uti possidetis* is primarily a political tenet rather than a rule of law demonstrates the utility of law. The drawing of boundaries is, in itself, an essentially political event that demonstrates agreeable physical limits to state sovereignty (Reeves 1944). In this context, the function of international law was to legitimate and order the process of colonial withdrawal. In western liberal societies, the concept of rule of law has been reified in that law appears to have a separate identity outside and above the political and social relations of society. This identity allows law to give the appearance of being independent of these relations and thereby present itself as universal. However, it could be argued that international law is a social construction of the political relations between states. These relationships arguably provide the basis for the law and can be ignored only at great peril (see generally Boyle 1994 and Hunt 1993). Further, modern international law, with its origins in western liberalism, embodies the notion of the rule of law as expressed in the need for the preservation of order. The colonial powers involved in the withdrawal from Latin America sought to legitimate the consequences of their withdrawal by reference to a relatively obscure Roman interdict. This convenient mechanism clothed the political consequences of withdrawal with the sanctity of law and this norm appears to have been accepted into international law without any noticeable dispute. The uncertainty raised in the *Beagle Channel* case highlights the true relationship between law and political actions of modern states and the attendant problems of ascribing firm legal valence to a doctrine framed in a specific political context.

In order to legitimate the political actions of withdrawing colonial powers, it is apparent that international law has been highly selective in its use of the Roman interdict. In this context international law could be considered an embodiment of the political motives of colonial powers, and in its application of the relatively obscure Roman interdict it has chosen to adopt only those parts that support its motives. The *nec vi, nec clam, nec precario* restrictions of the interdict have been ignored, as has the notion of its being an interim measure that does not award but rather keeps in abeyance the award of title to territory. It could be argued that perhaps this is because the colonial methods of territorial acquisition would not be able to satisfy such requirements and thus construction of a doctrine of this nature would erase this illegality (see Mazrui 1975: 1–21; Ali 1997: 219; and, with regard to acquisition of colonial property in Africa, Pakenham 1991).

Thus *uti possidetis* primarily sought to protect the existing international order. It remains a doctrine of merit – being highly useful in a difficult transitory period. In addition the nature of the colonial entity as highlighted above meant that the threat of fragmentation was very real as forces within sought to renegotiate externally imposed boundaries. The only option for the promotion of international order at the time was the imposition of a strict moratorium on such potentially violent modifications to international boundaries. In this scenario it is quite clear that the doctrine has played a vital role in preventing violent upheavals motivated by vested interests from flourishing on the withdrawal of colonial forces. Ideally, *uti possidetis* was seen as an approach that would guarantee short-term peace and security and buy the fledgling post-colonial state time to solidify its own 'national' identity within its new physical and conceptual parameters as an independent state. However, the problem is that in asserting this doctrine the international community has brought in a new rigidity that affects the very concept of the 'national'. The state was thus able to proclaim the juridically acceptable nature of its own territorial definition, internally as well as externally. The doctrine thus adds the thrust of territoriality to the already problematic discourse of statehood and sovereignty. It also, by way of this process, forecloses questions of legitimacy and recognition, restricting them to a purely territorial basis, in precedence over other legitimizing principles such as ethnicity, tradition, linguistics, religion, ideology or history. It thus seeks and attempts to induce a re-reading of history, based on the specific definition of a territory as the state, rather than an allegiance to a sovereign, as in the past (see generally Hinsley 1986). In addition, by allowing the only flexibility to this approach to be the consent of states, it makes the unsound assumption that the only entities entitled to participate in the process of boundary re-alignment are other states. In this sense it reinforces the colonial norm that the only personality in international law is the pre-existing colonial or post-colonial state.

This presents us with a number of problems. First and perhaps most important, it critically alters the norm of self-determination. While the Wilsonian vision of self-determination was based on the need to protect minorities by giving them recourse to forming autonomous states within which their interest would be better protected, the norm as interpreted through *uti possidetis* reverses this process. Thus instead of seeking a territorial settlement for a vulnerable people, it seeks to 'settle' people within a fixed territory. Judge Harry Dillard in the *Western Sahara* case (1975) suggested that 'it is for the people to determine the fate of the territory and not the territory the fate of the people'.[43] However, through the action of *uti possidetis* the territory is deemed to be a settled unit and the people who are sustained on it are asked to comply with this

---

[43] *Western Sahara case*, ICJ Reports (1975) 12 at 116–22 (sep. op. of Judge Harry Dillard).

requirement. Thus it reverses the Wilsonian vision which was originally based on concern for unrepresented minorities (Whelan 1994), and instead seems to treat the need for territorial 'order' as being more important to the 'identity' of a people (Franck 1996: 362). While this can be explained as further manifestation of the need to preserve order, it is arguable that it is a task doomed to failure even in this limited aim.

Second, the manner in which *uti possidetis* 'stops the clock' seems to suggest an extremely static view of history. Thus in the decolonization process one particular moment in time is considered vital or 'critical' and all the political processes that follow are subjugated to this defining moment. The concept of the 'critical date' in determining when boundaries have crystallized is highly contentious, especially since it is based on the exit of an artificial European influence. This European colonial occupation of property very often failed to respect local fault lines within peoples and instead merged them into spheres of influence with a view to preventing other European powers from 'grabbing' the same land (Pakenham 1991). Further, the UN Charter-based system outlaws the use of force within international law, thus removing the prime mechanism with which boundary issues have traditionally been settled.[44] Thus while European boundaries have evolved since the Peace of Westphalia,[45] often through the use of force, boundaries in Africa are deemed settled, based on a specific reading of history, which is frozen by the norms against the use of force, preventing the system from self-adjusting. As a result artificial entities abound, with the need for order, no matter how artificial, deemed superior to the requirement of cohesive identities based on existent fault lines and allegiances.

Third, it can be argued that with respect to its prime aim, that is the preservation of order, *uti possidetis* is beginning to falter. While it did provide 'order' in the short term, it is questionable whether it still provides this today. The number of conflicts wherein groups seek self-determination has been steadily increasing. Arguably none of these movements are 'new' since they are based on what Franck (1993) calls 'post-modern tribalism'. He defines this as a movement that:

> seeks to promote a political and legal environment conducive to the break-up of existing sovereign states . . . in a bid to constitute uni-cultural and uni-national units . . . by asserting a political, moral, historically determinist and legal claim to support this agenda.
>
> (Franck 1993: 5)

He suggests that this trend has forced upon us a growing need to 'rethink fundamental norms such as title to territory and its relation to human personality and group identity' (ibid.). It is primarily this quest that this book seeks to highlight in analysing the different strands of the issues of title to territory in international law. This is particularly relevant at this stage since what has empowered these groups in their fight against

---

[44] UN Charter, art. 2(4), art. 51. See also Simma *et al.* (1994).

[45] For a comparison between the Peace of Westphalia and the Monroe Doctrine see Chapter 3.

what they perceive as the unrepresentative state is the growth of the human rights agenda and in particular the movement for self-determination, which is the first human right given by the International Covenants of 1966.[46] This particular movement has itself transformed East Timor and Kosovo from entities within 'unrepresentative' states to the brink of sovereign statehood. These battles have been fought in the name of human rights and self-determination, fuelling the aspirations of other separatist groups who believe they have been hard done by in the external 'settlement' of their 'states' as expressed through *uti possidetis* or other manifestations of the need to preserve short-term order. These groups are, very often, willing to use force to achieve what they perceive as their right and it is they who in the immediate term threaten international peace and security, as best demonstrated by the attempt of Chechnya to secede from Russia. Thus it can be argued that while the doctrine of *uti possidetis* played a vital role in a transition period it has perhaps outlived is utility and is threatening the very 'order' it sought to preserve. However, to be able to effectively critique and re-examine the nuances of the packages of doctrines that govern the treatment of territory in modern international law, it is necessary to review their development in the specific contexts in which they evolved. For this purpose this book reviews developments during different eras to seek a temporal setting against which these doctrines can be located. The first step towards the examination of the doctrine is inevitably to retrace its place within Roman *jus civile* from which it originates. This will arguably provide the theoretical framework against which all subsequent development of the doctrine can be critically examined.

---

[46] Joint art. 1 of the International Covenant on Civil and Political Rights 1966 and the International Covenant on Economic, Social and Cultural Rights 1966 identifies the right to self-determination; see also Castellino (2000a).

2 The Impact of Roman Property Regimes on Territorial Acquisition in the Modern International Context

It is widely acknowledged that fundamental concepts of Roman law inspired European scholars in their task of formulating a modern law of nations (*jus gentium*). However, the precise nature of the Roman norms that served as the foundation for the modern system remains ambiguous (see generally Nicholas 1962, Sherman 1918 and 1921). This chapter is premised on the thesis that in order to fully comprehend the core principles of the modern international system it is necessary to acquire a thorough grasp of the underpinnings of ancient theory and practice. As such, this chapter examines critically select areas of Roman jurisprudence in a bid to enhance our appreciation of modern international doctrine with specific reference to the treatment of territory.

The difficulty of this task is compounded by three significant factors. First, the Romans themselves had a number of interpretations of the term *jus gentium*. One interpretation concerned the creation of a body of law developed exclusively to govern relations between nations or states on the grounds of the universality of natural reason (*jus naturale*), thus appearing to be a precursor of a modern public international system (Phillipson 1911: 69–99). In recognition of the personality principle,[1] which formed the basis of jurisdiction in the ancient world, another equally valid interpretation recognized *jus gentium* as a body of law applicable to all individuals, again by virtue of *jus naturale*. This source of jurisprudence stemmed from private law and was particularly significant in regulating the conduct of foreign nationals (peregrines). Although this body of law was open to both peregrines and Roman citizens alike, many of its features were consistent with an embryonic private international law. In the circumstances, this chapter will refer to the first interpretation of *jus gentium* as 'public *jus gentium*' and the second as 'private *jus gentium*'. This distinction is made purely for the sake of convenience as it is readily accepted that the Romans did not begin to recognize the existence of a public law until as late as the third century AD.[2]

---

[1] Essentially jurisdiction was dependent on nationality rather than territory. This issue is discussed below.

[2] Ulpian appears to have been the first to make the distinction between public and private law in Roman legal theory; see Stein (1999: 21).

Second, while devising his concept of an international system, both interpretations and the tenets of *jus civile* impressed Grotius, who is often referred to as the founding father of modern *jus gentium* (Grotius 1853). As a result, the modern system derives many of its core principles from private law analogy, despite the original norms often being created with very different purposes in mind.[3] Finally, the surviving fragments of Roman jurisprudence have left many vital questions unanswered, as Nicholas remarked:

> without [*jus gentium*] the Roman law would never have held the place in history that it does, and yet we know next to nothing of its origin or growth.
>
> (Nicholas 1962: 58)

Given the nature and extent of the seemingly insurmountable evidential barriers to legal research in this area, the fundamental aim of this chapter is to survey available sources of Roman jurisprudence in order to facilitate the task of evaluating the authenticity of modern interpretations of Roman norms used so extensively to justify the actions of states under modern international law.

To this end the first part of the chapter will concentrate on the theoretical background of *jus gentium* and the origins and tenets of its public interpretation in a bid to provide an assessment of its value as an international system worthy of transposition. The second section will then study the impact of *jus civile* on modern *jus gentium* with particular reference to the doctrine of the ownership and possession of interests in property. The third part will centre on private *jus gentium* in an attempt to assess its influence on modern *jus gentium* and in turn will discuss the utility of this mechanism for the regulation of peregrine relations and therefore its significance as an archetypal private international law. The final part will focus on the reception of Roman theories of possession and ownership into modern *jus gentium*, as characterized by state practice, and will ultimately consider the continuing ramifications of this process for territorial acquisition in modern international law.

Theoretical Origins of Modern *Jus Gentium*

The existence of an international system defined by reference to philosophical characteristics has not been a consistent feature throughout all periods of history (see generally Hershey 1911 and Korff 1924). In particular a law of nations was seemingly absent in medieval Europe where 'war in all its forms may be said to have been the law of the feudal world' (translated from Luchaire; Hershey 1911: 923). This state of

---

[3] Some scholars have doubted the utility of this exercise. See the opinions of Schwarzenberger (1957).

affairs inspired theologians and jurists to search for a universal legal order that could regulate the conduct of warfare and govern international relations in times of peace. In this regard, canonists such as Gratian, Thomas Aquinas and later the commentators and humanists of the Renaissance were profoundly influenced by the surviving sources of the *Corpus Juris* (Gordon and Robinson 1988, Mommsen and Kruger 1985, Birds and McLeod 1987). Subsequently, with the rise of the 'nation' state, the framers of the modern *jus gentium* also drew inspiration from these remnants of Roman jurisprudence (Sherman 1921: 357–9).

In their quest for universal concepts upon which to build a modern law of nations, these early scholars were influenced as much by the philosophy of the ancients as by their strict jurisprudence. To this end it was believed that any positive international legal order had to possess a moral dimension in order to provide the necessary legitimacy for an international system premised on good faith, reciprocity and the sanctity of obligations (ibid.). Clearly, given the nature of the exercise, the core principles of a modern law of nations had to reflect the philosophical and equitable characteristics apparent within the concept of civilization itself (Sherman 1918: 63). The idea of a universal law common to all peoples by virtue of natural reason derives from Aristotelian philosophy and was subsequently harnessed by Roman stoics, notably Cicero, to provide the foundations for the Roman concept of *jus gentium*.[4] According to Gaius:

> Every people that is governed by statutes and customs applies partly its own peculiar law and partly law which is common to all mankind. For all law which each people establishes for itself is peculiar to it and is called the [*jus civile*] as being the special law of that state (*civitas*); but the law which natural reason establishes among all mankind is observed equally by every people and is called the [*jus gentium*] as being the law applied by all nations (*gentes*). And so the Roman people applies partly its own peculiar law and partly that which is common to all mankind.[5]

Evidently, to the philosopher *jus naturale* referred to an ideal – the law, as it ought to be observed by all peoples; however, to the Roman jurist, *jus gentium* was perceived as that law which was actually applied universally and thus was perceived essentially as a practical body of jurisprudence (Phillipson 1911: 92; Sherman 1921: 356).

Although this concept of *jus gentium* clearly informs modern international law it would be erroneous to hold that the Romans were pioneers of a law of nations; previous international practice had significantly influenced them. Indeed Korff

---

[4] Nicholas quotes Gaius' *Institutes* in this respect (1962: 54). See also Sherman (1918: 57–8; 1921: 350–1).

[5] These words introduce Gaius' *Institutes* and are quoted by Nicholas (1962: 54); obviously slaves were excluded from the category of mankind.

(1924) suggests that the existence of an international legal system is the necessary corollary of attaining a certain standard of civilization. He focuses on regulatory international relations systems devised to govern relations between ancient civilizations such as those of Egypt, Babylon, Assyria and Greece to support his convincing argument that international systems have been a regular feature of world history since times immemorial. Interestingly he contends that such systems have demonstrated a remarkable uniformity in relation to their core values, which consistently included the sanctity of international contracts, obligations and the maintenance of recognized channels of communication between nations (Korff 1924: 254, 258–9).

The achievement of Roman supremacy with its ensuing *Pax Romana* promoted throughout the Mediterranean a distinctly Roman concept of international relations.[6] By the late Republic, Rome readily acknowledged the existence of certain formalities, procedures and ceremonies in relation to the conduct and protection of envoys, declaration of war, conclusion of peace and the drawing up of international treaties (Korff 1924; 254). While Rome clearly appreciated the core principles of existing international systems it nevertheless made important additions to pre-existing international practice and thereby created a relatively comprehensive array of norms which extended to provision for naturalization, extradition, asylum, treatment of captured enemy property, burial of the dead, payment of ransom, exchange of prisoners and the position of hostages (Phillipson 1911: 107–8). Further, during the early part of the Roman Empire these norms had acquired the status of a distinct body of law recognized as public *jus gentium*.[7]

Although a form of public international law clearly governed international relations during the era of Roman hegemony such a system was actually hampered by the might of Rome. It has been claimed that a key feature of any international system is that the nations involved have attained a comparable stage of cultural development resulting in a degree of equality between them. If a particular nation is in a position to impose its will by sheer military strength then the sanctity of international obligations and the reciprocity demanded by such a system would be fundamentally undermined (Korff 1924: 248–9). It is also clear that while in the earlier part of its history, Rome was prepared to recognize the juridical personality and sovereignty of other nations, after the Punic Wars Rome gradually began to assert its true supremacy in its political relations with other nations (Phillipson 1911: 104). In this respect Rome advanced a view that it was the 'Common Superior' of other nations, therefore precluding the existence of a truly international system of law (Hershey 1911: 919). Against this background it could be argued that the ingenuity of Roman international theory was conceived and developed in the period before supremacy was finally achieved, that is during an era marked by the relative equality of the participating nations and thus

---

6 *Paxa Romana* translates as 'Roman Peace'.
7 This body had certainly crystallized by the time of Livy; see Sherman (1918: 61–2).

amenable to the creation of a truly international jurisprudence. Nevertheless, while the ascendancy of Rome had ensured that Roman normative practice continued to evolve into a distinct body of law, by this stage Rome was capable of imposing her will by force if necessary. Thus to a great extent the Romans had already undermined the international dimension of public *jus gentium* that they sought to advance.

The credibility of any international system is arguably dependent on the existence of a certain degree of substantive equality between nations (Korff 1924: 252–5, 259). Although public *jus gentium* may, in some respects, have been the forerunner of a modern *jus gentium*, it clearly could never claim to be a legitimate law *between* nations during the period of Roman hegemony. Indeed it is possible to draw certain parallels between the positions of Rome and the European powers in the modern colonial context. Both civilizations shared military superiority that enabled them to impose their will irrespective of the views of other nations; both were responsible for developing self-serving doctrine in order to justify their actions in the international arena. Against this background one of Rome's greatest achievements in the sphere of public *jus gentium* was the articulation and codification of international norms into a modular system capable of transposition (Sherman 1921: 351). The modularity of this body of law partly explains the survival of the Roman interpretation of international legal theory. First, the spread of the *Pax Romana* ensured that the tenets of public *jus gentium* extended far beyond the parameters of Rome's political influence and in time were mirrored throughout the ancient world. Second, the coherent systemization of public *jus gentium* meant that it was liable to be transposed by subsequent civilizations, most notably at the hands of Grotius and other international scholars, which led to the creation of a modern *jus gentium* during the seventeenth century. From a critical perspective, however, the modularity of this distinctly Roman jurisprudence meant that its norms could also be imposed upon other nations or transposed to give the *appearance* of an international system when a truly international system did not actually exist.

The Influence of *Jus Civile* on Modern *Jus Gentium*

Although Grotius clearly modelled his concept of a modern *jus gentium* on the norms of public *jus gentium*, he did not draw inspiration from this source alone. In this regard it is perhaps significant that Grotius used the term *jus inter gentes* (the law *between* nations) rather than the Roman term *jus gentium* (the law shared by all nations, that is the universal law) to describe his interpretation of a modern international system.[8] In his attempt to create a body of law that acknowledged the value of natural reason,

---

[8] Vittoria also made this distinction in *Relectiones de Indis* (1532); see Stein (1999: 94). Grotius (1853) makes the same point; see Sherman (1918: 56).

Grotius also perceived a correlation between the *jus naturale* and the municipal law of Rome (Stein 1999: 99). As a result his discourse relies heavily on private law concepts for its central precepts, especially with regard to the acquisition of territory and the concepts of territorial sovereignty.

According to *jus civile*, the notion of ownership was premised on the concept of dominion (see generally Jolowicz and Nicholas 1972: 137–55; Buckland and McNair 1952: 60–126; Buckland 1963; Stein 1999: 180–281; Buckland 1925: 106–52). In this regard, ownership was an absolute phenomenon, the right to control a physical object irrespective of whether the owner has actual possession of the object or not. It appears that the mode of acquisition was primarily dependent on the nature of the property itself. Classically, Italian land, slaves, cattle and horses were referred to as *res mancipi* while the remaining forms of private property were deemed to be *res nec mancipi* (see Buckland and McNair 1952: 60–1 and Borkowski 1994: 156). *Res mancipi* could only be transferred by means of formal conveyance, namely *mancipatio*, whereas *res nec mancipi* could be transferred by mere delivery or the physical surrender of the goods (*traditio*) (Jolowicz and Nicholas 1972: 140–51 and Buckland 1925: 120–5). The distinction between different kinds of property appears to have been based upon the relative importance of certain types of property in what was principally an agrarian and warring society (see Jolowicz and Nicholas 1972: 137).[9]

The massive expansion that characterized the late Republic meant that compliance with the formal methods of transferring *res mancipi* declined and it became increasingly common for it to be transferred by *traditio* (Borkowski 1994: 158). The problem with this practice was that if the transfer as such had not been made in accordance with the requisite formalities the transferee would not obtain dominion over the property. *Jus civile* attempted to resolve this dilemma by recourse to the prescriptive mechanism of *usucapio* (see Jolowicz and Nicholas 1972: 151–5 and Buckland 1925: 126–31). This mechanism ensured that although dominion did not pass on delivery, it could be secured if the transferee maintained continuous and uninterrupted possession of the property for an appropriate period.[10] Alternatively, *usucapio* could also be considered applicable in a situation where an owner (the *dominus*) failed to assert his[11] dominion over the

---

[9] *Mancipatio* referred to the formal ceremony whereby ownership would be transferred; see Muirhead (1916: 120–36). Alternatively ownership of *res mancipi* could also be transferred by *jure cessio*, which allowed a magistrate to formally effect a conveyance in the presence of the transferor and transferee; see Borkowski (1994: 202).

[10] The requisite period was dependent on the nature of the property in question. During the classical era, the periods were one year in relation to moveable forms of property and two years for immoveable property. Later, the period for immoveable property became 10 years for Italian land and 20 years for provincial land. See Borkowski (1994: 203).

[11] It should be pointed out that a woman did not possess legal personality under Roman law and as such her interests would be protected or enforced through her husband or father; see Sinclair (1996: 190–3).

property to such an extent that another had already acquired possession and sought to claim ownership.

In any event, a claimant seeking such entitlement had to satisfy a number of stringent conditions before the mechanism attributable to *usucapio* could become applicable. First, unless the claimant had acted in good faith and could also prove just cause from the start of his possession, *usucapio* would not become available. Apparently just cause would be deemed to exist if the transfer had been carried out by 'an event or dealing which is normally the basis for acquisition' thus for example sale, legacy, gift and dowry (Buckland 1925: 129). Furthermore, the *usucapio* mechanism could not be applied if the property had been stolen, regardless of the good faith of a subsequent purchaser (Jolowicz and Nicholas 1972: 152). If the possessor demonstrated that he had satisfied these requirements and had maintained continuous and uninterrupted possession for the requisite period his actions would be deemed consistent with ownership and he could therefore obtain dominion. The primary justification behind the mechanism of *usucapio* was that the ownership of property should not remain uncertain for a significant period of time (Gaius *Digest* 2.44). Clearly, from an early stage, Roman society appreciated the importance of the continuance of undisturbed possession in maintaining public order and the integrity of the existing property regime.[12] Although speaking in the context of the possessory interdicts, Paul captured the essence of Roman property law when he said that 'every kind of possessor has by virtue of being a possessor more right than a non-possessor' (*Digest* 43.17.2, quoted in Borkowski 1994: 168). Thus while *jus civile* has emphasized the distinction between ownership and possession it was always understood that the roots of ownership lay in possession. The pragmatism of *jus civile* in recognizing the validity of prescriptive claims has been echoed by municipal jurisdictions through the ages and continues to be an important instrument for legitimating the status quo in modern municipal systems and in the field of international law.[13]

The phenomenal expansion of Rome especially after the Punic Wars resulted in a paradigm shift away from a relatively insular agrarian community to an international commercial centre and regional military power.[14] Such fundamental changes made the elaborate requirements of *jus civile* seem increasingly outmoded and therefore unlikely to be fulfilled. *Jus civile* was premised on the rigid actions recognized by the XII Tables,[15] a virtually exhaustive code which dated back to the fifth century BC, and political expediency dictated that it evolve in a bid to satisfy the demands of a rapidly

---

[12] Indeed *usucapio* was an ancient mechanism that actually preceded the XII Tables.

[13] This feature has manifest itself in English municipal law through the doctrine of adverse possession; see Ames (1913), Pollock and Maitland (1898: 29–80) and Ballantine (1918–19: 135–59). The utility of the doctrine of acquisitive prescription in international law is discussed later in this chapter.

[14] For a useful guide to the institutional history of Rome, see Muirhead (1916).

[15] For an extensive review of the history behind the XII Tables, see Muirhead (1916: 75–97).

developing society. To this end Rome developed the role of the praetor, a magistrate who was responsible for the administration of justice with the task of remoulding *jus civile* in a bid to adapt the ancient legal institutions of Rome to the changing socio-economic circumstances.

The praetors exercised their *imperium* to supplement the rigid actions of *jus civile* by developing equitable remedies and expanding their sphere of application (Muirhead 1916: 228).[16] The primary function of the magistrate was to define the issues to be resolved at the final determination of a case. If full proceedings were then instituted the matter would be assigned to a lay judge (*judex*) who would decide the case in the light of directions issued by the magistrate as to the nature of the case and the particular law to be applied.[17] A magistrate therefore possessed the authority to shape proceedings and grant interim relief. Although his function was technically declaratory, he nevertheless could grant remedy where a claim justified it, even where such a remedy was without precedent (Stein 1999: 9). Over time a body of law evolved (*jus honorarium* or *jus praetorium*) which soon became a part of the core jurisprudence of Rome (Sherman 1921: 354–5).

In this context, a prime mechanism available to a praetor was the edict, which allowed him to issue an injunction with the aim of protecting public order regardless of an alleged breach of *jus civile* (Muirhead 1916: 228–32). Although edicts originally related to a given case, a body of general edicts developed and crystallized in the form of the magistrate's album.[18] These edicts were ultimately codified during the Empire via the *Edictum Perpetuum*, which became a permanent annual announcement made by a praetor at the beginning of his term of office (Sherman 1921: 353–5).

The proliferation of these edicts transformed the private law of Rome and this transformation process was particularly apparent with regard to the possession and ownership of property. While numerous conditions guarded against any abuse of the *jus civile* prescriptive mechanism of *usucapio*, the evidence suggested that such extensive criteria could lead to inequitable results especially in situations where a transferee had not managed to satisfy the requisite period of time for *usucapio* (Jolowicz and Nicholas 1972: 263). In such situations the possessor could not claim any entitlement to ownership as he was unable to institute proceedings (*vindicatio*) and thus no remedy was available under *jus civile*. However, the evolution of *jus praetorium* resulted in the edict known as the *actio Publiciana*. This edict recognized the equity in circumstances where the possessor held the strongest claim and as such it provided

---

[16] Praetors were referred to as magistrates when carrying out their judicial functions. Regarding the nature of equity (*aequitas*), see Jolowicz (1957: 54–60).

[17] These instructions were known as *formulae* – a claimant would have to select the appropriate *formulae* from the magistrate's album and then apply to the magistrate for it to be granted; see Sherman (1921: 353), Muirhead (1916: 323–34) and Buckland (1925: 393–407).

[18] A statement made at the outset of his term establishing the principles and procedures according to which his administration will govern; see Stein (1999: 10).

a remedy premised on the fiction that the requisite period had already been satisfied (Thomas 1976: 136–7 and Jolowicz and Nicholas 1972: 263–7). The *actio Publiciana* was available to possessors in situations where the transfer had not been carried out in compliance with the requisite formalities, whereupon such a possessor, known as a 'bonitary owner', would be entitled to protection against the transferor.[19] Alternatively, the *actio Publiciana* could also be applied in situations where the possessor acquired the property from a transferor who was not the owner. In those cases the possessor would become a bona fide possessor whose possession would be valid against anyone who could not produce a better title.[20]

A central aspect of the Roman law of property was the distinction made between ownership and possession. As Ulpian infamously proclaimed, 'ownership has nothing in common with possession' (*Digest* 41.2.12.1, quoted in Borkowski 1994: 162). The theory of dominion, premised upon absolute ownership, knew nothing of the relativity underpinning most subsequent legal systems (see Buckland and McNair 1952 generally on this issue). However, in practice, the lack of a reliable mechanism for the registration of titles to land and the widespread failure to use title deeds uniformly was compounded by the absence of an equitably developed body of evidential rules. Consequently, at least during the Republic and early Empire, the concept of dominion must have rested on the notion of possession (Borkowski 1994: 162; Buckland and McNair 1952: 64). This interpretation is also supported by the relatively short periods of time required to obtain dominion by way of the mechanism of *usucapio* (Buckland and McNair 1952: 64). Furthermore it is evident that the connection between possession and ownership was still crucial at the height of classical jurisprudence as the position of bonitary owners and bona fide possessors demonstrated (ibid.: 62–3). Although the Roman law of property was clearly based on the notion of ownership rather than possession, the distinction made between these concepts is evidently not as marked as Ulpian would have us believe (ibid.: 62–88).

The Roman theory of possession was also fraught with other conceptual difficulties. The surviving Roman texts are silent as to its definition and as a result the subsequent debate on the issue by eminent Romanists has never been satisfactorily resolved (Muirhead 1916: 315–17 and, more extensively, Thomas 1976: 138–46). Although the theoretical subtleties are still the subject of controversy, the elements of possession are nevertheless clear: to acquire possession, a person had to secure physical control over the property (*corpus*) and have sufficient intention to possess it (*animus*) (Buckland and McNair 1952: 70).[21] The doctrine of possession did not, however, refer to a

---

[19] The transferor would, however, technically remain the *dominus*.

[20] Although his interest would be inferior to that of the *dominus*; see Jolowicz and Nicholas (1972: 264–5).

[21] Although in relation to possession protected by the interdicts the Roman jurists referred to the need for the appropriate kind of *iusta causa* rather than the need for *corpus* and *animus*. Buckland and McNair suggest, however, that objectively these elements were largely comparable (1952: 74–5).

continuing relationship with the property; rather it focused only on the acquisition or loss of possession. According to Lawson, Roman law regarded possession as being something obtained with the taking of possession, that is the appropriation of the practical and economic advantages of ownership irrespective of the issue of title.[22] Thus, for example, under Roman law a lessee did not obtain possession of the premises which formed the subject matter of the lease. Instead the owner retained possession on the grounds that he continued to derive practical and economic benefits from the property by virtue of the lease.[23]

It has been rightly suggested that to understand the notion of possession in Roman law the possessory interdicts must be fully appreciated (Jolowicz and Nicholas 1972: 259, 259–63; Buckland 1925: 412–18; Muirhead 1916: 334–9). It appears that the interdicts were divided into three distinct classes, those concerning the acquisition, retention and recovery of possession (Jolowicz and Nicholas 1972: 259). Of particular interest to scholars of public international law and the focus of this book is the interdict of *uti possidetis*, which was concerned with the retention of possession in respect of immoveable kinds of property, and was subsequently applied in the post-colonial context during the modern era. Other interdicts of note included the remedies of restitution, namely *unde vi* and *unde vi armata*, which provided for the recovery of immoveable property in situations where the possessor had been evicted by force. The evidence suggests that interdictory proceedings were basically concerned with the resolution of disputes as to the existing state of possession rather than the rightful entitlement to it (Jolowicz and Nicholas 1972: 259; Muirhead 1916: 334–6). It is clear that the maintenance of public order was uppermost in the mind of the praetor and his reasoning was thus grounded in the belief that a possessor had a presumptive right to possess. This connection with the maintenance of public order meant, however, that certain conditions would have to be observed for the remedy to be effective. These conditions essentially dictate that possession had to be acquired *nec vi, nec clam, nec precario* (without force, secrecy or permission) in order to allow an owner to challenge the legitimate claims of any would-be possessor (Jolowicz and Nicholas 1972: 260).

As a result of interdictory proceedings the praetor would issue an order forbidding interference with the declared state of possession. Interdictory proceedings were often a preliminary step before the commencement of full proceedings under *jus civile* concerning the rights of ownership (*vindicatio*). While it is clear that the praetorian order did not affect the result of any subsequent *vindicatio* proceedings regarding actual ownership it did nevertheless produce the result that the party that had been defeated at the interdictory stage would become the applicant whereas the actual

---

[22] See Lawson's analysis of possession in Buckland and McNair (1952: 75).
[23] Contrast with possession under the English legal system – the Roman legal system was a system based on ownership whereas the English system was one premised on possession; see generally Buckland and McNair (1952).

possessor would assume the enviable position of the respondent if *vindicatio* proceedings were instituted.[24] It is, however, interesting to note that the outcome of interdictory proceedings could also result in *vindicatio* proceedings not being brought (Jolowicz and Nicholas 1972: 260). In this respect interdictory proceedings could also be a terminal point for the treatment of the issue at law. Further, as the praetorian order regarding possession was final it is clear that it was the notion of possession that was provisional in Roman jurisprudence rather than the praetorian remedies that protected it (Buckland 1925: 412).

The Influence of Private *Jus Gentium* on Modern *Jus Gentium*

A second interpretation of *jus gentium* concerned its function as a municipal body of law created to regulate the private affairs of individuals (see generally Muirhead 1916: 215–45). The surviving Roman texts suggest that this aspect of *jus gentium* preceded the *jus civile*, the latter being developed under the guidance of the universal law according to natural reason. Indeed according to Gaius:

> Of some things we acquire ownership under the *jus gentium* which is observed, by natural reason, among all men generally, of others under the *jus civile* which is peculiar to our city . . . the *jus gentium* is the older, being the product of human nature itself . . .
> (*Digest* 41.1.1.pr., quoted in Borkowski 1994: 184)

Clearly, from a philosophical perspective, the tenets of *jus gentium* applied to all peoples by virtue of natural reason and were therefore open to both Roman citizens and foreign nationals (peregrines) alike. However, it is submitted that while the core principles of *jus naturale* may have had some impact on Roman jurisprudence, the claim that private *jus gentium* preceded the *jus civile* is a convenient fiction given that the rigid actions of the XII Tables actually predated the existence of a *jus gentium* possessing the characteristics of *jus naturale* (Jolowicz and Nicholas 1972: 143).[25]

Further, while an awareness of the natural order of things was deeply rooted in the Roman legal psyche,[26] the extent to which *jus naturale* actually influenced *jus gentium*

---

[24] 'The outcome of a dispute over possession is simply this: that the judge makes an interim finding that one of the parties possesses; the result will be that the party defeated on the issue of possession will take on the role of plaintiff when the question of ownership is contested', *Digest* 41.2.35, quoted in Borkowski (1994: 168).

[25] However, on the existence of a localized clan-based *jus gentium* that existed before the Republic and probably quite distinct, see Phillipson (1911: 70).

[26] It is evident that the natural order of things pervaded Roman jurisprudence. The Romans acknowledged that certain things were ownerless (*res nullius*), for example wild animals, and some were incapable of being owned as they were open to everyone as, for example, the oceans (*res communes*); see Nicholas (1962: 56–7).

remains uncertain.[27] Notwithstanding the prevalence of stoical philosophy throughout classical Roman literature, the tenets of *jus naturale* did not appear to hold practical ramifications for the jurists of Rome (Nicholas 1962: 54–9). This is perhaps unsurprising in view of the fact that the Roman character, though rich in cultural inheritance gained from other Mediterranean civilizations, remained intensely pragmatic and this quality tended to militate against any meaningful application of *jus naturale*. Therefore although the private *jus gentium* was a body of law available to all free persons within Roman jurisdiction, its political significance lay in its value as a specific mechanism to regulate and therefore control peregrine relations.

Unlike modern legal systems, jurisdiction in the ancient world was premised on a personal rather than a territorial basis. Thus a person was entitled to the benefits of the institutions of *jus civile* because he was a Roman citizen rather than because he happened to be in Roman territory (Muirhead 1916: 98). Although certain concessions were granted to nationals of foreign states that had concluded international treaties or alliances with Rome (ibid.: 101–5), outside these limited exceptions peregrines lacked legal personality under *jus civile* and were therefore denied access to the legal institutions of Rome (ibid.: 98–9).[82] This situation was particularly problematic as originally only citizens possessed the legal right to acquire or alienate private property and conclude contracts (*commercium*), had the capacity to marry (*conubium*) and to become a party to legal proceedings (*legis actio*) to enforce such rights (ibid.: 99–101).

However, with the expansion of the Roman Empire, these legal impediments were increasingly perceived as being contrary to Rome's commercial interests and public order. As a result Rome was forced to re-evaluate its institutional approach to foreign nationals, a reaction that was characterized by two principles (Phillipson 1911: 96). First, Rome recognized the need to remove certain legal impediments facing peregrines in order to facilitate commercial relations. This step required the revision of existing legal institutions in a bid to create a simpler more equitable system that could support such an inclusive approach. Second, the inhabitants of territories that had submitted to Rome were permitted to preserve their own laws insofar as they did not conflict with the interests of the Roman administration. While this concession was made, Rome reserved the right to adjudicate legal disputes in a manner consistent with Roman jurisprudence and policy (more generally, see Phillipson 1911: 100–21).

This development had a profound impact on Roman legal theory and practice that held significant ramifications for the doctrine of modern *jus gentium*. Given its subsequent importance the jurisprudential reaction to this development merits further consideration. By the late Republic two distinct praetorian offices had developed although each was part of a wider jurisprudential evolution. The praetor *urbanus* was charged with adapting the actions *jus civile* in the context of relations between citizens;

---

[27] For an extensive discussion as to the nature and meaning of *jus gentium* see Phillipson (1911: 69–99).

the praetor *peregrinus* was responsible for the same with regard to peregrine relations. Despite this formal distinction, given that praetors were also responsible for discharging other public functions, for example commanders of Roman legions or provincial governors, at times a single praetor would be responsible for both offices (Sherman 1918: 58–9). Thus given the equitable nature of *jus praetorium* and the lack of available evidence, it could be construed that in practice there was a significant amount of cross-fertilization between *jus civile* and *jus gentium* (Nicholas 1962: 58).

Further, the survival of the doctrine of private *jus gentium* was not helped by the promulgation of the *Constitutio Antoniniana* by Emperor Antoninus Caracalla in AD 212. Although this edict was the product of an ambitious fiscal policy rather than any liberating motive, it declared all residents of the Roman Empire to be Roman citizens (Stein 1999: 20). This paradigm shift was to have devastating consequences for private *jus gentium*, as once all the residents of the Empire became citizens jurisdictional issues premised on personality were rendered virtually redundant (Jolowicz 1957: 39). Furthermore, the general application of *jus civile* from the beginning of the third century also had implications for the survival of the literature relating to private *jus gentium*. The *Corpus Juris* was grounded in the legal doctrine pertinent to the late Empire and therefore was not concerned with preserving classical and pre-classical texts relating to the issue of jurisdiction and the practical application of *jus gentium* to peregrines (ibid.). Though this omission has been rectified to a certain extent by the works of Gaius and Ulpian, a considerable lacuna endures hampering modern interpretations of this body of jurisprudence (ibid.: 39–40).

While scholars have labelled private *jus gentium* a form of private international law – dealing with the relations of nationals of different states – this concept appears to be somewhat misleading (Phillipson 1911: 70–99). Although *jus gentium* in this sense did apply to foreign nationals it was clearly not conceived as a law of nations. *Jus gentium* as developed by the praetor *peregrinus* was the product of Roman legal theory and despite its radical approach was designed to compliment *jus civile* rather than create a distinct legal system (Sherman 1921: 355–6).[28] While there can be little doubt that the laws and customs of the peregrines influenced the development of *jus gentium* to some extent, it would be inaccurate to suggest that the jurisprudence of private *jus gentium* was forged by such sources or amounted to a comparative system of law (ibid.: 355). Indeed there is no evidence to suggest that a comparable system existed beyond the frontiers of Roman influence or that there was any reciprocity from other nations in this regard. Both the public and private aspects of *jus gentium* were clearly products of a strictly 'national' interpretation of 'international' law and thus were designed to serve national interests rather than to facilitate relations *between* nations (ibid.: 356).

---

[28] Modern day equivalents can be found between the English common law and the system of equity.

The Reception of Roman Property Regimes into Modern *Jus Gentium*

Peregrines were allowed to acquire property by virtue of the private *jus gentium*. However, it should be emphasized that modes of acquisition under *jus gentium* were not restricted to peregrines alone, the effective transfer of ownership of *res nec mancipi* by *traditio* being open to both peregrines and citizens alike. According to Justinian, private *jus gentium* was 'the source of almost all contracts, such as sale, hire, partnership, deposit, loan for consumption and very many other things' (Phillipson 1911: 237, 233–44). It was the apparent universality of private *jus gentium* that proved so appealing to the early international scholars charged with the task of formulating a set of norms on which to base the concept of territorial sovereignty and the modes of acquiring territory (Hershey 1911: 921). Despite claims that private *jus gentium* amounted to systematic expression of fundamental rights gained by reason of humanity, in reality it was devised by a 'Common Superior' to serve municipal political ends and as such failed to embrace the abstract philosophical tenets of *jus naturale*. Arguably therefore it remained an unsuitable template on which to base a truly international legal order.

Under private *jus gentium*, the Romans recognized that certain types of property belonged to no one and were therefore *res nullius*. Property that was capable of being declared *res nullius* was divided into *humani juris* and *divini juris* (Buckland 1963: 183–6).[29] Although, along with *res communes* and *res publicae*, *divini juris* could never be privately owned, *humani juris* (principal examples included wild animals, abandoned and enemy property) was wholly different in character (ibid.; Borkowski 1994: 184–7, 153–5).[30] Property within this category could be privately acquired by recourse to the doctrine of *occupatio*. This mechanism allowed the first person to seize *res nullius* with the requisite intention to become its owner for as long as they controlled it (Buckland 1963: 205–8).[31]

The doctrine was, however, beset by normative limitations; the jurists of Rome only conceived of *occupatio* in relation to movable forms of property and therefore *res nullius* had neither a territorial dimension nor any implications for the acquisition of sovereignty.[32] Nonetheless European scholars such as Vittoria and Grotius were quick to appreciate the theoretical utility of *res nullius* when considered in the international context. For them it followed that if legal title could be conferred on the first person to acquire movable property under the tenets of *jus naturale* then the

---

[29] *Divini juris* comprised sanctified, religious or sacred forms of property.

[30] *Res publicae* was concerned with forms of property belonging to the Roman public as a whole whereas *res communes* referred to property that belonged to all humanity on the grounds that it could not be owned, for example the ocean.

[31] The owner, if a citizen, would therefore acquire dominion over the claimed property.

[32] Interestingly new islands that formed in the sea were also considered to be *res nullius* although this clearly had no bearing on the issue of sovereignty; see Lindley (1926: 10).

doctrine could be extrapolated to apply to immovable property, thereby legitimating instances of territorial acquisition. Further, the alleged universality of *jus naturale* was perceived as enabling the doctrine to be conveniently transposed into modern *jus gentium*. Thus its international manifestation *terra nullius* could be used as a theoretical tenet to legitimate the acquisition of newly discovered territory in the New World and elsewhere. However, to achieve the desired result European scholars were required to undertake the task of promoting relatively obscure examples of *res nullius*, notably in relation to the acquisition of precious stones found on the seashore (Buckland 1925: 139 and Maine 1894: 248–300).[33] Evidently such steps were thought necessary to maintain an appearance of doctrinal coherence, given that Roman legal theory was widely acknowledged to provide the theoretical foundations for modern *jus gentium*.[34]

Faced with the apparent restrictions of ancient doctrine, framers of the modern system sought assistance from the related Roman theory of possession. This combined approach was justified on the grounds that the operation of *occupatio* in private *jus gentium* was clearly rooted in the notion of possession, albeit a form of *jus naturale* possession rather than one protected by the possessory interdicts in *jus civile* (Westlake 1910: 99 and Buckland 1963: 196–204). The European scholars sought to develop the notion of natural possession by analogy with its expression in *jus civile*, thereby allowing them to draw upon its theoretical flexibility and the proven territorial dimension, which had been so keenly protected by *jus praetorium* (Westlake 1910: 99). As a result of combining the strengths of the related Roman concepts of dominion and possession the first state to claim possession of *terra nullius* would be considered to have acquired valid title on the grounds that no state could establish a superior title.[35]

The merits of transposing the doctrine of *res nullius* into modern *jus gentium* were clearly twofold. First, as stated, the norm was useful in situations of unclaimed territory as it could be pressed into service to legitimate the acquisition of uninhabited territory. Second, its broader significance lay in the concept of statehood and its impact on the acquisition of territory (see Chapter 4 and, generally, Verzijl 1955). According to Vittoria, if the European powers recognized the juridical personality of indigenous societies the territories that they inhabited would not be *terra nullius* and, consequently,

---

[33] It is nevertheless clear that the seashore itself was not capable of being privately owned; see Borkowski (1994: 154–5).

[34] The validity of this exercise has been questioned subsequently. Maine (1894: 248) pointed out: 'In applying to the discovery of new countries the same principles which the Romans had applied to the finding of a jewel, the Publicists forced into their service a doctrine altogether unequal to the task expected of it.'

[35] Although the Roman concept of dominion was concerned with the ownership of property, in the *jus civile* it clearly informed the modern interpretation of *imperium* in the context of territorial acquisition; see Westlake (1910: 88–9).

not liable to acquisition by occupation or conquest without just cause.[36] In this regard Vittoria was building on the theory espoused by Acquinas that proprietary rights stem from *jus naturale* rather than divine law and thus were common to all peoples regardless of their religious belief (Lindley 1926: 11). Grotius clearly supported this view stating that:

> (Infidel) rulers, though heathen, are legitimate rulers, whether the people live under a monarchical or democratic regime. They are not to be deprived of sovereignty over their possessions because of their unbelief since sovereignty is a matter of positive law, and unbelief is a matter of divine law, which cannot annul positive law.
>
> *(Mare Liberum* (1609), cited in Umozurike 1979: 20)

The propagation of theories on this issue heralded the development of a whole literature concerning the valid reception of *res nullius* into modern *jus gentium* (see the work of Vittoria 1532, Gentilis *De Jure Belli* [1588] 1877, Pufendorf 1710 and Vattel 1916). Evidently the modern interpretation appears to have promoted the universality of *jus naturale* in its modes of acquisition while in practice it legitimized territorial acquisition by the European powers on the grounds of perceived levels of civilization. (This issue will be explored in Chapter 4.)

Nevertheless Roman legal theory was still problematic when applied to the practical acquisition of territory in the New World. Prime amongst these difficulties was the need to establish territorial parameters of a given claim. According to the Roman theory of possession both physical control (*corpus possidendi*) and an intention to possess (*animus possidendi*) had to be present before property could be possessed. Under Roman law, a new possessor was not obliged to traverse the parameters of the territorial unit on the grounds that the existing possessor could relate its spatial dimensions on the event of acquisition. If the requisite *animus possidendi* could be shown in respect of the entire territorial unit, no barriers existed to its effective transfer and it could therefore be taken over at any given point with reference to the unit as a whole (Westlake 1910: 99–100). The same, however, could not be said of acquisition of *terra nullius* in the international context. In situations where European representatives were faced with vast tracts of *terra nullius*, in the absence of previous possessors they were incapable of substantiating the extent of the territory being claimed. It has been argued that Roman legal theory was premised on the understanding that possessory rights were limited to the territory that a possessor could physically control. The belief that the possessory rights in *jus civile* did not extend to notional possession severely hampered the ability of Roman theory to determine the degree

---

[36] See the views of Vittoria, Grotius and other scholars as expressed in Lindley (1926: 12–17). Vittoria, however, believed that if the indigenous peoples of the Americas were not prepared to be converted to Christianity or barred Europeans from their rights to trade then such conduct would amount to just cause for conquest.

and kind of possession that was required to support a valid territorial claim in the New World.[37]

The Papal bull *Inter Caetera* (1492) granted Ferdinand and Isabella of Spain exclusive rights to acquire territory in the New World unless it was already in the possession of another Christian prince (Lindley 1926: 24). In return for an undertaking to convert its inhabitants to the Christian faith the Spanish *conquistadors* were thus granted unparalleled rights of territorial acquisition in the Americas (Waldock 1948: 319, 321–2). This Catholic *fait accompli* was extended to Portugal, which had already been given rights of discovery on the coast of West Africa by Pope Nicholas V in 1454 (Westlake 1910: 96). Against this background the Treaty of Tordesillas (1494) contrived to divide territories of the undiscovered world exclusively between the Iberian powers, an agreement that received Papal sanction in 1506.[38] However, the hegemony of the Iberian powers was openly challenged from the middle of the sixteenth century with the emergence of the new imperial powers of France, England and subsequently the Netherlands. The Protestant powers were unsympathetic to the Iberian territorial claims and despite Papal sanction the French were equally unmoved.[39]

Regardless of the increased competition for territory in the New World, the European powers nevertheless recognized the need to establish a framework for the development of international norms that would acknowledge the territorial claims of enterprising nations while preserving order within the European Family of Nations.[40] As a result it was generally recognized that the 'discoveries' of the fifteenth and sixteenth centuries were carried out on the understanding that territories of the New World not already in the actual possession of a Christian prince were open to acquisition. Early international practice appears to have reflected this understanding, evidenced by the instructions given by Emperor Charles V of the Holy Roman Empire to his ambassador concerning the dispute over the Molucca Islands in 1523:

> Although Mallucco had been discovered by ships of the King of Portugal, it could not on this account . . . be said that Mallucco has been found by him; for it was evident that to 'find'

---

[37] It should be pointed out that Westlake relied on the work of the nineteenth-century Romanist Savigny in this respect. Savigny believed that the above position reflects Roman practice and its faithful reception into medieval feudal law. However, it appears that scholars of the Renaissance misinterpreted such theories in favour of territorial acquisition by symbolic annexation (see below). See Savigny (1848: 173–4), Westlake (1910: 99–100), Lindley (1926: 139–41) and Buckland (1963: 196–204).

[38] Accordingly this line was drawn 370 leagues to the west of the Cape Verde Islands with all the territory to the west going to Spain and all to the east going to Portugal; see Waldock (1948: 319).

[39] As evident from the tenor of the negotiations between France and Spain at the conference held at Chateau-Cambresis in 1559; see Heydte (1935: 458).

[40] See the judgment of Chief Justice Marshall in *Johnson* v. *McIntosh* (1823) 8 Wheaton's Supreme Court Reports (21 U.S.) 573, cited in Lindley (1926: 129) and Westlake (1910: 92–3).

required possession, and that which was not taken or possessed could not be said to be found although seen or discovered (Waldock 1948: 323).

Not only did these instructions demonstrate the practical limitations of the Tordesillas line between the Iberian powers themselves, it appears to recognize that territorial claims premised on Papal authority had little impact on acquisitory practice in the New World.[41] However, while the validity of the doctrine of occupation was widely acknowledged, the nature and extent of the possession needed to constitute a claim of territorial acquisition remained uncertain. It is evident that the development of international principles largely depended on agreement being reached as to the degree of possession required to support a valid claim to territory. Against this background Grotius proclaimed that:

> No one is sovereign of a thing which he himself has never possessed and which no one else has ever held in his name . . . To discover a thing is not only to capture it with the eyes but to take real possession thereof . . . The act of discovery is sufficient to give a clear title of sovereignty only when it is accompanied by actual possession.
>
> (*Mare Liberum* (1609), quoted in Waldock 1948: 322)

It is clear that the views of Charles V and Grotius appear to have been consistent with Roman legal theory in this respect. According to Roman law a finder did not acquire title by the act of detection but by the act of appropriation, thereby manifesting an assumption of possession (ibid.). As such mere sightings of undiscovered territory or simple physical landings ('mere discovery') were not sufficient *per se* to establish a valid title to territory, although it is nevertheless difficult to determine the exact meaning of 'actual possession' in the international context.[42] To this end it was seemingly vital to establish whether the 'taking of possession' could be achieved by symbolic annexation or was subject to the requirement of effective occupation, that is a continuous occupation supported by actual settlements or military posts (ibid.: 322–3).

Portugal was the first European nation to embark on a concerted policy of overseas territorial expansion as evidenced by its discovery of Madeira in 1419 (Keller *et al.* 1938: 23–32). Although Portuguese explorers were invariably careful to erect pillars, crosses or other landmarks bearing the insignia of the king of Portugal, in some cases

---

[41] This, however, did not stop the Iberians from promoting their purported validity. Clearly such contentions were made only where the Iberians could not base their claims on better grounds. Bartolus questioned whether the Papal bulls granted absolute title in any event. He believed that the bulls converted *possessio* into dominion and as such by analogy with Roman private law only granted the Iberian powers an inchoate title which had to be perfected with occupation; see Heydte (1935: 451–2).

[42] Waldock (1948: 317) states that in Latin *occupatio* related to the act of appropriation not the act of settlement.

leaving domestic animals or taking clods of earth, their actions were characterized by a degree of informality.[43] In general there were no prescribed ceremonial procedures for taking possession of newly discovered territory and this absence of formality was to prove problematic with the emergence of European competition for title to territory.[44]

In marked contrast the territorial claims of the Spanish *conquistadors* were supported by extensive acts of symbolic annexation, which remained unparalleled throughout the classical 'Age of Discovery' (Keller *et al.* 1938: 33–48). Spanish acquisitory practice was articulated in art. XIII of the Royal Ordinance on New Discoveries and Settlements 1563, which provided that (ibid.: 35):

> The persons who should go to discoveries by sea or by land shall take possession in our name of all the lands of the province and parts where they should arrive and land; making the necessary solemnity and acts, of which they shall bring faith and testimony in public form and in such a manner that there should be faith.

The 'necessary solemnity and acts' included the performance of a formal ceremony wherein taking possession was formally declared in the name of the king of Spain; the act would then be formally documented by a notary public and signed by attendant witnesses. The king's representative would then exercise jurisdiction on his behalf, demonstrating the effectiveness of his newly acquired territorial sovereignty. This demonstration of sovereignty often involved judging a complaint brought before him or conferring land on persons specified according to Spanish municipal law (ibid.: 39).

Despite its variance, state practice suggests that between the fifteenth and eighteenth centuries the acquisition of sovereign rights over *terra nullius* was the product of purposeful acts of exploration by authorized state representatives who would acquire newly discovered territory on behalf of their national states through symbolic annexation, typically effected through the formal act of taking of possession supported by various physical manifestations as outlined above (ibid.: 148–9). Nonetheless the apparent consensus on symbolic annexation clearly favoured the established Iberian powers and while the emerging European powers acknowledged the existing acquisitory regime their frustrations were expressed by Queen Elizabeth I of England when she informed a Spanish Ambassador in 1580 that:

> She would not persuade herself that the Indies are the rightful property of Spain . . . only on the grounds that the Spaniards have touched here and there, have erected shelters, have given names to a river or promontory, acts which cannot confer property. So that . . . this

---

[43] See Cabral's annexation of Brazil on behalf of Portugal in 1500 (Keller *et al.* 1938: 25–6).
[44] For example, see the dispute with Spain over the Molucca Islands which was eventually resolved by the Treaty of Saragossa in 1529 (ibid.: 27–8 and Heydte 1935: 457). See also the dispute with Britain regarding the *Delagoa Bay arbitration* (Lindley 1926: 135–6).

imaginary proprietorship ought not to hinder other princes from carrying on commerce in these regions and from establishing colonies where Spaniards are not residing, without the least violations of the law of nations.[45]

England also locked horns with Portugal on this issue. The king of Portugal protested to Queen Elizabeth regarding English expeditions to territories claimed by Portugal in Africa and Guinea. It is revealing that when Queen Elizabeth rejected Portuguese claims based on discovery and possession, Portugal advanced its claims on the basis of the exercise of effective control. Interestingly, in response England seemed only prepared to recognize Portuguese title in situations where military positions had been clearly established or where indigenous peoples were paying tribute (Keller *et al.* 1938: 28–9).

In respect of Newfoundland, notwithstanding the existence of a charter authorizing him to acquire undiscovered territory in North America by effective occupation, Sir Hugh Gilbert clearly acted on the understanding that sovereignty had been acquired through the performance of symbolic acts of annexation. The provision within the charter allowing English representatives to inhabit any discovered territory simply expressed the purpose of the venture and had no bearing on any legal requirement to perfect title (ibid.: 62–6).[46] It could therefore be argued that despite occasional protests, English acquisitory practice largely reflected that of the Iberians in the New World. In addition, evidence of a tacit international practice in favour of the sufficiency of symbolic annexation can be gleaned from the international dispute in respect of the Spanish claim to Florida (ibid.: 148–9). In 1565 French Huguenots sought to colonize the territory of Florida discounting claims based on the Papal bulls. The (Spanish) Royal Council of the Indies was of the opinion that the representatives of Spain had acquired title to Florida by means of symbolic annexation at least since 1558, which provided the basis for the Spanish protestation to the French court. When the matter was relayed to Queen Elizabeth she quickly recognized the validity of the Spanish claim despite the absence of actual occupation in that territory (ibid.: 45–8). As such it cannot be maintained that between the fifteenth and eighteenth centuries a general principle was advanced from either side that effective occupation was a prerequisite for the acquisition of title to territory. Notwithstanding vast claims based on nothing more than symbolic annexation, the Iberian powers were convinced of the validity of their claims. This is borne out by the seminal work of Keller, Lissitzyn and Mann which suggests that the voluminous Spanish records of exploration do not produce a shadow of a doubt that anything

---

[45] See Heydte (1935: 459), citing Goebel (1927: 63). Indeed it should be recognized that the emerging powers were perhaps fortunate to acquire any territory in the New World in the light of the Treaty of Tordesillas and the strength of the Iberian powers.
[46] The same can be said of the acquisition of Trinidad by Sir Robert Dudley (Keller *et al.* 1938: 68–70) and of English acquisitory practice in general (ibid.: 49–99).

more than symbolic annexation was required to give valid title to territory during this period (ibid.: 45).[47]

Nevertheless the prevalence of extensive territorial claims based solely on symbolic annexation presented the acquisitional regime of the time with a sustained challenge. Coupled with the mounting international competition, this meant that the existing regime became increasingly unsustainable. This presented a backdrop to the development of a theory that symbolic annexation gave the claimant state an inchoate title that would need to be perfected by effective occupation within a reasonable period if territorial sovereignty were to be considered acquired.[48] Thus the implications of an inchoate title were that it only amounted to a declaration of intent, which allowed a state to claim a prior acquisitional interest over other European powers.[49] This theory began to influence state practice from the middle of the eighteenth century and Vattel captured this shift succinctly when he said that:

> Thus navigators who are invested with a commission from the sovereigns and going on a voyage of discovery come across islands or other vast lands, have always taken possession thereof on behalf of their nation; and usually that title has been respected, provided it has been followed later by actual possession.
>
> (*Les Droits des Gens* (1758), quoted in Heydte 1935: 462)[50]

It appears that by the nineteenth century the prerequisite of effective occupation for territorial acquisition had become conventional state practice. In this climate not only did a claimant state now need to prove possession in accordance with the tenets of Roman law, it also had to establish some form of administration to demonstrate actual governance of that territory (Oppenheim 1992: 689). In keeping with inchoate title theory, if the territory were not effectively occupied within a reasonable period putative title would be considered as being lost (ibid.: 689–90). Although it appears that the doctrine of occupation in international law was moving away from its Roman law origins, English jurists sought to challenge this trend. To this end Westlake, a

---

[47] It has already been stated that given the absence of a territorial dimension the doctrine of *res nullius* was not equipped to determine the territorial parameters of a claim. It is clear that modern *jus gentium* provided no adequate solutions in this respect and it is therefore not surprising that the powers were anxious to perform acts of symbolic annexation at frequent and regular intervals (ibid.: 150).

[48] An 'inchoate title' is a title that has begun but is incomplete.

[49] See the Award of Judge Huber in the *Island of Palmas arbitration*, *AJIL* 22(4) (1928) 867–912 at 883–4. Proponents of the theory of inchoate title included Westlake (1910: 100–111), Lindley (1926: 136–58) and Hall (1924: 126–39).

[50] Further, he added that 'The law of nations will not acknowledge the property and sovereignty of a nation over any uninhabited countries, except those of which it has really taken actual possession, in which it has formed settlements, or which it makes actual use'; see Lindley (1926: 140).

committed proponent of inchoate title theory, repeatedly questioned the legal validity
of the Iberian approach to territorial acquisition (1910: 103). In support of his
argument that effective occupation had always played a central role in gaining
conclusive title he turned to nineteenth-century interpretations of the Roman theory
of possession.[51] Westlake claimed that Renaissance scholars promoted the mistaken
belief that the *animus* for acquisition was determined by acts of symbolic annexation
applicable in respect of the surrounding area.[52] Relying on the theories of the eminent
Romanist Savigny, he asserted that such *animus* was limited to the actual position
adopted rather than its broader territorial parameters, thereby undermining the validity
of symbolic annexation in favour of the doctrine of effective occupation.[53] Westlake
concluded that the predominant theory of acquisition during the nineteenth century
was more faithful to Roman legal theory than the notion of symbolic annexation.
Perhaps the most interesting aspect of Westlake's position for present purposes has
less to do with the validity of symbolic annexation during the 'Age of Discovery' and
more to do with the continuing desire of eminent international jurists to justify their
views in terms of Roman legal theory. Although international legal theory may have
been moving away from its Roman origins, the tendency to rely on its core values
evidently persisted.

While it has been claimed that the doctrine of effective occupation was widespread
during the nineteenth century it is apparent that the convergence between theory and
practice was short-lived. From the perspective of the European powers the prerequisite
of effective occupation was problematic. Territorial claims were often made in respect
of uninhabited, largely unexplored or relatively inaccessible territory (see Chapter 3).
This added to the constraints of physical possession and combined with financial
costs of administration made the requirement of effective occupation seem prohibitive.[54]
Although the doctrine remained predominant throughout the nineteenth century, there
is evidence to suggest that the powers largely ignored it in the colonial context.[55] The
practical limits of the doctrine of effective occupation were even acknowledged by its
most fervent proponents. To this end the incremental nature of an inchoate title was

---

[51] Westlake (1910: 104–5) also refers to the statements of Vattel and Queen Elizabeth I in
support of the historic value of inchoate title theory.

[52] Westlake (1910: 100) transposes the *animus* of possession into the *animus* for ownership for
the present purposes.

[53] See Savigny *Possession*, Vol. II, (1848: 173–4) cited by Westlake (1910: 99–100). On effective
occupation see pp. 102–3 and 105.

[54] Further, given the physical constraints of acquisition in the colonial context the doctrine of
effective occupation did not resolve questions over the spatial dimensions of territorial claims.
Oppenheim (1992: 690–1) suggests that while it seems natural to suppose that the extent of
such claims would be dependent on effectiveness the powers were often keen to enhance their
claims by questionable instruments such as the hinterland doctrine or the notion of contiguity.

[55] The limits of effective occupation were glaringly apparent from the Berlin West Africa
Conference (1884–5) and the subsequent reception of its Final Act (see Chapter 4).

emphasized, stating that compliance with the requirement of effective occupation was the result of a gradual process dependent on the nature of the particular territory in issue (Westlake 1910: 108–11).

However, while this approach appreciated the circumstantial element of the march towards effective occupation it was accepted that territory would have to be effectively occupied eventually (ibid.: 111). In marked contrast scholars in the twentieth century began to acknowledge the importance of relativism in cases of territorial acquisition.[56] The requirement of effectiveness was still relevant in providing evidence of continuous and peaceful display of territorial sovereignty, ensuring that the maintenance of order and protection corresponded to the international standard. Nevertheless this standard was dependent on the nature of the territory under issue; the degree of occupation required in uninhabited or sparsely occupied regions will differ substantially from that expected in densely populated metropolitan areas (Heydte 1935: 463).[57]

During the twentieth century international tribunals began to emphasize corollary duties attendant to the exercise of territorial sovereignty including protection of rights of other states regarding their national security and the treatment of their nationals while in the territory (Waldock 1948: 317). According to Waldock the shift from effective occupation with its right to exclude others to the manifestation and exercise of governmental functions over territory comes as a result of the recognition that occupation in modern international law is the acquisition of sovereignty rather than property.[58] In the modern context he suggests that effective state activity either internally or externally provides the basis of a title acquired by occupation rather than settlement or exploitation of the territory.[59]

Another important mode of territorial acquisition in the international historical context is that of prescription. A prescriptive claim may arise through the continuous and undisturbed exercise of sovereignty over territory for such a period as is necessary to create the impression that the current position conforms to the requirements of international order (Oppenheim 1992: 706). In this respect the notion of prescription shares many similarities with the doctrine of occupation. Although both concepts reflect the wider concerns of the international community, they have traditionally been distinguished on the grounds that occupation relates to the acquisition of *terra nullius*

---

[56] Heydte (1935: 462) cites the views of French scholars Verdross and Smedal in this context. Accordingly 'It is owing to that new conception of effectiveness with its defining-lines drawn by the "international standard" and by the intrinsic aim of the rule, that the prospect was opened towards the wide world of facts, and the way was cleared for observations of political reality.'

[57] On this issue see the *Island of Palmas arbitration*, AJIL 22 (1928) 867–912; the *Clipperton Island arbitration*, AJIL 26 (1932) 390–4; the *Eastern Greenland case* (1933) PCIJ, Series A/B, no. 53, p. 52 and the *Minquiers and Ecrehos case*, ICJ Reports (1953) 47.

[58] The doctrine of occupation in modern international law relates to the appropriation of sovereignty rather than soil.

[59] For discussion of the modern approach, see generally Shaw (1997: 342–54), Brownlie (1998: 136–48) and Jennings (1962: 1–35).

and prescription to situations where the territory belonged to a state whose sovereignty was subsequently challenged by a competing state (Brownlie 1998: 137).

Grotius believed that prescription was characterized by a presumptive quality.[60] To this end the doctrine was considered to be applicable where the origins of a particular state of affairs were uncertain. In such cases the doctrine presumed that the existing situation was legal as a result of 'immemorial possession'. However, it is generally accepted that a prescriptive claim can give rise to good title under certain conditions if there is evidence of a continuous and undisturbed possession for a sufficient period (Oppenheim 1992: 706). To this end 'acquisitive prescription' fully recognizes the adverse nature of this form of possession and seeks to cure defective title in the broader interests of international peace and stability. In this regard the notion of acquisitive prescription draws heavily on its *jus civile* equivalent of *usucapio*. As already stated, this Roman norm became applicable where uninterrupted possession of property (albeit under putative title) existed for a period defined by law. To this extent the notion of *usucapio* clearly informed the doctrine of acquisitive prescription both in terms of its ultimate ends as well as the means by which they could be achieved.[61] Thus it can be categorically stated that the notion of *usucapio* has by transference significantly influenced international law and the acquisition of territory (Johnson 1950: 338).

However, despite such glaring doctrinal similarities the academic debate regarding the relevance of the notion of *usucapio* persisted (Oppenheim 1992: 706; Lindley 1926: 178). A particularly contentious issue stemmed from the fact that according to its classical interpretation a person would only be entitled to the action of *usucapio* if they had acted in good faith. Given that the justification for the existence of prescriptive claims in international law is widely accepted to be the need for order (see Chapter 1), it has been argued that a requirement of good faith would be contrary to the whole nature of the exercise (Johnson 1950: 337). On the function of acquisitive prescription in international law Hall stated:

> While under the conditions of civil life it is possible so to regulate its operation as to render it the handmaiden of justice, it must be frankly recognised that internationally it is allowed for the sake of interests which have hitherto been looked upon as supreme, to lend itself as a sanction for wrong, when wrong has shown itself to be strong enough not only to triumph for a moment but to establish itself permanently and solidly.
>
> (Hall 1924: 143–4, quoted in Johnson 1950: 337)

Although it must be acknowledged that no requirement of good faith exists in respect of international claims, this element alone cannot be considered sufficient to diminish the impact of Roman legal theory in this regard (Johnson 1950: 338). Furthermore

---

[60] For the views of Grotius on this subject, see Johnson (1950: 336–7).

[61] It is clear that modern scholars rely heavily on the notion of *usucapio* in their consideration of acquisitive prescription; see Johnson (1950) and Brownlie (1998: 151).

there is reliable evidence to suggest that the earliest conception of *usucapio* was not subject to the condition of good faith in any event.[62]

In order to make a successful prescriptive claim a state is required to satisfy a number of stringent conditions.[63] First, the possession of the prescribing state must be exercised *a titre de souverain*, that is there must be a display of state authority and the absence of recognition of sovereignty of another state (Brownlie 1998: 153). Second, the possession must be peaceful and uninterrupted, as such there has to be a continuous and peaceful display of state authority. It is clear that this requirement manifests itself in two respects, the display of authority by the prescribing state and the necessary acquiescence of the other state (Johnson 1950: 345). This same condition gives rise to questions regarding the use of force within the confines of territorial acquisition. Johnson points out that acquisitive prescription could not operate in situations where possession was maintained by force since such a state of affairs would be contrary to the purposes of the doctrine. However, acquisitive prescription could be applied in cases where the original act of taking possession was affected by the use of force as long as subsequent possession was peaceful (ibid.: 346).[64] Against this background the related issue of how such a possession may be challenged needs to be considered. Academic debate has dwelt on the value of diplomatic protest in this context, yet although such protests have been held to be sufficient it is nevertheless clear that continued protests unsupported by other acts may prove to be fruitless given the existence of available machinery designed to resolve international disputes.[65]

Third, the possession must be public. According to Johnson (1950: 347) 'publicity is essential because acquiescence is essential', suggesting that without knowledge there can be no acquiescence, a factor that goes to the root of acquisitive prescription and one that has significantly impacted on the doctrine of *terra nullius* globally.[66] Finally the possession must persist for a sufficient period of time. Clearly, as with the issue of publicity, the matter of duration derives its importance in relation to knowledge and acquiescence, nonetheless the exact period required under international law has always remained an open question.[67] Given the nature of the international

---

[62] Johnson (1950: 338, footnote 1) refers to the conception of *usucapio* existing at the time of the XII Tables.

[63] Ibid.: 344–8, adopting the work of Fauchille (1925: 759).

[64] This is obviously subject to the caveat of intertemporal rule since the Kellogg-Brand Pact (1928) and subsequently art. 2(4) of the UN Charter. On the application of the intertemporal rule, see Jennings (1962: 28–31).

[65] On this issue see the *Chamizal arbitration*, AJIL 5(3) (1911) 782–833. Further, see MacGibbon (1953).

[66] Publicity does not, however, equate to a duty to notify, although states have often sought to publicize their acquisitions in this context; see the *Clipperton Island arbitration*, AJIL 26 (1932) 390–4.

[67] The *British Guiana–Venezuela arbitration*, British and Foreign State Papers, 87, pp. 1061–107 used the yardstick of 50 years. Commenting on this case Lindley (1926: 178–80) thought the period could be shorter in appropriate cases.

system and the potential scope of acquiescence this is perhaps understandable, and indeed the apparent reluctance of modern scholars to hanker after the certainty of municipal regimes has much to recommend it.

It is clear that the above conditions have been substantially influenced by Roman legal theory in that they appear to constitute a blend of the elements of *usucapio* (in the sense that a possession must manifest an intention to own over a sufficient period) and the requirement of the possessory interdicts that a possession must be *nec vi, nec clam, nec precario*. Clearly, as with the transposition of *res nullius* into modern *jus gentium*, the various elements of *usucapio* and the possessory interdicts have been significantly adapted to fulfil their functions in the international context. However, the fact that ancient theories have been subjected to a process of thorough revision does not in any way undermine the importance of their contribution to the development of international law.

The increasing reluctance of international tribunals to reach their decisions in accordance with classical modes of territorial acquisition with preference for more pragmatic approaches has fuelled the academic debate regarding the continuing value of the traditional classification (Johnson 1950: 348–9).[68] This trend is reflected in the attitude of modern scholars who favour the use of broader frameworks premised on effective control rather than performing the difficult task of deciding between occupation and prescription in cases where the parties may indeed be asserting concurrent claims to territory (Brownlie 1998: 136–56; Shaw 1997: 342–54). The importance of acquisitive prescription as a means of territorial acquisition has also been challenged by recourse to notions of acquiescence, recognition and estoppel (Brownlie 1998: 156–9).[69] In this context Oppenheim stated:

> In short, prescription is not so much now a singular mode of acquisition, or loss, of territorial sovereignty, as a convenient term for one group of elements, which go together to make or break a title. And this leads into the consideration of modern developments in a law beginning to outgrow its origins in the categories of classical Roman law.
>
> (Oppenheim 1992: 708)

Brownlie suggests that it is clear that modern international law now chooses to attach greater weight to considerations of international stability and pragmatism than maintaining its doctrinal links with Roman legal theory (1998: 141). However, while in an era characterized by national self-determination the core values of the current international regime are rightly changing, it is nevertheless clear that modern interpretations of Roman legal theory have always perceived their core value as being

---

[68] Johnson amplifies his arguments (1955: 219–22). See also Jennings (1962: 23). The main cases cited in this debate are the *Island of Palmas arbitration* (1928), *Eastern Greenland* (1933) and the *Minquiers and Ecrehos case* (1953) (see footnote 57).
[69] On the issue of acquiescence see MacGibbon (1957a and 1957b). See also Jennings (1962: 36–51).

the promotion of order and to this extent it is suggested that Roman property regimes continue to inform the doctrine of territoriality in the modern international context.

Conclusions

This chapter has examined key aspects of Roman legal theory with specific reference to Roman property regimes in an attempt to provide a thorough assessment of their importance to the development of modern international law. The reception of Roman jurisprudence into modern *jus gentium* was clearly not the product of a process of simple transposition from an ancient 'international' system. Rather, modern *jus gentium* was heavily reliant on strained analogies with private *jus gentium* and *jus civile* in a bid to serve its own ends, that is the legitimation of territorial acquisition in the colonial context. Further, the eclectic selection and theoretical intermingling of Roman norms by European scholars in order to create a modern system has been exacerbated by the lack of surviving evidence, thus ensuring that the task of analysing the continuing validity of these ancient norms remains extremely difficult.

Regardless of the vagaries of subsequent doctrinal revision the characteristics of Roman legal theory were deeply entrenched within the jurisprudence of modern *jus gentium*, particularly in the sphere of territorial acquisition. Evidently the mechanism of occupation closely resembled *occupatio* in private *jus gentium*, notwithstanding its subsequent territorial expression. Further, the international manifestation clearly drew upon Roman conceptions of ownership and possession and as a result was profoundly influenced by the strict requirements of *jus civile* as well as by the tenets of *jus naturale*. The continuing importance of Roman theories of ownership and possession was apparent during the fifteenth and sixteenth centuries when the European powers first embarked on their process of territorial acquisition in the New World. European states and scholars turned to Roman legal theory in an effort to justify their actions and to provide a framework for territorial acquisition *inter se*. Consequently they promoted the doctrine of occupation, which led to the apparent dispute as to the constitution of 'possession' in modern *jus gentium*. Interestingly, the resultant debate remained largely faithful to Roman legal theory as reflected by international consensus on the effect of symbolic annexation in cases of territorial acquisition. Although the nineteenth century with its preference for inchoate titles perfected by effective occupation arguably denoted a shift away from the confines of Roman legal theory, eminent scholars maintained that such doctrinal changes actually rendered international practice more consistent with Roman theories of possession and its territorial expression.

Clearly there were limits regarding the utility of Roman jurisprudence in the international context. Irrespective of the historical dispute over whether symbolic annexation was sufficient to secure valid title, Roman law proved to be of limited assistance in delimiting the actual parameters of territorial claims – a lacuna modern *jus gentium* also struggled to fill. Against this background it must not be forgotten that the norms of ownership and possession were the products of Roman private law and were not conceived with the acquisition of territorial sovereignty in mind. Thus the purpose of this chapter is not to demonstrate that Roman legal theory provided a blueprint for the modern international system; rather it demonstrates how the variety of sources and norms were combined and revised to provide the foundations of an international system.

The events of the twentieth century have clearly unleashed both centrifugal and centripetal forces in the guise of the norms of self-determination, democratic governance and human rights, thereby threatening the inviolability of the nineteenth-century paradigms of statehood and sovereignty (see generally Davis 1996). Nevertheless, as the following chapters will demonstrate, in the face of these pervasive forces the current international regime explicitly maintains its commitment to the doctrine of territoriality in a bid to preserve its version of international order. Accordingly, by seeking to promote the doctrine of territoriality at the expense of other equally valid determinants, 'modern international law' has in fact preserved the efficacy of key sources that provided the theoretical foundations for the existing international regime. Consequently, despite its subsequent revision and selective reinterpretation, Roman jurisprudence did make an immense contribution to the treatment of territory within modern *jus gentium*; the process of decolonization and the events surrounding the break up of states in the former Soviet Union and Yugoslavia have shown that it continues to hold ramifications for the doctrine of territoriality within modern international law.[70]

---

[70] The continuing value of *terra nullius* in modern international law can be seen in the judgment of the ICJ in the *Western Sahara case*, ICJ Reports (1975) 12. Further, the continuing relevance of Roman legal theory can be seen in the validity ascribed to the norm of *uti possidetis* regarding the formation of new states (see Chapter 5).

3 Spanish America and the Treatment of Territory in International Law

This general principle offered the advantage of establishing an absolute rule that there was not in the law of the old Spanish America any *terra nullius*; while there might exist many regions which have never been occupied by the Spaniards and many unexplored or inhabited by non-civilised natives, these regions were reputed to belong in law to whichever Republic succeeded to the Spanish province to which these territories were attached by virtue of the old Royal ordinances of the Spanish mother country. These territories, although not occupied in fact were by common consent deemed to be occupied in law from the first hour by the new Republic.

Arbitral Award of the Swiss Federal Council of 24 March 1922 concerning boundary questions between Colombia and Venezuela (UN *RIAA* I 228)

No study of the treatment of territory in international law can be complete without a thorough review of the contribution made by the Latin American states to the development of the international legal principles guiding the treatment of territory in international law. As has been seen in the discussion on the doctrine of *uti possidetis de jure* and *de facto*, the first real transposition of the Roman norms governing territory within international law came in the Creole action in seeking liberation of Latin American territories from the aegis of imperial Spain.[1] This process was extremely significant in terms of international law for a variety of reasons. To understand the context in which these developments took place it is vital to analyse the background that motivated the Creoles to seek secession and independence from Spain and the subsequent development of the relevant norms.[2] It needs to be noted that the Creole action was the first instance of 'decolonization' in the sense that it is currently understood.[3] Until the Creole action in Latin America it was more common for imperial European powers to acquire territory abroad than to be forced to defend themselves against inhabitants of a territory seeking its own government. This is not to suggest that the acquisition of territory elsewhere took place amicably. Indeed the numerous wars and skirmishes that took place under the aegis of the so-called 'Scramble for

---

[1] For general reading on the subject of the colonization of Latin America, see Picon-Salas (1962), Pastor (1992) and Boggs (1980).

[2] For a general reading about the Creoles' motivations see Brading (1983).

[3] For the dynamics of the principle of decolonization see Sureda (1973).

Africa' are documented elsewhere (Pakenham 1991). Also documented are the numerous brutal battles fought by imperial powers in other theatres around the globe as they sought to disseminate their 'three Cs' policy of christianity, commerce and 'civilization' (see Chapter 4). However, these could be considered struggles to acquire territory rather than in defence of territory against a concerted effort of resistance, which in the case of Africa and Asia only came much later.

Having examined the genesis of norms of Roman law governing the acquisition of territory in international law, it is appropriate to examine how these norms affected the acquisition and subsequent relinquishment of territory by the imperial powers of Spain and Portugal. The rest of this book focuses on the manner in which these norms have affected the treatment of territory in the face of different turning points in the history of a given territory. The importance of the Creole action in defining the interpretation of these norms make this a particularly compelling place to start.

The importance of Latin America to the development of international law governing territory can be analysed by studying three different eras identified within the nineteenth century by Alejandro Alvarez (1909). The first era begins at 'independence' and runs to the middle of the century, the second extends from the middle of the century until the last third, while the third consists of the remainder of the century. In analysing the relationships between Latin American countries as well as their relations with states outside the continent, a clear picture emerges of the legal and political climate surrounding the newly formed states. This analysis casts direct and indirect insights into the development of the notion of *uti possidetis*, the view of territory and the notion of *terra nullius* and the factors influential in transposing these Roman law concepts into modern international law. It needs to be stated at the outset that one of the biggest contributions made by Latin American states identified by Alvarez is the denial of the notion of *terra nullius* (1909: 321). He identifies and discusses this in the context of the Monroe Doctrine on which considerable emphasis will be laid in the latter parts of this chapter. However, the first section of this chapter seeks to identify the preconditions and motivations of the Creole action and their potential impact on legal regimes. The second section then traces the specificities of the decolonization of Spanish America and the manner in which the principle of *terra nullius* and the doctrine of *uti possidetis* were used. This process is informed by attempts made by the newly formed states to establish a legal regime for the treatment of territory through means of confederation. The final section then locates these doctrinal developments alongside two major contributions ascribable to Spanish American states, namely the enunciation of the Monroe Doctrine and the creation of an arbitration mechanism in a bid to regulate conflict. However, to understand these principles one needs to understand the factors and conditions which engendered their development in Latin America. While the former reiterates the fundamental principles in support of a denial of *terra nullius*, the latter provides an early insight into the resolution of boundary disputes and other disputes over territory.

Historical Background to the Creole Action

In seeking to demonstrate that the Latin American states were different from the European states that governed them Alvarez described them thus:

> Europe is formed of men of a single race, the white; while Latin America is composed of a native population to which in colonial times was added in varying proportions an admixture of the conquering race and emigrants from the mother country, Negroes imported from Africa, and the Creoles, that is those born in America but of European parents. Out of this amalgamation of races (the Aborigines, the Whites, and the Negroes, together with the Creole element), the Latin American continent presented an ethnical product which was no less peculiar than its physical environment. The resultant *colonial society* . . . is completely *sui generis*; in it the whites, born in the mother country, although in the minority, exercised the control and guided a multitude which was in great part illiterate and ignorant.
>
> (Alvarez 1909: 271–2)

While the tone of the language locates the discourse in its rightful place as writing of the early part of the twentieth century, it reveals the extent to which theorists could generalize about given situations. Such theorizing, as has been pointed out elsewhere, was often the underlying basis for the prejudicial and often incorrect views of specific peoples.[4] Nonetheless as an early review of the influence exercised by Latin American states this work remains significant for its breadth and analysis. Besides, as the native indigenous population continues to be marginalized across modern Latin America, the crux of the issues raised by Alvarez remain relevant today. Also significant is the setting described above which propelled the Creoles, themselves European descendants, into the forefront of the movement for independence from Europe. Endowed with European values and education, the Creoles quickly became the dominant force in the wresting of independence away from the Spanish. They formed the intellectual elite on whom the main thrust of the pro-independence movement fell. For Alvarez, this responsibility was natural enough since he identified them as the 'only thinking part of the population' (1909: 274), yet the failure to include other groups (notably indigenous peoples) within the quest has left a long legacy in many of the inter-American states.[5] The prime motivation for Creole independence was identified as being the injustice with which the mother country treated its colonies. The role of this elite cannot be understated and its parallel to independence movements during the UN sponsored decolonization has been explored elsewhere (Grovogui 1996). Instructed by travel and greatly

---

[4] See, for instance, Gellner (1972). Gellner makes the essential point that the vision of North Africa that was perceived in Europe came from personal accounts of travellers and explorers and therefore was influenced by their own prejudice.

[5] See *Yanoamani Indian case*, Case 7615 IACHR 24, OEA/Ser.L/V/11.66, doc. 10 Rev. 1 (1985). For this and other cases concerning indigenous peoples in the Americas see Davis (1988).

influenced by the philosophical writings of the eighteenth century, the Creoles seized on the opportunity presented by the embarrassment of Spain in the Napoleonic Wars to launch their bid for emancipation (Brading 1983: 16). The unity for this struggle amongst the different populations of Spanish descent is difficult to determine. Alvarez himself suggested a rather ambiguous 'law of historical psychology' may have played a part (1909: 272). According to him this 'law' consists of the notion that a people will 'take advantage of the difficult situation of another people in order to exercise against that other, any rights to which it believes itself entitled' (ibid.). However, whatever the support from within for the Creoles, their action proved decisive and the regions of Latin America came to independence almost solely as a result of their action.

Charles Tilly in examining the preconditions for 'revolution' suggested that certain essential factors needed satisfaction:

a)   Active support of a significant segment of the subject population
b)   Coalition appearance of new contenders for governmental power
c)   Insider and outsider challenges to power
d)   Incumbent government's inability or unwillingness to suppress the threat to its monopoly of power

(Tilly 1975: 521)

These conditions seemed ideally suited to the French Revolution, which informed Tilly's analysis to a certain extent. But that revolution, in the quest for self-determination, had at heart similar notions about self-governance to those that motivated the Creole action in Spanish America. The French Revolution basically sought to reconstruct a political system around a unitary national community and a democratic decision-making process (Hayward 1991: 1). In this quest plural identities were submerged in the interest of the creation of a supervening unifying identity with the emotional, spiritual and physical appeal to overthrow the existing notions of governance (Castellino 1999a). Neuberger in analysing these norms from a historical perspective highlights the importance of the precursors, suggesting that they go back further than the French Revolution. He traces them to the late Middle Ages and the early Renaissance when Marsilus of Padua enunciated the notion of 'legitimate government' based on the 'consent of the governed'. He also refers to Dante who raised the issue of autonomy for cultural groups (Neuberger 1986: 4–5; see also Rabl 1973: 5). Indeed Neuberger suggests that jurists and philosophers prepared the ground for democratic ideas as early as the seventeenth and eighteenth centuries when discussing the right of resistance to tyrannical authority. This right, framed as *jus resistendi ac secessionis* or the right to resistance and secession, was reflected succinctly in the works of Grotius who saw it as a right for the oppressed (*De Jure Pacis Bella*, as quoted in Neuberger 1986: 5).

Thus the Creoles with their exposure to European educational institutions would have been well aware of the philosophical and historical underpinnings of secession. Further, in the dramatic events of the French Revolution, they would have been inspired by the romantic notion of self-determination (Koskenniemi 1994: 241; Castellino 2000a: ch. 1) and would have seized on the opportunity to rid 'their continent' of Spanish influence. However, in returning to Tilly's analysis of revolution and applying it to Creole action in the emancipation of Spanish America, an interesting view emerges. First, as regards the condition of an 'active segment of the subject population', it could be argued that the 'subject' of that population only included other Creoles and did not include other tribes and groups that may have lived on the same territory. This reveals a view of the indigenous populations that is borne out especially in Alvarez's analysis as being too ignorant to partake of these matters. Thus redefining the population arguably satisfied the first condition for revolution. The second precondition concerned the appearance of coalitions of new contenders. This took place within the Creoles themselves and as they consolidated their moral arguments based on notions of democracy and the 'consent of the governed' they managed to promote real contenders for governmental power that eventually succeeded in overthrowing the colonial regime. The third factor, concerning the insider and outsider challenges to power, can be seen in the subsequent development of legal norms and principles concerning territory. While the 'inside' challenge to Spanish rule consisted of the Creoles, the 'external' challenge presented to the fledgling states was the constant fear of being reconquered. This was at the heart of the development of a legal regime in protection of the independence gained. Finally, the colonial government's inability and unwillingness to suppress the threat to its monopoly of power was partly dictated by the ravages of the Napoleonic Wars and also the 'law of historical psychology' as suggested by Alvarez (1909: 272).

On seizing power the Creoles, seeking to empower the new states with a real legal regime, attempted to consolidate a constitutional regime that could be identified as being republican, liberal and democratic (ibid.: 273). However, the sudden change in the dynamics of political power had significant consequences. Without an educated populace the practice of democratic values was also going to be difficult. The inevitable result was continent-wide 'civil wars, dictatorships and constant modifications of the fundamental ordinances of those countries in the first period of their independence' (ibid.). Nonetheless, despite continuous unrest, an almost fraternal spirit existed within the new states. They had distinct similarities in that they were fighting a common colonial enemy, had similar population dynamics with large indigenous populations existing beyond the franchise of the new states, had inherited shared common cultural backgrounds from Europe and had similar fears and insecurities in terms of the state-building process within the continent.[6] Thus although there were numerous wars and more importantly boundary skirmishes amongst the protagonists, it is important to bear in mind that the states were:

---

[6] Similar sentiments led to the creation of the International Union of American Republics of 1890 and subsequently the Organisation of American States in May 1948. For more on the inter-American system of human rights, see Harris and Livingstone (1998).

... born into political life simultaneously, forming a family of states in which the pride of independence, the love of liberty and the spirit of fraternity, developed an implacable hatred towards all foreign domination, and an eager striving for the formation of a political entity which would protect them against all attacks on their sovereignty and maintain peace amongst themselves.

(ibid.)

These factors remained central to the growth of the independent countries of Latin America throughout the nineteenth century and in this sense had a direct impact on the development of the notions of territory throughout the continent. Thus, similar to that of fifteenth- and sixteenth-century European jurists, the regime governing territory that the Creoles sought to imbibe and elaborate had its foundations in a quest for the justification of the stability of possessions. The significance of this legal regime beyond the continent was twofold: first the doctrines adopted in this process of Spanish decolonization came to take on great resonance and were subsequently applied as international legal principles. Second, the Creole-inspired action in quest of independence from European empires was the first of its kind in modern international law (Schwarzenberger 1968). The only identifiable event of this nature preceding it was the revolt in the Low Countries against the suzerainty of Spain at the end of the sixteenth century. On that occasion the seven provinces of the north formed a Perpetual Confederation and declared themselves independent of Spain. They then set themselves up with a republican form of government and by 1581 considered themselves fully independent. Spain contested the situation for half a century though ultimately recognizing the independence of the provinces via the Treaty of Münster, signed in 1648 (Alvarez 1909: 274). Thus the Creoles, acting between 1810 and 1824, had no significant precedent to fall back on since the Low Country action was different for a number of reasons, and in any case was on a completely different territorial scale.

The distance was clearly one of the chief differences in the two situations. But this was compounded by numerous other factors such as the make-up of the population of the Latin American countries, their proximity to the United States of America, and the control exercised by the Creole numerical minority over the newly emergent states. In asserting their independence the new states maintained that their actions were a natural consequence of their individual liberty, which, they argued, gave them the right to form sovereign states (ibid.: 275). Interestingly they were keen to distinguish this right from one of a civil struggle, insisting rather that it be considered as an international war. This is particularly relevant to our current study since it can be argued that while Latin American independence from Spain was achieved outside the rubric of civil liberties and human rights, modern struggles over territory and their governance are integral to the growing relevance of human rights[7] and humanitarian law (see generally

---

[7] Issues concerning land rights within the UN system come under the auspices of the Fourth Committee on Decolonisation, before the Human Rights Committee claiming violations of arts. 1 and/or 27 of the International Covenant on Civil and Political Rights 1966, or before the International Court of Justice when concerned with strict territorial disputes between states.

Murphy 2000). For instance, the debate still rages as to the extent to which non-state combatants such as liberation movements could be considered as fighting an international rather than internal war (Chadwick 1996). Suffice to state at this stage that the notion of independence from Spain for the Latin American countries was not perceived and highlighted at the time as being one of providing a more representative regime.[8] Rather, since the Creoles were themselves of European origin, it was more a triumph of notions of territoriality over considerations of identity, since the Creoles' ties to the territory overrode any emotional attachment they might have had to the mother country from which their parents first emerged: a situation markedly different from modern manifestations of decolonization.

Legal Impact of the Creole Action

The first threat faced by the new regimes in Latin America was that of renewed European conquest. To be able to harvest the fruits of the independence struggle the Creoles had to find a way to buttress themselves in law and fact against any renewed European interest in what they saw as 'their' lands. While the ideas of self-governance that motivated the struggle could be seen to come from their European-based education, they were now in a position to use this education to consolidate and cement their hold over the territory that could be deemed to belong to them. This process had both internal and external ramifications. Internally it was important for the Creoles to come to some agreement amongst themselves with regard to the extent of their territorial limits so as to prevent infighting and forceful renegotiation of boundaries between themselves. Accordingly it was necessary to build the geographical parameters of the new state into its constitution to forestall territorial disputes that might arise between states.[9] The process was coupled with attempts to foster co-operation between the states by agreeing to forge regional pacts for defence and co-operation. One of the prime objectives envisaged for this regional co-operation was the creation of an institution that could mediate in potential boundary disputes. Based on the manner in which Latin American states were administered by the imperial regime of Spain, the fledgling states were highly aware that boundary disputes were more than likely. This awareness in tandem with the external threat to territory was the *prima facie* cause for the attempts to create a continent-wide arbitration procedure. In terms of the treatment of territory in international law this too is significant since it has subsequently been used in different formats in territorial disputes between states.[10] The external

---

[8] In this sense it differs from the American and French Revolutions; see Hayward (1991), Franck (1992: 46) and Castellino (1999a).

[9] This can be seen in numerous Latin American constitutions; see the Constitution of El Salvador 1981, referred to in the *Case concerning the land, island and maritime frontier dispute (El Salvador v. Honduras case)*, ICJ Reports (1992) 351; see also Chapter 5.

[10] Most notably in the Opinions of the Badinter Arbitration Commission that was created by the European Community Conference on Yugoslavia; see Shaw (1997); Radan (2000) and Terrett (2000).

ramifications of the consolidation process were affected by the attempt at continent-wide pacts. However, to be able to justify title to territory the more significant ramification is the development of the doctrine of *terra nullius* and its expression in the international sphere. This development sought to prevent the acquisition of territory by Europeans in Latin America by way of a legal mechanism that has since been consolidated as a principle within international law.[11] Although the concept of *terra nullius* was not new to international law at that point, it had not constricted imperial states in their quest to consolidate their overseas empires elsewhere. While in international law at the time the principle of unfair occupation of occupied territory was not necessarily acceptable, it was nonetheless subject to the power dynamic of expansionists. In addition, by way of justification these powers saw fit to occupy lands where there was no 'recognizable' form of government, even if in a strict legal sense these lands were not *terra nullius* in that they had upon them inhabitants who could lay claim to them. That the inhabitants had not formed themselves into units 'recognizable' to the colonists, in addition to other factors in the power struggle between colonists, meant that the territories were deemed *terra nullius* and therefore open to occupation by competition if necessary under international legal principles. Thus the prime utility of the principle of *terra nullius* lay, at the time, in the identification by the international community of the geographic space available for its occupation and colonization. However, in seeking to declare that all Latin American territories were considered occupied territory the Creoles made some salient points that directly challenged and undermined the international perception of *terra nullius*.

Their first point was that all territory within the continent, whether viewed from an internal continent-wide perspective or from an external perspective, was under the guise of an existing sovereign power. This claim is essentially one of 'effective control' over territory. It can be categorically proven that many of the new states did not exercise effective jurisdiction to the extent of the territory claimed within their respective boundaries. Indeed parallels can be drawn here with what Jackson (1992) sought to describe in his controversial analysis of the sub-Saharan African state. The Creoles in declaring their independence and insisting that all territory within Latin America came under the auspices of sovereign states were clearly not reflecting a *de facto* situation since there was often no way in which some of the tribes of the interior could be said to be paying allegiance to any specific government. Externally such a *diktat* would ostensibly have no validity since it was not based on the notion of 'democratic entitlement' that could be said to give an entity its 'international legitimacy' based on principles of the American Revolution in the late eighteenth century (Franck 1992: 46). However, within the international legal climate of the time, the rejection of the principle of *terra nullius* was accepted since it was considered to have been made by a government and thereby the very laying of such a claim would seem to prove that

---

[11] As discussed earlier in Chapter 1 and as will be demonstrated in the case law of the ICJ in Chapter 5.

the territory concerned could not be considered *terra nullius* despite the lack of evidence as to effective control within the stated boundaries. From this acceptance it can be inferred that the Latin American states had achieved the status of being recognizable international entities. In addition, their own understanding of the mechanics of the European state regime was instrumental in the making and subsequent acceptance of their statements. Of course in the middle of the nineteenth century when this process was taking place the focus of the imperial powers had already begun to shift eastward towards Africa and Asia. While Spain and Portugal had been active in seeking out overseas territories before this point, the formal colonization process, especially in terms of ownership and possession against other similar claims, could be said to have commenced only later with the quest to gain control in Africa.[12]

The second important point within the Creole declaration of independence related to the notion that although they viewed their actions as an extension of personal liberty, they did not feel the need to include other groups within the continent in the process. Modelling their approach upon the virtues of the Westphalian state, they believed that the most suitable strategy for state building on the new continent was to accept the administrative boundaries created by the Spanish and to leave them uncontested. This action had the prime purpose of preserving order,[13] and although the new states continued to hold claims against each other these claims were nevertheless subject to two factors: first, a general belief that the Spanish (and Portuguese in the case of Brazil) lines were sacrosanct and, second, that these disputes could be susceptible to arbitration through a mechanism set up under the *aegis* of a regional pact.[14] The first factor is significant to the extent that Latin American boundaries were ostensibly required to adhere to the *uti possidetis juris* boundaries established under the *diktat* of the Spanish colonial administration. The war of succession that ensued between the Brazilians, who claimed status of successor to the Portuguese Empire on the continent, and the former Spanish states cast some doubt on the validity of this principle but only to the extent that the parties disputed whether the lines to be sanctified and preserved were *de jure* or *de facto* lines at the time of the creation of the independent states (Shaw 1996). The actual principle that the line (whether *de facto* or *de jure*) should remain sacrosanct was essentially uncontested between the new states. Indeed many of the cases that came up for arbitration and have since come up for adjudication before international tribunals concern the quest to determine the original line that needs to be delimited between the new states (Menon 1978; Maier 1969). Thus the

---

[12] For more on such literature see Gann and Duignan (1978).

[13] 'Order' as defined by Hedley Bull consists of an arrangement of life that promotes given goals and values. The three things he lists as being essential for this are security against violence, assurance of maintenance of promises and stable possession of things (Bull 1995: 4).

[14] See, for instance, *Arbitration of the boundary dispute between the Republics of Costa Rica & Panama provided by the Convention between Costa Rica and Panama of March 17th 1910*, *AJIL* 8 (4) (1914) 913–41.

principle of the sanctity of boundaries can be ascribed with some certainty to the Creole discussion of statecraft post-decolonization.

This chapter seeks to analyse some of the factors under these two headings to gauge the origins of principles governing the law of territory that have since been passed down as sacrosanct, and in doing so to demonstrate some important issues. First, that the principles that have been so rigorously and rigidly stated in different forums concerning territory in international law have their origin in the very specific instances of the Creole action in Latin America (as recognized in Shaw 1996: 75). Second, to identify the parameters against which their application in other contexts and circumstances can be measured so as to evaluate the extent and manner in which their application was appropriate and accurate. Third, to highlight that the interpretation of these 'laws' often varied with political situations and while the events taking place in Latin America could be seen to point the way in terms of modern international law of territory, it needs to be borne in mind that these events preceded the 'Scramble for Africa' by nearly 50 years. Thus it is hoped that what will emerge is a picture of inconsistent application of laws and principles which will prove that the rigid laws claimed to exist within international law are themselves the result of specific political events and that the circumstances in which they have subsequently been enforced do not necessarily reflect the specificity of their original application. A secondary aim is to tackle the question of the laws of territory against the appropriate temporal law in order to assess their validity.

Ideas of Confederation: Consolidation of *Res Nullius* and *Uti Possidetis*

In Latin America growing *opinio juris* and state practice against the concept of *terra nullius* developed in parallel to the idea of independence from Spain. In his overview of the Latin American contribution to international law Alvarez (1909: 321) highlights this notion as being the most significant. This section highlights the Creole action in gaining independence against the notion of *terra nullius* and then analyses its importance to the subsequent development of international law. In the process it also focuses on the doctrine of *uti possidetis*, analysing its original manifestation in the temporal space created immediately after independence.

A central feature within the independence from Spain of the new states was the notion that no part of their territory, however unexplored, would be allowed to be open to European annexation or acquisition.[15] At the time this concept was new in its application within contemporary international law. As established in the previous chapter the international community had used the principle to justify imperial expansion

---

[15] This principle was subsequently expressed as the Monroe Doctrine and was also contained in a declaration concomitant to the Pan American Conference documents. This is discussed in the final section of this chapter. See Lenoir (1942).

into territories. This territory included the South American continent, which the Spanish and Portuguese had sought to colonize, armed with Papal bulls giving them this right (Wright 1962). Thus not only were the colonial powers forced to relinquish their hold of these territories but were further confronted with the declaration by independent Latin American states that none of their territories were amenable to future colonization. As will be argued in the final chapter of this book, the intertemporal rule that has constantly been invoked by imperial powers can be seen as simply a handmaiden to this political principle, derived from the need for domination. The main pillar to this argument is bolstered by the denial of the notion of *terra nullius* by the Latin American countries as early as 1824 (see generally Kunz 1946 and also News and Notes 1908). In fact a significant component of the diplomatic history of nineteenth-century Latin America is this assertion against European expansion (see, for example, Fenwick 1942). It was this singular notion that was at the heart of the significant efforts of the newly independent states to form themselves into a confederation (Manger 1928). This idea evolved from statements by Chilean statesmen who, in 1810, first enunciated the aims of a potential confederation (Alvarez 1909: 276–9). They sought five main objectives. The first and foremost was to reiterate the sovereign autonomy of each state. This aim seems contradictory since it seeks to assuage the sovereignty of a state by ostensibly creating a superstructure in abeyance above the sovereign state, and in this sense highlights the very nature of inter-regional or international law.[16] Rather than a system regulated by a supreme body that can sit in judgment above the sovereign government of every state, the system is conceptualized as being self-regulatory and in this sense for it to function effectively states need to respect and recognize each other's sovereignty. The second important aim of the notion of a confederacy addressed the fear of external domination and in this sense reveals the *realpolitik* of the notion. Towards this aim the confederacy was viewed as a defence pact wherein each new state would undertake collective action in the event of an armed attack by a European state against their sovereignty. The third and fourth aims were, respectively, to fix the courses of domestic or foreign policies and to harmonize interests. These issues were always liable to provoke disagreement and such mechanisms are considered to be outside the purview of this present study. The final perceived aim of the Latin American confederation was to provide a system of conflict resolution by which all potential disagreement within the confederacy would be regulated. The impact of this particular aim is significant to the development of the notion of territory in international law since the arbitration system that emanated from Latin America played a significant role in the treatment of territorial disputes between the newly emergent states and continues to do so today, as we shall see in the next section (see also Chapter 6). A significant parallel can also be drawn between the notions of continental agreements in Latin America and Africa, first with the Pan-African movement and subsequently

---

[16] For early writing on the European Union, see Briggs (1954).

with the notion of African unity, as best evinced by the Organization for African Unity.

The idea of continent-wide agreement was not a new one. Within Europe itself such moves predate the Treaty of Rome by nearly a century and a half. This treaty regime includes the Treaty of Quadruple Alliance of Chaumont 1814, the Treaty of Paris 1814 (both cited in Alvarez 1909: 277) and the Congress of Vienna of the following year (Barkin and Cronin 1994). Clearly these arrangements sought to achieve Europe-wide co-operation, which nonetheless always fell short of any coherent system (see Eulau 1941 for a history of European confederation). Of course, moves for any cogent co-operation were always likely to be doomed in view of the 'Scramble for Africa', which was essentially adversarial rather than co-operative in nature (Fisch 1988 and Chapter 3). The Latin American plans for a confederacy, expressed in or around the same time, were markedly different especially with regard to the stated aims identified above. The spur to this notion of confederacy came from Simon Bolivar, the great liberator, who in his role as President of Columbia worked hard to create such a confederacy (Alvarez 1909: 277). His vision involved a congress that would meet in Panama, and the first significant step towards that aim came in the treaties of Union, Alliance and Confederation that he signed with several countries in 1825 (ibid.: 277–8). The first congress finally met in Panama in 1826 and refined the earlier Bolivarian treaty. The new pact agreed by representatives from Mexico, Central America, Columbia and Peru was the pact of Union, Alliance and Perpetual Confederation (ibid.: 278–80). While it sought to augment the notions of confederation it gave rise to a number of salient features that cast first light on the issue of territory and boundaries and remained significant to the development of regional law in Latin America.

The pact was primarily defensive in support of fledgling sovereignty and the territorial integrity of the countries against European ambition and expansion, but in art. 22 it nonetheless addressed the issue of delimitation of boundaries. This article merely reinforced the notion of *uti possidetis* though not necessarily choosing either the *de facto* or the *de juris* position as being superior. Article 22 sought agreement amongst the parties that as soon as the boundaries were agreed by the new states they should be delimited, guaranteed and secured under the protection of the confederation. This article especially seems to cast doubt on the application of the concept of *uti possidetis* to African nations in the following century. While not illuminating the peculiarity of the *uti possidetis de facto/de jure* debate, it questions the notion that the boundaries inherited from the Spanish Empire were as sacrosanct as the literature surrounding the doctrine of *uti possidetis* seemed to suggest (Shaw 1996: 105). The practical significance of the treaty, however, remained incidental since only Columbia ratified it. According to Alvarez this trend of agreeing treaties but failing to ratify them plagued the process of confederacy in the region throughout the nineteenth century. One of the reasons for this he identifies is that the treaties were usually negotiated under threat and as soon as that particular threat dissipated the new states failed to return to the theme and ratify it. Thus these treaties are not necessarily part of codified international law. However, in their agreement and negotiation it is easy to gauge the *opinio juris* of states and also the development of a uniquely Latin American flavour of customary international law. This is further evidenced by the events leading up to another congress in 1847.[17] This time the impetus came from the threat of an expedition planned in Spain by the Ecuadorian General Flores that had, as its expressed purpose, his recovery of the government of Ecuador (Alvarez 1909: 280). The Spanish American states perceived this mission as being orchestrated by Spain in a bid to recapture power by recreating a Spanish suzerainty over Latin America. To unify their response to this process the congress met in Lima in 1847 (Baldwin 1907).

In contrast to the Panama Congress of 1826, the Lima Congress was attended only by the states that perceived themselves as being immediately threatened by the return of General Flores and his ostensibly Spanish agenda. These included New Granada, Ecuador, Peru, Bolivia and Chile (Alvarez 1909: 281). The twenty or so sessions of the Congress were intensive and yielded two treaties and two conventions. Of these the Treaty of Confederation of February 1848 (Wright 1919) is most significant since it highlights the importance of the Monroe Doctrine, which will form a significant part of the next section (for basic reading on the doctrine see Hughes 1923). The object of the pact was the unification of the signatory powers in repelling any attack against their independence or territorial sovereignty (Alvarez 1909: 281). In tone and nature it is arts. 1 and 2 of this treaty that closely mirror the sentiments of the Monroe Doctrine enunciated by President Monroe of the United States of America a few years earlier (see pp. 85–7). However, one other impact of the treaty that needs to be highlighted concerns the contents of art. 7. This article aims to regulate conflict arising amongst members of the confederacy with regard to their mutual boundaries. Towards this end it establishes, in default of special stipulations between any of the interested parties, that:

> . . . the boundaries should be possessed by the respective countries in the epoch of the conquest of independence from Spain, and further provid[es] rules for their demarcation.

This particular article thus seems to suggest a degree of support for the Brazilian notion of *uti possidetis de facto* wherein the boundaries maintained are the ones held at the time of independence (Shaw 1996: 100). However, rather than viewing this as tacit support for one interpretation of the doctrine of *uti possidetis* over the other, the extent of the agreement needs to be borne in mind. Instead of encompassing the entire breadth of Latin America it only pertained to the states that felt immediately threatened by the perceived *reconquista* by the Spanish through General Flores. In this sense it is a restricted interpretation and in any case, like the Bolivar induced pact, it failed to gain ratification (Alvarez 1909: 282).

---

[17] See Arbitration Convention between the United States and Ecuador, in *AJIL* 4(4) (1910) 347–8.

Another significant element of the treaty is the contents of art. 8. This article locates the aim of the treaty in the context of the imminent fear of Spanish motives. Article 8 thus states:

> If an attempt should be made to unite two or more of the confederated Republics in a single State, or divide into several States any of the said Republics, or to separate one or more ports, cities or provinces, from any of them to unite with another or with a foreign power, it will be necessary, in order to make such a change effective, that the Governments of the other confederated Republics shall expressly declare, either directly or by their plenipotentiaries in the Congress, that such a change is not prejudicial to the interests and security of the Confederation.

When compared with the modern regime with regards to issues of self-determination of peoples and the subsequent treatment of territory as given by General Assembly Resolution 1541, the differences are striking. The latter suggests that a state emerging out of decolonization in a bid for self-government has three options, namely:

a) Constitution into a sovereign independent State
b) Free association with an independent State
c) Integration with an existing independent State

(GAOR 1541 (XV) December 1960)

However, art. 8 suggests that any changes made to existing territories, whether to unite or divide different components of existing states, would be subject to the veto of the confederation. Thus the subtleties of art. 8 suggest an important distinction between the Latin American system and the modern UN system of sovereign states. While both systems are overtly concerned with issues of peace and security, which were a clearly discernible motive for the formation of the respective regimes, the Latin American system suggests that even the consent of the parties subject to such division or integration could be overridden by the veto exercisable directly by governments of other confederated states or by their plenipotentiaries in congress. This veto could be exercised at any time if delegates believed that the perceived action was prejudicial to the overall interests of peace and security of the confederation. Thus while in the UN system of sovereign states the notion of consent between disputants essentially trumps the doctrine of *uti possidetis* (Bolintineanu 1974), in the Latin American confederation any violation of the doctrine was subject to veto by the whole confederation.

The next opportunity for continent-wide discussion about confederacy and issues of territory came with the negotiation of a Treaty of Union of the American States – essentially consisting of two separate treaty mechanisms signed in Santiago and Washington in 1858 with different states, towards the promotion of relations between the north and south (Alvarez 1909: 284). This treaty is significant in showing the importance of a consensus on issues pertaining to the treatment of territory. While this in itself provides no clues as to the view of the American states as a whole towards territory, there are certain indicators that reveal consensus on issues dealing with territory. The prime purpose of the north–south treaty was the creation of allegiances that would at once strengthen the alliance against European interference while (as far as southern American states were concerned) at the same time seeking to regulate the influence of the USA within Latin America. The US–Mexican war of 1848 provided the impetus for such a move by showing that the threat faced by the new states was not merely from European powers. In the context of strengthening opposition to hostile takeovers of territory (obviously less likely in the north than in the south) art. 13 of the pact stipulates that:

> . . . each one of the contracting parties binds itself not to cede nor to alienate to another State, under any form, any part of its territory, nor to permit any nationality foreign to . . . dominat[e] . . . to establish itself within its boundaries, and promises not to recognise in this character, any that stand in the way of any cession that may be made by the interested States for the purpose of regulating their geographical boundaries or in fixing their natural limits or in determining with mutual advantage their frontiers.

The difference between art. 13 of the Treaty of Union 1858 and art. 8 of the Treaty of Confederation 1848 is essentially that art. 13, although reinforcing the earlier principle about restrictions on changing geographical composition of states with regards to outsiders, nonetheless explicitly legislates for the exception of negotiation between two or more states in seeking to regulate or demarcate existing frontiers between themselves to gain best advantage. The central feature within this system that brings it within the realm of the modern UN system is that boundary negotiations are consent driven (Shaw 1996: 105). However, rather than an expression of a change in policy this document should more accurately be read as a post-decolonization document that while seeking to consolidate relationships between the new states and the USA also appreciated the nature of the inherited boundaries and the difficulty of identifying and demarcating the *uti possidetis* line. The objection to this treaty entered by the government of Argentina provides a fascinating insight on the issues at stake in its negotiation. Communicated via an official note in 1862 the objection essentially suggests that Argentina could not agree with the treaty since it believed that the provisions of art. 13 imposed an unacceptable limitation on state sovereignty (Alvarez 1909: 285 and Root 1914). Not party to the earlier treaty that sought to provide the veto power to the confederacy in matters considered prejudicial to the security of the confederation, Argentina believed that the function of sovereignty ought to include the power of the government to determine the destiny of its own territory.

The consensus within this all-American congress was strengthened in the face of Spanish attempts to reconquer and reoccupy the Chinchas Islands belonging to Peru (Alvarez 1909: 285).[18] Faced with this threat Peru summoned the congress, which met in Lima in 1864 and sought to further strengthen and codify the relationships

---

[18] *The Chaco dispute*, AJIL 28(4) (1934) 137–208.

between the states (Alvarez 1909: 285). This included the aim of adopting principles that it was hoped would put an end to boundary disputes within the continent and also to create an arbitration mechanism that could regulate this and other conflicts that might arise between the state parties. Although negotiations were affected by the Spanish–Peruvian tussle over possession of the Chinchas Islands, the congress signed two separate pacts in 1865, namely the Union and Defensive Alliance and Preservation of Peace. Both these pacts provide significant insights into the treatment of territory and the issue of boundary disputes within the continent.

The Pact of Union and Defensive Alliance identified some of the main purposes of the regional alliances. Article 1 stated that parties were to:

> . . . defend together their independence, sovereignty and territorial integrity against all aggressions whether foreign powers, those signing the pact, or on the part of foreign forces that are directed by no recognised government.

Article 2 stipulated that the alliance would become operative in the event of an attempt being made to:

> . . . bring any of the High Contracting Parties under a Protectorate or force it to sell or cede territory or to establish or impair the free and complete exercise of its sovereignty and independence.

In addition, via art. 9 of the treaty the parties promised 'not to alienate to another nation or government any part of their territory'. Predictably, in the Latin American context and keeping in mind the spirit of art. 13 of the Treaty of Union 1858, the renegotiation of boundaries and exchanges of territory between parties with a view to agreement of boundaries was once again made exempt from this notion.

The significance of the second part of the Pact for the Preservation of Peace 1865 lies in its institution of the norm of arbitration as the main means to conflict resolution. In this pact the parties bound themselves via arts. 1, 2 and 3 to use pacific measures exclusively to put an end to all their differences – including boundary disagreements. Through the agreement parties were compulsorily required to submit these disputes to an arbitrator when the dispute could not be settled through bilateral discussion. The impact of the two pacts is difficult to determine since, as with the other conventions and pacts, they were not ratified by the contracting states (Alvares 1909: 287). According to Alvarez the issue of ratification is not wholly significant. He suggests that even had they been ratified the agreements would not have been able to achieve what they set out to for a number of reasons (ibid.: 289). These include the obstacles of the distance and lack of communication. In a continent the size of Latin America there was an obvious need for strong lines of communication to make a confederacy of any kind work. However, technology had not yet developed to the extent that this would be feasible and the general lack of infrastructure meant that traditional means of communication would take an inordinate amount of time and resources. However, the resources-driven obstacles as well as other physical difficulties paled in comparison with other real impediments to the effective working of such a confederacy. Chief amongst these was the nature of the relationship between the new states. While at a superficial level the agreement to form a confederacy was strong, it was underpinned by numerous disputes and problems that were a grave threat to any form of inter-state relations. The spirit of national independence was strong in the aftermath of the Creole action and thus any attempt to cede sovereignty away from the immediate rulers was not considered a strong option. The states were engaged in the task of uniting peoples within their respective territories behind the leaders, and thus the added complications of creating continental allegiances were significantly lower on their list of priorities. In addition, such allegiances required a commonality of purpose that was lacking in the context of Latin American states (ibid.: 290). Instead, owing to the difficulty of interpreting the doctrine of *uti possidetis* and the immediate fall-out of the controversy over the demarcation of boundaries, the states continued to harbour a large number of boundary disputes amongst themselves.[19]

According to Alvarez (p. 290), there were very few states within Latin America that were not plagued by the problem of boundary disputes, which consequently affected their ability to form meaningful relationships with their most immediate neighbours. Accompanying boundary disputes were two other related factors. First, disagreements about river navigation, which in interior Latin America was the only traditional route to facilitate commerce, and second, the constant civil wars relating to this and other disputes between the states (ibid.). These factors suggest that at the very outset, irrespective of the willingness of states to ratify pacts cementing continent-wide relationships and allegiances, the end objective of a functioning confederacy was not necessarily conceivable. Alvarez also suggests other important factors that would have played a role in blocking the notion of a confederacy. These are the lack of preparation of the peoples of the new states for political life and the lack of common political traditions (ibid.: 289). The latter reason is indicative of the ambiguous nature of custom with regards to international law. On the one hand the treaties signed and the continental agreements seem to point towards the existence of a form of custom that bound the states of Latin America together. This was especially true in their external relations and the manner in which they perceived their role *vis-à-vis* each other and the international community as a whole. Thus despite the significant achievement of initiating a regional focus group of new states, the pronouncements for unions, alliances and confederations only ever had moral force rather than strict legal complicity. Nonetheless in terms of the treatment of territory in international law these pronouncements remain highly significant since not only were the relevant articles of the treaties discussed above the subject of intense negotiation that reveals

---

[19] The best example of this is the *El Salvador–Honduras* case that recently came before the International Court of Justice. This case is introduced in this chapter and discussed in some length in Chapter 5.

the new states' perceptions of territory, but it needs to be reiterated that these negotiations also took place in the context of the members of the different forums holding claims against each other's boundaries.

The Doctrine of Uti Possidetis

While the doctrine of *uti possidetis* clearly stated that the colonial and administrative boundaries on departure of the Spanish would be adhered to, there were numerous associated issues that had to be resolved. The biggest issue remained the actual discovery of the so-called *uti possidetis* line and its subsequent validation and demarcation. In the context of the Creole action, however, this took place against a background of growing nationalism. This difficulty is best demonstrated in the following paragraph:

> At the time of the struggle for emancipation, there were four vice royalties in Spanish America (Mexico, New Granada, Peru and Buenos Aires) and seven *Capitanias Generales* (Yucatan, Cuba, Puerto Rico, Santo Domingo, Guatemala, Venezuela and Chile). Bolivar formed of New Granada, Venezuela and Northern Peru, the United States of Columbia, which fell away in 1830 into three States: New Granada, Venezuela and Ecuador. The old vice royalty of Buenos Aires became sub-divided into four States: Bolivia (which was separated from the vice-royalty by Bolivar in 1825), Uruguay, Paraguay, and the United Provinces of the River Plate. The United States of Central America, founded in 1823 split up into five separate States in 1839.
>
> (Alvarez 1909: 289)

Thus what were emerging out of the Creole action were not single unitary states that could be neatly categorized, but different alliances, mergers and groupings of states. The further break-up of these states along predetermined administrative boundaries proved to be extremely difficult. Despite the above discussions about confederacies, they had no significant impact on the amalgamation of states in Latin America. On the contrary there is evidence in the later Additional and Explanatory Convention 1833 which was appended to the Treaty of Peace, Friendship, Commerce and Navigation 1832, signed between Chile and the USA, that a case was provided wherein new states should only be formed in America by the dismemberment of the old, in direct contradiction to the perception of self-determination as it was developing in Europe and to which purpose the doctrine of *uti possidetis* had been brought into use.

Irrespective of whether a wider point about regional customary international law can be made, there is little doubt that the doctrine of *uti possidetis* remained central to the conduct of governance and territorial demarcations in Latin America. With doubt surrounding many of the boundaries inherited by the new states, a system had to be devised that would seek to regulate order within the continent. In this regard all the emergent states agreed on the need to adhere to the norm of *uti possidetis*. In modern international law discussions of *uti possidetis* as famously expressed in the *Burkina*

Faso/Mali case hinge on the notion of the 'snapshot' of the territory (see Chapter 5), bringing into play the grave importance of a 'critical date' (see Goldie 1963: 568 and ICJ Reports (1986) 554 at 568). While the importance of the critical date remained in Latin America, as highlighted above, the discussion centred on which line, the *uti possidetis juris* line or the *uti possidetis de facto* line, was to be respected. The constitutions of many states reveal that they fixed their boundaries on the basis of the 1810 line, which is bolstered by the agreement achieved in the Congress of Lima 1848 (Brown 1927). This in itself does not cast further light on whether the doctrine of *uti possidetis juris* or *uti possidetis de facto* was favoured. Instead, it locates the debate rather more within the 'critical date' discussion, with the year being identified as 1810.[20] In this sense it could be argued that this favours a *de facto* situation of 1810, which by way of constitutional expression is made *de jure*. The outstanding boundary disputes in Latin America suggest that this would be a simplistic explanation, especially since many of the 1810 boundaries were extremely vague and often conflicted with one another. The reason for this was the lack of awareness about the geographic lay of the land especially in interior regions where boundaries were difficult to demarcate in areas that had never been penetrated from the outside.[21] As in Africa, the situation was also compounded by the nature of the territory, which was essentially located on the coast and extended inwards into hinterland regions. As Alvarez points out:

> . . . the peculiar geographical situation of these countries, located on the coast and with territory extending in toward the centre of the continent and delimiting several states at the same time, made such a clash inevitable. Brazil, for example, touches the frontiers of all states of South America and three Guianas with the exception of Chile. Thus the Brazilian delimitation itself along the lines of the *uti possidetis de facto* line would cause a dispute in potentially every state except Chile.[22]
>
> (Alvarez 1910: 290)

The significance of the boundary disputes, while following the *uti possidetis juris/de facto* discussion, clearly put the destiny of the territory above the destiny of the people.[23]

---

[20] In subsequent cases this date is later (e.g. *El Salvador/Honduras case*) but this has to do with the break-up of the alliances that originally gained independence from the Spanish; see ICJ Reports (1992) 351.

[21] With regard to African colonization Lord Salisbury stated: 'We [the colonial powers] have engaged . . . in drawing lines upon maps where no white man's feet have ever trod; we have been giving away mountains and rivers and lakes to each other, but we have only been hindered by the small impediment that we never knew exactly where those mountains and rivers and lakes were'; as cited by Judge Ajibola, *Case concerning the territorial dispute (Libyan Arab Jamahiriya v. Chad)*, ICJ Reports (1994) 6 at 53.

[22] While on a modern map Ecuador does not share a boundary with Brazil, Ecuador was at one time part of the United States of Columbia and only became separate in 1830.

[23] Contrast this with the statement of Judge Dillard in the *Western Sahara case*, ICJ Reports (1975) 12 at 116–26.

The demarcation and delimitation of boundaries did not take any notice of populations that inhabited the region, instead relying exclusively on theoretical occupation of the land by the state – colonial at first instance and subsequently the post-colonial successor. The fact that many of these disputes have subsequently been resolved by arbitral sentence is further evidence of the subjugation of the rights of peoples to the importance of territory. This is because in passing an arbitral sentence in these boundary dispute contests the notions taken into account were titles of occupation, possession and prescription and none of these adequately explained the situation facing people in frontier regions or on impenetrable hinterlands.[24] Especially affected were the indigenous peoples of Latin America whose voice was not heard by either the Spanish or their successors. These indigenous peoples, whose livelihood depends on the territory on which they live, were paradoxically the ones most disenfranchised through the process of emancipation.[25] This issue is looked at in the context of the discussion of *terra nullius* later in this book. However, even in cases where the arbitral sentence had ostensibly resolved the matter these resolutions remain far from satisfactory since in taking into account a strict reading of territory as actual possession they failed to adequately address the problem, and many of these boundary disputes still persist today.

One of the disputes that was suitably resolved provides a further insight into the working of the system. This concerned the war that broke out in 1825 between the Brazilian Empire and the United Province of the River Plate, which could be considered the precursor to modern Argentina. The dispute concerned possession of a territory situated around the province of Montevideo. This province had been part of the United Province of the River Plate until its annexation by Brazil in 1822 under the name of 'Provincia Cisplatina' (Alvarez 1909: 293). Thus in terms of the *uti possidetis* line of 1810 the Brazilian annexation was null and void since it had occurred 12 years after the original designation of the critical date. However, as still transpires in international politics, the superior military power of the Empire of Brazil held sway and as a result the province was successfully annexed and held for three years until 1825, when it declared its independence and sought to secede from the Brazilian Empire. The result of this proclamation was the start of a war between Brazil and the United Provinces of the River Plate, which utilizing the argument of the 1810 *uti possidetis* boundary line sought to reincorporate the territory within the United Provinces on its declaration of independence. In the meantime the Province itself sought to assert its independence from both the powers and thus sought recognition as a separate entity. A bilateral treaty between the River Plate Provinces resolved the issue initially and Brazil signed in 1828. This set up a system of mediation under the

---

[24] See Pleadings in the *Case concerning the land, island and maritime frontier dispute (El Salvador v. Honduras case)*, ICJ Reports (1992) 351, as discussed in Chapter 5.
[25] *Yanoamani Indian case*, Case 7615 IACHR 24, OEA/Ser.L/V/11.66, doc. 10 Rev. 1 (1985); see also Chapter 7.

auspices of the British government. This mediation finally came to fruition as that government gained the agreement of the two powers and the new entity of Uruguay was introduced via a convention signed in 1859. Prior to that there had already been a tacit agreement between Brazil and the United Provinces of the River Plate with regard to the need to maintain an independent and neutral Uruguayan entity around the former province of Montevideo. This agreement had already been included in the more general Treaty of Peace and Friendship 1856, though the Treaty of 1859 only secured the ramifications of the agreement subsequently. This latter convention not only reiterated the two powers' agreement regarding the neutrality of Uruguay but also bound them as guarantors of its independence and territorial integrity. In return for this guarantee the sovereignty of the government of Uruguay was restricted in many other ways. The agreement was not enough in principle to prevent Brazil from declaring war on Uruguay in 1864, although that particular dispute was not related to the possession of territory and thus did not repudiate the principle of the 1859 treaty. In fact the 1864 war was actually terminated by the creation of an alliance between Brazil, Uruguay and Argentina with regard to declaring war against Paraguay. Thus the nature of allegiances in Latin America continued to be founded on the basis of immediate threats thus further substantiating the fact that notions of confederacy were doomed to failure.

One other commonality shared by the states of Latin America was their general belief in the need to maintain relationships with the old countries of Europe. The reason for this link is apparent: the Creoles, as descendants of European stock, were keen to assert their independence while at the same time relying on the knowledge of their forefathers in Spain and Portugal. It also highlights the composition of the new Latin American rulers who by using the notion of self-determination sought to overthrow their colonizing forefathers and install themselves – their sons – in their place. Thus the indigenous peoples of the continent had no part to play in the subsequent demarcation of the states of the New World. As a result the boundaries of the new states failed to take into account the needs of the indigenous peoples or those of the slaves who had been forcibly transferred onto the shores of the continent through Spanish and Portuguese activity (Hugh 1997).

The Extent of the Doctrine of Terra Nullius

The relationship with the Old World continued to be affected by notions of territory. The best example of this and one that has had continued resonance since is the dispute over the territorial possession of the Malvinas Islands (Franck 1983). The dispute between the British government and the United Provinces of the River Plate essentially concerned the right to exercise sovereignty on the island, beginning with its occupation by Britain in 1823. As such this is merely an indicator of the uneasy relationship between the newly emergent states of the New World and the imperial powers in Europe, and does not throw any light on the notion of boundaries. However, it does reveal that the notion of occupation remained central to the ownership of territory even after the gaining of independence in 1810. The dispute over the Malvinas suggests that despite the gains made by the Creoles in terms of their ownership of the territory of Latin America, and despite the attempted dissipation of the notion of *terra nullius*, the British government still believed it could lay claim to these remote islands, suggesting that not all territory benefited from the dissipation of *terra nullius* or that the British government had directly violated emerging international custom and the explicit wishes of new sovereign states. What is proven by subsequent events in Africa towards the last two decades of the nineteenth century is that rather than dispel the notion of *terra nullius* as a principle of international law, the Latin American decolonization had merely rid its own continent of that problematic notion. Elsewhere in Africa and Asia the concept of *terra nullius* provided a degree of legal justification for the large colonial gains made by the imperial European powers in the late nineteenth century. The dispute over the Malvinas, however, suggests that even in the limited aim of declaring the continent populated by socially and politically organized peoples, the newly emergent Latin American states met with uncertain results. The dispute over the Malvinas was not the only territorial dispute with the Old World either. There were disputes between the USA and Haiti over the possession of the Island of Navassa in 1856 and between Venezuela and Holland with regard to the possession of the Island of Aves (Alvares 1909: 298). This particular dispute was only resolved by an arbitral decision by the king of Spain in 1865, which gave ownership of the island to Venezuela (Clarke 1907). While the issue of ownership was central to these disputes it also needs to be borne in mind that the disputes over boundaries continued to reverberate in relations between the New and Old World states.

As pointed out by Alvarez, the continued disputes of Latin America with the imperialist states highlight a fourfold violation of international law. These four violations were:

a)   Unjust declaration of war or violation of sovereignty
b)   Unfounded claims for damages on behalf of citizens
c)   Diplomatic pursuit against Latin American countries with regards to unjustified claims
d)   Use of force including seizure of property, to obtain compliance with claims.

(Alvarez 1909: 299–300)

Of these only the first and fourth violation affect the treatment of territory. Both demonstrate, however, that even though the Latin American states had achieved their independence the notion of territory continued to be shrouded within colonial rhetoric. This permeated relationships at every level between the states, which were not really considered as being equal to the states of Europe.[26] In many of their international relations the imperial states treated the Latin American states in much the same way as they did 'the weaker states of Europe or semi-civilised countries' (ibid.: 303). Indeed

---

[26] This dilemma was confronted by Turkey who since the time of the Ottoman Empire has faced a similar struggle; see Bull (1995) and Chapter 4.

in comparing the relationship within Europe and that between the European states and Latin America, Alvarez finds that 'in the former case they were inspired by the dictates of broad policy, humanity or religion, while in the latter they acted with the sole purpose of assuring unduly for their citizens who came to those countries a specially privileged situation' (ibid.).

The Development of the Doctrines of *Uti Possidetis* and *Terra Nullius* Prior to the 'Scramble for Africa'

The international life of the Latin American countries from the middle to the end of the nineteenth century is also instructive in throwing more light upon the treatment of territory and its relationship to the doctrine of *uti possidetis*. This is particularly relevant since although the doctrine of *uti possidetis* was applied nearly half a century later in African decolonization, the doctrine of *terra nullius* was directly violated by the imperial powers in expanding their empires into Africa and Asia (see especially Gifford and Louis 1971). It is common practice to excuse these events as lying within the realm of the intertemporal rule of international law, which suggests that actions of a particular era should be judged only against the laws and standards prevalent at the time (Elias 1980). By focusing on the development of these doctrines towards the second half of the nineteenth century it is hoped to portray some of temporal settings against which these norms can be gauged. Thus this section will address two main issues: first, the developments of legal norms concerning territory in Latin America after the consolidation of independence by the Creoles and, second, whether these developments can be considered to form a regime indicative of the development of international legal principles in the period immediately prior to the twentieth century quest of imperial European powers for overseas territories. For this purpose the remainder of this chapter will focus on two notions that developed within Latin America and have given rise to considerable international legal discourse. The ramifications of these two issues for territory, it is hoped, will demonstrate that a suitable regime covering the treatment of territory could be ascertained as having existed towards the end of the nineteenth century and prior to the colonization of Africa and Asia. Ideas of confederation that were integral to efforts in the post-decolonization phase faded in the face of the diminishing threat of external conquest by the European states. This could be attributed to the increasing statecraft of the fledgling states and also to the European gaze being drawn elsewhere (Pakenham 1991). The continental congresses were still held but their focus had changed considerably (see Baldwin 1907).

The Regional Custom of Arbitration

The development of the notion of arbitration to settle disputes was arguably one of the greatest contributions made by Latin America to general international law (Alvarez

1909: 344). This contribution can be traced back to the congress of eminent Latin American jurists that met in Lima in 1877 with a view to codifying rules of private international law (ibid.: 343). In terms of its ambit this in itself excluded questions of public international law such as the treatment of territory. However, in the way that this particular aspect of relations developed, the norm was set in place to ensure that arbitration became the port of call in every dispute, and since many of the disputes between the states were over territory or territorial demarcations, or the physical existence of the *uti possidetis* line, the study of this issue is central to understanding the resolution of territorial disputes in Latin America. With this in mind the Bogotá Convention 1880, signed between Chile and Columbia, is significant (ibid.: 328). This convention essentially identified arbitration both general and absolute as the means for settling disputes between the two states. Also interestingly, in art. 2, it identified the President of the USA as arbitrator in disputes. Article 3, however, contains the seeds for the development of regional custom with regard to arbitration when it calls on the two governments to sign similar treaties with other Latin American countries:

> . . . in order that the solution of every international conflict by means of arbitration may come to be a principle of American Public Law.

With the principle enunciated, the call to a conference in 1881 to further these means as a conflict resolution mechanism met with general enthusiasm (ibid.: 322). The only two exceptions in Latin America were Argentina, who was concerned with notions of territorial integrity, and Brazil, who was not invited to the conference. The Argentinian exclusion could easily be explained by reference to its dissenting role in previous conferences citing notions of state sovereignty (see p. 71). The Brazilian exclusion probably had more to do with the distinction of it being a successor state to the Portuguese rather than the Spanish and therefore not party to the same issues as emanated from Spanish decolonization. A treaty was signed in 1883 in Caracas highlighting agreement on the issue on the birth centennial of Simon Bolivar (ibid.: 326). Thus while the notion of confederacy proclaimed by Bolivar had largely failed, it had been replaced in principle at least by a more practical agreement: the creation of a mechanism for dispute settlement that primarily addressed the reason for the failure of the confederation in the first place, namely the proliferation of wide-scale and regular conflict between the members of the proposed confederacy.

The importance of arbitration was evident in the First Pan-American Conference of 1889, held in Washington, where arbitration was reiterated and was the only issue fully discussed (ibid.: 326–8). Held as a meeting of the states of the all-Americas, it identified a project wherein the republics of America essentially adopted arbitration as a principle of American international law for the solution of all difficulties between two or more of them. Article 1, which expresses this principle, also goes on to stress that arbitration ought to be obligatory, permanent and general and extend to all conflicts. Unfortunately a loophole was provided in the acceptable exceptions (arts. 2–5):

> ... those questions which, in the exclusive judgement of one of the nations interested in the contest, compromise the independence of that nation; in such case, the arbitration will be voluntary on the party of that nation, but will be obligatory for the other party.

By permitting this exception it would seem that the entire mechanism was weakened, since it was open to any state concerned about its liability in an arbitration process to use its prerogative and deem the proceedings voluntary upon itself since the issues discussed could be claimed prejudicial to the independence of that state. Nonetheless as a document negotiated by the Pan-American Conference it had great resonance. Besides, as pointed out by Alvarez, the project of arbitration, no matter how flawed, had no precedent in the diplomatic history of the world (ibid.: 328).

   In addition, the conference discussed the issue of conquests and adopted the following declaration:

1. The principle of conquest is eliminated from American Public Law, for as long as the treaty of arbitration remains in force.
2. The grants of territory which may be made during the time that the treaty of arbitration subsists, shall be null and void if made under menace of war or because of force of arms.
3. The nation making such grants shall have the right to demand that their validity be decided by arbitration.
4. The renunciation of the right to demand arbitration, if made under the conditions set forth in article 2, shall be without value or efficacy.

This declaration, adopted as part of the documents signed concomitant to the Treaty of Arbitration 1890, shows very clearly the developing norms of territory and territorial acquisition. However, although widely subscribed to, the treaty was never ratified. The issues were revisited in the second and third Pan-American Conferences, discussion of which is aptly captured in much academic writing (ibid.: 330). These agreements essentially identified the notion of arbitration as being the best mechanism for the settlement of disputes between states. Despite its imperfections, the system came into immediate use as the boundary disputes between the new states continued. A good manifestation of the process can be viewed in the dispute between Argentina and Paraguay over the possession of territory. The territory concerned was nestled between the River Verde and the main branch of the Pilcomayo together with the Villa Occidental. Pursuant to the treaty signed in 1883, and notwithstanding initial Argentinian objections in 1880 with regard to limitations to sovereignty, the dispute was referred to the President of the USA for arbitration and was resolved by his decision in 1878 (ibid.).

Another dispute that has particular resonance to our study of territory concerns the issues surrounding the war fought between 1879 and 1885 by Chile against the secretly aligned forces of Bolivia and Peru. The significance of this particular conflict is that it changed the territorial map of western Latin America and also bears resonance to the ongoing efforts of resolution to the Western Sahara situation (see Castellino 1999c). The war of 1879–85 was halted temporarily by the signing of a treaty in 1883. In this treaty the province of Tarapacá was ceded by Peru to Chile (via art. 2) while deferring decision on Tacna and Arica for ten years, placing it under temporary Chilean sovereignty in the interim pending a plebiscite (art. 3) (Coolidge 1926). However, not unlike the situation following the *Western Sahara* case, the actual determination of the terms of the plebiscite remained problematic and the situation rapidly deteriorated. The conflict continued to rage beyond the signing of the 1883 treaty and was only finally terminated by a treaty of peace signed between the countries in 1904, which ultimately recognized the sovereignty of Chile over the areas.[27]

A corollary issue in terms of the nature of identity to territory in the region concerns the principles of nationality. While the traditional European view of *jus sanguinis* suggested that even the occupiers of Latin America were entitled to European nationalities,[28] the principle of sovereignty developed in Latin America focused more on the notion of *jus soli* distinction.[29] In this sense the ethnic content of Latin America changed dramatically with the award of Latin American nationalities to the descendants of the European colonizers. As a result of this policy and notions of territoriality, enormous tracts of territory were turned over to newcomers resulting in 'large districts . . . thus peopled exclusively by Europeans of the same nationality' (Alvarez 1909: 306). As a result the initial view of the Latin countries was that even though they may have shed the immediate shackles of colonialism they were perceived, in Europe at least, almost as colonies and in this sense there remained a moral influence in terms of institutions. The notion of immigration and control over the territory and its accompanying foreign influence on Latin America still essentially brings into sharp focus the dismissal of the notion of *terra nullius*. While on the one hand the Creole action, by asserting independence from Spain, may have decimated the notion of *terra nullius* within Latin America, it essentially did so by itself treating the continent as *terra nullius*. By virtue of the fact that they themselves were of foreign origin, and by virtue of maintaining links with the colonizers at the cost of indigenous peoples and other peoples in Latin America, the message the Creoles seemed to be communicating was that *terra nullius* as a principle was inapplicable only from the time of their own occupation. However, occupying the territory and continuing

---

[27] Peace Treaty of 1904 between Peru and Chile. See also 'Memorandum on Tacna-Arica Delivered by the Secretary of State of the United States to the Governments of Chile and Peru', *AJIL* 21(1) [Supplement: Official Documents] (1927) 11–15.
[28] For general reading on this issue, see Gamberale (1995).
[29] For citizenship and its changing guises, see Aleinikoff and Klusmeyer (2000).

colonial traditions as such leaves open the possibility that for them the territory was indeed *terra nullius*, that is consisting of no recognizable jurisdiction or ownership until their own arrival. This is of course manifestly untrue but unpacking that particular situation *vis-à-vis* the indigenous peoples of the continent is a process that is only just beginning, nearly two centuries after the original 'emancipation' of 1810.

Thus looked at from the perspective of the indigenous peoples of Latin America the notion of arbitration was merely an agreement between neo-colonizers to settle their disputes through the means of another foreign power. While it did take the territorial disputes outside the realms of direct state-interest politics and within a *quasi-legal* setting, it nonetheless failed to take into consideration an important issue in the determination of the territorial question: the allegiance of the people of the territory. Rather, it relied on essentially colonial precepts of possession, occupation and external treaties in the grant of the award of territories through the arbitration process. The fact that many of the boundaries failed to be properly demarcated has meant that while the process of arbitration may have been preferable to full-fledged war, it nonetheless was a less than satisfactory means of settling these disputes. This is best demonstrated in the particular case concerning the land, island and maritime frontier between El Salvador and Honduras to which we shall now turn.[30]

El Salvador–Honduras Case

This dispute, resolved recently by the International Court of Justice and examined in more depth in Chapter 5, is a good example of a dispute in Spanish America that still reverberates. It demonstrates that it is simplistic to suggest that the doctrine of *uti possidetis* was responsible for stable boundaries following the withdrawal of the Spanish Empire. Rather this case reveals a lasting legacy of boundary disputes that essentially revert to the issue of the location of the 1821 *uti possidetis juris* line.[31] To understand this dispute better it is instructive to identify a few historical aspects of the case. Formed as a result of the break-up of the Spanish Empire in Central America, the territories of the two protagonists, namely El Salvador and Honduras, correspond to administrative sub-divisions that existed within that empire. In the case that was brought before the ICJ in 1992, this similarity with many of the other boundary disputes in Spanish America was highlighted, that is that the problem was not whether the doctrine of *uti possidetis* applied, rather it concerned the exact location of the line that would give rise to the principle.[32]

---

[30] *Case concerning the land, island and maritime frontier dispute (El Salvador v. Honduras; Nicaragua intervening)*, ICJ Reports (1992) 351. This case is also reviewed in Chapter 5 in a bid to show the continued resonance of these unresolved issues in Latin America.

[31] As mentioned earlier, while the original *uti possidetis* line may have been considered as the 1810 line, many states that subsequently emerged out of central unions had later critical dates.

[32] ICJ Reports (1992) 351 at 380, para. 28.

As pointed out by the court in reviewing and adjudicating upon the case in 1992, different kinds of administrative boundaries abounded in Central America at the time of the withdrawal of the Spanish. For instance there were 'provinces' whose meaning varied through the ages, *Alcaldias Mayores* and *Corregimientos* and towards the eighteenth century there were *Intendencias* and territorial jurisdictions of higher courts (*Audiencias*). There were also Captaincy-Generals such as that of the Kingdom of Guatemala which comprised the five states of Nicaragua, Honduras, El Salvador, Costa Rica and Guatemala, which came to independence as a Federal Republic in 1821, as well as Vice-Royalties. In addition, the jurisdictions of administrative bodies did not always pertain to territorial scopes and there were many overlaps especially as far as military commands were concerned. Finally there was the notion of ecclesiastical jurisdictions designating territory as parishes. These parishes, although in principle supposed to correspond to the civil administrative units, did not always adhere to these.[33] Thus the withdrawal of Spain in 1821 could not be deemed to have left clear-cut boundaries that could be established as the 1821 *uti possidetis* line.

The court also quoted a similar issue in the Guatemala–Honduras arbitration that confronted the arbitrator in 1933:

> It must be noted that particular difficulties are encountered in drawing the line of *uti possidetis* of 1821, by reason of the lack of trustworthy information during colonial times with respect to a large part of the territory in dispute. Much of this territory was unexplored. Other parts which had occasionally been visited were but vaguely known. In consequence, not only had boundaries of jurisdiction not been fixed with precision by the Crown, but there were great areas in which there had been no effort to assert any semblance of administrative authority.
>
> (UN *RIAA* II 1325)

With the independence of Central America from the Spanish Crown on 15 September 1821, Honduras, El Salvador, Costa Rica, Guatemala and Nicaragua constituted the state of the Federal Republic of Central America. This republic pertained to what was recognizable as the Spanish Captaincy-General of Guatemala and survived until 1839 when the component states gained independence as separate states. Since then the dispute has continued and despite many other attempts to resolve the issue, including a judgment delivered by the Central American Court of Arbitration in 1917, the issue has continued to be complex and unresolved. While efforts to arbitrate did result in some success, managing to delimit certain segments of the boundary between the states, other issues remained to be tackled. The 1980 Treaty of Friendship negotiated and signed bilaterally between the state parties finally resolved some of those outstanding issues and thus formed the basis for the dispute that came before the International Court of Justice in 1992.[34] However, three main issues remained

---

[32] ICJ Reports (1992) 351 at 380, para. 28.

[33] Ibid. at 387, para. 43.

[34] For other attempts to resolve the dispute, see ICJ Reports (1992) 351 at 382–6, paras. 33–9.

unresolved. The first pertained to six segments of the land boundary that had not received satisfactory treatment under the 1980 treaty; the second alluded to three islands, El Tigre, Meanguera and Meanguerita, over which both parties laid claim and asserted sovereignty based on the doctrine of *uti possidetis*; and finally there were factors pertaining to maritime delimitation – an issue which in the case before the International Court of Justice in 1992 was considered relevant to Nicaragua, which was allowed to intervene and present its own arguments with respect to the treatment of the Gulf of Fonseca. While the salient features within the case are dealt with later, it is instructive to highlight this case to show that the two issues identified in this chapter with regard to territorial disputes in Latin America – the doctrine of *uti possidetis* with its related concept of *terra nullius* and the notion of arbitration that was central to the resolution of those territorial problems – continued to reverberate beyond the Latin American epoch itself.

The Impact of the Monroe Doctrine on Treatment of Territory

A second important development during this period of Latin American international legal history was the enunciation and general support as regional custom of the Monroe Doctrine of 1823. This declaration, enunciated by the then American President, was intended as a message from the New World to the Old World. It was well subscribed to in Latin America, which essentially sought to portray the same message to the imperial powers. The doctrine itself can be summarized in a few key points.

First and foremost it stressed the notion of the independence and complete sovereignty of the states of the New World from the European states. In this sense its gravity can almost be compared to the notion of state sovereignty as first expressed in the Peace of Westphalia in 1648 (Gross 1948). There the Calvinist states essentially declared themselves separate entities from the Catholic Church and thus disjoined their foreign policy from that of Rome. Also of significance with regard to the Peace of Westphalia was that it created the terms of the order that would endure in Europe for a significant period, and contained notions of state sovereignty (ibid.: 24). The Monroe Doctrine arguably resulted in similar effects. It was a statement by which the states of the New World sought to do lay down their independence *vis-à-vis* the states of the Old World. By its enunciation the Monroe Doctrine sought to exclude the new states and territories of America from the balance of power mechanisms prevalent in Europe. In doing so it condemned and barred any potential European intervention in affairs within the New World, resolving instead to set up mechanisms which would deal with these issues amongst the New World states themselves. Thus in many ways the Monroe Doctrine, like the Peace of Westphalia, was concerned about setting out the parameters for an ordered existence. Finally it stressed the idea that under no circumstances could the states of Europe acquire any territory in the New World. This was further evidence of the denial of the principle of *terra nullius*. Further corollaries to this essential doctrine involved:

1   Recognition of existing European colonies on the continent
2   Political equality of all the states on the continent
3   Non-interference from the United States of America in the affairs of European states.

As pointed out by Alvarez, in declaring that the continent of America was no longer open to European conquest and colonization, the Monroe Doctrine essentially challenged two important notions of international law: first, the notion of intervention and, second, that of *terra nullius*. While the sentiment had been growing since the 1810 Creole action, this was the first real international enunciation of the idea and in this sense merits special attention. As mentioned earlier the threat that hung over the Latin American countries at the time was the reconquest of 'their' territories by the European powers. This had, in the first instance, instilled in the new states the perceived desire to form confederations. With the original threat of European annexation dissipating and with the enunciation of the Monroe Doctrine, the states now sought to locate that agreement in international law, even if it challenged the existing belief. By doing so, the Monroe Doctrine essentially implied that all territories in America whether explored, peopled, or not, were essentially the exclusive 'property' of the American state within whose jurisdiction the territory was contained, and that in no circumstance could any of the territory within the continent be considered *res nullius*. Ironically the support for the American states in the form discussed above was ultimately a reification of the notion of colonization only through occupation rather than through renewed conquest. This contradiction was conveniently lost on the new incumbents of power. The internal ramification of the Monroe Doctrine was that the new American states now essentially needed to conquer parts of their own territory that had previously been outside their *de facto* jurisdiction without the threat of such a conquest being externally challenged either from outside the continent or from their neighbours, unless a dispute existed with regard to the location of the *uti possidetis* lines of 1810 or 1821. In this sense the parallel with the situation in sub-Saharan Africa is striking (Herbst 1992). However, rather than gaining the keys to the state machinery as a result of a decolonization process that was imperfect, the new states gained the state machinery by agreeing that no other Europeans could challenge their own jurisdiction. This view essentially informed the premise that the territory of the Americas had already been distributed amongst the states and that each one of the new states had the unqualified power to extend their sovereignty to all of the regions demarcated to them even if these regions were problematically delimited and largely unpeopled. The latter point needs to be especially stressed since there remain large tracts of land today, especially in the Amazon Basin, where tribes exist isolated from the events of the last two centuries.[35] To declare that the notion of *terra nullius* was no longer relevant is perhaps appropriate. However, to suggest that the

---

[35] See <http://www.amazonalliance.org/>.

sovereignty of the successor states extended to the entirety of the territory is manifestly inadequate.

The resonance of the Monroe Doctrine principles can be clearly seen in state practice. The message, even though expressed through the auspices of an American President, was essentially a message echoed by all America. The public support for it in Latin America can be gauged as early as the Panama Congress of 1826 (Baldwin 1907: 814), and is also pursuant to the 1826 dispute between the Provinces of the River Plate and Brazil with regards to the neutrality of Uruguay (see pp. 76–7). As pointed out by Alvarez, the understanding of the Monroe Doctrine as merely a hegemonic expression of the USA over all America is largely a misreading of the doctrine in traditional literature (1909: 317). Rather it emanates from the more rapid development of the USA in contrast to its southern neighbours.

Thus the doctrine could be summarized as developing along two main axes: first and foremost through the general principle of the prevention of any European state acquiring under any pretext, sovereignty over any American territory. Alavarez supports this by highlighting a few central cases:

> . . . the declaration of Polk in 1848 as to Yucatan; the declaration of 1895 upon the proposal of Nicaragua to cede to England Corn Island as a Naval Station; declaration of 1904 and 1905 in connection with the coercive measures of England, Italy and Germany against Venezuela.
>
> (ibid.: 315)

The second important axis along which the doctrine developed was the parallel norm of preventing European states from entering upon any permanent occupation of territory within the continent. The ambit of this principle also extended to the transfer from one state to another of its colonies in the New World. It also essentially prevented any European intervention in the formation of new states in America whether this process was achieved through emancipation, secession or other means. Notwithstanding either of these two issues the lasting legacy of the Monroe Doctrine to international law concerned with notions of territory and its acquisition remains the enunciation of the eradication of the principle of *terra nullius* (ibid.: 321). As outlined above, while this principle is essentially sound, it was born of a contradiction in itself. Nonetheless the legacy can still be viewed, ironically, in the cases of indigenous peoples' land rights today (see Chapter 7).

Conclusions

When the African leadership met in Cairo to extend the principle of *uti possidetis* to their territories, they justified this in the interests of protecting the African states from fragmenting.[36] However, in extending the notions concomitant to decolonization in

---

[36] See the Cairo Declaration, OAU Document AHG/Res.16(1) (1964); see also Brownlie (1979: 10–11).

Spanish America nearly a century and a half prior to their own actions in ridding their territory of colonizers, they arguably set in place the seeds for modern conflict over territory. As has been seen in this chapter the manner in which the concepts of *uti possidetis* and *terra nullius* were developed in the decolonization process was an indicator of many political factors at play. Association with similar principles has exported some of these negative factors to Africa. Some positive features of the use of the doctrine, such as its relative success in maintaining states in the immediate aftermath of decolonization, have also accompanied the process. However, the main aim of this chapter was to demonstrate two issues. First, that the doctrines and principles that were handed down and reapplied in a different context a century and a half later were not as firm and settled as they are often made out to be. In many ways discussions surrounding the doctrines of *uti possidetis* and *terra nullius* suggest that they are closed issues that do not need to be debated but are accepted as firm rules governing territory. Since their application forms the basis of the identities of more than 80 per cent of the world's population it is suggested that such debates will become increasingly important. Thus there is great benefit in re-examining the norms as they were first applied in a bid to ascertain their precise nuances and application then. Although *uti possidetis* cannot be considered a norm of *jus cogens*, its increasing applications in diverse situations cries out for more understanding of issues related to its use and reapplication. In addition, the principle of *terra nullius* has particular resonance for indigenous peoples, and in this context, too, it is important to identify the problematic beginnings of this doctrine and the manner in which it has affected the development of indigenous peoples' rights. The second aim of this chapter has been to focus on the era immediately before the colonization of Africa and Asia. Very often in discussing issues pertaining to colonization the intertemporal rule is called upon. This rule is usually highly appropriate since unfettered application of modern law to ancient situations is patently unfair under the legal doctrine of protection from retrospective laws. Nonetheless it is arguable that the doctrine has been often used as a handmaiden for political interests. By focusing on the period immediately preceding the African and Asian colonial era it can be argued that even via laws and principles of the pertinent time, subsequent colonization could be seen as violating international law. While the thrust of this argument is not necessarily to reassess and gain redress for such action,[37] the overuse of the intertemporal law arguably weakens international law in favour of dubious political interests.

Thus, in summary, the following points could be made with regard to the development of laws governing and affecting territory post-decolonization in Spanish America.

First, it set a precedent for challenging territories held by European nations at a distance from their own continent. Second, the doctrine of *uti possidetis* was

---

[37] This discussion could mirror the discussion that took place in South Africa at the International Conference against Racism in September 2001 with regard to compensation for slavery.

problematically applied in the decolonization process; although it sought to maintain order, it did so on the basis of questionable jurisdictions established under colonial law. Third, the principle of *terra nullius* while ostensibly defeated by the Monroe Doctrine was nonetheless the basis for the original occupation of the land by the Creoles. Fourth, the process of arbitration suggested that title to territory could be challenged and addressed by legal processes. Fifth, the declaration passed in 1890 concomitant to the Monroe Doctrine seeks to explicitly outlaw conquest of territory.

The importance of this declaration to the 'Scramble for Africa' is obvious. Any notion questioning the legitimacy of the European scramble for African territory in international law can usually be dismissed by reference to the intertemporal rule. The argument being put forward here and elaborated upon in the next chapter is essentially this: if the 'Scramble for Africa' is beyond the reach of international law by virtue of the notion of the intertemporal rule, then first this rule will need to be examined against its appropriate temporal context. However, even if this rule is accepted as being appropriate to the situation, its reference to time suggests that the contemporaneous development of principles should be applied to the given situation. The declaration quoted above was made in 1890. In a purely temporal sense this essentially meant that while the 'Scramble for Africa' was taking place there was development in customary international law that argued convincingly that acquisition of territory in another continent was illegal. This occurred primarily through the Monroe Doctrine, first expressed in 1823 and reinforced through state practice throughout the nineteenth century in Latin America. In addition it was also codified further in the above declaration passed unanimously in 1890. The states of Europe at the heart of the 'Scramble for Africa' might suggest that the intertemporal rule essentially puts the legality of their acquisition of these territories beyond the pale of international law. But to do this effectively one would need to understand the developing notions of international law of that given time and it is this task that has been attempted in this particular chapter.

4 African Treaty Regimes in the Nineteenth Century

An Examination of the Impact of Acquisitory Colonial Treaties on African State Formation

This chapter will examine the validity of certain African treaties during the period that became known as the 'Scramble for Africa'. Armed with the aims of free commerce, christianity and civilization, European powers sought to gain a foothold in sub-Saharan Africa ostensibly to satisfy their burgeoning markets (see generally Gann and Duignan 1969–75: vol. 1). In return, African entities were to be welcomed into the Family of Nations as equals under the classical tenets of *jus gentium* (see generally Alexandrowicz 1971). This 'bargain' was initially affected through treaties made with African rulers. However, these treaties were of dubious validity not only due to serious questions regarding their form and substance but also in view of their long-term ramifications as contributors to the process of colonization.

It could be argued that the nineteenth-century process of territorial acquisition held immense significance not only for the sovereignty of the African entities of that time but also for the formation of modern African states post-decolonization. This is principally due to the acquisitory treaties being recognized by the powers as title deeds *inter se* during the partition of the territory. Ultimately through this process of colonization the powers fixed the vast majority of existing boundaries in modern African states. This chapter will therefore provide a useful background to the continuing dilemma for African states today of achieving a balance between the competing concepts of territorial integrity and national self-determination.

To this end the chapter will be divided into six sections. The first assesses the nature of 'free market imperialism' and its application in the African context. The classical doctrine regarding territorial acquisition, protectorates and jurisdictional capitulations will then be introduced accompanied by a study of the notion of personality within international law. The third section examines the validity of the mechanisms used to legitimate the acquisition of territory in the light of such classical doctrine. In turn, the status of acquisitory treaties will then be determined according to the tenets of the customary law of treaties. In the fifth section the process by which the resultant territorial entities were transformed into colonial 'states' is analysed. The final section then confronts the cultural relativity apparent in the notions of territoriality and sovereignty, thereby attempting to extrapolate the manifestation of the acquisitory process on state formation and post-colonial 'national' identity. This is especially significant in view of the doctrine of *uti possidetis*, which is central to the creation of the modern African state.

Commerce, Christianity and Civilization

For the greater part of the nineteenth century European–African relations were purely commercial. 'Free trade imperialism' was characterized by the extension of global commercial influence under the guise of private enterprise (see generally Gifford and Louis 1971, Gann and Duigan 1969–75, 1978a and Hargreaves 1974). However, rather than express interest in purely commercial terms, the European powers proclaimed that *civilization* of the 'Dark Continent' was at the heart of their involvement. This view was classically expressed, as 'Commerce plus Christianity equals Civilisation'. The notion of the 'civilising mission' manifest itself in a policy of aggressive imperial philanthropy justified by the 'improvement of the moral and material well-being' of the indigenous peoples of Africa. The Europeans' belief in their own superiority meant that they could not accept the premise that Africans were capable of the art of government (for example see Westlake 1910: 107 and also Gann and Duigan 1969–75: vol. 1: 6–7, 24), and thus the perceived burden of bringing the 'blessings of civilisation' to the continent served to mask the true nature of European interest.[1] It is noteworthy that 'Colonisation' was never marketed as part of the civilizing mission (Flint 1988: 73). Indeed the conspicuous absence of the colonial process was a conscious effort by established powers who understood that colonial acquisition brought with it financial responsibility. The costs of colonial administration were deemed prohibitive and 'free trade imperialism' was therefore preferred wherever possible (Hargreaves 1985).

The naval supremacy of Britain ensured that it was the dominant continental power in the post-Napoleonic era and this arch proponent of free trade imperialism was committed to maintaining its 'informal sway' without the burden of territorial responsibility. It is submitted that the British media accurately reflected British policy when *The Standard* newspaper stated on 11 October 1884 that:

> Our ambition is to find markets, not to assert dominion; we do not want to extend our Empire, but to find outlets for our industries and avenues for our trade.
>
> (quoted in Louis 1971: 167–220)

Although there is evidence to suggest that, in a bid to maintain commercial hegemony, Britain did make some attempt to formalize its territorial position, it was nevertheless

---

[1] These phrases are taken from art. VI of the Final Act of the Berlin West Africa Conference 1885; Hertslet (1909: vol. II: 473).

reluctant to embark on a policy of widespread colonization. Instead it preferred to rely on the art of diplomacy in a rather belated attempt to re-establish principles equating to a 'Monroe Doctrine' to be applied in Africa for British benefit. However, regardless of such official inactivity, fundamental changes in the balance of power in Europe in the 1870s heralded a return to a period of normality in international relations. This shift gave rise to a 'new imperialism' that enabled emerging powers to realize their imperial ambitions by provoking conflict between the European powers in Africa.[2] With increased competition, the only way to secure monopolized access to African markets was via territorial acquisition and as a result the 'Scramble for Africa' began during the last few decades of the nineteenth century (Pakenham 1991; Fage 1995: 213–388; and Wessling 1996).

While the powers were prepared to engage in a scramble for territory, they were nonetheless reluctant to bear responsibility for the acquisitory process. Britain was especially concerned that the process of territorial acquisition would result in substantial administrative costs.[3] Ultimately, the prospective returns from Africa were not considered to be worthy of governmental commitment and in any event did not warrant direct conflict with other European powers. Therefore, the powers sought a mechanism that mutually recognized evidence of state authority (and thus acquisition *inter se*) without the expense of formal colonial rule. The solution lay in the institution of the 'chartered company'.

The use of such private concerns incorporated by royal charter for the purpose of overseas colonization found its origins in the English and Dutch trading companies of the seventeenth century. However, by the mid-eighteenth century the institution, dependent on monopolies, privileges and tariffs and associated with slavery, came to represent the unacceptable face of economic organization (Flint 1988: 70). While the chartered company was still predominant in the colonization of both British North America and India, the ramifications of the Indian 'Mutiny' of 1857 and the creation of the Federal Dominion of Canada (1867) suggested that it was an institutional relic of a past colonial age (ibid.: 69–72).

The 'Scramble for Africa', however, resulted in a new period of imperial expansion that led the powers to revive the institutions of the previous colonial era and as a

---

[2] The participation of a unified Germany in the Scramble led to conflicts with Britain, for example, in the Cameroons and Angra Pequena in 1884.

[3] As imperial municipal law would be automatically applied to the territory of a new colony such acquisitions were potentially costly. This issue was of paramount concern to the British government at the Berlin West Africa Conference (1884–5) where it was suggested that acquisition should take the form of annexation as a matter of course. Lord Chancellor Selbourne was anxious to avoid the creation of such a rule of law, not least for the consequences for British colonial policy outside Africa; see Louis (1971). The importance of this point was not lost on the Foreign Secretary, Lord Salisbury, in the context of the governance of the Oil Rivers Protectorate, which was reconsidered in 1888–9. When formal annexation was recommended, Salisbury, aware of the difficulty of enforcing anti-slavery laws, ensured that the territory remained a protectorate; see Flint (1960: 235–6).

result the phenomenon of the chartered company once again proved to be the preferred instrument of colonization. While these companies had been granted wide commercial privileges and monopolies they also exercised rights of delegated sovereignty allowing them to conclude treaties with African rulers which resulted in the acquisition of territorial sovereignty on behalf of their states.[4] The application of the chartered company in the African context thus engendered a paradigm shift away from free trade imperialism towards privately motivated territorial aggrandisement that was exploited to the full during the Scramble (see generally Flint 1960, Williams 1921 and Stead 1902). The institutional importance of the chartered companies was demonstrated by the fact that they were responsible for securing nearly 75 per cent of British territory in sub-Saharan Africa (Flint 1988: 71). French and German chartered companies were similarly productive on behalf of their national states as well as others such as the Sultan of Zanzibar. This institutional development satisfied the 'milomania' of new imperialism and thus presented the continent to European commerce.[5] The chartered company with its combination of private enterprise and indirect state authority became the symbol of effective colonization during this period (Gann and Duigan 1969–75: vol. 1: 100–29.

Nonetheless, it is clear that the commercial success of chartered companies was more often perceived than actual. The strongly held convictions of imperialist-financiers that empire, investment and profits all went together were wholly unfounded. Indeed arguably the most successful chartered company, the British South Africa Company, was generally unprofitable and paid no dividends to its shareholders between 1890 and 1923 (ibid.: 102). Further, the economic viability of chartered companies was compromised by the substantial costs of the acquisitory process itself, as evidenced by the £300 000 claim made by the National Africa Company for costs incurred in its battle to keep the Niger region in British hands.[6]

The Classical Doctrine of Territoriality and the Notion of Personality within International Law

The classical tenets of international law provided that the mode of territorial acquisition was determined by the nature of the territory in issue (see generally

---

[4] These privileges and monopolies were less common after the Berlin Conference 1885. See the struggle of the National Africa Company (later the Royal Niger Company) for its charter in Flint (1960: 68–87). See also Hertslet (1909: Vol. I: 125–7).

[5] 'Milomania' was a term coined to describe the imperialist policy of acquiring territory for its own sake; see Gann and Duignan (1969–75: vo. 1: 9). More generally for a discussion of the antics of King Leopold of Belgium, see Brittain (1999: 133).

[6] While this was obviously a negotiating figure arrived at for the purposes of securing a charter, the claim was accepted in principle by the British government; see Flint (1960: 79–85).

Oppenheim 1992: 677–718; Jennings 1962: 1–35; and Shaw 1986: 1–26). Essentially, if the territory was unoccupied (being *terra nullius*) it could be acquired by occupation alone. However, if a people possessing social or political organization inhabited the territory then occupation of that territory could not amount to valid title. As this society would be recognized as having personality under international law, the territory would have to be acquired by way of a treaty of cession thus ensuring the transfer of sovereignty between the contracting parties and the acquisition of derivative title. Thus in terms of the development of international law it could be argued that progress had been made from the settlement of the Americas since in that instance the territory of the continent had been considered *terra nullius*. That the imperial powers agreed that treaties of cession had to be signed to legitimate transfer of territory in Africa suggests a greater respect for the existence of a people than was granted to Latin American indigenous peoples, even though in both cases the imperial powers ultimately achieved their end result – the acquisition of territory.

While the classical modes of territorial acquisition were certainly used in the African context,[7] in general the powers preferred other mechanisms to assert their territorial and political influence. Prime amongst these was the institution of the classical protectorate in which external sovereignty was vested in the protecting state while internal sovereignty remained with the protected state.[8] The protecting state thus provided shelter from external threat while the protected state was allowed relative freedom in the conduct of its internal affairs (Alexandrowicz 1973b: 54–60). According to the arch-colonialist Lord Lugard, the institution of the protectorate was especially well suited to the African context as it allowed the powers to gain a foothold on the continent in return for introducing the African political entities into the Family of Nations (ibid.: 51). Further, it has also been suggested that the institution required the powers to secure the benefits of European civilization for African entities without impairing African national or cultural identity (Alexandrowicz 1971: 152).

Another classical institution favoured by the powers in their relations with African entities was the instrument of jurisdictional capitulations (Alexandrowicz 1975: 61–3). The original mechanism of capitulations ensured that a foreign community established in the territory of another state would be granted the privilege of self-government according to their own laws, with jurisdiction vested in the head of that community. These privileges were eventually included in bilateral treaties thereby presenting obligations for the signatories in the form of jurisdictional capitulations. While by accommodating differing forms of civilization this classical institution was a manifestation of the notion of equality between states, capitulation treaties were also arguably entirely consistent with the spirit of free trade imperialism. Indeed,

---

[7] For example, see the cession of the Port and Island of Lagos by King Docemo to Britain in 1861 in Hertslet (1909: vol. I: 93–5).

[8] For the present purposes, leaving aside the thorny issue of whether sovereignty can theoretically be divided, see generally Andrews (1978).

according to Protocol 13 the Paris Peace Convention 1856, capitulations provided the conditions for the

> peaceful residence of Christians within [such] countries and the successful prosecution of commerce with their people.
>
> (Schwarzenberger 1962: 55)

Despite some notable exceptions (for example the Vatican State and the Order of St John), it was generally accepted until very recently that only states had legal personality in international law.[9] The natural law view embodied in *jus gentium*, however, took a broad view of statehood. According to Cicero, a state was defined as a 'numerous society united by a common sense of right and a mutual participation in advantage' and his conception of statehood clearly influenced Grotius and Vattel.[10] Modern *jus gentium* promoted the notion of the equality of states and accordingly any society would be recognized as possessing sovereign authority over its territory regardless of the level of civilization it had reached. It followed therefore that 'primitive societies' too ought to have been considered capable of transferring territorial sovereignty within international society.[11] Furthermore European relations with Morocco, Algeria and Tunisia through the seventeenth and eighteenth centuries suggests that there was at least a degree of support for the universal theories of modern *jus gentium* in early state practice (Alexandrowicz 1975: 33–7).

This position, however, was to be revised by international society of the late nineteenth century.[12] During this period legal theory was dominated by the positivist school, which arguably represented the most blatant expression of Euro-centricity within international law (Verzijl 1955). Positivists held that organized non-European societies possessed no sovereign rights over the territory they inhabited (Westlake 1910: 91–111). As such, this *de facto* occupation was not legally effective and the territory (being *terra nullius*) was therefore open to acquisition by occupation. Justification for this view lay in the reinterpretation of the definition of statehood. Admission into the 'Family of Nations' was the preserve of the existing membership (in effect, the European powers) and thus so was the definition of statehood. Rather than maintaining the classical view, positivists asserted that a state could be defined as:

---

[9] See the *Island of Palmas arbitration, AJIL* 22(4) (1928) 867–912. On the subject of statehood in general, see Crawford (1979).

[10] *De Re Publica* Lib. 1, XXV.39, cited in Andrews (1979: 410). See also Crawford (1979: 5–10).

[11] See the views of Grotius and Vattel as discussed in Lindley (1926: 12–17). Vattel did, however, qualify his view of the territorial sovereignty of 'primitive' peoples by allowing another society to acquire any 'excess' territory if it was required.

[12] For a definition of 'international society' see Bull (1984).

A people permanently occupying a fixed territory bound together by common laws, habits and customs into one body politic, exercising, through the medium of an organised government, independent sovereignty and control over all the persons and things within its boundaries, capable of making war and peace and of entering into all international relations with the other communities of the globe.[13]

(Phillimore 1879: 81, quoted in Andrews 1978: 411)

Essentially, these criteria reflected the fundamental characteristics of the Westphalian state. The more remote the society from this model, the less chance it had of becoming a subject of international law. Indeed even well-established entities such as Turkey struggled for acceptance within international society.[14] It appears that a core justification for prescribing such criteria was the requirement of being able to establish and maintain international relations. If an entity did not possess the stable governmental institutions necessary to protect the life, liberty and property of foreign nationals, admission would be denied.[15] In such situations, the powers were thereby 'entitled' to protect their nationals either by applying their own laws through the liberal interpretation of jurisdictional capitulations or by simply asserting their own *de facto* authority over the territory in an effort to maintain the rule of law in their favour (Schwarzenberger 1962: 77).

Other motives were also at work in the exclusion of African entities from international society. In keeping with the missionary spirit of the age, it was initially claimed that adherence to Christianity was material consideration for admission into the Family of Nations. However, this view is not supported by facts: both Ethiopia and Liberia were Christian entities during the period of the Scramble and neither was granted membership of the Family on these grounds.[16] The exclusion of African entities it seems, was motivated by pure racism as evidenced by the positivist claim that international society consisted of 'all the states of European blood, that is all the European and American states except Turkey, and of Japan' (Westlake 1910: 40 and Umozurike 1979: 21). The gaze of the Family of Nations was evidently coloured by the cause of 'civilization' and the link between civilization and international personality was thus an express feature of positivist theory. The argument was that political communities capable of civil association intended territory to be used for the purpose

---

[13] This view has continued to receive credence in the twentieth century; see art. 1 of the Convention on Rights and Duties of States ('Montevideo Convention'), *AJIL* 28 (1934) 75–8.

[14] According to Alexandrowicz (1973a: 129–30), the Ottoman Empire was admitted to the Family of Nations as a result of the Treaty of Paris 1856, which allowed Turkey into the Concert of Europe.

[15] According to Schwarzenberger (1962: 71) such requirements became embodied in a multitude of treaties, which gradually became rules of customary international law.

[16] An issue discussed in Umozurike (1979: 21). Alexandrowicz (1973a: 129–30) asserts that Liberia achieved recognition during the early nineteenth century. However, in view of the writings of the positivist school it is submitted that this assertion is to be doubted.

of occupation and since only states organized on the European model could meet such requirements it followed that no civilization was possible in their absence. In addition, with the high valence granted to the notion of civilization within international society,[17] the lack of it was considered a threat to human association (Fisch 1988: 362). Therefore 'international law' demanded that primitive societies achieve civilization before gaining recognition as members of the Family of Nations with rights to territorial sovereignty (Lindley 1926: 20). Thus 'civilization' became the acid test for personality in international law thereby reflecting the philosophical change away from the classical tenets of *jus gentium*.

Classical Doctrine and the Acquisition of Territory in the 'Scramble for Africa'

The Nature of Acquisitory Treaties

It has been suggested that Africa could not be regarded as *terra nullius*, the presence of acquisitory treaties providing crucial evidence that African entities were deemed to possess territorial sovereignty (Alexandrowicz 1973b: 96–7 and Shaw 1986: 37). However, this factor could have no direct bearing on the *ideology* behind colonial acquisition (Fisch 1988: 360–3).[18] The powers decided to perceive Africa as *terra nullius* because in practice they possessed the military strength to do so.[19] At no point did the powers question their right to colonize Africa; the history of the period reveals that the question was always *how* and not *why* (ibid.: 348). This is particularly relevant in light of the Declaration on Conquests as appended to the Lima Declaration 1890 (see Chapter 3). It could be argued that the sentiments expressed in that declaration as well as the growing discussion about the status of territory ever since the 1810 Creole action and subsequent events had led to these norms being questioned. Nevertheless, the colonization of Africa was only superficially cloaked in an aura of legality – perhaps more to reflect synergy with ever-growing norms of democracy at home than in compliance with international legal thought and philosophy. Thus while the positivist school proved a useful source of justification, it was more convincing to treat African entities as if they possessed legal personality in international law. It is therefore arguable that international society recognized the territorial sovereignty of

---

[17] It is important to note that this terminology of 'civilization' persists as conspicuous in art. 38 of the Statute of the International Court of Justice, as appended to the UN Charter 1945.

[18] See also the judgment of Judge Ammoun in *Legal consequences for States of the continued presence of South Africa in Namibia (South West Africa) notwithstanding Security Council Resolution 276 (1970)*, ICJ Reports (1971) 86, quoted in Umozurike (1979: 26).

[19] The converse was also true. Italy recognized the sovereignty of Ethiopia in 1896 when its attempt to enforce its 'protectorate' against Ethiopia led to military defeat at the Battle of Adowa.

African entities but only for the limited purpose of being able to transfer it to the European powers.[20]

While the powers were prepared to conclude treaties directly with African rulers they were reluctant to follow this course unless vital commercial interests were threatened or territory was in danger of being seized by another power.[21] In general, they preferred to delegate restricted sovereign rights to chartered companies to act on their behalf (Lindley 1926: 90–109; Flint 1988; and Alexandrowicz 1975: 43–4). Although chartered companies were granted *passive legitimation* (that is the capacity to receive sovereign rights from the indigenous rulers) they could not alienate sovereignty once acquired. Thus they automatically assumed the role of agents for their national states.[22] Sovereignty in this context was also limited to internal authority over the territory in question, the capacity to act in the international arena being reserved exclusively for the respective national government (Alexandrowicz 1973b: 41).

While there are grounds for believing that African rulers wished to establish friendly relations with European agents, there is much less clarity about the precise nature of such relations. African leaders that recognized the advantages of European commercialism often expressed their value by concluding ceremonial blood pacts. It was these symbolic expressions of friendly relations that provided the basis for the conclusion of acquisitory treaties with African entities (Mwa Bawele 1988). Lord Lugard believed that in the blood pact he had found the African equivalent of the *jus civile* notion of the law of contract and that the binding nature of such pacts mirrored the rule of *pacta sunt servanda* in international law.[23] Accordingly, in his view this ceremony amounted to a treaty of protection wherein the European agent offered protection in return for recognition of him, and by association his state, as overlord. Although from the African perspective, blood pacts were never intended to signify the surrender of territorial authority, they presented the Europeans, under the pretext of ceremonial reciprocity, with an ideal opportunity for territorial acquisition. African leaders were thus 'invited' to participate in this European custom of 'friendship', which, in reality, amounted to the deceitful transfer of their territorial sovereignty (ibid.: 471).

---

[20] According to Judge Huber 'Sovereignty in the relation between states signifies independence. Independence in regard to a portion of the globe is the right to exercise therein, to the exclusion of any other state, the function of a state'; *Island of Palmas arbitration, AJIL* 22 (1928) 875. In the circumstances such a limited interpretation of the concept of territorial sovereignty cannot be justified under international law.

[21] An example of the former would be the annexation of Lagos by Britain in 1861 and as for the latter, the creation of the Oil Rivers Protectorate due to an impending threat from France; see Flint (1969: 230).

[22] This was the view of the German scholar Dr Hesse in relation to German chartered companies; see Alexandrowicz (1973b: 39).

[23] *Pacta sunt servanda* is generally interpreted as meaning that every treaty in force is binding on the parties and must be performed in good faith; see Alexandrowicz (1973b: 50–4 and Lugard (1893).

The form of acquisitory treaties used on the African continent varied enormously and was often dependent on the status of the parties involved. Thus larger African entities were often better placed in negotiations than leaders of smaller communities.[24] It followed therefore that some treaties were of a highly individualized character and products of lengthy negotiations while others were concluded on the spot by the use of standard forms (Hertslet 1909: vol. I: 137–53).[25] Many of these standard form treaties concluded by chartered companies provided for the 'cession' of territory and the transfer of full jurisdiction. However, it is clear that such treaties could not legally amount to cession of territory under international law. Acquisitory practice demonstrated that the powers would not usually effect cessions directly due to the consequent burden of jurisdiction and the accompanying imperial policy of avoiding colonial responsibility wherever possible. Further, as standard form treaties usually included clauses relating to protection, it can be safely assumed that these treaties were actually implying the creation of protectorates rather than true cessions of territory under international law (Lindley 1926: 185). It has been suggested, however, that even standard form treaties complied with the requirements of international law. They usually contained clauses providing that the African signatories fully understood and consented to the terms of the treaty and that European negotiators, with the assistance of interpreters, had explained the documents, which were then signed in the presence of witnesses (for examples, see Alexandrowicz 1973b: 45–54). However, it should be appreciated that the inclusion of such provisions, especially in advance of the events themselves, seldom ensured that true consent had been obtained.[26] Perhaps the lowest point of the acquisitory process was expressed by the account of an agent in Uganda:

> A ragged untidy European, who in any civilised country would be in danger of being taken up by the police as a vagrant, lands at a native village, the people run away; he shouts out after them to come back, holding before them a shilling's worth of beads . . . the so-called interpreter pretends to explain the treaty to the chief. The chief does not understand a word of it, but he looks pleased as he receives another present of beads; a mark is made on a printed treaty by the chief, and another by the interpreter, the vagrant, who professes to be the representative of a great empire, signs his name. The boat sails away, and the new ally and protégé of England or France immediately throws the treaty into the fire.
>
> (Thruston 1900: 170–1, quoted in McEwen 1971: 12)

---

[24] Notable examples here include the protectorate over the territory of Opoboland concluded between Britain and King Ja Ja and British negotiations with King Lobengula of Mashonaland and Matabeleland and the Sultan of Zanzibar.

[25] This source provides a number of standardized forms used in the conclusion of treaties of protection between the National African Company (later Royal Niger Company) and African entities in the area of Nigeria.

[26] This point has been readily conceded by modern authors; see Shaw (1986: 42).

Not only did the lack of informed consent have severe consequences for the validity of these treaties;[27] but central misrepresentations regarding the subject matter arguably amounted to evidence of bad faith and would therefore create a fundamental illegality in any event.

Acquisitory Practice and the International Context: The Berlin West Africa Conference (1884–5)

Historically, the acquisition of colonial territory was legitimated without the need for actual possession. This was manifest in the Catholic *fait accompli* between the Pope, Spain and Portugal regarding the New World.[28] While the Protestant states of Europe were prepared to challenge this approach, the notion that valid title to territory could be acquired by symbolic annexation continued to be a feature of territorial acquisition in the modern colonial era.[29]

However, by the late nineteenth century, the emerging and re-emerging powers were only too aware that unsubstantiated territorial claims deprived them of their imperial ambitions. Thus vague or fictional protectorates only served to intensify demands for an international regime to determine valid territorial claims. The Berlin West Africa Conference of 1884–5 therefore provided the powers with an ideal opportunity for fashioning legal principles upon which territorial acquisition would be recognized under international law. Although the conference was grounded in the principles of free trade imperialism,[30] it was ultimately concerned with creating standardized criteria for legitimating territorial acquisition through the lens of West Africa for the continent as a whole.

To this end, the chairman of the conference, Prince Bismarck, was intent on securing the requirement of effective occupation as evidenced primarily through the consequent responsibility of jurisdiction, for all territorial acquisitions, in an attempt to end the practice of creating paper protectorates with nominal or notional administration. The

---

[27] According to Vattel, freedom of consent was held to be sacrosanct in the cession of territory in modern *jus gentium*; see *Le Droit des Gens*, vol. 2, ch. 12, para. 163, cited in Alexandrowicz (1975: 46).

[28] The Papal bull *Inter Caetera* (1492) granted Ferdinand and Isabella of Spain exclusive right of territorial acquisition in the New World. By the Treaty of Tordesillas (1494) Spain and Portugal purported to divide the undiscovered territories of the world between themselves. The treaty received Papal sanction in 1506. See Lindley (1926: 24) and Westlake (1910: 96–7).

[29] See the *Island of Palmas arbitration, AJIL* 22(4) (1928) 897–8. See also the *Minquiers and Ecrehos case (France v. UK)*, ICJ Reports (1953) 47 and the *Clipperton Island arbitration, AJIL* 26 (1932) 390–4.

[30] According to Bismarck at the first session of the conference, the aims of the conference were (1) freedom of commerce on the Congo; (2) freedom of navigation on the Congo and Niger; and (3) agreement about the formalities of valid annexation of territory in the future; see generally Louis (1971).

British, mindful of the financial implications of effecting jurisdiction in Africa and elsewhere, vehemently argued that as the indigenous authority retained territorial sovereignty, the creation of a protectorate could not amount to the acquisition of title under international law. It was argued therefore that the requirement of effective occupation was unwarranted (Louis 1971: 208–14; Fisch 1988: 352–3, 364). Despite threatening to adjourn the conference, Bismarck ultimately conceded and art. XXXV of the Berlin Final Act provided that:

> The Signatory Powers of the present Act recognise the obligation to insure the establishment of authority in the regions occupied by them on the coasts of the African Continent sufficient to protect existing rights, and, as the case may be, freedom of trade and of transit under conditions agreed upon.[31]

By refusing to acknowledge the colonial interpretation of the protectorate, the conference allowed the practice of creating paper protectorates and thus *de facto* territorial acquisition to continue unabated.

The evidence suggests that the ramifications of acquisitory practice rather than the spirit of free trade imperialism drove the conference. Indeed the history of colonization reveals that political factors and other circumstances invariably determined the manner of territorial acquisition rather than abstract legal principles designed for general application. The requirement of effective occupation was only mooted with regard to the acquisition of new coastal territory post-Berlin, primarily because none of the powers were in a position to establish effective occupation of the African interior (Shaw 1986: 49). More cynically, there was precious little coastal territory left to acquire by this time in any event, since one or other of the powers could account for most African territory. So while the powers were anxious to construct an *a priori* framework for the legitimation of territorial acquisition, they were wary of creating an international regime that would hamper their own colonial ambitions. The main concern at the time was therefore the establishment of an interim framework so as not to restrict future opportunities for acquisition while at the same time seeking to order the events until that point.

Interestingly, in the context of the validity of acquisitory treaties, the delegation from the USA insisted upon the adoption of principles ensuring the voluntary nature of African consent during acquisition (Fisch 1988: 362–2):

> Modern International Law steadily follows the road which leads to the recognition of the right of native races (African communities) to dispose freely of themselves and their hereditary soil. Conformably to this principle my Government would be willing to support the more extended rule – one which should apply to the said occupation (of territory) in Africa, a principle looking to the voluntary consent of the natives of whose country

---

[31] See Hertslet (1909: vol. I: 485). The requirement of notifying other signatories of a territorial acquisition did, however, apply to protectorates; see art. XXXIV.

possession is taken (by treaty) in all cases when they may not have provoked an act of aggression.[32]

Although it has been claimed in some quarters that this principle was tacitly accepted by the conference,[33] the refusal of the USA to ratify the Final Act suggests otherwise. Evidently the powers remained sensitive about the true nature of the acquisitory process. While they appreciated the incumbent flaws they remained circumspect in testing the validity of these treaties under international law. As discussed earlier, the powers in Africa replicated the approach adopted by the Iberians in the New World (see Chapter 3): they claimed the entire continent before it was effectively occupied. Clearly they were only concerned with territorial acquisition *inter se* and the interests of the indigenous peoples, as was the case in Latin America, were marginalized as a result. While the conference and its Final Act failed to fulfil its objectives spectacularly, the very nature of its ostensible aims meant that it was never likely to succeed in practice. Evidently the participants saw the conference more as an opportunity for developing the international customary law of treaties than as a vehicle for the creation of a new source of law (Fisch 1988: 351). In fact the British concluded that the Final Act laid down no new rules of international law, a view that seems to have been supported by subsequent British practice.[34] While the Berlin Conference did at least provide the international legitimation for the actions of the powers during the Scramble, it failed to establish an effective framework for this process (Crowe 1942; Forster *et al.* 1988: vi–vii; and Hargreaves 1988: 74). In any event, the powers tended to ignore the territorial regimes established, preferring instead to rely on spheres of influence and protectorates to achieve their colonial objectives.

Protectorates, Capitulations and Spheres of Influence

The relations established by treaties of protection ensured that the protected states transferred all or part of their international capacity or personality to the protecting state, thus enabling the effective protection of a given state within the international arena. Nevertheless, according to classical theory, relations would be restricted to the sole purpose of providing protection, and further the power of the protecting state

---

[32] Declaration of John Kasson, head of the US delegation, which he asked to be included as a Protocol of the Berlin Final Act, quoted in Alexandrowicz (1975: 47).

[33] Alexandrowicz (1973b: 47) draws on Lugard's view that the conference tacitly supported this principle. Shaw (1986: 42), however, believes this view to be rather optimistic; see also Hargreaves (1988: 319) and Westlake (1910: 93). For the text of the General Act of the Conference of Berlin 1885, see Hertslet (1909: vol. II: 468–87 and the extensive compilation of documents in Gavin and Betley (1973).

[34] Britain took the view that art. XXXV merely restated the existing principles of customary international law and therefore would also apply to acquisitions in the interior of Africa; see Allott (1973: 112).

would be limited to that permitted by the empowering treaty.[35] In the event of breach, the protected state would be considered entitled to regard the treaty as being broken and thus voidable. While the institution of the protectorate possessed legal validity according to the tenets of *jus gentium*, the definition of the institution in the positivist era was liable to reinterpretation. According to Hall, the term 'protectorate' was

> somewhat indefinite, or rather perhaps it may be said to have different meanings in different circumstances in the mouths of different people.
>
> (Hall 1894: 204, quoted in Morris 1972: 42)

Indeed, that the apparent elasticity of the protectorate was exploited to the full during the period of the Scramble is best demonstrated by the British protectorate established over the territory of King Ja Ja of Opoboland in 1884. During negotiations, King Ja Ja sought a definition of the term 'protection'. In response Consul Hewett of the Niger Coast Protectorate assured the King that

> in the proposed treaty . . . the Queen (of England) does not want to take your country or your markets, but at the same time is anxious that no other nation take them. She undertakes to extend her gracious favour and protection, which will leave your country (Opoboland) still under your government.[36]

While this interpretation seems to be in accord with the classical notion of a protectorate, when Ja Ja began to interfere with the commercial interests of British traders the true form of the colonial protectorate was swiftly revealed. According to the British Colonial Office in 1886, 'protection' was deemed as meaning:

> The promotion of the welfare of the natives of all the territories *taken as a whole* by ensuring the peaceful development of trade and facilitating their intercourse with Europeans (superseding any contrary obligation).[37]

By resorting to this approach the British government let the pretence to classical theory slip (Flint 1969: 234). It is evident that in this case Britain openly acknowledged its mission to 'civilize' the continent. The powers claimed the right to be the arbiters of the welfare of the African people taken together as a whole. It followed that the provisions of individual treaties concluded with specific African rulers were therefore of no significance *per se* and could be disregarded if contrary to the 'welfare of the

---

[35] Alexandrowicz (1973b: 62) derives authority from Vattel, *Le Droit des Gens*, vol. 1, 16, and vol. 2, para. 204.

[36] 1 July 1884, enclosed in Ja Ja to Salisbury, 5 May 1887, F.O. 84/1862; see Anene (1966: 66), quoted in Umozurike (1979: 44).

[37] Roseberry to Hewett, 15 April 1886; see Anene (1966: 74), quoted in Umozurike (1979: 44) and Flint (1969: 234). For a fuller account of Ja Ja's actions see Flint (1969: 232–5).

natives' or more realistically, the interests of the European powers. In general, however, the powers tried to maintain the illusion of the classical form. The appearance of its legal validity under international law assured, the colonial protectorate could serve the interests of the European powers in a number of important ways. First, in general, this guise of colonialism deflected attention away from the power on to the chartered company. Second, by establishing protectorates the powers maintained territorial claims valid against all other powers but without the prohibitive expenses of formal colonial annexation. Finally, such claims also reserved authority for the concerned power to interfere in the internal sovereignty of the protected state at will and ultimately to absorb it by annexation (Lindley 1926: 183; Westlake 1910: 121–9).[38]

From a municipal perspective it is notable that in English constitutional law, for instance, the distinction between 'protected states' and 'protectorates' was maintained.[39] The former appears to concur with the classical institution of *jus gentium*, the protected state transferring all or part of its external sovereignty to the protecting state. However, this conception is far broader than the notion of statehood within international law during the nineteenth century. The crucial significance of the term 'state' could be understood as lying in the recognition that the territorial integrity of the protected 'state' remained after the conclusion of the treaty of protection. In short, the boundaries of the protected 'state' continued to reflect the territorial parameters of the pre-existing political entity. Thus British agents were prepared to confer the status of a 'protected state' on the larger and more powerful entities with which they concluded acquisitory treaties, such societies being in a stronger position to negotiate the terms of their treaties of protection while retaining their territorial integrity.

In contrast, a British 'protectorate' was the product of the amalgamation and consolidation of the territories of numerous smaller African entities with which British agents had concluded treaties of protection (Allott 1973: 121).[40] This process eventually led to the creation of the 'protectorate', an artificial entity manufactured through its territorial parameters at the hands of an imperial government rather than through any pre-existing political communities (ibid.). Thus it is evident that a 'protectorate' under English law approximated to the phenomenon of the colonial protectorate in international law. While the distinction may have carried validity during the initial phases of the Scramble, as the powers began to assume greater authority in the internal affairs of protected 'states' and 'protectorates' alike, the distinction became increasingly insignificant.

Besides concluding these acquisitory treaties with African rulers, the powers also acquired territorial interests by way of bilateral or multilateral treaties between

---

[38] Interestingly Hall (1894) saw the territorial character of the colonial protectorate as comparable to conquest.

[39] For examples, see acquisitory practice with regard to Buganda and Barotse in Allott (1973: 121).

[40] For a fuller account of protectorates, see Crawford (1979: 186–214).

themselves. These third party treaties[41] or conventions gave rise to 'spheres of influence' (Rutherford 1926) by which the parties agreed not to interfere in the territorial sphere of the other party.[42] Spheres of influence would sometimes pre-empt protectorates in a given area although more often pre-existing protectorates would provide the basis for the conclusion of such treaties.[43] The prime importance of acquisitory treaties made with African entities can only be understood effectively through the lens of these third party treaties since their true value could only be realized in the context of European relations. It can therefore be argued that both mechanisms taken together affected the partition of Africa between the European powers. This partition of territory is particularly important since the vast majority of state boundaries in modern Africa are the products of this process. While the Berlin Final Act formally sanctioned this practice,[44] these third party treaties were clearly products of political expediency rather than sound legal principle.[45]

Another important instrument in the process of colonization was the implementation of jurisdictional capitulations. Clearly premised on the *jus gentium* notion of equality between states, capitulations were not considered to be evidence of cultural superiority or inferiority; rather they were the doctrinal expression of the existence of a mutual respect for different forms of civilization (Alexandrowicz 1973b: 83). Indeed the European states originally adhered to the spirit of reciprocity by allowing communities from Asia and Africa to exercise such jurisdictional rights in the territories of the European states.[46] Capitulations in the African context provided for the division of jurisdiction between the native ruler and the European authority. In principle, both civil and criminal disputes between Europeans in African territory were subject to the

---

[41] For an example of a third party treaty see the *Case concerning the territorial dispute (Libyan Arab Jamahiriya v. Chad)*, ICJ Reports (1994) 6, also referred to in Chapter 5.

[42] See also the arrangement for the delimitation of spheres of influence between Britain and France on the West Coast of Africa, 10 August 1889 in Hertslet (1909: vol. II: 729); the convention between Britain and France for the delimitation of their respective possessions to the west of the Niger and their respective possessions and spheres of influence to the east of the Niger (14 June 1898) in Hertslet (1909: vol. II: 783); and generally Brownlie (1979).

[43] For example, a treaty of protection was concluded between the Emir of Yola and the Royal Niger Company in 1893 using standard Form 10 (Flint (1960: 177–8) and Hertslet (1909: vol. I: 152). The efforts of the company led to the Anglo-German Agreement of 1893, which provided that Germany recognized the British sphere of influence as including Yola and Bornu and Britain recognized the German sphere east of Bornu as far as the Shari River. See the text of the treaty in Hertslet (1909: vol. III: 914). See also Flint (1960: 179–86).

[44] See arts. VI and IX of the Berlin Final Act (1885) in Shaw (1986: 48); see also Uzoigwe (1976).

[45] The positivists themselves admitted this; see Westlake (1910: 130–5). The USA did not recognize the legality of spheres of influence; see Lindley (1926: 212).

[46] For example, see the French treaties concluded with Morocco, Algeria and Tunisia in the seventeenth century; see Alexandrowicz (1975: 36–7).

jurisdiction of the European Consul. However, in mixed disputes, the matter would be resolved by the principle of *actor sequitur forum rei* or by referral to mixed courts where both authorities were represented. *Actor sequitur forum rei* provided that jurisdiction was dependent on the nationality of the offender in any particular case. Thus, if a European national were accused of an offence, the European authority would exercise jurisdiction and vice versa. Along with classical protectorates, capitulations were generally a feature of relations between the Europeans and the more powerful African entities (for example Morocco, Algeria, Tunisia and Zanzibar). Weaker 'village' entities were more likely to be subjected to standard form treaties, creating implied protectorates where jurisdiction was vested in the European authority and therefore the issue of capitulations did not arise (Alexandrowicz 1975: 63). Nonetheless, the application of capitulatory provisions was significant for the entire continent, as they were barometers of the inequality apparent within Euro-African relations throughout the nineteenth century (Alexandrowicz 1973b: 83).

Although, classically, capitulations ensured that African rulers retained a significant degree of judicial authority within their territory, the Scramble led to fundamental changes in capitulatory practice. During this period the rush for territory precluded any pretence to the norms of *jus gentium*, which had been observed in the context of North Africa earlier in the century. Indeed, the new approach appeared to be a complete reversal of the original practice, as now the powers decided whether or not to concede a degree of jurisdiction to the native ruler in relation to internal matters. Thus treaties concluded in this period often curbed native jurisdiction by providing that civil disputes between Africans were subject to appeal to an imperial court or, in criminal cases, liable to interference by imperial officials.[47] Further, existing capitulations were often revised and replaced during this period. For example, the treaty between Britain and Zanzibar of 1886 recognized the principle of *actor sequitur forum rei* with regard to mixed disputes. However, when Zanzibar became a British protectorate in 1890, the treaty provided that mixed disputes, in situations where jurisdiction would previously have rested with the Sultan, would henceforth be transferred to mixed courts.[48] It is clear that the actions of the powers during the Scramble transformed this natural institution into an artificial instrument of colonialism thereby mirroring the decimation of the protectorate in this era of new imperialism (Alexandrowicz 1975: 125).

Acquisitory Treaties and Customary International Law

It is evident that the formation of treaties in international law has been greatly influenced

---

[47] See the British treaties of protection with Uganda (1893 and 1895) cited in Alexandrowicz (1973b: 88).

[48] Article XVI, Treaty of Protection, cited in Alexandrowicz (1975: 62).

by *jus civile*.[49] Thus the general principles of the law of contract such as free consent, capacity, privity and good faith have arguably provided the foundation for the customary international law of treaties (see generally McNair 1961 and Elias 1974). However, with international law premised on the sovereignty of independent states, international regimes remain largely consensual in nature. In the province of treaties, this reality has found expression in the rule *pacta sunt servanda*. A core principle of customary international law, this rule implies that good faith must be observed at the time of conclusion and throughout the existence of any given treaty. Despite assurances that the blood pacts (and thus treaties of protection) were made in the spirit *of pacta sunt servanda*, evidence suggests that acquisitory treaties were in general crude and misleading imitations of customary international law. It is apparent that these quasi-treaties were binding on the European powers only in a moral sense; when they proved useful they could be enforced, if not they would be disregarded. However, while treaties of protection may not strictly have been treaties in international law they were significant in the political context of the Family of Nations. Judge Huber recognized their value when he stated that

> As regards contracts between a state or a company such as the Dutch East India Company and native princes or chiefs of peoples not recognized as members of the community of nations, they are not, in an international law sense, treaties or conventions capable of creating rights and obligations such as may, in international law, arise out of treaties. But, on the other hand, contracts of this nature are not wholly void of indirect effects on situations governed by international law; if they do not constitute titles in international law; they are none-the-less facts which the law must in certain circumstances take into account.[50]

It is thus submitted that treaties concluded with African entities were primarily political – providing evidence of territorial claims against other European powers and thereby allowing for the partition of the continent (McEwen 1971: 14). This contention is supported by the non-application of certain principles of customary international law in the African context. First, as African signatories were neither party to nor represented at the Berlin Conference, the provisions relating to territorial acquisition contained in the Berlin Final Act could have been invalidated under the rule of *pacta tertiis nec nocent nec prosunt*. This principle derived from Roman law asserts that where a treaty purports to impose an obligation on a third party without its consent the offending provisions are liable to be rendered null and void.[51] The norm was originally adopted into modern *jus gentium* as it symbolized not only the contractual nature of international

---

[49] While this analogy has been attributed to Grotius it has been consistently maintained throughout the development of international law; see Lauterpacht (1970: 159–60) and Brierly (1963: 315).

[50] *Island of Palmas arbitration*, AJIL 22(4) (1928), 897–8.

[51] For examples of the modern application of this principle see the *Island of Palmas arbitration* (1928). See also the *Free Zones of Upper Savoy and the District of Gex* (1932) PCIJ Series A/ B, no. 46, p. 141 and Elias (1974: 59–70).

treaties but also the independence and equality of states within international society (Elias 1974: 59–60).

Second, even the most favourable interpretation of treaties of protection could not justify the steps taken in their name. Thus the actions of the powers at Berlin and elsewhere could result in the potential application of *rebus sic stantibus*. This principle originated in *jus civile* and was explored in the writings of Thomas Aquinas before being introduced into the modern *jus gentium* by Gentilis (Sinclair 1984: 192). The norm acknowledged the existence of ethical considerations for the revision of treaties on the grounds that the application of a treaty has ceased to accord with the shared intentions, expectations and objectives of the parties at the time the treaty was concluded (Lissitzyn 1967: 896).[52] Therefore it envisaged situations where the actions of one party resulted in a fundamental change of circumstances, which destroyed the foundations on which the treaty was based, thereby entitling the affected party to disregard the treaty (Alexandrowicz 1975: 51).[53] While *rebus sic stantibus* has been criticized for providing parties with a vague licence to avoid inconvenient or onerous obligations (Elias 1974: 119), this argument clearly carries little weight in relation to the dubious acquisitory practices of the powers in the African context.

It has been claimed that any acceptance of the inequality of colonial treaties (and therefore grounds for readjustment) would be injurious to the principle of *pacta sunt servanda*.[54] Such an argument fails to appreciate the essential correlation between *rebus sic stantibus* and *pacta sunt servanda*. Rather than jeopardizing the sanctity of treaties, *rebus sic stantibus* seeks to ensure that the application of a treaty continues to accord with the original intentions of the parties. Its objective therefore is wholly consistent with the fundamental requirement of performance in good faith (Lissitzyn 1967: 896). *Rebus sic stantibus* actually amounts to a concession to achieve a balance between the institutional requirement of enforcing treaty obligations and the avoidance of oppressive treaties, which would otherwise undermine the integrity and stability of a system premised on good faith (Brierly 1963: 332–4). It is clear that international society sanctioned the Berlin Final Act and other acquisitory practices while ignoring the legal 'rights' of African peoples who lacked the political might to challenge these mechanisms by other means. Thus evidently international society was not concerned with acquisitory treaties beyond their validity within the European arena.

In a search for the origins of the validity of acquisitory treaties, scholars have often turned to municipal sources. In the context of English private law, Alexandrowicz claims that the evidence reveals a clear distinction between these acquisitory treaties

---

[52] The theoretical dimensions of *clausula rebus sic stantibus* are nevertheless somewhat controversial.

[53] The application of this principle is also rather notorious. In customary international law it is, however, not without precedent. See the *Nationality Decrees case* and the *Case Concerning the denunciation of the Sino-Belgium Treaty of 1865 PCIJ* Series C., no. 16, vol. 1, p. 52. See also Lauterpacht (1970): 167–75), Brierly (1963: 327–45) and Elias (1974: 119–34).

[54] For example, see the view expressed by Evans (1995: 690).

and private law agreements for the transfer of real property (1975: 96–9). Indeed support for this view can gleaned in the Privy Council decision of *Ahmodu Tijani* v. *Secretary of State of South Nigeria* where it was said that

> this cession appears to have been made on the footing that the rights of property of the inhabitants were to be fully respected. This principle is a usual one under British policy and law when such occupations take place . . . A mere change in Sovereignty is not to be presumed as meant to disturb rights of private owners.[55]

Although this position should be accepted with regard to the sphere of private law, the doctrine of English public law also needs to be examined. In this context, Morris suggests that such treaties were unenforceable and therefore invalid.[56] Despite this opinion it is generally accepted that as the authority to make treaties derives from the Crown by virtue of its prerogative powers, these 'Acts of State' are not justiciable in municipal courts.[57] Therefore in the British context the lack of municipal jurisdiction provided the means to legitimate territorial acquisition, which could not have been justified according to the principles that informed customary international law.

The Process of Formal Colonization

Perhaps unsurprisingly, measures taken to achieve formal colonization continued to derive support from the sources used to justify the abandoned policy of free trade imperialism. For example, the Brussels Conference of 1890 decided that the most effective means of abolishing the slave trade in the African interior included the development of administrative, judicial, religious and military organs in the territories that were under the sovereignty or protection of the powers.[58] As the powers were committed to seeking the abolition of the slave trade, effective control and administration of their protectorates was therefore essential in stamping out the practice. While they seized on such opportunities to extend their control over African territories, it is notable that imperial policy was often dictated by the avoidance of making good on this initial commitment.[59] Despite being initially reluctant to administer protectorate

---

[55] [1921] 2 AC 399 (PC); see also *In re Southern Rhodesia* [1919] AC 211 (PC). Alexandrowicz (1973b: 99–105) also cites the legal theories of Dr Hermann Hesse and their application in the context of South West Africa.

[56] *Ol Le Njogo and Others* v. *AG* (1913) 5 EALR, 70; *Sobhuza II* v. *Miller* [1926] AC 518 (PC); *R* v. *The Baganda Cotton Company* (1930) 4 ULR 34; *Nyali Ltd* v. *AG* [1956] QB 1; see Morris (1972).

[57] See *R* v. *the Earl of Crewe*, ex parte Sekgome (CA) [1910] 2 KB 576; *Sobhuza II* v. *Miller* [1926] AC 518; *Nyali Ltd* v. *AG* [1956] 1 QB 1; and *Blackburn* v. *Attorney General* [1971] 1 WLR 1037. See also Roberts-Wray (1966: 187–92).

[58] See arts. I and III of the Brussels General Act 1890 in Roberts-Wray (1966: 112–16, 185).

[59] For example, see the positions adopted by the British government at Berlin, Salisbury in the Oil Rivers and the problems faced in East Africa as discussed below.

territory, it was inevitable that the powers would have to effectively occupy such territory if their protectorates were ever to yield the returns demanded by them.[60] Although in certain cases the powers had obtained substantial capitulatory 'concessions' enabling them to assert their authority, the establishment of modern colonial administrative systems could rarely be justified by the favourable reinterpretation of acquisitory treaties. The powers resolved this problem by recourse to their municipal law. In the British context, the Crown exercised inherent authority in foreign affairs by virtue of its royal prerogative and the Foreign Jurisdiction Acts (1843–90) clarified the application of this authority in respect of foreign territory. The effect of the legislation was that 'usage, sufferance or other lawful means' could extend the original jurisdiction acquired *inter alia* by way of treaties.[61]

However, while the original jurisdictional parameters could be exceeded, it was clear that such authority could only be exercised in respect of British subjects resident in or resorting to the territory in issue.[62] According to local imperial commissioners, the absence of jurisdiction over indigenous peoples and foreign nationals caused serious difficulties for the effective administration of protectorates. In such circumstances, Britain quickly adopted the policy favoured by Germany and France of assuming jurisdiction over *all* persons in the territory of a protectorate (Roberts-Wray 1966: 114). A useful example of this process can be found in the East Africa and Uganda Protectorates. By 1902, the East Africa and Uganda Orders were promulgated, authorizing commissioners to make ordinances for 'the peace, order and good government of all persons in the protectorate'.[63] Thus, with regard to British protectorates, the extension of jurisdiction was a unilateral process achieved by recourse to the vagaries of municipal law.[64] Although the indigenous peoples and territory were still foreign to the protecting power, according to its municipal law, they were subject to the full measure of *colonial* administration.

In any event, it was only a question of time before formal colonial rule was established and by the turn of the twentieth century even the British government was beginning to address the issue of whether protectorates should be formally annexed. By this stage, many protectorates were being administered along colonial lines; the

---

[60] This was especially the case once the chartered companies had outlived their usefulness and the costs of administration had to be met by public funds directly. For coverage of the demise of the Royal Niger Company, see generally Flint (1969).

[61] According to the Preamble of the 1843 Act jurisdiction could be derived from treaty, capitulations, grant, sufferance or other lawful means; see Roberts-Wray (1966: 112–16, 185).

[62] See the opinions of Hall and Law Officers of the Crown in Morris (1972: 47–9).

[63] Article 12(1) of both Orders; see Roberts-Wray (1966: 115).

[64] See Morris (1972: 48). See also see the judgments of Lords Justices Vaughan Williams and Kennedy in *R* v. *the Earl of Crewe, ex parte Sekgome* (CA) [1910] 2 KB 576; *Sobhuza II* v. *Miller* [1926] AC 518; *Nyali Ltd* v. *AG* [1956] 1 QB 1 and more generally *In re Southern Rhodesia* [1919] AC 211.

fact that they did not attract colonial status gave rise to certain legal anomalies.[65] Nevertheless, the jealousies of international society and, more immediately, the requirement of enforcing municipal anti-slavery laws were prohibitive.[66] The anticipated administrative impact of formal colonial status can be gleaned from the revealing comments of the Governor of the Nyasaland protectorate when asked for his opinion on its annexation in 1917:

> for years now, the Protectorate has been administered by the Colonial Office and all the legislative, judicial and executive functions have been applied fully and directly as would be the case were Nyasaland a British possession. This being so it will be well to dispose once and for all of a somewhat fictitious and complicated legal position which has little or no relation to administrative facts.
>
> (quoted in Morris 1972: 66–7)

Eventually, by 1920, the interior of the East Africa Protectorate was annexed to become the Colony of Kenya. Due to insurmountable technical difficulties, the coastal strip remained a protectorate although it was renamed the Protectorate of Kenya (see generally Allott 1973). The introduction of a formal policy of colonization followed official recognition that the pretence of protectorate status was no longer tenable especially where full jurisdiction had been acquired and modern colonial systems of administration were in place. Although minor legal anomalies were eliminated, the process of conversion did not carry any significant changes of administrative policy, the *de facto* colonization having already been achieved.

Post-colonial Ramifications

Since the Peace of Westphalia, the European view of statehood has been grounded in the concept of territorial sovereignty and the European powers have ensured that international law has maintained this traditional view. Accordingly, political authority in any society can only be made coherent when viewed through this lens (Shaw 1986: 27–30).[67] It

---

[65] These anomalies included problems of naturalization, which were claimed to hinder the development of settlement populations, the extradition of criminals, the validity of marriages and agreements with other powers, for example the Declaration in 1862 between Britain and France to respect the independence of the Sultan of Zanzibar. A particular difficulty was faced in the East Africa Protectorate due to extra territorial rights granted by the Sultan of Zanzibar to the nationals of other powers, which were guaranteed by the treaty of protection and caused difficulties in the administration of the areas affected; see Morris (1972: 61–2).

[66] According to the Foreign Secretary, Lord Lansdowne, in 1902 the disadvantages of conversion were prohibitive; see Morris (1972: 60–1).

[67] However, it is evident that modern international law is beginning to recognize the relativity apparent within the notion of territoriality; see the *Western Sahara* case and more recently the dispute between Eritrea and Yemen (Antunes 1999).

follows that without the existence of given territorial parameters the state lacks spatial expressions of certainty and permanence demanded by western political philosophy. While the utility of territory in any society cannot be ignored, the values ascribed to it in pre-colonial Africa did not reflect the characteristics found in the European model. Rather than performing strategic or ideological functions, territory provided the context for the expression of social relations (Allott 1973: 117; 1975: 76–8; and Castellino 1999c). While this perception of territory was assisted by demographic and topographical factors, the fluidity of African identities perplexed the powers during the period of the Scramble. For example, in 1899 British Military Intelligence concluded that:

> The tribes . . . have . . . no idea of territorial limits, their locations are constantly changing, and there often exist small tribes between the large ones which owe allegiance sometimes to the one and sometimes to the other.[68]

The absence of unambiguous territorial boundaries made the process of partition problematic. Topographical mistakes were often effected by widespread ignorance of demographic and ethnographic factors and resulted in arbitrary and haphazard boundaries.[69] The abstract nature of the process has been supported by statistical analysis that has found that 44 per cent of modern African boundaries are astronomical lines (meridian parallels), 30 per cent mathematical lines (arcs, curves, etc.) and only 26 per cent are geographical features.[70] Evidently the powers were driven by a belief that arbitrary lines were better than no lines at all (Hargreaves 1985: 23). Further this process clearly demonstrates that the identity of the African entities affected was not a material factor in the minds of the powers as they carved up the continent. The prime purpose of boundaries was the avoidance of conflict between themselves (Herbst 1989: 682). Post-colonial Africa was thus faced with the dilemma of whether to embark on a fundamental revision of the colonial boundaries provided on independence or to acquiesce in the boundary regimes of its predecessors. The former could potentially lead to chaos within while the latter would amount to the loss of an opportunity to establish representative state formations. The African leadership, largely trained in western political thought, decided to accept existing boundaries on the attainment of national independence. This decision was incorporated into the

---

[68] FO.84/1899, Memo by Lake and Darwin (M.I.D.) 16 July 1899, cited in Hargreaves (1985: 23).

[69] This cavalier approach was compounded in some instances by representatives of the powers encouraging African chiefs to make exaggerated claims about the extent of their territorial authority which, of course, could then be claimed as against other powers; see Anene (1970: 15).

[70] Calculated approximately in Barbour and Prothero (1961: 305), cited in Kapil (1966: 660). See also Nugent and Asiwaju (1996: 35–67).

Charter of the Organization of African Unity[71] with its juridical basis founded in the classical principle of *uti possidetis*.[72]

The principle was designed to protect the territorial status quo in situations of state succession by recognizing the sanctity of existing boundaries (see generally Shaw 1996, Ratner 1996, Kaikobad 1983 and Naldi 1987). In particular, the operation of *uti possidetis* in modern international law centred on the creation of international boundaries from the internal administrative lines developed by the previous colonial power, which were subsequently used to divide the region into distinct independent states on decolonization. The merit of the norm was undeniable in that it sought to maintain territorial integrity at a time when fledgling states were vulnerable to both internal and external threat. However, this interpretation of *uti possidetis* arguably reinforces the territorial basis of statehood – restricting questions of legitimacy and recognition by rating territoriality above other legitimizing principles such as ethnicity, tradition, linguistics, religion and ideology. Judge Dillard in the *Western Sahara* case said that 'it is for the people to determine the fate of the territory and not the territory the fate of the people'.[73] However, instead of seeking territorial settlement, *uti possidetis* seeks to 'settle' people within fixed territories. Thus the norm treats the need for territorial 'order' as being more important than the 'identity' of a people.

It is evident that customary international law accepts that boundary treaties operate along similar lines to a conveyance of realty in private law; the transfer of territorial sovereignty once effective becomes entirely independent of the means by which it was achieved.[74] Thus in situations of state succession the newly independent state inherits the territory of the previous colonial entity rather than its constituent boundary treaties, thereby making any process of treaty revision (and territorial readjustment)

---

[71] Article 3 (3) of the OAU Charter (1963) provides that states must show 'respect for the sovereignty and territorial integrity of each State and for its inalienable right to independent existence'. While support for *uti possidetis* was originally implied in the Charter by art. 3 (3), the principle was expressly affirmed by resolution 16(1) of the OAU Assembly of Heads of State and Government at Cairo in July 1964. This provided that 'all Member States pledge themselves to respect the borders existing on their achievement of national independence'; cited in Brownlie (1971: 360–1). See generally Woronoff (1970), Chime (1969) and Touval (1969).

[72] The adoption of *uti possidetis* was affected by Pan-African ideology. The influence of Pan-Africanism was clearly evident at the All-African Peoples Conference (1958) with its commitment to the early abolition and readjustment of existing boundaries and in the OAU Resolution on Border Disputes 1964 that proclaimed that the borders constituted 'a grave and permanent factor of dissension' – Brownlie (1971: 360). See generally Legum (1965) and Mazrui (1967).

[73] ICJ Reports (1975) 12 at 116 (sep. op. of Judge Dillard).

[74] See *Case concerning territorial dispute (Libyan Arab Jamahiriya v. Chad)* ICJ Reports (1994) 6, for a discussion of the opinions of the International Law Association and International Law Commission on this issue. See also Kaikobad (1983: 127).

legally impossible. The ultimate denial of the right to renegotiate boundary treaties under modern international law came with the advent of the Vienna Convention on the Law of Treaties in 1969. In an attempt to limit the potential ramifications of state succession, the conference sought to restrict the scope for redressing post-colonial territorial claims by entrenching the notion of the permanence of boundaries within the convention (Sinclair 1984: 98–106). The revisionist cause, championed by a number of delegations, challenged the credibility of this norm especially with regard to the post-colonization dimension. Syria argued that the proposed exceptional status of boundary treaties would be in contravention of *jus cogens* on the grounds that colonial occupation could not be legalized with the passage of time. Poland also reached the same conclusion by asserting that unequal colonial treaties were void *ab initio* and thus outside the scope of the convention in any event (Elias 1974: 126). Nevertheless, the overwhelming opinion of the conference was that the customary norm of *rebus sic stantibus* could have no application with regard to treaties establishing a boundary.[75]

Nonetheless, both the International Law Commission (ILC) and the Vienna Convention refused to sanction the creation of 'objective regimes', which would have implications for third states by recognizing the *erga omnes* validity of treaties intended *inter alia* to create permanent rights of a territorial character (Sinclair 1984: 104). Clearly the creation of such regimes would restrict the potential territorial application of *pacta tertiis* in the post-colonial context.[76] By the early 1970s, however, the ILC was prepared to accept the cogency of arguments in favour of objective regimes in appropriate cases and its findings were sanctioned by the Vienna Convention on Succession of States in respect of Treaties 1978 (see the commentary of the ILC in the *Yearbook of the ILC* (1974: vol. 2: 196–208). To this end, the ILC doubted the applicability of *pacta tertiis* in relation to situations of state succession. The ILC was of the opinion that in situations of state succession, the successor state could not properly be deemed a third state with regard to a treaty affecting its territory because of the legal nexus that existed between the treaty and the territory prior to the event of succession (Sinclair 1984: 105). The perception that succession occurs in relation to territory rather than to the treaties by which the territory was constituted clearly underpins the opinion of the ILC in this regard. In the circumstances, it was not considered possible for a successor state to allege invalidity on the grounds that it had not consented to the obligations created by such a treaty (art. 35 of the 1969 Convention). To this end, art. 11(a) of the 1978 Convention provides that state succession does not as such affect the validity of a boundary established by a treaty (see also art. 12 and Sinclair 1984: 104–5). Thus, taken together, these two conventions amount to an attempt to rule out the possibility of principled boundary readjustment in the post-colonial era (Kaikobad 1983: 128).

---

[75] See art. 62(2)(a), cited in Kaikobad (1983: 129).
[76] Articles 34–8 of the 1969 Vienna Convention deal with the operation of *pacta tertiis* in modern international law.

It is clear that the perceived threat to international order underlies much of the juridical reasoning of the ILC and explains to a greater extent the actions of modern developed states in this context (ibid.: 129). Under the current international regime, irredentist claims by post-colonial states will be hard pressed to successfully challenge the mechanisms established to safeguard vested interests acquired before the existing territorial regime fossilized. Evidently the mechanisms developed to preserve the territorial status quo have been fuelled by international society's deep-rooted fear of wholesale post-colonial revision. It is suggested that this fear has proved to be groundless even within the colonial period itself, when post-colonial idealism had arguably reached its highest point. The radical All African Conference of 1958, which called for the readjustment of boundaries at the earliest opportunity, was nevertheless primarily concerned with a piecemeal process of revision as opposed to a latter-day Scramble *in* Africa (Touval 1966: 641).

The difficulties confronting the modern African state when advancing claims for territorial revision were demonstrated in the *Libyan Arab Jamahiriya/Chad* case in which the International Court of Justice reinforced the non-recognition of the doctrine of unequal treaties in modern international law.[77] In this case the court was unwilling to accept the validity of a submission regarding Libya's diplomatic inexperience (and therefore inequality) in relation to the conclusion of a post-colonial treaty with France.[78] It is at least arguable that Libya's naivety in the conduct of its international relations could be likened to that of the African signatories to acquisitory treaties in the late nineteenth century. While the process of concluding a post-colonial treaty in 1951 was significantly different from that of a treaty of 'protection' concluded during the Scramble, the difference was perhaps a matter of degree rather than kind. In any event, the case does raise questions regarding the continuing ramifications of colonial subordination for fledgling states within international society.

Indeed some scholars have argued that the attainment of national independence has merely resulted in the abandonment of the blatant territorial dimension of colonialism in favour of more subtle means of subjugation (Jackson 1992: 1). Needless to say, in keeping with the principle of the equality of states as proclaimed by art. 2(1) of the UN Charter, former colonial powers have been careful to draft the provisions of treaties with their former colonies. However, it is clear that such legal formalism has not been reflected in the substantive relations between the parties. In this regard, Osnitskaya (1962) provides an excellent example of the neo-colonial policies of the British government in its relations with the newly independent Nigeria. Pursuant to independence, in 1960 Britain concluded a treaty with Nigeria under which Britain obtained control over Nigerian military forces. Britain was also empowered to establish military bases on Nigerian territory and to conduct military training in respect of

---

[77] ICJ Reports (1994) 6 at para. 36. See also Evans (1995: 689–90) and, for a comprehensive analysis of this case, Chapter 5.

[78] France was the colonial power with regard to the territory of Chad.

Nigerian forces. In particular, the treaty granted both parties mutual rights enabling them to carry out unlimited military flights with landing rights (including the exemption from local jurisdiction, tax regimes and visa requirements for military formations on visit) over the territory of both states. Osnitskaya suggests that while it is difficult to envisage Nigerian military planes flying over British air space during this period, clearly British missions over Nigerian territory simply amounted to the perpetuation of colonial practice with all the obvious implications for sovereignty that it entailed. Perhaps even more alarming is the fact that the conclusion of this defence treaty was a precondition for Nigerian independence.[79] The legal formalism underpinning modern international law clearly masks the true relations that underlie contemporary institutional arrangements (Talalayev and Boyarshinov 1961). Although the current international regime has evidently adopted the precepts of the 'rule of law' as developed by western liberal philosophy the resultant social inequalities are so stark that post-colonial states cannot internalize them. However, while post-colonial states are prepared to question the legitimacy of the tenets of modern international law, as with African entities during the Scramble they lack the political strength to successfully challenge the fundamental norms of the current regime.

Conclusions

It is suggested that despite the assistance of positivist legal theory, acquisitory treaties in the African context failed to comply with the standards set by international law in the late nineteenth century. The European powers were prepared to acknowledge the classical modes of territorial acquisition and the principles of the customary international law of treaties *inter se*. However, they were unwilling to extend the advantages of membership of the Family of Nations to those societies that did not reflect European norms of civilization. The fact that the powers relied primarily on illusory institutions, third party political conventions and jurisdictional measures to legitimate their gains is a powerful indicator of the true nature of territorial acquisition during the 'Scramble for Africa'. In the circumstances the acquisition of African territory during this period was achieved more through the underlying phenomenon of occupation than by way of acquisitory treaties governed by international law (Fisch 1988: 366). This view has been reinforced by the continuing reluctance of the existing international regime to provide an effective means of redress against the international boundaries forged by the powers in disregard of pre-colonial territorial and ethnographic parameters.

The value of maintaining existing territorial boundaries as a fundamental contributor to present-day international peace and security cannot, however, be underestimated.

---

[79] Osnitskaya points out that this policy of conditional independence was not uniquely British as France adopted a similar strategy in relation to Algeria. See GAOR 1514 and 2625 for developments in this regard.

In this regard modern international law continues to reflect its significance by adhering to the presumption of the continuity of existing boundaries (see generally Kaikobad 1983 and Touval 1966). The primacy of this norm was expressed in the *Libyan Arab Jamahiriya/Chad* case where the ICJ held that 'once agreed, the boundary stands, for any other approach would vitiate the fundamental principle of the stability of boundaries, the importance of which has been repeatedly emphasised by the Court'.[80] In the light of this statement it is perhaps unsurprising that modern international law should be prepared to deny a fledgling state its pre-colonial territorial integrity on the basis of the actions of colonial powers which have gained legitimacy with passage of time. Nonetheless this approach is far from satisfactory against the backdrop of an international regime struggling to resolve the fundamental contradictions within the competing norms of territorial sovereignty and self-determination. It follows that a territorial regime that does not countenance the legitimacy of claims for readjusting colonial boundaries in a bid to reflect its constituent societies sacrifices the values of enduring stability, cultural identity and national development in favour of a momentary and fragile peace (see Chapter 1).

---

[80] ICJ Reports (1994) 6 at 37.

5 Cases Concerning Territoriality before the International Court of Justice

Having examined the manner in which the treatment of territory varied in different temporal contexts, it is now useful to turn to its treatment by the International Court of Justice in the post-colonial phase.[1] This exercise, useful for a number of reasons, has to be undertaken bearing in mind certain caveats. First, with respect to the usefulness of studying the documentation of the ICJ, it needs to be pointed out that this is a forum whereby inter-state complaints can be adjudicated upon by a panel of international judges and, in this sense, it provides a clear view of the direction in which modern international law of territory is moving. Second, the ICJ judgments and pleadings provide a rich source for studying not only the manner in which the doctrines are seen to have evolved, but also the manner in which the parties to the disputes perceive them to be applicable to them. These judgments thus provide clear indicators of the parameters and limitations of the respective doctrines and laws and their perceived evolution and application, as viewed by the judges. The pleadings, on the other hand, provide arguments by the parties, usually documented by an interesting list of sources, on the history of their own territory and the manner in which various events were perceived and recorded in their 'national' psyche. This is particularly interesting in post-colonial situations since it presents an alternative view of the history of regions that have traditionally been viewed in academic literature through the lens of the colonial power (Burke 1972: 177–204). Third, a review of the ICJ materials not only demonstrates the extent to which state parties accept the treatment of territory within modern international law, notably the doctrines outlined in the preceding chapters, but also provides an insight into the extent to which they extrapolate and apply them to their own situations.

A number of issues need to be noted with respect to the limitations of the process before the ICJ. First, being a system that is in place purely to regulate inter-state conflict, the biggest flaw of the ICJ is that non-state parties cannot be represented in the proceedings.[2] This particular feature colours the nature of the proceedings when dealing with issues of rights of 'indigenous peoples' or of national minorities since they are not always represented by the state within which they happen to be

---

[1] For a general reading on the functioning of the court see Rosenne (1995).
[2] Article 34(1) of the ICJ Statute, as appended to the UN Charter 1945, states 'Only States may be parties in cases before the Court.'

geographically located. Second, the judgments provide evidence that many of the issues that come before the court for jurisdiction are questions of a verification of facts rather than laws. This is particularly true of issues pertaining to territoriality since, as will be seen, all the cases discussed here demonstrate that the parties accept the validity of the doctrine of *uti possidetis* and the principle of *terra nullius*. However, what the court is often asked to determine is not an interpretation of these, but rather the actual demarcation of boundaries based on the factual evidence presented. Thus, rather than commenting on and analysing the law, the court is often weighing up the quality of evidence of one particular party against that of the other in reaching its decision. This weighing up exercise provides an interesting insight into the extent to which judicial mechanisms such as the ICJ can adjudicate upon issues that are perceived to be about contradictory historical facts. A final issue to be borne in mind is that access to the ICJ is not necessarily universal, with states having to accede, if only temporarily at times, to the jurisdiction of the court pursuant to art. 36 of the statute.[3] Having said that, the court has witnessed a trend towards being increasingly accessible with more flexibility in its procedures (Muller *et al.* 1997).

This chapter will consist of a review of eight cases that have come before the ICJ, chosen because they fulfil certain criteria. First and foremost they are all disputes over territory at some level. Second, they all reflect, to different extents, either exposés on doctrines that are the subject matter of this book, or if not expressed in those terms, sentiments that could be construed as indicating such doctrines and values. Third, the cases all take place within the United Nations era. This was considered important in view of the historical chronology maintained throughout the book. Thus, important cases such as the referenda that took place under the League of Nations system have been omitted as not fulfilling this requirement (see generally Baker and Dodd 1925–7). This exclusion can be justified on the basis that the current system of treatment of territory has evolved beyond the League of Nations system, which primarily pertained to European states and entities.[4]

A number of factors determined the exclusion of other cases that might deal equally well with the issues addressed in this chapter. For a start, cases concerning property rights such as those manifest in *Certain property (Liechenstein v. Germany) 2001*,[5] *Oil platforms (Islamic Republic of Iran v. United States of America) (1992–)*[6] and

---

[3] Article 36(2) of the ICJ Statute states that 'The State Parties to the present Statute may at any time declare that they recognise as compulsory *ipso facto* and without special agreement, in relation to any other State accepting the same obligation, the jurisdiction of the Court in all legal disputes.'

[4] The *Island of Palmas* case, often quoted in discussion of *uti possidetis*, is also excluded for similar reasons. See Jessup (1928).

[5] See <http://www.icj-cij.org> accessed on 31 August 2001.

[6] <http://www.icj-cij.org/icjwww/idocket/iop/iopframe.htm>.

Certain phosphate lands in Nauru (Nauru v. *Australia) (1989–93)*[7] were ruled out for not falling strictly within the parameters of this current enquiry even though they pertain to issues of ownership and possession. Also excluded were numerous cases that pertain to territorial issues that fall primarily under the purview of the Law of the Sea. This condition, ultimately, resulted in the exclusion of the following cases: *Maritime delimitation between Nicaragua and Honduras in the Caribbean Sea (Nicaragua* v. *Honduras) (1999–);*[8] *Maritime delimitation and territorial questions between Qatar and Bahrain (Qatar* v. *Bahrain) (1991–2001);*[9] *Maritime delimitation in the area between Greenland and Jan Mayen (Denmark* v. *Norway) (1988–93);*[10] *Aegean Sea continental shelf (Greece* v. *Turkey) (1976–8);*[11] *North Sea continental shelf (Federal Republic of Germany/Denmark) (1967–9);*[12] *Federal Republic of Germany/Netherlands (1967–9).*[13] Many of these cases contain valuable information on the manner in which the issues discussed within this chapter are interpreted within non-land jurisdictions. However, these questions were considered to be beyond the parameters of this present enquiry. The *South West Africa* cases (1949–50) (1954–5) (1955–6) (1970–1) [Advisory] (see also Dugard 1972) were excluded since they pertain to issues of mandates which, it could be argued, in theory, were strictly not within the purview of the treatment of territory between independent states. Finally, cases such as the *Western Sahara* case, which discusses the principle of *terra nullius* in particular, and the *Temple of Preah Vihear* case[14] and its discussions on issues of the stability of boundaries have been excluded since material abounds in terms of their treatment of issues of territoriality (see, for instance, Castellino 2000a: ch. 6 and 7). The only current case included is the *Cameroon* v. *Nigeria* case since it presents some interesting issues that are due to come up for discussion. Other outstanding cases within the court's docket are excluded since the judgments and pleadings are not yet complete enough to allow analysis.[15]

With regard to the order of the cases below, by and large they are set out in chronological order, although this is not always possible since the commencement dates do not necessarily correspond to the final judgment dates. With this in mind, discretion has been exercised, as also with the review of facts that pertain directly to the issues of territoriality. It is for this reason that the two continental shelf cases are grouped together after the *Frontier dispute* case with a view to providing cases, around

---

[7] <http://www.icj-cij.org/icjwww/Icases/inaus/inausframe.htm>.

[8] <http://www.icj-cij.org/icjwww/idocket/iNH/iNHframe.htm>.

[9] <http://www.icj-cij.org/icjwww/idocket/iqb/iqbframe.htm>.

[10] <http://www.icj-cij.org/icjwww/Icases/igjm/igjmframe.htm>.

[11] ICJ Reports (1976) 3.

[12] ICJ Reports (1969) 3.

[13] ICJ Reports (1969) 3.

[14] <http://www.icj-cij.org/icjwww/idecisions/isummaries/ictsummary610526.htm>.

[15] For instance *Sovereignty over Pulau Litigan and Pulau Sipadan (Indonesia/Malaysia) (1998–)*, <http://www.icj-cij.org/icjwww/idocket/iinma/iinmaframe.htm>.

the same time, that looked at a different perspective of territoriality. In addition, rather than following a standard format the case reviews focus on issues considered most pertinent in each case to this current enquiry.

Case Concerning Sovereignty over Certain Frontier Land (Belgium/Netherlands) 20 June 1959[16]

This case, brought before the court by the governments of Belgium and the Netherlands and governed by a Special Agreement signed between the parties on 7 March 1957, called upon the court to determine sovereignty over land that formed the frontier between the two state parties. The court was requested to determine whether sovereignty over that land, identified as plots shown in a survey and known from 1836 to 1843 as Nos. 91 and 92, Section A, Zondereygen, belonged to Belgium or to the Netherlands.

In its judgment, the court found that in the area north of the Belgian town of Turnhout a number of enclaves existed formed by the Belgian commune of Baerle-Duc and the Netherlands commune of Baarle-Nassau. Baerle-Duc was found to consist of a series of plots of land many of which were actually enclosed within the commune of Baarle-Nassau. Thus, there were sections of Baerle-Duc isolated from both the rest of the territory of Belgium and from other parts of Baerle-Duc itself. Attempts had been made in the past, notably between 1836 and 1841, to establish the boundary between the two regions and determine the question of sovereignty between the two kingdoms. This past attempt referred to as the 'Communal Minute' was presented to the court as evidence relied upon by both parties.[17] A further complexity to the case was that the Netherlands itself only separated from the Kingdom of Belgium in 1839, after which a Mixed Boundary Commission had been set up between the two entities to determine the exact limitations to their respective territorial sovereignties. The deliberations of this committee resulted in a Boundary Treaty being concluded between the parties in 1842, which entered into force the following year. Article 14 of that treaty suggests that:

> The *status quo* shall be maintained both with regard to the villages of Baarle-Nassau (Netherlands) and Baerle-Duc (Belgium) and with regard to the ways crossing them.
>
> (p. 211)

Thus, while not addressing the issue of sovereignty and possession, this clearly suggests that demarcations of Belgian and Dutch territory already existed and that that particular status quo would continue to endure.

---

[16] ICJ Reports (1959) 209. All subsequent page references in this section refer to this text.
[17] ICJ Reports (1959) as given on <http://www.icj-cij.org/icjwww/idecisions/isummaries/ibnlsummary590620.htm>, p. 211.

The court's judgment addressed three contentions.

First, as to whether the Convention of 1843 itself already determined sovereignty over the plots or whether it merely confined itself to a reference to the status quo. In addressing this issue, the work of the Boundary Commission was examined. Analysis revealed that the delimitation of the boundary initially took place based on the existing status quo rather than procedure, which questioned sovereignty over territory. However, further examination suggested that from 4 September 1841, the work of delimitation proceeded on the basis of this maintenance of status quo and that, as noted in minutes of a meeting on 4 April 1843, the Mixed Boundary Commission adopted the text of an article which attributed the disputed plots to Belgium. Thus, the court concluded that the convention did in fact determine the sovereignty of the plots and awarded this to Belgium (p. 211).

The second contention addressed by the court concerned the convention and whether it was vitiated by mistake. The court's judgment described this contention as follows:

> The Descriptive Minute of 1843 specified that the Communal Minute of 1841 noting the plots composing the communes of Baerle-Duc and Baarle-Nassau should be transcribed 'word for word' in Article 90 of the Descriptive Minute. A comparison of the copy of the Communal Minute produced by the Netherlands with the Descriptive Minute discloses, however, that *there was not a 'word for word' transcription of the former*, inasmuch as the Descriptive Minute attributes plots Nos. 91 and 92 to Belgium, whereas this copy of the Communal Minute attributes them to Baarle-Nassau.
>
> (p. 218)

Thus, the contention sought to suggest that in transcription of the Minutes, a mistake was made and it was based on that mistake that the final determination of the plots took place.[18] The court considered that comparison between the two documents would not necessarily establish the existence of a mistake. Instead, it required the Netherlands to establish that the intention of the Mixed Boundary Commission was that the Descriptive Minute attached to and forming part of the Convention of 1843 should set out the text of the Communal Minute contained in the copy produced by the Netherlands. In this context, the court also pointed out that the prima facie duty of the Mixed Commission had been to determine the existing status quo.

The third and final contention of the Netherlands was that via acts of sovereignty exercised by the Netherlands since 1843, it ought to be deemed to have established sovereignty over the plots. Thus, the court in pursuing this argument would need to address the issue of whether Belgium had lost its sovereignty over the territory as had been determined by the Mixed Boundary Commission. This loss would have occurred

---

[18] The issue of an error in demarcation is also pertinent to the *Temple of Preah Vihear case (Cambodia v. Thailand)*, ICJ Reports (1962) 6, where the court determined that in the interests of stability the original error was made irrelevant.

had Belgium not asserted its rights of sovereignty in the region or by its acquiescence in acts of sovereignty alleged to have been exercised by the Netherlands at different times since 1843. In examining this contention, the court ruled that via different acts performed in the territory by Belgium it could categorically be proved that it had not abandoned sovereignty over the territory. In coming to this conclusion the court examined numerous documents including military staff maps, survey records that clearly showed the plots within Belgian territory and records of Survey Authorities transferring deeds. In contrast, it found that the claim by the Netherlands was based upon acts that were largely routine and administrative in nature and that would have accrued, mainly, as a consequence of the inclusion of the territories within its own by the Netherlands, contrary to the findings of the Boundary Commission. Thus, the court categorically found that these acts were insufficient to displace the sovereignty established by Belgium (p. 230).

The court also addressed the issues raised by an unratified convention between the two states signed in 1892. According to this convention, Belgium had agreed to cede to the Netherlands two of the disputed plots. However, since the convention remained unratified it did not create legal rights and obligations. Further, the court saw this as evidence that the Netherlands was clearly aware that Belgium had, up to that point, asserted its sovereignty over the territory. This Belgian claim had not been repudiated at any time since that treaty of 1892 until the dispute arose between the states in 1922. Thus, the court was satisfied that Belgian sovereignty, once established, had not been extinguished and on that basis awarded the territory to Belgium.[19]

This case is instructive since it addressed issues of status quo and territory without invoking the doctrine of *uti possidetis*. In terms of international law, the time period of the case is relevant since the process of decolonization had already begun. Looked at strictly in terms of the international regime and the manner in which the doctrine of *uti possidetis* has been interpreted, it could be argued that the doctrine was not directly applicable to this particular dispute. However, if the peculiar aspect of its relevance to situations of independence is removed and the doctrine is allowed to revert to its original manifestation in Roman law then it takes on great relevance in this case. A vital factor was the decision of the Mixed Boundary Commission, which ruled in favour of Belgium, and this raises questions about the function of that committee. The fact that that has been established in the case as being the determination of the status quo suggests that the doctrine of *uti possidetis* in its Roman manifestation of 'as you possess so you possess' was operating. However, since this case was adjudicated upon before the full advent of modern decolonization movements, it provides an interesting perspective of the motives of the court and an indicator of the value of stability as perceived by the judges. In addition, the manner in which the court proceeded after having established that the sovereignty over the territory was Belgian suggests the

---

[19] By 10 votes to 4, p. 230.

very advantage provided to the possessor by the Roman law principle of *uti possidetis* as expressed by the praetor (see Chapter 2).

Case Concerning the Frontier Dispute (Burkina Faso/Republic of Mali) 22 December 1986[20]

This case is one of the most oft-cited cases in the discussion of issues pertaining to territoriality. It has even been argued that it provides a watershed to the treatment of the doctrine of *uti possidetis* (Radan 2000). This discussion will be explored in more depth in the concluding comments to the case. As it is not possible to capture the full richness of the case within a few pages, this review will focus primarily on the establishment of rules applicable to the conflict, since it is the court's judgment on these issues that is most often cited.

Intangibility of Frontiers inherited from Colonization

This principle, accepted by both parties and included in the preamble, is inherently contained in the joint statement by the parties that the settlement of the dispute should be 'based in particular on respect for the principle of the intangibility of frontiers inherited from colonisation' (p. 557). This statement echoes precisely the sentiments expressed by the heads of African governments when they met under the auspices of the Organization of African Unity in Cairo in 1964. According to the document emanating from that meeting, known as the Cairo Declaration, member states:

> solemnly . . . pledge themselves to respect the frontiers existing on their achievement of national independence.
>
> (ASGH/Res. 16(1) July 1964)

In this context, therefore, it is certain that Burkina Faso, which corresponds in territory to the former French colony of Upper Volta, and the Republic of Mali, which corresponds to the former French colony of Sudan (or French Sudan), are fully compliant for the purpose of this case with the rule that the boundaries inherited by them from France shall remain inviolable.

The Principle of Uti Possidetis Juris

In these circumstances, the chamber decided that it could not disregard the principle of *uti possidetis juris*, 'the application of which gives rise to this respect for intangibility of frontiers' (p. 566, para. 20). It went on to emphasize the general scope of the principle

---

[20] ICJ Reports (1986) 554. All subsequent page references in this section refer to this text.

in matters of decolonization and especially highlighted the exceptional importance of the doctrine for the African continent, including the two parties to this case. Interestingly, the chamber made the following pronouncement on the doctrine of *uti possidetis*:

> Although this principle was invoked for the first time in Spanish America, it is not a rule pertaining solely to one specific system of international law. It is a principle of general scope, logically connected with the phenomenon of the obtaining of independence, wherever it occurs. Its obvious purpose is to prevent the independence and stability of new States being endangered by fratricidal struggles provoked by the challenging of frontiers following the withdrawal of the administering power. The fact that the new African States have respected the territorial *status quo* which existed when they obtained independence must, therefore, be seen not as a mere practice but as the application in Africa of a rule of general scope which is firmly established in matters of decolonisation; and the Chamber does not find it necessary to demonstrate this for the purposes of the case.
>
> (p. 566, para. 23)

Thus, the chamber not only extended the doctrine to the case at hand, it also suggested that it had validity beyond the case at hand to all cases of independence wherever they occurred. It is this quote that is referred to by the Badinter Commission in justification of the validity of the principle of *uti possidetis*. However, as pointed out by Radan (2000) and as examined in more detail in the penultimate chapter of this book, this reference was premised on a selective reading of the case, its implications and background. The court's ruling in the paragraph above sought to reiterate that the *prima facie* purpose of the rule, namely that of preventing fratricidal struggles by the challenging of frontiers following withdrawal of the administering power, brings it within the remit of the rule first invoked in Spanish America in similar circumstances of decolonization. In addition, the chamber pronounced that:

> The principle of *uti possidetis juris* accords pre-eminence to legal tide over effective possession as a basis of sovereignty. Its primary aim is to secure respect for the territorial boundaries, which existed at the time when independence was achieved. When those boundaries were no more than delimitations between different administrative divisions or colonies all subject to the same sovereign, the application of this principle resulted in their being transformed into international frontiers, and this is what occurred with the States Parties to the present case, which both took shape within the territories of French West Africa. Where such boundaries already had the status of international frontiers at the time of decolonisation, the obligation to respect pre-existing international frontiers derives from a general rule of international law relating to State succession. The many solemn affirmations of the intangibility of frontiers, made by African statesmen or by organs of the OAU, should therefore be taken as references to a principle already in existence, not as affirmations seeking to consecrate a new principle or to extend to Africa a rule previously applicable only in another continent.
>
> (p. 565, para. 20)

Thus, the chamber reflected not only the will of the parties who had extended the rule upon themselves in the preamble but stressed the nature of the process attendant to the stability of boundaries. In substantiating the rule, it went on to reiterate the commitment of the African leaders to the principle, as expressed in the Cairo Declaration, and referred once again to the rule's known pedigree, having already been used in Spanish America (see Chapter 3).

The chamber also tackled the issue of the conflict between the doctrine of *uti possidetis* and the principle that brought it into play in the first place: the right of peoples to self-determination. While not substantiating the nature and extent of this particular conflict, it found that the requirement of stability of frontiers and maintenance of the territorial status quo in Africa 'is often seen as the wisest course' (p. 566, para. 25). This requirement of stability is considered basic to the very survival of the new state in order to give it the space to develop and consolidate its independence. Thus, the chamber stressed that while the right of self-determination is important it has, by deliberate choice of African rulers, been interpreted within the requirements of *uti possidetis*, which seeks to guarantee external frontiers (p. 567, para. 26).

The Role of Equity (pp. 567–8, paras. 27–8)

A third important rule that was deemed applicable in the case was the role of equity. Although not strictly concerned with the determination of territory, it nonetheless proves interesting in presenting the regime, as interpreted in this particular case. In pronouncing the rule applicable the chamber stated:

> Obviously, the Chamber cannot decide *ex aequo et bono*, since the Parties have not requested it to do so. It will, however, have regard to equity *infra legem*, that is, that form of equity which constitutes a method of interpretation of the law in force, and which is based on law. How the Chamber will, in practice, approach its consideration of this form of equity will become clear from its application of the principles and rules, which it finds to be applicable.
> (p. 567, para. 27)

Thus the tone of the judgment stresses that, whilst it will be based on the law in force, the interpretation of that law will also be subject to a form of equity that is based on law. This issue of equity has met with differing treatment in the different cases[21] and is revisited in the concluding comments to this chapter.

French Colonial Law (droit d'outre-mer) *(p. 568, paras. 29–30)*

A final aspect of this case, in terms of the identification of rules, is the statement on the issue of colonial law. In discussing the status of French colonial law, the chamber

---

[21] See especially the *continental shelf* cases (Tunisia/Libya 1982 and Libya/Malta 1985).

ascertained that the inviolable frontier being discussed was one that was determined by French colonial law and was said to have existed in 1959–60. This administrative boundary divided the French colony of Upper Volta from the French colony of Sudan. Being of an internal administrative nature, the chamber stated that the boundary was not strictly within the purview of international law of the time but would have been subject to French colonial law *droit d'outre-mer*. The chamber went on to explain that modern international law – and therefore the principle of *uti possidetis* – applies to the new state as from its accession to independence, but has no retroactive effect. It freezes the territorial title. International law does not affect any *renvoi* to the law of the colonizing state. If it has any part to play at all, it is merely as one factual element among others, or as evidence indicative of the 'colonial heritage' at the critical date.

The Task before the Court (pp. 569–70, paras. 31–3)

The judgment briefly reviews how territorial administration was organized in French West Africa – to which both parties previously belonged – with its hierarchy of administrative units (colonies, *cercles*, subdivisions, cantons, villages), before recapitulating the history of both the colonies since 1919 to determine, for each of the two parties, the colonial heritage to which the doctrine of *uti possidetis* could be made to apply. Mali gained its independence in 1960 under the name of the Federation of Mali, succeeding the Sudanese Republic that had emerged in 1959 from the overseas territory called the French Sudan. The history of Upper Volta is more complicated. Although it came into being in 1919, it was abolished in 1932. It was later reconstituted by a law of 4 September 1947, which stated that the boundaries of 'the re-established territory of Upper Volta' were to be 'those of the former colony of Upper Volta on 5th September 1932'. It was this reconstituted Upper Volta that subsequently obtained independence in 1960 and took the name of Burkina Faso in 1984. In the present case, therefore, the problem faced by the chamber was in ascertaining the exact location of the frontier inherited from the French administration. This task involved an examination of the location of the 1950–60 frontier that existed in French colonial law between the *territoires d'outre-mer* of Sudan and Upper Volta – which both parties agreed was the official boundary between the new states – so as to deem it the international frontier between the two modern states of Burkina Faso and Mali. In seeking resolution of this, the parties concerned and the chamber relied on different kinds of evidence. This included legislative and regulative texts from French colonial times, administrative documents from the same period and 'abundant and varied' cartographic materials that seemed to contradict each other (pp. 580–8, paras. 51–65). Another source of evidence for the determination of the frontier was the parties invoking of '*colonial effectivités*'. This is best described as 'the conduct of the administrative authorities as proof of the effective exercise of territorial jurisdiction in the region during the colonial period' (p. 586, para. 63).

The Role of Evidence in Territorial Disputes

With regard to the value of the evidence presented by the parties, notably maps, the court ruled that:

> . . . maps merely constitute information, which varies in accuracy from case to case; of themselves, and by virtue solely of their existence, they cannot constitute a territorial title, that is, a document endowed by international law with intrinsic legal force for the purpose of establishing territorial rights. Of course, in some cases maps may acquire such legal force, but where this is so the legal force does not arise solely from their intrinsic merits: it is because such maps fall into the category of physical expressions of the will of the State or States concerned. This is the case, for example, when maps are annexed to an official text of which they form an integral part. Except in this clearly defined case, maps are only extrinsic evidence of varying reliability or unreliability, which may be used, along with other evidence of a circumstantial kind, to establish or reconstitute the real facts.
>
> (p. 582, para. 54)

The Chamber's Finding

In its final judgment, the chamber emphasized the unusual nature of the case. Whilst cases before the international tribunals often tend to focus on differences in interpretation of law, this case concerned facts that needed to be proven after the analysis of the evidence produced by both sides. In this sense, the case was one of the first contentious cases to request a decision based on review of fact.[22] Since then, however, as is demonstrated in the later cases reviewed, this process has become much more common. Of course, to the extent that the case concerned issues of fact, it proved difficult to adjudicate since the chamber could not be certain that it had been able to ascertain all the relevant facts. This was particularly true since much of the evidence, such as maps, was contradictory and there were inconsistencies and shortcomings in much of the material before the chamber. The dilemma of the court was best captured in this statement:

> The systematic application of the rule concerning the burden of proof cannot always provide a solution, and the rejection of any particular argument for lack of proof is not sufficient to warrant upholding the contrary argument.
>
> (p. 576, para. 44)

In a separate opinion appended to the judgment, Judge Georges Abi-Saab *ad hoc* especially focused on the declaratory nature of one of the sources of evidence that was relied upon by the chamber in the determination of the frontier (pp. 659–63). He

---

[22] The *Western Sahara* case did consider issues of fact as well, but that case was submitted as an advisory and not a contentious case.

pointed out that this source, like other sources, was merely an indicator of possible frontiers that had 'not [been] hardened to certainty by any evidence'. Having emphasized the difficulties that sometimes arise in applying the principle of *uti possidetis*, he also noted that the chamber had adopted a possible legal solution within the bounds of the degrees of freedom that existed in the case. While this was found legally acceptable, Judge Abi-Saab suggested that greater emphasis should have been laid on considerations of equity *infra legem* in the interpretation and application of the law, especially considering the nomadic population that exists in the region and the scarcity of water resources.

Case Concerning the Continental Shelf (Tunisia/Libyan Arab Jamahiriya) 24 February 1982[23]

This case, brought by Tunisia and Libya, called upon the court to delimit and ascertain the status of the continental shelf that ran adjacent to both states. Article 1, para. 1 of the Special Agreement signed between the states for the purposes of this case called upon the court to state 'the principles and rules of international law' which might 'be applied for the delimitation of the areas of the continental shelf' (p. 37, para. 22). In addition to this determination the court was also requested by the parties via the Special Agreement to take account of three factors in rendering its final decision, namely:

1   Equitable principles
2   Relevant circumstances that characterize the area
3   New trends in the Third United Nations Conference on the Law of the Sea.

Thus, the mandate given to the court by the parties consisted of the dual role of ascertaining any existing legal regime that could be found to apply to the delimitation of the continental shelf, but also to ensure, in this process, that the three factors above were applied.

The conclusions reached by the court are indicated in the operative paragraph of the judgment. Therein the court found (by 10 votes to 4):

> . . . that the principles and rules of international law applicable . . . are as follows:
>
> (1) Delimitation is to be effected in accordance with equitable principles, and taking account of all relevant circumstances.
>
> (2) Area relevant for the delimitation constitutes a single continental shelf as the natural prolongation of the land territory of both Parties, so that in the present case, no criterion for delimitation of shelf areas can be derived from the principle of natural prolongation, as such.

---

[23] ICJ Reports (1982) 37. All subsequent page references in this section refer to this text.

(3) Particular geographical circumstances of the present case, the physical structure of the continental shelf areas, is not such as to determine an equitable line of delimitation.

(p. 92, para. 133)[24]

This case was particularly interesting and has been especially chosen for inclusion in this chapter since it presents a view of equity in issues concerning continental shelf proceedings that are often explicitly dismissed in dealing with cases of territorial demarcations. Thus, the role ascribed to equity and equitable treatment in the delimitation of the continental shelf is somehow considered more important than correspondingly in issues dealing with the land.

Case Concerning the Continental Shelf (Libyan Arab Jamahiriya/Malta) 3 June 1985[25]

The *Libya–Malta* case of 1985, also concerning the delimitation of a continental shelf, is particularly interesting in the determination of the regime governing international law and its treatment of territory.[26] In this case, the court specifically addressed a question pursuant to art. 1 of the Special Agreement between the parties:

> What principles and rules of international law are applicable to the delimitation of the area of continental shelf which appertains to the Republic of Malta and the area of continental shelf which appertains to the Libyan Arab Republic, and how in practice such principles and rules can be applied by the two Parties in this particular case in order that they may without difficulty delimit such area by an agreement as provided in Article III.

Once again the case concerned the identification of applicable principles and rules and the examination of evidence against these by the court. With this mandate in mind the court sought to identify the principles applicable to the determination of territory in modern international law, which will be our main focus in the examination of this case.

Rules and Principles Applicable (paras. 26–35)

The two parties agreed that the dispute needed to be governed by customary international law. In further justification of applicable principles, it was reiterated that

---

[24] See also a later case that revisited the issue, namely *Application for Revision and Interpretation of the Judgment of 24 February in the Case Concerning the Continental Shelf (Tunisia/Libyan Arab Jamahiriya)* of 10 December 1985.

[25] ICJ Reports (1985) 13. All subsequent page references in this section refer to this text.

[26] There are a number of cases that deal with the delimitation of continental shelves – Libya/Malta (1982–5), Tunisia/Libya (1978–82), Greece/Turkey (1976–8), Germany/Netherlands and Germany/Denmark (1967–9).

Malta is party to the Geneva Convention on the Continental Shelf 1958 while Libya is not. Nonetheless, both states were signatories to the United Nations Convention on the Law of the Sea (UNCLOS) 1982, although the convention had not entered force at the time of the case. To counter this, the parties agreed in principle that some of the provisions contained in UNCLOS 1982 could be considered to constitute an expression of customary international law. The difficulty though lay in the fact that the parties could not agree which provisions of the convention were entitled to be treated as concurrent with this status. Thus, it was left to the court to consider the nature of the provisions and the extent to which they could be considered to reflect customary international law – appropriate in a convention that had been widely signed at the time of the case.

However, as to agreement on the legal basis of title to continental shelf, the views of the parties proved irreconcilable. For Libya, the natural prolongation of the land territory of a state into the sea is the fundamental basis on which legal title to continental shelf areas can be entertained. For Malta, however, continental shelf rights are no longer defined in the light of physical criteria, being controlled rather by the concept of distance from the coast. Within the case the Libyans introduced the 'rift zone' argument, which was rejected by the court (paras. 36–41). The court also rejected the Maltese argument with regard to the respect for primacy of the 'equidistance principle' (paras. 42–4). Instead, interestingly, the parties agreed that the delimitation of the shelf ought to be effected by the application of equitable principles in all the relevant circumstances so as to achieve a result that was as equitable and fair as possible. Thus, the role of equity was considered important in the territorial settlement of this particular case. In enunciating some of concepts related to its treatment of this principle of equity and its application in this case, the court stated that the following factors need to be borne in mind:

- That there is no question of refashioning geography
- That of non-encroachment by one party on areas appertaining to the other
- That respect was due to all relevant circumstances
- That 'Equity does not necessarily imply equality'
- That there is no question of distributive justice.

(paras. 45–7)

and

- That the doctrine of proportionality was important.

(paras. 55–9)

Having identified these caveats, the court, as requested by art. 1 of the Special Agreement between the parties, sought to identify the principle and rules of modern international law that would be applicable to the case before it. These were as follows:

(1) Delimitation is to be effected in accordance with equitable principles and taking account of all relevant circumstances, so as to arrive at an equitable result.

(2) Area of continental shelf to be found to appertain to either Party not extending more than 200 miles from the coast of the Party concerned, no criterion for delimitation of shelf areas can be derived from the principle of natural prolongation in the physical sense.

(para. 60)

Thus, as in the previous continental shelf case, the court stressed the role of equitable principles. In this case though, the court went further, identifying the substantive content of the notion of equity and how it relates to disputes concerning boundary delimitations that occur with regard to continental shelves. In addition, the court focused on the doctrine of natural prolongation. Although it rejected the idea in this case, it demonstrated that this principle too plays a part in the treatment of territory in international law. It is of special note that in this discussion the court did not use the language of *uti possidetis* and to this extent, even though it was dealing with issues of delimitation, it did not see any role for this doctrine.

Case Concerning the Land, Island and Maritime Frontier Dispute (El Salvador *v.* Honduras; Nicaragua intervening) 1992[27]

This case pertained to a dispute that had a long history between the two parties – both successor states to the Spanish Crown (see Chapter 3). The disputants requested the chamber to adjudge two main issues:

1. To delimit the boundary line in the zones or sections not described in Article 16 of the General Treaty of Peace of 30 October 1980.
2. To determine the legal situation of the islands and maritime spaces.[28]

Two points need to be made at this stage. First, the history of the dispute is contained in the judgment (pp. 362–86, paras. 23–39) and has been referred to in Chapter 3 and thus will not form the focus of this review except to mention that past disputes over these issues had resulted in the General Treaty of Peace of 1980 mentioned above. This treaty had succeeded in delimiting all but six sectors of the boundary between the parties. Second, as far as the relevance of this case to the current project is concerned, we shall focus exclusively on the issue of the land border inasmuch as it pertains to the Court's view on the issues of title to territory and *uti possidetis juris*.

---

[27] ICJ Reports (1992) 351. All subsequent page references in this section refer to this text. This is the first case in the history of international adjudication of this kind (ICJ or PCIJ) where a third state was allowed to intervene pursuant to art. 62 of the Statute of the International Court of Justice.

[28] As given by art. 2 of the Special Agreement; see ICJ Reports (1992) 351 at 357.

The parties asked the court to adjudicate on the dispute based on two prime sources, namely the Treaty of Peace mentioned above and the 'rules of international law applicable between the Parties'.[29] A notable factor in this case which is of importance to historians of international jurisprudence is the 13 September 1990 judgment of the court where, after having ascertained that Nicaragua had a legitimate interest in the case, it was permitted to intervene pursuant to art. 62 of the Statute of the ICJ and subject to the rule of *res inter acta alios*.[30] After an initial analysis of the parties' arguments, the chamber requested submissions based on three aspects of the dispute:

(a)   The whole of the general question
(b)   Each of the six sectors of the land frontier
(c)   The islands and maritime spaces.

(p. 360, para. 17)

The main thrust of the pleadings that are the focus of this section will pertain to issue (a) and the first half of issue (c).

In presenting its case El Salvador sought to prove:

(i)   . . . that the land boundaries defined by the Formal Title-Deeds to the Commons of the indigenous communities . . . presented by El Salvador are absolutely identical with the international frontiers of each State;

(ii)   . . . that [it] has completely established . . . that the Formal Title-Deeds to Commons which support the claims . . . were executed by the Spanish Crown in accordance with the necessary judicial procedures and requirements and . . . [that] these form the fundamental basis of the *uti possidetis juris* in that they indicate jurisdictional boundaries, that is to say the boundaries of territories and settlements;

(iii) . . . that Honduras has presented Title-Deeds to private proprietary interests which in no case permitted the exercise of administrative control or implied the exercise of acts of sovereignty;

(iv)   . . . that the majority of the Title-Deeds presented by Honduras relate to lands which are situated either outside the disputed sectors or in sectors . . . already . . . delimited by the General Peace Treaty of 1980.

(p. 363, para. 1)

Honduras countered the above allegations and referring to the 1980 treaty requested the court to reject the El Salvadorian arguments. As regards the issue of the disputed islands, Honduras contended that El Tigre (one of the three islands identified by El Salvador as being disputed) was Honduran and that there was no dispute about its

---

[29]   Article 5 of the Special Agreement; see ICJ Reports (1992) 351 at 357–8.
[30]   ICJ Reports (1992) 351 at 360, para. 15; see also 609–10, paras. 421–4 and ICJ Reports (1994) 6 at 17, para. 24.

ownership. As regards the other two islands (Meanguera and Meanguerita), Honduras agreed that the dispute was pertinent and claimed sovereignty over them.

In discussing the issues pertinent to the case, the court noted that the doctrine of *uti possidetis* was central to the determination of the case. In referring to the importance of the principle, the court noted that it had been used extensively in Central and South America and had resulted in stable frontiers. However, it pointed out that 'these certain and stable frontiers are not the ones that find their way before international tribunals for decision'. In describing the conflicts that come before the tribunals the court stated that these are:

> . . . almost invariably the ones in respect of which *uti possidetis* speaks for once with an uncertain voice. It can indeed be assumed that boundaries, which, like the ones in this case, have remained unsettled since independence, are themselves the subject of dispute.
>
> (p. 386, para. 41)

Relying on the meaning attributed to the doctrine in the *Burkina Faso/Mali* case and Arbitral Award of 1922 between Colombia and Venezuela,[31] the court reiterated that the principle is concerned as much with title to territory as with the location of boundaries, and thus a key aspect to the principle is the denial of the possibility of *terra nullius* (p. 387, para. 42). The court also highlighted the difficulties with the determination of the 1821 *uti possidetis* line as identified in Chapter 3, and stressed that the doctrine is essentially a retrospective principle that invests administrative boundaries intended for different purposes as international frontiers (p. 388, para. 43). Thus while both parties sought to furnish evidence as to the exact location of the 1821 line, the issue was always going to prove difficult to resolve. Aware of this task, the chamber recognized that it was:

> . . . asked, in effect, to conclude, in the absence of other evidence of the position of the provincial boundary, that where a boundary can be identified between the lands granted by the authorities of the neighbouring province, this boundary maybe taken to have been the provincial boundary and thus the line of *uti possidetis juris*.
>
> (p. 388, para. 44)

The court also echoed the *Burkina Faso/Mali* case in discussing the nature and substantive content of the concept of 'title'. This discussion, of particular relevance in this case, was reiterated as not being limited to documentary evidence alone but also including evidence that could be seen as establishing the existence of rights and their respective sources.[32] It was applied in this case with regard to the court's analysis of the formal title deeds presented by El Salvador (pp. 393–4, paras. 51–3). One of the interesting aspects of the El Salvadorian arguments concerned the issue of equity in

---

[31] ICJ Reports (1986) 554 at 566, para. 23 and UN *RIAA* I 228, respectively.

[32] ICJ Reports (1986) 554 at 564.

the judgment. This issue had come before the courts on previous occasions where equity *infra legem* had been found of limited value as a subsidiary means to the limitation of the doctrine of *uti possidetis*.[33] Nonetheless El Salvador put forward an argument pertaining to demographic pressures that created a need for territory. This met with predictable failure as the court reiterated its earlier judgment[34] in reasserting that economic considerations could not be taken into account for the delimitation of boundary regimes in accordance with the doctrine of *uti possidetis juris*.

On the issue of the 'critical date', the chamber made some interesting observations (p. 401, para. 67). Stressing the importance of this concept to the doctrine of *uti possidetis*, it nonetheless questioned the perception of the absolute value of the concept. Acknowledging that whilst the critical date is usually construed as the date on which independence occurred, for the purpose of the *uti possidetis* regime to take over, the court suggested that this rule may not always be determinative. In this case, for instance, the boundary regime was reconditioned by negotiation and adjudication between the parties subsequent to the date of independence. The court argued that although these processes were undoubtedly based on a reading of the critical date that would have focused around 1821, the notion of consent in the proceedings would suggest that the new critical date must be interpreted as being the Peace Treaty of 1980 to the extent to which it casts light on the existence of the boundary. This would seem a logical extension of the notion of the 'critical date' but it is instructive to re-emphasize its importance in ascribing meaning to the date of independence.[35]

With regard to the question of sovereignty over the islands, El Salvador based its claim on the title it claimed to have inherited from the Spanish Crown. Thus the El Salvadorians argued that the doctrine of *uti possidetis* was at the heart of their territorial claim. This was contested by Honduras, who pointed to art. 84 of the El Salvadorian Constitution of 1983 pursuant to the ruling of the Central American Court of Justice in 1917 (p. 557, para. 330; see also *AJIL* (1917), p. 702). This article was meant to identify the territory that comprised El Salvador but was read differently by the two parties. Honduras based its own claim to the islands on *uti possidetis* suggesting through evidence of the display of sovereignty that the *uti possidetis* line of 1821 included the islands within the territory of Honduras (p. 557, para. 331). In analysing the relative arguments of the two parties, the chamber reiterated an important point about the law referred to in the doctrine of *uti possidetis*, namely the colonial laws of the departing administrative power (p. 559, para. 333). However, with the difficulty in determining that law, especially in the manner in which it contradicted territorial jurisdiction, the

---

[33]   Ibid. at 633, para. 149.

[34]   ICJ Reports (1982) 37 at 77, para. 107.

[35]   It could then be argued that in the adjudication of boundary regimes the Badinter Commission, rather than being forced to adhere to boundaries set historically and administratively, could have sought consent and created a regime for which the subsequent critical date would be 1991–2 rather than the constitution of the state of Yugoslavia from the six republics and the two autonomous regions.

court accepted that it may be perfectly possible that the 'law itself gave no clear and definite answer to the appurtenance of marginal areas, or sparsely populated areas of minimal economic significance' (ibid.). Relying on arguments analysed in the *Minquiers and Ecrehos Islands* case,[36] the chamber ruled that the islands could not be considered *terra nullius*. This was backed up by the growing norms concerning the doctrine of *terra nullius* as elaborated in Chapter 3. Thus, the court ruled that with the uncertainty of the administrative and constitutional law of the colonial power being unable to provide the clear answers, possession backed by the exercise of sovereignty could be construed as evidence of confirmation of the *uti possidetis* line. This is controversial since it would arguably favour the *uti possidetis de facto* position over the *uti possidetis juris* doctrine that was arguably at the heart of principle that informed the treatment of boundaries in Spanish America. Based upon this assertion, the chamber ruled by four votes to one in favour of Honduras with respect to the island of El Tigre, whilst ruling unanimously that Meanguera and its appendage island Meanguerita could be considered as the sovereign territory of El Salvador (p. 579, para. 368).

Case Concerning the Territorial Dispute (Libyan Arab Jamahiriya *v.* Chad) 1994[37]

This particular case focuses on the interpretation of the Treaty of Friendship and Good Neighbourliness 1955 signed between Libya and France. The relevance of the treaty was that it was deemed to have established the boundary between the modern states of Libya and Chad. The case as a whole is significant in terms of the treatment of territory for a number of reasons.

First, the two parties started from different premises. Libya believed that there was no boundary in place, since it held that the Treaty of 1955 was not relevant to the given situation, Chad meanwhile held that the boundary established by treaty was already in existence and wished to be able to effectively delimit it. Thus, this case too concerned a request by both parties of the court with regards to the delimitation of a boundary. As seen in other cases, this raised a host of fascinating legal issues worthy of further attention. However, from the perspective of title to territory in modern international law it, once more, raises the question of the validity of colonial treaties – an issue dealt with by the court in the *Guinea-Bissau v. Senegal* case[38] and also in Chapter 4 of this book.

Second, the case very briefly raised the issue of indigenous peoples. In terms of the judgment the reference itself was sporadic and fleeting, but it would be instructive to examine the court's response to the issue and to compare it with other pronouncements,

---

[36] ICJ Reports (1953) 47, especially at 53, 67 and 72.

[37] ICJ Reports (1994) 6. All subsequent page references in this section refer to this text.

[38] Arbitral Award of 31 July 1989 (Guinea-Bissau *v.* Senegal) (1989–91), ICJ Reports (1995); see order of 8 November 1995.

notably on the Masubian people who intermittently lived on the Kasikili/Sedudu Island.[39]

Third, it contains an interesting argument as to an alternative source of the provider of titles to territory. This argument was made by Libya, which claimed the frontier zone under the dispute by reference to the legacy of the Ottoman Empire. Libya held that, as successor to this empire, it had historical rights to the territory that needed to be addressed. In terms of the discussion concerning the title to territory it would seem that Libya was presenting evidence in support of the establishment of a right, and its source, and thus the court's treatment of this discussion is illuminating.[40]

With regard to indigenous peoples, discussion centred around the activities of the Senoussi tribe. This tribe was involved in numerous battles with the French as it sought a worthwhile place to settle down around Lake Chad and further south. The Libyan argument is based on the alleged non-ability of the French to pacify this tribe, resulting in doubt being cast on France's claim to have gained the title to this territory.[41] The Libyans argued that numerous tribes who maintained close links to each other populated the Sahara and Sudan.[42] They argued that based on the sharing of cultures and internal structures of these tribes they could be identified as politically organized societies. In referring to its own history, Libya put forward the view that its predecessor entity was such a politically organized society, referred to by the Ottomans when describing the territories south of the Lake Chad as 'Tripolitania'. This entity consisted of numerous groups and sultanates that had united themselves against the French incursions into their territory. These movements against the French were spearheaded by the Senoussi Order that was also later instrumental in organizing resistance against the Italian invasion in the north.

In contrast to many of the other pleadings of post-colonial states, the Libyans argued that the lines drawn in Africa reflected only European aims and diplomatic strategies and that they did not pertain to real situations on the ground. Further support is ascertained in the Ottoman objection to the French occupation, as a result of which the Ottomans are alleged to have built numerous military outposts in the area to protect their interests. Thus the Libyans stated:

---

[39] See the *Kasiliki/Sedudu* case as examined on pp. 140–41.

[40] See *Libyan Written Memorial*, vol. 1 Submitted on 26 August 1991, especially Chapter IV 'Impact of Colonial Expansion on the Indigenous Peoples', pp. 69–158.

[41] A similar claim was made by Morocco in suggesting that the Spanish never managed to conquer the more interior tribes of the Western Sahara territory. The Spanish themselves countered this by suggesting that the Bled es-Siba part of the Sherifian Empire and precursor to modern Morocco did not spread as far as the Western Sahara and that even if it did there was no demonstration of effective control from the imperial cities over the tribes resident there; see Castellino (2000c).

[42] For a similar discussion see the *Western Sahara case*, ICJ Reports (1975) 12 at 57–8, para. 132.

. . . the historical evidence shows that when the Anglo-French agreements from 1890 to 1899 were concluded, neither France nor Great Britain had any effective authority over the African territories and peoples included in their respective 'spheres of influence' and, indeed, no meaningful presence at all in the region. When France created the *circonscription spéciale dite territoire militaire des pays et protectorates du Tchad* in September 1900, within what were then called the French Congo Territories, it had neither effective authority nor any real presence in the areas surrounding or extending north of Bir Alali in Kanem or in the regions of Borkou, Tibesti, Ounianga, Erdi and Ennnedi. At the moment of entry into force of the Treaty of Ouchy in 1912 between Italy and the Ottoman Empire, when the Sultan in the *Firman* made part of the treaty arrangements give full autonomy to the populations of Tripolitania and Cyrenaica, the local peoples under Senoussi leadership and the Ottoman military forces had effective control of the territories north of a line running east . . . A *modus vivendi* was reached at the time accepting this as the *de facto* boundary between French forces and the Senoussi and Ottomans.

(p. 17, para. 24)

This strong rebuttal of the treaties as accurate reflections of the situations faced by the colonial powers was followed by a distinction made in the pleadings between treaties that sought to establish 'spheres of influence' and those which set out to achieve boundary regimes.[43] The latter, it was suggested, presupposed the existence of two organized political communities on either side of the frontier, which was clearly not the case in most parts of Africa. In addition, these treaties were, in any case, concluded before the administrative machinery of the concerned colonial power would have arrived in the territory and thus there would have been no way of establishing the exact parameters of the boundary (see Chapter 4). The Libyan pleadings also make interesting points about the functions of treaties demarcating spheres of influence. In discussing the different aspects of these treaties, the Libyans argued that they were primarily in place to serve as warnings to trespassers (that is other European powers) to abstain from the territory (Holdich 1916: 96–7). In this scenario, when territorial conflicts arose with third parties, such as the Ottoman Empire or Zanzibar, Libya argued it would be obvious that the treaties would lack legal effect not only towards their object but also under the principle of *res inter alios acta*.[44] In support of this statement, the Libyans cited the negotiations that had been agreed to between France and the Ottoman Empire in 1910–11 to negotiate the southern borders of Tripolitania even though they were clearly under the French 'sphere of influence' according to treaties it had signed with Britain in 1890 and 1899. This proposed negotiation was argued in the pleadings as being candid admission by the colonialists that the 'spheres of influence' agreements had not created territorial boundaries *vis-à-vis* the Ottoman

---

[43] For the original usage of this term, see Rutherford (1926: 300).

[44] The doctrine of *res inter alios acta alteri nocere non debet* suggests that 'a transaction between others does not prejudice a person (or entity in this case) who was not party to it'; as given by Murdoch (1993: 457).

Empire.[45] Had the treaties demarcating these borders had strict legal force then, it could be argued, there would be no reason for France to negotiate with the Ottoman Empire. That the negotiations did not actually take place is attributed to the war that broke out between the Ottoman Empire and Italy (see Shaw 1986: 49).

Thus in summarizing the central elements of this case, the following points need to be made. First, with regard to the facts accepted by both sides it could be said that both parties accepted that there was an absence of a conventional boundary and that the substantive issue at stake was the attribution of territory based on an analysis of the competing claims with a view to ascertaining the better one. Second, the law applicable to the case, as in other cases already examined, concerned first and foremost the attribution of territory, rather than boundary delimitation. In addition, it included the analysis of the two titles, both of which were argued as being derivative. In this context, whilst the Libyan claims were based on the arguments discussed above, Chad argued that its title derived directly from its succession to France. A third issue in terms of the law applicable was the importance of an agreeable 'critical date' by which to test the validity of title and, finally, other factors already discussed in earlier cases and in previous chapters such as issues of effective occupation and the sanctity of colonial boundaries.

Case Concerning Kasikili/Sedudu Island (Botswana/Namibia) 13 December 1999[46]

This case came before the ICJ as a result of a Special Agreement between Botswana and Namibia agreed to at Gaborone, signed on 15 February 1996 and entered into force on 15 May 1996. Article I of this agreement reads as follows:

> The Court is asked to determine, on the basis of the Anglo-German Treaty of 1st July 1890 [an agreement between Great Britain and Germany respecting the spheres of influence of the two countries in Africa] and the rules and principles of international law, the boundary between Namibia and Botswana around Kasikili/Sedudu Island and the legal status of the island.[47]

The Special Agreement sets out the following issues that have been agreed by the parties as being relevant to the determination of the legal status of Kasikili/Sedudu Island. First, that the spirit of the colonial treaty signed between Britain and Germany in 1890 be adhered to and, second, that the case be determined in accordance with rules and principles of modern international law governing the treatment of territory.

---

[45] Libyan Written Pleadings at p. 88 para. 4.46.
[46] See ICJ website <http://www.icj-cij.org/icjwww/idocket/ibona/ibonaframe.htm>.
[47] ICJ Reports (1999) paras, 1–10. Subsequent paragraph references in this section refer to this text.

In Botswana's final submission (5 March 1999), it called upon the court to:

(1) Adjudge and declare:
   (a) That the northern and western channel of the Chobe River in the vicinity of Kasikili/
Sedudu Island constitutes the 'main channel' of the Chobe River in accordance with the
provisions of Article III (2) of the Anglo-German Agreement of 1890; and
   (b) Consequently, sovereignty in respect of Kasikili/Sedudu Island vests exclusively in
the Republic of Botswana; and further

(2) To determine the boundary around Kasikili/Sedudu Island on the basis of the thalweg in
the northern and western channel of the Chobe River.

Namibia, on the other hand, called upon the court to reject all claims and submissions
to the contrary and instead to adjudge and declare:

1. The channel that lies to the south of Kasikili/Sedudu Island is the main channel of the
Chobe River.

2. The channel that lies to the north of Kasikili/Sedudu Island is not the main channel of the
Chobe River.

3. Namibia and its predecessors have occupied and used Kasikili Island and exercised
sovereign jurisdiction over it, with the knowledge and acquiescence of Botswana and its
predecessors, since at least 1890.

4. The boundary between Namibia and Botswana around Kasikili/Sedudu Island lies in the
centre (that is to say, the thalweg) of the southern channel of the Chobe River.

5. The legal status of Kasikili/Sedudu Island is that it is a part of the territory under the
sovereignty of Namibia.

(para. 23)

In seeking to adjudicate upon this matter, the court examined historical material useful
to the determination of the case (paras. 11–16). From this material it is clear that the
dispute between the parties is set against the background of the nineteenth-century
race among the European colonial powers for the partition of Africa (see Chapter 4).
The document listed as prime material for the case, namely the agreement between
Germany and Britain in 1890, was arrived at after negotiations between the parties
concerning their respective trade and spheres of influence in Africa. Those negotiations
resulted in the Treaty of 1 July 1890 that delimited *inter alia* the spheres of influence
of Germany and Great Britain in South West Africa. It is that specific delimitation
which is the primary focus of this case.

   In the ensuing century, the territories experienced various mutations in their political
and legal status. Whilst the Republic of Botswana came into being as an independent
republic on 30 September 1966, on the territory of the former British Bechuanaland
Protectorate, Namibia, including the Caprivi Strip, only gained its independence from

South Africa as late as 21 March 1990.[48] The current dispute between the states thus arose shortly after Namibian independence in 1990. The main cause of this dispute concerned the exact location of the boundary around Kasikili/Sedudu Island. The dispute was submitted to a Joint Team of Technical Experts after agreement was reached between the parties in 1992. By 1995, the team had announced its failure to find a solution and as a result the dispute was submitted to the ICJ. In seeking to analyse and interpret the rules applicable to the 1890 treaty, the court reiterated that both parties had accepted it as binding (paras. 18–20). Thus the need to question the validity of that particular treaty, as had been the case in the *Libya–Chad* and *Guinea-Bissau* cases was obviated.[49] In terms of the interpretation of that treaty, however, the court relied on the Vienna Convention on the Laws of Treaties 1969.[50] The use of this convention has to be subject to two caveats. First, that the two parties are not parties to it, as stated in the judgment, and second, that application of art. 31 of the Vienna Convention would be subject to the intertemporal rule. While the second issue was not addressed in the judgment, the first caveat was overcome by the parties' admission that the Vienna Convention was believed to be a reflection of customary international law. The applicability of this to the second caveat has already been covered in a discussion in Chapter 3 (pp. 87–9).

The court indicated that it would proceed to interpret the provisions of the 1890 treaty by applying the rules of interpretation set forth in the 1969 Vienna Convention, especially art. 31, and also quoted from the *Libya–Chad* case to the effect that:

> . . . a treaty must be interpreted in good faith, in accordance with the ordinary meaning to be given to its terms in their context and in the light of its object and purpose. Interpretation must be based above all upon the text of the treaty. As a supplementary measure, recourse may be had to means of interpretation such as the preparatory work of the treaty.[51]

Thus the court concluded that, in accordance with the ordinary meaning of the terms that appear in the pertinent provision of the 1890 treaty, the northern channel of the River Chobe around Kasikili/Sedudu Island would have to be regarded as its main channel. This conclusion it suggested was supported by the results of three on-site

---

[48]   The South Africans invaded and took over the territory formerly known as South West Africa (modern Namibia) as part of the First World War conquest of German colonies. The territory continued to be held by South Africa in exercise of a 'Class C' mandate given to Britain by the League of Nations and exercised on its behalf by South Africa. The continued presence of South Africa proved controversial during the UN era and was the subject matter of three cases before the ICJ. For more information, see Dugard (1972) and (1996: 549).

[49]   ICJ Reports (1994) 6 and ICJ Reports (1985) 636 respectively.

[50]   In a separate opinion appended to the judgment Judge Oda found the analysis based on the Vienna Treaty excessive; see sep.op. <http://www.icj-cij.org/icjwww/idocket/ibona/ibonaframe.htm>.

[51]   ICJ Reports (1994) 6 at 21–2, para. 41.

surveys carried out in 1912, 1948 and 1985 establishing that the main channel of the River Chobe was its northern channel. The court also examined the object and purpose of the treaty, considering this important for the clarification of any meaning that could be ascertained to have arisen from the treaty itself. In doing so it observed that though the treaty was not actually framed as a boundary treaty it had been accepted by the parties as determining the boundary between their respective territories (paras. 43–6). Nonetheless, the court highlighted that one of the main objects and purposes of the treaty was actually the issue of navigation. In examining subsequent practice, the court noted that while both parties accepted that interpretative agreements and subsequent practice constitute elements of treaty interpretation, they disagreed on the consequences that could be inferred from the facts concerning the interpretation of the purposes of the treaty. The court then examined various documents provided by the parties to suggest an interpretation of the treaty (paras. 47–80). Botswana premised its argument on three documents:

1. Report on a reconnaissance of the Chobe produced in August 1912 by an officer of the Bechuanaland Protectorate Police, Captain Eason.

2. Arrangement arrived at in August 1951 between Major Trollope, Magistrate for the Eastern Caprivi, and Mr. Dickinson, a District Commissioner in the Bechuanaland Protectorate, together with the correspondence that preceded and followed that arrangement.

3. An agreement concluded in December 1984 between the authorities of Botswana and South Africa for the conduct of a Joint Survey of the Chobe, together with the resultant Survey Report.

(paras. 64–8)

Of these, of particular note was the 1951 document that contained a 'gentleman's agreement' between Trollope and Dickinson to the following effect:

(a) That we agree to differ on the legal aspect regarding Kasikili Island, and the concomitant question of the Northern Waterway;

(b) That the administrative arrangements which we hereafter make are entirely without prejudice to the rights of the Protectorate and the Strip to pursue the legal question mentioned in (a) should it at any time seem desirable to do so and will not be used as an argument that either territory has made any admissions or abandoned any claims; and

(c) That, having regard to the foregoing, the position revert to what it was *de facto* before the whole question was made an issue in 1947 – i.e. that Kasikili Island continue to be used by Caprivi tribesmen and that the Northern Waterway continue to be used as a 'free for all' thoroughfare.

The court thus concluded from its examination of the extended correspondence that the events between 1947 and 1951 resulting in the 'gentleman's agreement' demonstrated the absence of agreement between South Africa and Bechuanaland with regard to the location of the boundary around Kasikili/Sedudu Island and the status of the island. The issue raised in point (b) above is of special note since despite agreeing to administrative arrangements between the protagonists, stress is laid that these arrangements are not to prejudice any subsequent legal question with regard to sovereignty issues over the island. The question that needs to be highlighted at this point is the basic difference between this administrative arrangement and those resorted to under colonial rule that essentially set out the administrative boundaries of territories, which subsequently became international frontiers. However, in seeking subsequent practice the court ruled that those events could not be considered to constitute 'subsequent practice in the application of the treaty [of 1890] which establishes the agreement of the parties regarding its interpretation', nor could it have given rise to an 'agreement between the parties regarding the interpretation of the treaty or the application of its provisions'.[52]

An additional factor considered relevant by the court and of significant value to this current project was the discussion surrounding the issue of the presence of the Masubia peoples on the island (paras. 71–5). It is indeed indicative of the process of the international legal treatment of territorial disputes that the presence of these peoples was not identified within art. 1 of the Special Agreement, which instead asked the court to rule on the issue based on the 1890 treaty and applicable rules of international law concerning the treatment of territory. In discussing the issue of subsequent practice Namibia contended that this conduct:

> . . . is relevant to the present controversy in three distinct ways. In the first place, it corroborates the interpretation of the Treaty . . . Second, it gives rise to a second and entirely independent basis for Namibia's claim under the doctrines concerning acquisition of territory by prescription, acquiescence and recognition. Finally, the conduct of the parties shows that Namibia was in possession of the Island at the time of termination of colonial rule, a fact that is pertinent to the application of the principle of *uti possidetis*.

The subsequent practice relied on by Namibia consisted mainly of:

> . . . [t]he control and use of Kasikili Island by the Masubia of Caprivi, the exercise of jurisdiction over the Island by the Namibian governing authorities, and the silence by Botswana and its predecessors persisting for almost a century with full knowledge of the facts . . .

The court opted out of an examination of Namibia's argument concerning prescription. It instead focused on ascertaining whether the long-standing and unopposed presence of Masubian tribes on Kasikili/Sedudu Island constituted adequate 'subsequent practice' to the 1890 treaty to the extent required by art. 31, para. 3(b) of the Vienna Convention

---

[52] As given by the Vienna Convention on the Law of Treaties 1969, art. 31, para. 3(b) and para. 3(a) respectively.

on the Laws of Treaties 1969.[53] In seeking to establish this, the court ruled that two conditions would need to be satisfied. First, the occupation of the island by the Masubia would need to be linked to a belief on the part of the Caprivi authorities that the boundary laid down by the 1890 treaty followed the southern channel of the Chobe. Second, that the Bechuanaland authorities were fully aware of and concomitant to the situation, accepting this as confirmation of the treaty boundary. However, in examining this feature against the intermittent population of the island, the court found no demonstrable link to territorial claims by Caprivi authorities. In fact, the court ruled that Bechunaland and subsequently Botswana seemed content that the intermittent presence of the Masubia on the island did not trouble anyone and was thus tolerated, not least because it did not appear to be connected with interpretation of the terms of the 1890 treaty. The court thus ruled out this factor as providing subsequent practice in the application of the 1890 treaty. Having thoroughly reviewed the issues arising from the 1890 treaty as required by the parties in art. 1, the court then concluded that the treaty did not result in any agreement between the parties with regard to its interpretation or application, nor was the subsequent practice of the parties sufficient to allow interpretation of it.[54]

Thus, having failed to gain any indication from the treaty the court proceeded to review the relevant maps provided by the parties (paras. 81–7). This review took place keeping in mind the principle already established in the *Burkina Faso/Mali* case that maps were merely constitutive of information and not indicative of 'territorial title of intrinsic legal force for the purpose of establishing territorial rights'.[55] In this case too, with the contradictions present in different maps they failed to provide definitive guidance and the court found itself unable to draw adequate conclusions from the maps presented.

An interesting feature of this case, however, was Namibia's claim that it had title to Kasikili/Sedudu not only on the basis of the 1890 treaty but also by virtue of the doctrine of prescription. This doctrine has been examined before but it is, nonetheless, instructive to view the manner in which the argument of acquisitive prescription was dealt with in this case (paras. 90–99). Namibia's argument was that:

> ... by virtue of continuous and exclusive occupation and use of Kasikili Island and exercise of sovereign jurisdiction over it from the beginning of the century, with full knowledge, acceptance and acquiescence by the governing authorities in Bechuanaland and Botswana, Namibia has prescriptive title to the Island.
>
> (para. 90)

---

[53] Article 31, para. 3(b) of the Vienna Convention 1969 reads: [There shall be taken into account, together with the context:] 'any subsequent practice in the application of the treaty which establishes the agreement of the parties regarding its interpretation'.

[54] This discussion also took place in the context of Libya/Chad; see ICJ Reports (1994) 6.

[55] ICJ Reports (1986) 554 at 582, para. 54.

Botswana sought to prevent the court from taking account of this particular Namibian claim by arguing that it had not been included within the scope of the original question submitted to the court under the Special Agreement. The Special Agreement, as quoted on p. 140–41, suggested that the court was required to take into account the 1890 treaty and the 'rules and principles of international law'. The court interpreted the latter phrase as providing justification for the examination of the Namibian claim for prescriptive acquisition.[56] After summarizing the arguments advanced by each of the parties, the court stated that there was discernable agreement between them that acquisitive prescription was a recognized principle in international law governing the treatment of territory.[57] Further, the parties were also in agreement as to the conditions under which title to a given territory may be said to have been acquired by prescription. However, the source of tension between them on this issue lay in a disagreement as to whether those conditions were suitably satisfied in this given case. A prime source of this tension was the aforementioned presence of Masubian tribes originally of Eastern Caprivi on the island. Namibia's claim of acquisitive prescription is premised on that presence, identifying it as 'indirect rule' and claiming that its predecessors had exercised 'title-generating State authority' over the island. Botswana strongly contested this claim describing the presence of the Masubia as merely a manifestation of 'private' activity not giving rise to any title generation and, therefore, not of relevance within the ambit of modern international law. The court rejected the Namibian claim stating that the conditions cited by Namibia were not satisfied fully. In support of this conclusion it ruled that

> if links of allegiance may have existed between the Masubia and the Caprivi authorities, it has not been established that the members of this tribe occupied the Island *à titre de souverain*, i.e., that they were exercising functions of State authority there on behalf of those authorities.
>
> (para. 98)

Further support for this conclusion was identified as evidence that presented the Masubia as using the land only intermittently and exclusively for agriculture, depending on seasons and needs. This intermittent use is said to have commenced prior to the establishment of colonial administration in the Caprivi Strip and appears to have continued throughout the colonial period without being linked to territorial claims on the part of the colonial authority that governed the Caprivi Strip. This scenario only changed in 1947–8 when the boundary question arose between the Bechunaland Protectorate and the regime in South Africa. In that instance, even though the main channel of the Chobe was considered its northern channel and, therefore, indicative of the boundary, the South African authorities held that it possessed the title to the island based on prescription – a claim based on the Masubian presence. This led to the

---

[56] In a separate opinion Judge Kooijmans, questioned the merits of this interpretation; see <http://www.icj-cij.org/icjwww/idocket/ibona/ibonaframe.htm> at para. 18.

[57] For more on prescription, see Jennings and Watt (1992: 561–71).

original debate as to the precise location of the boundary with the colonial authority in Bechunaland insisting that, based on the interpretation of the northern channel of the river Chobe as a boundary line, the island fell within its colonial ambit. The court's judgment suggests that 'after some hesitation, they declined to satisfy South Africa's claims to the Island', whilst maintaining the need for protection of the Caprivi tribes. For the court, two inferences could be made from this. First, that the activities of the Masubian peoples on the island were, for the authorities of the Bechunaland, an issue independent of the title to the island. Second, that the authorities in Bechunaland did, however, reject immediately the South African claim to title, which precluded acquiescence on its part. Thus in the final analysis the court ruled that:

> . . . the boundary between the Republic of Botswana and the Republic of Namibia follows the line of deepest soundings in the northern channel of the Chobe River around Kasikili/ Sedudu Island.
>
> > (para. 104, 11 votes to 4)
>
> . . . Kasikili/Sedudu Island forms part of the territory of the Republic of Botswana.
>
> > (para. 104, 11 votes to 4)
>
> . . . in the two channels around Kasikili/Sedudu Island, the nationals of, and vessels flying the flags of, the Republic of Botswana and the Republic of Namibia shall enjoy equal national treatment.
>
> > (para. 104, unanimously)

The case provided an interesting insight into how the court dealt with the presence of the Masubia on the island. Some of the dissenting opinions provide more guidance on this issue, but what is of prime importance is that the court ruled that the activity of the Masubia did not amount to title-generating capacity. This in itself is not as problematic as the implication that even had there been title-generation activity these rights would have accrued for the authorities of the Caprivi Strip or the predecessor to the state of Namibia. It reveals the link made in international legal cases to the 'ownership' of a given land by territorially based authorities of peoples that existed in one part of that territory that has been deemed a unit. This 'ownership' was considered the real basis for the authorities to claim subsequent title-generation from the intermittent activities of a group that essentially used the island for agricultural purposes. This claim was not addressed within the case. Further, the ruling is also synonymous with the manner in which the court ruled in the *Western Sahara* case when examining the issue of the Tekna Confederation (see Castellino 2000a: 239–42). In that particular case it was held that since there were nomadic and settled tribes who bore the same name as the confederation, and since the former existed largely in the Western Sahara while the latter were based in Morocco, this was reason enough to suggest that the settled Tekna had a link to the nomadic Tekna. It was on this basis that the court ruled that links had existed between the territory of the Western Sahara and Morocco.[58] Thus it can be

---

[58] ICJ Reports (1975) 12.

seen that when issues of identity come up against issues of territoriality, the treatment of the former is essentially subservient to that of the latter, in sharp contrast to the statement of Judge Dillard who in the *Western Sahara* case deemed that 'it was for the people to determine the fate of the territory and not the territory the fate of the people'.[59]

Case Concerning the Land and Maritime Boundary between Cameroon and Nigeria (Cameroon *v.* Nigeria) 15 March 1996[60]

This case came before the court in 1994 after a dispute arose between Cameroon and Nigeria over the sovereignty of the Bakassi Peninsula in the Lake Chad area, claimed by both parties. Cameroon sought to gain adjudication on a host of issues, not all of which are relevant to our present study. This review will focus on the request for the following relief, as indicated by Cameroon in its application of 6 June 1994:

(a)   that sovereignty over the disputed parcel in the area of Lake Chad is Cameroonian, by virtue of international law, and that that parcel is an integral part of the territory of Cameroon;

(b)   that the Federal Republic of Nigeria has violated and is violating the fundamental principle of respect for frontiers inherited from colonization (*uti possidetis juris*), and its recent legal commitments concerning the demarcation of frontiers in Lake Chad;

(c)   that the Federal Republic of Nigeria, by occupying, with the support of its security forces, parcels of Cameroonian territory in the area of Lake Chad, has violated and is violating its obligations under treaty law and customary law;

(d)   that in view of these legal obligations, mentioned above, the Federal Republic of Nigeria has the express duty of effecting an immediate and unconditional withdrawal of its troops from Cameroonian territory in the area of Lake Chad.

Nigeria entered eight preliminary objections in this case, some of which throw an interesting light on the potential arguments that are still pending as this case unfolds.[61] The first two objections, rejected by the court, dealt with the appropriateness of the ICJ as a body to adjudicate in this matter (paras. 21–60). The substance for this argument was presented as a bilateral agreement between the parties to resolve their differences. A third objection, also rejected by the court, claimed that the Lake Chad Basin Commission had exclusive competence to deal with the issue of the territorial dispute (paras. 61–73). However, the court found that the commission had never been given

---

[59]   Ibid. at 116–22.
[60]   ICJ Reports (1998) <http://www.icj-cij.org/icjwww/idocket/icn/icnjudgment/icn_ijudgment_980611_frame.htm>.
[61]   ICJ Reports, Preliminary Objections Stage Summary of the Judgment of 11 June (1998). All subsequent paragraph references in this section refer to this text.

a fortiori exclusive jurisdiction. The fourth and fifth objections entered by Nigeria concerned the issue of the boundary. Via objection four, the Nigerians sought to suggest that the boundary was already established, based on the tri-point in the lake (paras. 74–83). Since this was one of the issues being questioned by the Cameroonian authorities, this objection too was rejected. Objection five reinforces the suggestion that there is no dispute concerning boundary delimitation, subject to the question of the title over Darak and adjacent islands, without prejudice to the title over the Bakassi Peninsula (paras. 84–94). The sixth objection, also rejected by the court, sought to argue that there could be no judicial basis for the determination of Nigeria's international responsibility for alleged frontier incursions (paras. 95–102). The seventh objection stays on the theme of there not being a legal dispute with regard to the delimitation of the boundary between the parties (paras. 103–11). In this objection, Nigeria argued that, first, determination of the maritime boundary was not possible without prior determination of the title to the Bakassi Peninsula and, second, that when that title is determined the issue of maritime delimitation will not be admissible 'in the absence of prior sufficient action by the Parties . . . by agreement on the basis of international law'. The court also rejected this objection since it considered matters already discussed in earlier objections. The eighth objection sought to provide supplementary information to the seventh by suggesting that interests of third party states might be violated by a discussion between the two parties with regard to the boundary (paras. 112–17). With this objection rejected as well, the court gave its ruling to the preliminary objections in February 2001. This order contained authorization for the submission of additional pleadings by the Republic to be filed as counter-claims to those submitted by Nigeria and set 4 July 2001 as the deadline for this submission.[62]

The main issue raised by this case, which will hopefully be elucidated with its progress before the courts, is that of modern occupation. This is not an issue that has been discussed at any length in this book, but it is important to highlight that in discussing issues of territorial treatment emphasis has been laid on the notions of the manner in which the doctrine of *uti possidetis* dispels the notion of *terra nullius* and guarantees the international frontiers of former colonial entities. This case presents a dispute about territory wherein one of the parties, namely Nigeria, is also accused by the other of using force to occupy the Bakassi Peninsula. If this dispute is to be interpreted strictly under the guise of Roman law, it could be summarized as a dispute over territory in the current possession of one of the parties though title over it is claimed by both. Thus, in these circumstances the current incumbent would have the advantage granted to the possessor whilst the claimant would need to prove a compelling case as to why the situation should be reversed and possession handed over. However, with the evolution of modern international law, these activities take place under the shadow of the UN Charter and the efforts to outlaw the use of force.[63]

---

[62] At the time of writing the memorials had yet to be filed.
[63] See the Pact of Paris 1928; Brownlie (1963).

Article 2(4) of the UN Charter states clearly that states will not use force in the conduct of their activities.[64] In addition, the use of force is generally considered a violation of UN Charter norms unless undertaken by a state in self-defence or in fulfilment of a mandate authorized by the Security Council acting under the mandate provided by Chapter 7 of the UN Charter.[65] Unilateral use of force is considered a violation of modern international law and the use of force beyond territorial boundaries is particularly susceptible to censure.[66]

Thus, what this case demonstrates is an action that took place in the last decade of the twentieth century being judged by modern standards that have evolved in the UN system. However, a part of those modern standards is the doctrine of *uti possidetis* as stressed by the court in preceding cases. That particular doctrine accepted the nature of colonial rule as a given and sought to freeze the situation at the moment of departure of that rule to provide legitimacy and definition to newly formed states in the interests of order. The justification for this comes from the intertemporal rule of modern international law, which suggests that actions of an era need to be governed against the laws prevalent in that era, and that to apply them across eras would be incorrect.[67] In the face of the intertemporal rule the use of the doctrine of *uti possidetis* is justified on the grounds that it was made to apply to modern situations by the consent of states and in the modern international legal system this consent remains supreme.[68]

Conclusions

Thus, as can be seen from the selection of cases presented above, the doctrine of *uti possidetis* has been used by the courts on numerous occasions. In contrast, the principle of *terra nullius* is referred to much less. This is perhaps an indication that in many of the cases what are often at question are state-centric views of the history of a territory. Thus, while the *Western Sahara* case, which directly used the terminology of *terra nullius*, was about the future of a territory which was at the time not in the possession

---

[64] Article 2(4) of the UN Charter (1945) states: '[The Organisation and its Members, in pursuit of the Purposes stated in Article 1, shall act in accordance with the following Principles:] All Members shall refrain in their international relations from the threat or use of force against the territorial integrity or political independence of any State, or in any other manner inconsistent with the Purposes of the United Nations.'

[65] There is growing evidence to suggest a third acceptable means of the use of force – in the case of humanitarian intervention – though this is yet to crystallize in legal terms.

[66] Security Council resolutions provide an interesting review of illicit use of force; see <http://www.un.org>.

[67] For a more indepth discussion on intertemporal law see Chapter 3. See also Elias (1980).

[68] These issues of intertemporal law are revisited in the concluding chapter of this book.

of either of the claimants to it,[69] in other cases the territory is already in the possession of a state. This presence is not always deemed *de jure*.[70] However, in terms of the doctrine of *uti possidetis* a strict reading would seem to suggest that the incumbent within the territory would continue to hold title in the interdict until the opponent establishes the legal basis for their own claim. This situation was reflected in the first case reviewed in this chapter, namely the *Belgium/Netherlands* case of 1959, where attention focused on the findings of a Mixed Boundary Commission that essentially sought to preserve the status quo. In seeking final justification for the territory the court began from the premise that sovereignty over the territory was held by Belgium, as established by the Mixed Commission, and then sought to examine whether there was proof of a subsequent extinguishment of this sovereignty.

One issue pointed out by Bekker (1998) in his commentary on cases is that although the concept of 'title' is used widely in international legal cases its actual meaning is yet to be determined. The best elaboration of the concept from the ICJ comes by way of a statement in the *Burkina Faso/Mali* case (1986) where title is deemed as:

> generally not restricted to documentary evidence alone, but comprehends both any evidence which may establish the existence of a right, and the actual source of that right.[71]

This definition of title remains inadequate both as an explanation and as a statement of clear legal intent but is accurate in that it reflects the grey area that title to territory in modern international law presents. To examine the explanation further, it can be isolated as representing the following factors.

Title is not restricted to Documentary Evidence

This factor itself is significant. On examining the pleadings to the cases before the ICJ concerning title to territory it is instructive to note that vast amounts of time and effort are devoted to 'proving ownership' over a particular territory. Whilst not every state claiming territory has been able to produce evidence that could satisfy the strict needs of being 'documentary', the fact remains that states have relied extensively on various documents of an external nature that allegedly show them to own or possess a certain tract of territory or demonstrate respect from others to the notion that they possess

---

[69] The two claimants at the time were Morocco and Mauritania. Spain had accepted its need to decolonize and the Saharawis, represented by the Polisario, were not allowed to be represented in proceedings.

[70] For instance, Nigerian 'occupation' of the Bakassi Peninsula or the occupation of Northern Cyprus leading to the 'Turkish Northern Republic of Cyprus'. For a historical precedent see the situation concerning Manchukuo in Harris (1998: 109).

[71] ICJ Reports (1986) 554 at 565, para. 18.

certain tracts of land.[72] First, the fact that the court has engaged this material at all suggests that it believes a certain internal validity can be assuaged through the respect of a frontier externally. Second, the fact that it has examined this 'documentary evidence' against specific norms of law suggests that the measure of a title can be gauged against objective legal criteria. This is problematic, at best, owing to a number of factors including the power dynamic present in unequal treaties signed by colonial powers with the colonized, treaties signed between colonial powers designating spheres of influence, the issue of the lack of effective control over territory claimed by documents and the differences in culture and tradition that were often misrepresented in cultural anthologies of different territories and peoples (see Gellner 1972). Nonetheless, when a dispute over territory occurs and the court is called upon to adjudicate it needs to ensure that the evidence, in these cases usually the 'facts', are verifiable. This proves extremely hard owing to some of the negative anthologies presented in literature and popular culture. As a result, the court is forced to give credence to evidence of a documentary nature and in verifying this evidence needs to subjectively ascertain its resonance.

Evidence that may establish Existence of a Right

When dealing with the lawful treatment of territory, the court has to rely on reliable evidence. However, it is difficult to understand the parameters of evidence that 'may establish the existence of a right'. While not questioning the need for evidence in these proceedings, the court seems willing to engage issues of a historical nature, the history of which are bitterly contested by the parties in the first place. Thus, the court is often left badly exposed in terms of verifying the details of non-documentary evidence *per se*. When this is added to the fact that the evidence requested for proof of title ought to establish existence of a right, we have a further clouding of issues. The fact remains that in many of the cases before the ICJ, the evidence presented by both sides seems equally compelling. This situation was witnessed in the Advisory Opinion on the *Western Sahara* case where both the Mauritanian entity and Morocco produced different kinds of evidence to support their respective territorial claim to the Western Sahara (Castellino 2000c: 263–7). The fact that the court seemed to base its decision with regard to the links between the two entities and the territory on factors that could be considered dubious suggests that it is extremely difficult to produce evidence of the establishment of a right. This was also true in the *Burkina Faso/Mali* case where in seeking to examine the evidence establishing a right the court was forced to engage the issue of *colonial effectivités*.

The Sources of Rights

The Court seems to have engaged in the rights discourse without necessarily laying

---

[72] For instance, Moroccan justifications in the *Western Sahara case*, ICJ Reports (1975) 12 at 49, para. 108.

down the parameters of what it anticipates this particular discourse to entail. When it talks about the sources of rights, for instance, exactly what kind of sources is it referring to? In the *Western Sahara* case, for example, Morocco sought to prove its title to territory by focusing on certain issues to demonstrate exercise of internal sovereignty. One such issue was the appointment of caids, which it considered an important factor in the proof of the role of the Sultan's influence over the region.[73] The discussion concerning the presence and activities of the Masubian people and their title-generation capacities in the *Kasiliki/Sedudu Island* case indicates similar sentiments (see p. 147). While setting aside the merits of these arguments themselves, it can be seen that they have their sources in religion, tradition and culture and their different interpretations. However, it is not always so easy to determine the source of each right presented since not all sources are as well established as the notion of religion. The rights of nomadic peoples, for instance, have been consistently disregarded. Modern international law seems inflexible to the rights of these peoples, an argument that was made in a dissenting opinion to the *Western Sahara* case.[74]

Another issue that needs to be highlighted in concluding this review of cases is the notion of *colonial effectivités* as it was deemed in the *Burkina Faso/Mali* case. As defined in the case, this pertains to the 'conduct of the administrative authorities as proof of the effective exercise of territorial jurisdiction in the region during the colonial period'.[75] Thus the principle of *colonial effectivités* forms an important tool for the propagation of the doctrine of *uti possidetis*. The relationship between the two needs to be intricately understood. Whilst *colonial effectivités* essentially represents the 'title to territory' under colonial law to a territory, it sets in place limits to this jurisdiction which are subsequently protected by the doctrine of *uti possdetis* on the withdrawal of the colonial power. Thus, it can be categorically stated that proof of *colonial effectivités*, in the face of a failure of the parties to come to any other agreement by consent, essentially informs the sanctifying of colonial boundaries within international law.

There are a number of important sub-issues related to the issue of colonial rule or colonial law that need to be highlighted at this stage. For a start there is the issue, highlighted in the *Libya–Chad* case, that application of colonial law is the determining factor in the delimitation of the *uti possidetis* line within territories. Thus, these territorial boundaries come from within a colonial system of administrative law. Yet a similar argument made in the *Kasiliki/Sedudu Island* case with respect to an administrative agreement between the Caprivi authorities and those in Bechunaland was not considered indicative of an agreement. Another sub-issue that emerges from the case law is that the doctrine of *uti possidetis* is, essentially, a retrospective doctrine that applies after the event. It is therefore subject to all the features that retrospectivity in law generates. In fact, it is to escape the judgment always entailed in retrospection

---

[73] ICJ Reports (1975) 12 at 45–9.
[74] *Western Sahara case*, ICJ Reports (1975) 12 at 83–101 (dis. op. of Judge Ammoun).
[75] ICJ Reports (1986) 554 at 586, para. 63.

in modern international law that the rule of intertemporal law is called upon. Yet the doctrine of *uti possidetis* seems unproblematic when applied without this question being considered. Once again, the overriding reason for this is states' consent to its use. A third sub-plot already identified concerns the issue of whether *colonial effectivités* was as extensive and exclusive as was often claimed. This is usually the underlying argument in cases where modern post-colonial entities seek to argue that the *uti possidetis* line varies since the colonial power could not demonstrate its occupation of some of the border regions. Thus *colonial effectivités* itself is open to criticism on a number of grounds:

1   Its appropriateness in a debate about post-colonial boundary situations
2   The precise nature of the concept itself
3   The inclusiveness of *colonial effectivités*.

First, with regard to the appropriateness of *colonial effectivités* to post-colonial boundary negotiations, this issue is easily answered within modern international law itself in the justification for *uti possidetis*, namely, that it is fundamentally a means by which order can be pursued without running the risk of fragmentation. Thus, criticisms of *colonial effectivités* would follow similar grounds to criticisms of *uti possidetis*. Second, the nature of the concept itself presents fascinating possibilities. Does *colonial effectivités*, for instance, represent title deeds to the commons or is it a reference of ownership of private property? Depending on the answer to that question, its treatment in law could entail completely different issues. In the *Burkina Faso/Mali* case, the court ruled that *colonial effectivités* represented the lands conveyed to municipal authorities under Spanish colonial law and as a result it reduced the weight given to the notion.[76] This, in turn, raises the question as to how *uti possidetis* can be considered a valid principle when there is doubt raised about the extent and scope of the notion of *colonial effectivités* upon which it is based. This particular debate needs to also bear in mind the court's decision with regard to 'title to territory' in general. Thus, if the only 'effective' title that can be proven as establishing rights is a colonial title of limited value, then what exactly is the legal basis of the doctrine of *uti possidetis*? Even if the answer to that question is merely the protection of existing order, it would arguably reduce the role of law from one that is about justice to one that is merely concerned with the protection and promotion of order, a conclusion that would not perhaps sit equally at ease in every setting. Finally, the issue of the inclusiveness of *colonial effectivités* runs parallel to the previous argument in that it seeks to question the extent of *colonial effectivités*. If the colonial state had managed to gain the consent of the governed, a doctrine that was being preached and readily accepted at home in the state of the colonists after the American and French Revolutions (Castellino 1999a), the legacy of *colonial effectivités* would have been potentially less harmful. Even if

---

[76]   ICJ Reports (1986) 554 at 620–33, paras. 124–50.

colonial effectivités had included different people within the colony, the side effects of the regime would have been restricted. However, by including certain groups and excluding others, notably indigenous peoples, seeds were sown for conflict on the withdrawal of the colonial power, further undermining the use of this particular principle in the post-colonial distribution of territory in modern international law.

6 The Badinter Commission and the Treatment of Territory in the Former Yugoslavia

Having examined the genesis of the doctrine of *uti possidetis* and its related concept of *terra nullius* and its application through different eras, it is now time to examine two modern manifestations of these doctrines governing territory in modern international law. From the outset, it should be borne in mind that the current impact of the doctrine is not merely restricted to these two issues: namely the dissolution of Yugoslavia, which is the subject matter of this chapter, and the issues contained in following chapter, namely indigenous rights of title to territory. Rather, it can be argued that the doctrines remain pertinent to most post-colonial states in which ethnic groups or national minorities are seeking to use the heavily validated but, nonetheless, contested right of self-determination to gain self-governance, autonomy and, in many instances, secession.[1] In many of these conflicts, one of the primary issues remains the sanctity of the territory for a particular group and, in this sense, the manner in which the doctrines regarding territory have affected them is that they have often been placed, sometimes artificially, within the bounds of a sovereign state to which they perceive no allegiance. This lack of allegiance has been countered to a certain extent by the principles of nation building (Deutsch 1963) but with the process less than half a century old in many instances, the fault lines of identity persist and could continue as a major cause of disruption to international peace and security. Whether the consequences of this eruption would be as disruptive or worse than the events witnessed in the former Yugoslavia remains to be seen, and feared. However, the events in Yugoslavia themselves offer us a view of the treatment of territory that merits close attention. While this was not a case of decolonization, the doctrine of *uti possidetis*, in particular, was made applicable to it, and presents a view of the application of this doctrine in a completely different setting.

Though the issues at the start of the conflict in Yugoslavia were polarized around whether the events transpiring amounted to the dissolution of the state of Yugoslavia or the secession of the republics, the conflict brings home various complexities

---

[1] For example, Kashmir, West Papua, Ambom, Aceh, Western Sahara and Kurdistan. This does not include problematic situations that cannot be considered technically 'colonial', such as Dagestan, Chechnya, Abkhazia, Kosovo, Northern Ireland and the Basque Country.

regarding the treatment of territory in modern international law. The growing phenomenon of 'post-modern tribalism' requires that these issues be discussed and resolved within modern international law to provide clarity on the treatment of territory. Thus, the significance of the conflict in Yugoslavia is manifold. First, it provides an example of a situation where ethnically induced tension has resulted in the creation of new states. This process of state creation has attendant to it the allocation and challenge with regard to title to the territory that is integral to the state. Second, in normal circumstances the principle of state sovereignty forecloses the issue from the aegis of modern international law.[2] The potential dissolution of states or secession from a state tends to fall strictly within the parameters of domestic jurisdiction.[3] However, in Yugoslavia various political factors and the allegations of genocide essentially pierced the veil of domestic sovereignty and forced the issue within the realms of modern international law,[4] as is best demonstrated by the recent spate of cases before the International Court of Justice.[5] This in itself is significant and although the processes that enabled such action are interesting, they remain beyond the scope of the present chapter. Third, and most crucial from our current perspective, are the pronouncements on the treatment to territory in this conflict made by the arbitration committee set up under the guidance of Robert Badinter.[6] These comments, essentially made by lawyers working with constitutional rather than international law (since the commission was initially set up to draw up a new constitution for Yugoslavia, before being overtaken by events), cast light on the title to territory that merits further analysis. It is this last issue that will form the major portion of this inquiry. It can be argued that the workings of the commission and the intricacies of their decisions with regard to the specific question of the treatment of territory in the former Yugoslavia form an important part of the development of modern international law, even though this is not to the satisfaction of all.[7]

For the purpose of our inquiry, this chapter will be divided into four main parts. The first part examines the formation of the Badinter Commission and its originally defined role. This section is presented by way of background to the work of the commission and is intended as an opportunity to place it in the appropriate context. The second part focuses on the issues before the commission in the form of the three questions that they were initially requested to comment upon. While not being exhaustive on

---

[2] This is also governed by art. 2(7) of the UN Charter 1945. For a general reading on state sovereignty see Castellino (2000a: 90–107 and Lapidoth (1992).

[3] For example, Biafra and Nigeria; see Heraclides (1991: 82–91).

[4] For an exhaustive review of the work of the Badinter Commission, see Terrett (2000).

[5] See ICJ website <http://www.icj-cij.org>.

[6] For a general reading on the subject of the Badinter Opinions see Terrett (2000), Shaw (1996 and 1997b), Pellet (1992) and Radan (2000).

[7] Radan (2000) and Ratner (1996), for instance, dismiss the tribunal's work.

the requests of the commission, this section highlights the issues with regard to the inquiry into the treatment of territory in the former Yugoslavia and their perception by the main protagonists in the conflict. The third part addresses the specific references to the treatment of territory within the Opinions of the commission and analyses these against the backdrop of existing international law. The final part then draws up a set of conclusions concerning the implications for title to territory within modern international law of the work of the Badinter Commission.

The Badinter Commission: An Introduction[8]

The Badinter Commission consisted of five members chosen from the presidents of the constitutional courts of the EC Member States. The composition of the commission was significant and it was to comprise:

(i)   Two members . . . appointed unanimously by the [Yugoslav] Federal Presidency;
(ii) Three members . . . appointed by the Community and its Member States.

(Terrett 2000: 122)[9]

The main function of the Arbitration Commission was identified in the European Public Commission's Declaration on 28 August 1991. That declaration suggested that the Arbitration Commission would be the body to which 'relevant authorities' would 'submit their differences'. It envisaged a time limit of two months for deliberations within the commission. While the issue of the proceedings of the commission and how they fit into general modern international law of arbitration are interesting, they remain outside the scope of the present inquiry.[10] Suffice to say that the written texts and commentaries prove less helpful in the analysis of the commission's works than the actual text of the commission's Opinions (Ragazzi 1992; Terrett 2000: 121). Also, vitally, from the perspective of modern international law, rather than providing judgments that fully engage the different issues, the Badinter Opinions are tersely worded and not necessarily in the language of other international bodies of adjudication such as the International Court of Justice (see Chapter 5). It is in this respect that it needs to be noted that the Badinter Commission's original mandate was to draw up a constitution for the Federal Republic of Yugoslavia that would enable the peaceful co-existence within the state of different threatening and threatened national minorities

---

[8] For other general documents on Yugoslavia, see also EC Declaration on Yugoslavia, 27 August 1991, reproduced in Trifunovska (1994: 333–4); *EC Declaration on Recognition*, UN Doc 2/23293 Annex 1 (1991); *ILM* 31 (1992) 1485; *EC Declaration on Guidelines on the Recognition of New States in Eastern Europe and in the Soviet Union* 16 December 1991, UN Soc. S/23293, Annex 2; *ILM* 31 (1992) 1486.

[9] For issues related to the appointment of judges, see Terrett (2000: 122–5).

[10] For general reading on arbitration in international law, see Clarke (1907) and Jessup (1928).

(Terrett 2000: 121–2). As the events in Yugoslavia began to unfold these issues became difficult to separate and as a result, the Arbitration Commission found itself thrust into the role of an international adjudication organ for which it had little experience. Further, the changed conditions of operation signalled a grave dilution in the powers attributable to the body (ibid.: 122–4). Thus, while the 'relevant authorities' who could access the commission were not defined, it had originally been envisaged that these would be territorially based representatives from within the republics affected by the process of disintegration within the former Yugoslavia. These relevant authorities would have had to include the previously autonomous regions of Kosovo and Vojvodina since the revocation of their constitutionally autonomous status played a significant role in provoking the conflict in the first instance.[11]

Interestingly, from the perspective of title to territory, the role envisaged for the commission by the European Communities Conference on Yugoslavia (ECCY) was one of arbitration. Drawing on concepts that developed during the decolonization of Latin America (see Chapter 3), the mechanism of arbitration was recognized as an efficient means of resolving different kinds of disputes (see generally Stuyt 1972). The arbitration process was therefore considered superior to bringing proceedings before the International Court of Justice since it was designed to engage factual issues concerning the specific situation as it was unfolding and to provide decisions that were deemed binding upon the parties who had brought the dispute before it.[12] The actual arbitration process involved consultation between the parties and the arbitrators, further justifying the binding nature of the award on the parties. In this sense, the award itself was envisioned as a legal one demarcating territorial adjustments (if any) and ruling on the subject of differences brought before it. The circumstances that led to the dilution of this originally envisaged role are examined elsewhere (Terrett 2000: 126–38) but the force of events in Yugoslavia dictated a change in role. In its new guise, rather than function as an arbitration body with the power to bind parties to decisions, the commission diminished to being an organ with merely advisory capacities. Thus, rather than rendering binding decisions, it handed out opinions on the matters posed to it.

The events in the former Yugoslavia are of extreme importance to the inquiry into the title to territory. In terms of modern international law, until that point, any crisis concerning title to territory had been contained within a sovereign state, but this crisis has suddenly revealed it as an issue with potential to traverse international boundaries.[13] From the viewpoint of the commission, this raised numerous issues that are attendant to conflicts over territory in modern international law. These included the issues of

---

[11] Craven (1995) argues for others to be included.

[12] The reason that the arbitration process is not focused upon in this book is that the issues being dealt with are more 'issues of law' than of 'fact'.

[13] Issues that involve self-determination and claims for separate status often cross this line; see Castellino (2000b).

recognition and state succession, among others. The issue of recognition, for instance, was vital since with a commission set in place it would inevitably have to provide the lead on whether the new republics could be recognized as sovereign independent states and, based on this recognition, the entire nature of the conflict would be altered. One of the most controversial aspects of the crisis was the recognition of Croatia by Germany as early as December 1991. Although the ECCY was discussing the issue and although the consensus within the organization and the international community tended towards awaiting the outcome of the situation before conferring recognition, Germany stepped out of line to recognize Croatia. This recognition, it could be argued, was highly significant since it changed the parameters of the conflict by raising the spectre of it being more than civil unrest within a given state (Weller 1992).

In addition, the commission had to consider whether what was transpiring in the former Yugoslavia could be deemed secession – namely independent republics breaking away from the parent state to form new independent entities – or whether the events amounted to dissolution of the old state and the birth of newer states. The significance of this distinction is that if what was transpiring was secession, a number of issues would be raised. First, the act of secession itself is not one that is recognized directly in modern international law. Although it is considered to be one of the routes identified as being available in the process of self-determination by the General Assembly Resolution 1541 (XV), that was strictly within the context of decolonization. Besides, even the action of decolonization was required to adhere to the principles of *uti possidetis*. To rule that what was transpiring in the former Yugoslavia was secession would basically suggest that the new republics were breaking away from the parent state in direct confrontation with the state's right to territorial integrity.[14] Second, the concept of secession would imply that the state of Yugoslavia endured and the implications of that for state succession were significant. A ruling in favour of secession would leave the concept of the existence of the state of Yugoslavia unmolested (albeit territorially reduced), while the breakaway republics could be seen as exercising a new and separate right. The advantage of this from the perspective of the federal authorities was that they would not need to seek separate recognition since the republics of Serbia and Montenegro would simply gain the mantle of Yugoslavia while the other republics forged their own international identity and sought recognition from the international community. Thus, the representatives of the Former Serbian Republic of Yugoslavia (FSRY) favoured the route of secession. This in itself is unique, since the manner in which secession compromises the principle of state sovereignty is usually enough for the state concerned to vehemently oppose notions of self-determination in this, its most extreme guise (Quane 1998: 537; Brilmayer 1991). However, in the case of this unfolding situation the parent state of the former Yugoslavia had clear-cut reasons for insisting that the disintegration of the state was as a result of the process of secession.

---

[14] For more on the status of secession, see Buchheit (1978 and 1979–80).

However, if the commission ruled that the events in the former Yugoslavia amounted to dissolution of the old state a whole different set of implications would arise. First, it would mean that all the republics emerging out of the conflict could be considered new entities, each with a need to seek recognition of their status from the international community. While in theory this would depend on whether the declaratory or constitutive model of recognition was at work (see Dugard 1992 and Opinion 2 of the Badinter Commission, pp. 972–3 below), in practice the emerging republics would need to be recognized externally to gain full legitimacy within the international community of states.[15] This in itself would present problems for some of the republics, most notably for Serbia and Montenegro who constituted 'Yugoslavia'. Second, dissolution would also imply that the state of Yugoslavia had ceased to exist. This was never stated as the aim of events as far as the Serbian leadership within the Socialist Federal Republic of Yugoslavia (SFRY) was concerned. They saw the challenge to the existing state as coming from the republics that wanted to break away from the federal state and the question of dissolution of the state itself did not arise. Finally, in terms of the republics, the notion of dissolution rather than secession from the federal state was attractive due to the presence in all of the republics of national minorities owing allegiance to sides other than the numerically dominant group within the territory of the given republic. Accordingly, they feared that should the premise of their new statehood be based on their rights as an ethnic minority, it would open the door for a continuously evolving process by which territorial minorities living in enclaves within the new states would progressively challenge each new parent state until uni-ethnic states would be achieved.[16] However, if what was transpiring was the dissolution of the state of Yugoslavia then the national minorities within the resultant states would not have an implied claim with regard to further secession, since the basis for the new state would be the old federated structures within Federal Yugoslavia, leaving no room for arguments in favour of ethnically induced secession (for more on this see Terrett 2000: 142–3).

While at first there was no clarity as to the nature of the conflict, it was clear in references made within the European Political Cooperation (EPC) forum that its dynamics had changed.[17] Although initially a conflict over the allocation of constitutional

---

[15] There is no threshold that states have to cross before recognition allows them a full role in the international community. The contrast presented by the 'Turkish Northern Republic of Cyprus', recognized only by Turkey, and the Saharan Arab Democratic Republic, recognized by as many as 74 states, is a case in point.

[16] It could be argued that the events in Kosovo are further attempts at secession in a bid to constitute ethnically 'pure' states.

[17] See, for instance, the EC's response to the takeover of the Federal Presidency by Serbia and Montenegro, which was classed as an 'illegal action' in contravention of the CSCE Charter of Paris as well as the constitution of Yugoslavia; see *EC Bulletin* 19 (1991) 86, statement of 5 October 1991.

rights, the failure of that particular discussion and the subsequent recourse to use of force by the various parties rapidly took it beyond this mandate (see generally Chadwick 1996). However, even though it recognized that the conflict was coming increasingly within the scope of modern international law, the EPC nonetheless stressed the continuing role of the Badinter Commission. As pointed out by Terrett, the statement of 6 October 1991 even emphasized that the:

> ... right to self-determination of all the peoples of Yugoslavia cannot be exercised in isolation from the interests and rights of ethnic minorities within the individual republics ... [and that such interests could only be sought to be protected through peaceful negotiations for which the] 'Arbitration Commission ha[s] been convened'.
>
> (Terrett 2000: 139)

Contrasted with the original mandate of the commission, this clearly was a 'creative reinterpretation' of its role (ibid.). However, support for the commission came not merely from the ECCY. It was also expressly backed by both the USA and the (former) USSR.[18] That particular support, expressed as a joint statement, provides further evidence of the recognition of the change in the dynamic of the conflict since if it was a purely internal conflict, international bodies would be slower to make such statements. While strongly backing the activities of the Badinter Commission, the joint communiqué stressed the emergence of an international dimension (with recognition of the republics as states) to a conflict that was initially intra-state. In addition to rejecting the use of force to change internal or external boundaries, it also referred to the CSCE principles dealing with inviolability of boundaries, respect for minority rights and the importance of political pluralism (Terrett 2000: 79).

  Thus, it is clear that the flow of events after the constitution of the Badinter Arbitration Commission under the auspices of the ECCY made the task before the commission a difficult one. Rather than changing the constituents of the task addressed to the commission, the ECCY and the major powers stressed their backing for it. The rationale for this was clearly the fact that since consent for the functioning of the commission had already been gained, attempting to change its mandate would require further negotiation. In the circumstances of continued violence and bloodshed, negotiations about its technical mandate seemed inappropriate and inadequate. Thus, the wisest course of action was seen as validation of the commission and a 'creative interpretation' of its role. As a result, the commission found itself ruling on issues of self-determination, secession and the status of boundaries, all of which were well beyond its original constitutional mandate. In addition, since the process was no longer consensual to the same extent, the findings of the body were deemed to be of little more than moral force since although the combatants were bound to the process, the material change in circumstances prevented implementation of hard judgments on the ground.[19]

---

[18] See *EC Bulletin* 10 (1991) 87.
[19] For a general reading on the history of the Balkans, see Gleny (1999).

The Issues Before the Badinter Commission

While many of the issues continued to reverberate around the international community, the commission received its first request from Lord Carrington. Having evaluated the events up to that point (5 November 1991) and concluded that the fundamental aspects of the peace plan were not being observed, he urged the EC to impose economic sanctions upon the FSRY.[20] With the imposition of these, the nature of the process was now contentious rather than consensual. Lord Carrington, Special Representative of the ECCY then issued a letter to the commission with a number of questions, which are the main focus of this section. However, it is important to bear in mind the ramifications of the consultation process under the auspices of the Badinter Commission after the imposition of sanctions. While the negotiations and consultations had, until this point, taken place with the consensus of the parties, the imposition of economic sanctions changed the status of these discussions. The use of economic sanctions comes under the rubric of Chapter VII of the UN Charter 1945[21] and is usually designed to ensure state compliance. Marginally less devastating than the use of full force, they, nonetheless, amount to an act of aggression or defence by the international community against a state that fails to comply with its consensus by seeking to break the peace or threatening to break the peace in violation of its Charter obligations. Although these sanctions were not applied under the auspices of the UN, it could be argued that their effect and purpose was the same. Thus, in this context it is evident that any rulings by the commission would not be accepted as binding by the parties.

Having solicited a list of differences from the republics and the Federal Presidency, Lord Carrington addressed three questions, enunciated originally by President Milosevic, to the commission for consideration. It is very clear that even at this stage the commission had the express backing of the SFRY. In fact, in a statement President Milosevic had noted the existence of '. . . a number of disputes . . . over issues representing vital principles in international law and constituting the entire basis of the world order today'.[22] He went on to request a ruling from the Commission on three questions:

1. Who should be the entity of the right to self-determination – the people or the federal unit?
2. Legality of secession in international law and the conditions under which the secession can be realised.
3. The status of internal or administrative frontiers and of external or State frontiers from the aspect of universal international law, the *Helsinki Final Act* and the *Charter of Paris*.
                                                        (quoted in Terrett 2000: 142)

---

[20] *EC Bulletin* (1991) 87.

[21] Chapter VII of the UN Charter deals with issues of the use of force and economic sanctions; see generally Simma *et al.* (1994).

[22] See President Milosevic's address (post rejection of the Carrington Plan) to the ECCY of 18 October 1991, as quoted in Terrett (2000: 142) and Trifunovska (1994: 363–5).

In requesting a ruling on these three questions, President Milosevic suggested he was seeking a solution that was based on law and justice – and he believed that the commission was the ideal body to provide such a solution. Thus, President Milosevic sought clarification on the whole issue within modern international law with regard to the treatment of the territory of the former Yugoslavia.

Dealing with these questions in turn, with respect to the notion of self-determination, the issue can be broken down into two segments: first, the general status of self-determination[23] and, second, its application in federal states. Regarding its general status, documentary sources suggest that the right of self-determination exists for all peoples.[24] However, although modern international law does not define the notion of a people, state practice reveals that the prime beneficiaries of this title are people under colonial rule (Thornberry 1989). In various opinions, consideration has been given to whether national minorities constitute a people[25] and the overwhelming response is that they do not (ibid.: 887–9), though there have been notable exceptions (see Castellino 1999b). With regard to self-determination in post-colonial states there is a lack of clarity, with practice revealing that while East Timor succeeded in gaining independence from Indonesia through a UN organized referendum, the same privilege has not been accorded to Ambon, Aceh or West Papua. Practice also varies from state to state depending on the state's own attitude and reading of the right to self-determination. Usually states interpret self-determination as being valid only in its internal form, that is to the extent that it allows participation within the decision-making processes within the boundaries of the sovereign state (Thornberry 1994) and in many cases even this issue continues to be controversial (see Halperin 1992). Thus, overall the status of self-determination as a right in modern international law is extremely hard to assuage and is highly dependent on the political perspective of the respective state. In relation to the application of self-determination to federal states even less information is available that could be construed as existing within the 'international' domain. The definitive case on the subject is a Quebec case that came before the Canadian Supreme Court.[26] This case addressed the dual issues of the right to self-determination of the territory of Quebec from Canada and the determination of its boundaries if the secession were to take place. Whilst providing rich material for comparison of the treatment of territory in federal states, the case came after the

---

[23] With regard to its general status, the following documents provide sources of modern international law by which self-determination can be examined: UN Charter 1945, GAOR 1514 (XV), GAOR 1541 (XV), ICCPR 1966, ICESCR 1966, GAOR 2625 (XXV) and Helsinki Final Act 1975; see generally Castellino (2000a: 22–43).

[24] Joint art. 1, ICCPR and ICESCR 1966.

[25] See, for example, *MiqMaq Tribal Society* v. *Canada* (No. 205/1986) UN Doc. A/47/40, p. 213; *Lubicon Lake Band (Bernard Ominiyak)* v. *Canada* (No. 167/1974) UN Doc. A/45/40, Vol. I, p. 1 (1990).

[26] *Legality of Secession of Quebec case* (1998) *Can. Rep.* 52.

Badinter Commission's deliberation and in that sense could not inform precedent. As a result, it can be argued conclusively that the first question addressed to the Badinter Commission in its entirety could not find a definitive answer within modern international law.

In terms of the status of secession within modern international law the situation is significantly different. The first enunciation of the principle of secession can be traced back to Grotius and *jus secessionis resistendi* or the right to resist and secede in the face of oppression. Grotius was very clear that such a right could be deemed to exist based on the principles of modern *jus gentium*. However, when examined under the lens of UN documents, the right to secession is heavily restricted. Although it is listed as one of the options given by General Assembly Resolution 1541 in facing a 'people' seeking self-determination, it has to be interpreted against the strength of art. 2(7) of the UN Charter and the principle of territorial sovereignty. Many of the later documents that deal with the issue of secession, such as Resolution 2625, have the claw-back phrase that the principle of territorial sovereignty must override any other considerations. The strength of the principle of territorial sovereignty usually means that the issue of secession is foreclosed. The notable exceptions to this are when 'crimes against humanity' take place wherein the entity concerned could argue that it has a right to secession as a manifestation of a right to self-defence (Castellino 2000b). Thus, when seeking the status of the right of secession in modern international law one would have to first qualify it against the notion of territorial sovereignty. Thereafter, an examination of the situation is necessary to determine whether non-secession could result in a violation of the right to self-defence. In terms of a federal state such as Yugoslavia, one applicable precedent would be the situation arising in Bangladesh where former East Pakistan argued that in the face of alleged genocide perpetrated by the Pakistani army it had no choice but to seek help from its neighbour India and secede from the federal state (ibid.: 105).

Finally, in relation to the status of frontiers the principle of territorial sovereignty is once more applicable. Modern international law does not prescribe rules with regard to the location of frontiers. However, as we have seen in the course of this book, the doctrine of *uti possidetis* has been used in colonial contexts to determine the location of post-colonial frontiers. The application of this principle in non-colonial scenarios is highly problematic, and this will be examined in the third section of this chapter with regard to Badinter Opinion No. 3 and the formulations of the so-called Badinter Principles.

Rather than submit the three queries posed above to the commission, Lord Carrington, after soliciting opinions from other participants in the ECCY modified the questions. Thus he stated:

> Serbia considers that those Republics, which have declared or would declare themselves independent or sovereign have *seceded* or would *secede* from the SFRY, which would continue to exist. Other Republics, on the contrary, indicate that there is no question of

secession but the question is one of *disintegration* or *breaking-up* of the SFRY as the result of the concurring will of a number of Republics . . . the six Republics [however believe that they] are to be considered equal successors to the SFRY, without any of them or group of them being able to claim to be the continuation thereof.

Therefore the two questions addressed to the commission were:

1. Does the Serbian population in Croatia and Bosnia-Herzegovina, as one of the constituent peoples of Yugoslavia, have the right to self-determination?

2. Can the internal boundaries between Croatia and Serbia and between Bosnia-Herzegovina and Serbia be regarded as frontiers in terms of public international law?

(Terrett 2000: 143)

In discussing these questions a number of inherent assumptions need to be highlighted. First, by determining that the commission was competent to discuss the issue, Lord Carrington and Serbia essentially believed that the resolution to these issues could come within the paradigm of modern international law. Clearly, having physically and metaphorically crossed the domestic boundaries within the dispute, the question was to be subject to modern international law. This raises questions as to the nature of the proceedings themselves which are beyond the scope of the current inquiry.[27] Second, it sets a precedent for the discussion within an international setting of the norms of self-determination and secession of groups within a federal structure. This suggests that the parties concerned had already tacitly accepted that the state of Federal Yugoslavia had ceased to exist. The importance of this conclusion stems from the fact that if it were still to exist, such a discussion would be in violation of the norms of territorial sovereignty as enshrined in art. 2(7) of the UN Charter. Clearly within the international community at large such a stance would be unacceptable since most sovereign states would be overcome by fear that ethnic or other groups within their own structures might, at some future point, seek to destabilize the state and thereby seek such a solution from an extra-state tribunal.[28] Third, the nature of the questions essentially links the question of self-determination to the rights of peoples and minorities. As stated earlier, modern international law has long resisted the argument that minorities, as a people, have the right to self-determination.[29] This has been primarily interpreted in the preservation of the interests of order and the state system. As a result the rights of national minorities have tended to be classified as separate

---

[27] For the importance of the notion of consent in modern international law, see Bolintineanu (1974).

[28] See especially the reservation by India to art. 1 in <http://www.hri.ca/partners/sahrdc/hrfeatures/HRF26.htm>.

[29] See arts. 1 and 27 of the ICCPR 1966 and the General Comment of the Human Rights Committee on art. 27, available at <http://www.minnesota.edu/un>.

from rights accruing to a 'people' seeking self-determination. However, in addressing the question of self-determination for the Serbian populations within two republics in particular, the commission was basically asked to comment on the link between the two discourses. Fourth, and most crucially in terms of this inquiry, the questions address the fact that the conflict concerned the treatment of territory in modern international law. By focusing on the internal boundaries of the republics and their potential transference to international status, the commission was indirectly asked to comment on the nature of the state and its title to territory. However, this discussion was predicated by the commission's response to the first question. If the commission ruled in favour of the rights of minorities (in this case the Serbian populations in the republics) to self-determination then this might have an impact on the second question as to the current boundaries between the three entities in question.

In terms of the re-phrasing of the questions by Lord Carrington it is instructive to examine the manner in which the questions differed from those initially addressed by Serbia. First, the questions framed by Lord Carrington were clearly targeted while the questions offered by the Federal Presidency were more general. This development is synonymous with the manner in which modern international law often treats questions of territory. Being slow to frame norms around the issue, modern international law proceeds cautiously, fully aware of the precedent-setting nature of these exercises. While the sources of modern international law are perhaps less explicit than within domestic jurisdictions,[30] the precedent-creating potential of such questions would deeply concern international lawyers. Thus, the specificity of the questions asked of the commission goes some way towards negating the fear of the creation of a blanket right to secession and self-determination away from that already existing in modern international law for colonial peoples (see generally Castellino 2000a). Second, in framing the questions the reference to secession has been removed and placed in the preamble, expressed as the Serbian view, the republics believing that the action transpiring was the dissolution of the states. This is significant since it would bring the conflict more within the auspices of modern international law. As originally framed, the question posed by the SFRY with regard to secession would be extremely difficult to tackle. While modern international law would clearly be against the notion of secession *per se*, such action by consent would be treated differently. Indeed, any response to the second question as framed by the SFRY would have to take into account the notion of consent since without consent there would be, in theory, no right to secession within modern international law. Although there have been some exceptions in practice,[31] and as highlighted above, it is possible to make the argument that in

---

[30] See art. 38 of the Statue of the International Court of Justice, as appended to the UN Charter 1945.

[31] For discussion of the situation in Eritrea, see Gayim (1993); for East Timor see Drew, 'The East Timor Popular Consultation: Self-determination Denied' at <http://www.nottingham. ac.uk/law/hrlc/hrnews/july99/DREW.HTM>.

some circumstances secession as an option of self-defence would have to exist,[32] but this view is not widespread. Nonetheless, with international action subsequently taking place in Kosovo the relevance of this particular question endures (Henkin 1999). As for the second part of the original SFRY question relating to the 'conditions' under which such secession can be realized, once again modern international law suggests that, if consensual, the details would need to be agreed between the parties themselves. While providing guiding principles including the need for order, the general principle of inviolability of boundaries, the adequate protection of national minorities *et al.*, modern international law would be unlikely to be prescriptive on the subject. However, with the questions as reframed by Lord Carrington, the commission did not need to rule on the issue generally but were instead asked to focus on the specific issues of the boundaries between Croatia and Serbia and Bosnia-Herzegovina and Serbia.

In terms of the treatment of territory within modern international law the following issues become apparent.

First, how does the action of secession or dissolution affect the application of the doctrine of *uti possidetis*? Second, to what extent can modern international law adjudicate in the midst of a crisis and how appropriate is this intervention when events continue to unfold beyond the control of a legal regime? Finally, what are the factors that need to be taken into account in the dissolution of a territory? These issues will be addressed in the context of the Opinions of the Badinter Commission.

The Opinions of the Badinter Commission

The commission's response to the two questions posed by Lord Carrington was divided into three separate Opinions and by this stage the tone had already moved away from the notion of binding judicial decisions (Terrett 2000: 147). As highlighted above, the reasons for this change could be attributed to the force of events, which made intervention on the behalf of the Yugoslav constitution impossible. In addition, in the light of the imposition of sanctions the findings of the commission were no longer accepted by the parties as binding. Rather than following the model of the judgments emanating from international bodies such as the ICJ, the Opinions were worded tersely and lack definitional clarity. Further, the decisions lack reference to international legal authority and as a result, while the Opinions clearly deal with issues of modern international law, they have met with little recognition within the discipline.[33]

In its first Opinion, the commission sought to define the conditions under which an entity would constitute a state. The ostensible reason for this Opinion was perhaps to consider whether the Serbian populations existing within Croatia and Bosnia-Herzegovina would be entitled to such a right. In addition, a secondary ramification

---

[32] See note 13.
[33] For a host of criticism see Ratner (1996) and Radan (2000).

of such consideration would arguably have a bearing on the issue of boundaries of the state. However, by delivering an Opinion on the nuances of statehood without prefacing its motive for doing so, the commission seemed to suggest that self-determination was essentially about the creation of states although this is merely one of three avenues available in self-determination (Castellino 2000a).

The text of the Opinion reads as follows:

Opinion No. 1
Events in Yugoslavia

1) The Committee considers:
a) that the answer to the question should be based on the principles of public international law which serve to define the conditions on which an entity constitutes a state; that in this respect, the existence or disappearance of the state is a question of fact; that the effects of recognition by other states are purely declaratory;

b) that the state is commonly defined as a community which consists of a territory and a population subject to an organized political authority; that such a state is characterized by sovereignty;

c) that, for the purpose of applying these criteria, the form of internal political organization and the constitutional provisions are mere facts, although it is necessary to take them into consideration in order to determine the Government's way over the population and the territory;

d) that in the case of a federal-type state, which embraces communities that possess a degree of autonomy and, moreover, participate in the exercise of political power within the framework of institutions common to the Federation, the existence of the state implies that the federal organs represent the components of the Federation and wield effective power;

e) that, in compliance with the accepted definition in international law, the expression 'state succession' means the replacement of one state by another in the responsibility for the international relations of territory. This occurs whenever there is a change in the territory of the state. The phenomenon of state succession is governed by the principles of international law, from which the Vienna Conventions of 23 August 1978 and 8 April 1983 have drawn inspiration. In compliance with these principles, the outcome of succession should be equitable, the states concerned being free of terms of settlement and conditions by agreement. Moreover, the peremptory norms of general international law and, in particular, respect for the fundamental rights of the individual and the rights of peoples and minorities, are binding on all the parties to the succession.

2) The Arbitration Committee notes that:
a) – although the SFRY has until now retained its international personality, notably inside international organizations, the Republics have expressed their desire for independence;

b) – The composition and workings of the essential organs of the Federation, be they the Federal Presidency, the Federal Council, the Council of the Republics and the Provinces, the Federal Executive Council, the Constitutional Court or the Federal Army, no longer meet the criteria of participation and representatives inherent in a federal state;

c) – The recourse to force has led to armed conflict between the different elements of the Federation which has caused the death of thousands of people and wrought considerable destruction within a few months. The authorities of the Federation and the Republics have shown themselves to be powerless to enforce respect for the succeeding ceasefire agreements concluded under the auspices of the European Communities or the United Nations Organization.

3) – Consequently, the Arbitration Committee is of the opinion:

– that the Socialist Federal Republic of Yugoslavia is in the process of dissolution;

– that it is incumbent upon the Republics to settle such problems of state succession as may arise from this process in keeping with the principles and rules of international law, with particular regard for human rights and the rights of peoples and minorities;

– that it is up to those Republics that so wish, to work together to form a new association endowed with the democratic institutions of their choice.

Thus, Opinion No. 1 of the Badinter Commission comprised three main sections. The first section concerned the issues the commission considered important to its finding, the second highlighted the issues considered relevant to the findings and the third is the actual opinion of the commission. There are a number of issues in the finding that need to be isolated for the purposes of our current inquiry into the treatment of territory in modern international law and its manifestations in the former Yugoslavia. In the first section the following issues have relevance to our discourse:

1   The principles of modern international law that serve to define the constituents of statehood
2   The issue of the existence or disappearance of a state
3   The definition of a state in modern international law
4   The notion of effective control
5   Issues of state succession.

The actual text of the Opinion suggests that the response is based on 'principles of public international law, which serve to define the conditions on which an entity constitutes a state'. Yet no reference was made to the Montevideo Convention on the Rights and Duties of States 1933, which remains the only authority on the constituents of a state in international law.[34] Secondary sources of modern international law that outline the principles governing statehood are also ignored. This includes the jurisprudence emanating from the *Admissions* case before the ICJ[35] and the *travaux*

---

[34] Montevideo Convention (1933) art. 1 reads: 'The State as a person of international law should possess the following qualifications: (a) a permanent population; (b) a defined territory; (c) government: and (d) capacity to enter into relations with other States.'
[35] *Admissions case*, ICJ Reports (1948) 57.

préparatoires and discussion of the norms of admissions to the United Nations (Simma *et al.* 1994). Thus, despite seeking to base its Opinion on principles of modern international law, no reference has been made to these sources. Instead, consideration is given to the idea that the existence or disappearance of a state is a matter of fact and not law. This is problematic since it is a highly selective, restricted reading of elements of state recognition and its treatment in international legal theory (see Dugard 1987; Crawford 1979). The issue is also complicated by the debate that took place with regard to the recognition of Croatia by Germany, an issue already highlighted. If the issue of 'fact' was beyond question, it need not have led to a difference in opinion regarding the recognition of the new entity among the members of the conference. Instead the Opinion goes on to state that a state is 'commonly defined as a community which consists of a territory and a population subject to an organized political authority [and] that such a state is characterized by sovereignty'. While this reflects aspects of the definition contained in art. 1 of the Montevideo Convention, the richness of the discussion on these issues within modern international law is sacrificed to a mere statement of law which has been found problematic in many cases, not least the *Western Sahara* case.[36] Also clearly, the last criteria identified, namely the characteristic of sovereignty, is predicated on the exercise of this sovereignty being recognized externally. With regard to ascertaining the effectiveness of the federal authorities' control over the territory, the commission makes two salient points: first, that while the form of internal political organization of a state was beyond the scope of modern international law, the notion of effective control was the ultimate test of a government's capabilities and, second, that in the case of a federal state this could be measured by the ability of the state's organ to wield effective power. While it is true that modern international law does not feel competent to determine the type of political organization within states, the discourse of human rights law is increasingly making inroads into this notion. The best demonstration of this is Franck's (1992) reference to an emerging right of democratic governance. Although this cannot be said to be part of customary international law, the growing importance of international human rights law would give some credibility to this argument. With regard to the ability of a state's organs to wield effective power, it needs to be stressed that this is true only in so far as it occurs *de jure*. Should a situation arise where the organs of a federal state wield effective power beyond their territorial demarcation, this would result in violation of modern international law and, therefore, the test of effective control could no longer be considered valid. Finally, unlike its treatment of issues concerning statehood, the commission clearly identifies its sources in dealing with issues of state succession. It identifies the process as being the replacement of one state by another in the responsibility for international relations of a territory, though this must clearly also include the responsibility for internal aspects of governance.

---

[36] ICJ Reports (1975) 12.

The second part of the Opinion deals with issues the Commission felt ought to be taken note of in arriving at its decision. These can be summarized as encompassing three main areas:

1 The republics' desire for independence
2 The inability of essential federal organs to meet the criteria for participation and representation
3 The impotence of these organs to control the destruction occurring in the republics.

This section of the Opinion casts light on the kinds of pressure placed upon the commission. As noted in point 3 above, these discussions were conducted against the backdrop of armed conflict. Yet in the final analysis, these negotiations were only one of a host of other measures taking place concomitant to the process. The difficulties highlighted by this situation are primarily that if an international organ is participating in a process at this level it ought to be empowered by the certainty of its decisions being capable of implementation. If not the work of the commission can merely be used to arm whichever side considers it to be to its advantage. However, the major problem as events unfolded in Yugoslavia was the extent to which emerging regimes could be vested with authority externally in a bid to gain agreement. While this was possible in the context of international politics where different parties could be engaged, modern international law as an institution was less flexible in this regard. Thus, the validity of subjecting an organ of this kind to the vagaries of the situation needs to be questioned.

In delivering its Opinions, the commission seemed overwrought by the evolving considerations and merely ruled that what was transpiring in Yugoslavia was dissolution rather than disintegration or secession. In this sense Opinion No. 1 sought the middle ground between the option of secession as suggested by the FSRY and the option of complete disintegration as suggested by the republics. Rather, it left room for subsequent actions by the republics themselves to determine this issue. Having thus ruled that the dissolution of the state had begun and that subsequent events would need to be examined, it seemed appropriate that the commission chose to withhold its opinion on the questions of internal boundaries and self-determination. In contrast to other international judicial bodies, the commission also did not include any statements on its own procedural criteria for admission.

The second Opinion of the Badinter Commission was delivered on 11 January 1992. It dealt with self-determination in direct response to the Serbian question even though Lord Carrington had modified the original question before transmission to the commission. The opinion was phrased as follows:

Opinion No. 2
Self-determination and the Serb minorities

1. The Committee considers that, whatever the circumstances, the right to self-determination

must not involve changes to existing frontiers at the time of independence (*uti possidetis juris*) except where the states concerned agree otherwise.

2. Where there are one or more groups within a state constituting one or more ethnic, religious or language communities, they have the right to recognition of their identity under international law.

As the Committee emphasized in its Opinion No. 1 of 29th November 1991, published on 7th December, the – now peremptory – norms of international law require states to ensure respect for the rights of minorities. This requirement applies to all the Republics vis-à-vis the minorities on their territory.

The Serbian population in Bosnia-Herzegovina and Croatia must, therefore, be afforded every right accorded to minorities under international convention as well as national and international guarantees consistent with the principles of international law and the provisions of Chapter II of the draft Convention of 4th November 1991, which has been accepted by these Republics.

3. Article 1 of the two 1966 International Covenants on human rights establishes that the principle of the right to self-determination serves to safeguard human rights. By virtue of that right, every individual may choose to belong to whatever ethnic, religious or language community he or she wishes.

In the Committee's view, one possible consequence of this principle might be for the members of the Serbian population in Bosnia-Herzegovina and Croatia to be recognized under agreements between the Republics as having the nationality of their choice, with all the rights and obligations which entails with respect to the states concerned.

4. The Arbitration Committee is, therefore, of the opinion:

(i) that the Serbian population in Bosnia-Herzegovina and Croatia is entitled to all the rights concerned to minorities and ethnic groups under international law and under the provisions of the draft Convention of the Conference on Yugoslavia of 4th November 1991, to which the Republics of Bosnia-Herzegovina and Croatia have undertaken to give effect; and

(ii) that the Republics must afford the members of those minorities and ethnic groups all the human rights and fundamental freedoms recognized in international law, including, where appropriate, the right to choose their nationality.

Opinion No. 2 is thus divided into four sections. The first section cited the doctrine of *uti possidetis juris* to the extent that it restricts self-determination to the existing frontiers unless express consent deems otherwise. The second section articulated the right to recognition of identity for minority groups comprising different ethnicity, professing different faiths or speaking different languages. The commission drew attention to the respect for the rights of minorities as peremptory norms of modern international law applicable to all minorities within the territories of the republics and identified the Serbian population in both Bosnia-Herzegovina and Croatia as such minorities. The third section highlighted the discourse of self-determination as given by the joint article of the International Covenants, suggesting that this right entitles every individual to choose to belong to whatever ethnic, religious or linguistic community he or she wishes. This is read to have the possible consequence that the Serbian populations in both states have the right to chose the nationality of their choice. Finally, the Opinion contained two exhortations: first, that the Serbian population in both states be accorded all the rights of minorities in modern international law and, second, that these rights ought to include, where appropriate, the choice of nationality.

Of the three Opinions, Opinion No. 2 is perhaps the most disappointing in the manner in which it sought to deal with the issues as a legal problem. In the first instance, it needs to be noted that the commission was originally asked to determine whether the Serb population had the right to self-determination. In this sense, as identified earlier, the commission ought to have been measuring whether the Serb populations had the right to either a) integrate with the Federal Presidency; b) form an association with the Federal Presidency; or c) secede from their existing physical arrangement to form an independent state.[37] However, none of these issues were tackled; instead the Opinion weakly discusses whether the population could have a right to choice of nationality where appropriate. Interpreting self-determination as being merely a choice of nationality is clearly an inadequate reading of international law.[38]

Other points of issue covered by this Opinion include:

a   The interpretation of *uti possidetis juris*
b   The discussion on the rights of minorities
c   The expression of a right to identity.

The Opinion identified *uti possidetis juris* as the principle that prevents changes being made to frontiers at the time of independence unless expressly consented to by the parties. On the face of it this appears a reasonable statement since the doctrine clearly seeks to create the preconditions for the perpetuation of order at a time of transition. This debate is revisited in discussing the effect of this doctrine in the so-called Badinter Principles expressed in Opinion No. 3. However, the most pertinent question to be raised at this stage is the appropriateness of applying this doctrine to a situation that did not involve the gaining of independence. Based on its earlier Opinion of 29 November, the commission clearly identified that what was transpiring on the territory of the former Yugoslavia was dissolution rather than disintegration or secession. The application of concepts of 'independence' to a process that involves dissolution is inherently flawed since it involves entities that were voluntarily subsumed within reasserting their right to separateness. This has to be differentiated from a process where entities initially suppressed by a colonial power were in a position to gain 'independence' from that power. An example that demonstrates this better is the

---

[37] As given by GAOR 1541 (XV).
[38] For other literature on self-determination see Cassese (1995), Hannum (1980) and Neuberger (1986).

'velvet divorce' between the Czech Republic and Slovakia. Associated with each other in the state of Czechoslovakia, the two components of the union decided to separate themselves to form two different states. To suggest that one state gained independence from the other would be manifestly inaccurate even if, in actual fact, it enabled Slovakia to gain more representation in terms of public institutions and governmental agencies. This situation would have to be differentiated from colonizing events of the kind seen in Latin America, Africa or Asia. In those circumstances the colonizing power, without the consent of the population at large, attacked and forcibly occupied territories. Decolonization in that context would need to be perceived as 'independence' and differentiated from the process involved in the dissolution of a federal state. Thus, it is in this context that the application of *uti possidetis juris* needs to be questioned (see Opinion No. 3, p. 179).

As regards the discussion on the rights to minorities contained in point two of the Opinion, the applicable minority rights regime needs to be identified. While it is true that the right to respect minorities is fast becoming a norm of peremptory international law, the components of that principle need to be articulated. There is no convention in international human rights law that deals with the rights of minorities, though the declaration passed in 1993 could be seen as providing moral voice to this debate.[39] In addition, emanating from ancient treaties as long ago as 1250,[40] the principle that the few should be protected from the tyranny of the many has been established in the international context. Modern international law for the protection of minorities can be ascertained as resting on art. 27 of the ICCPR 1966 which states:

> In those States in which ethnic, religious or linguistic minorities exist, persons belonging to such minorities shall not be denied the right, in community with the other members of their group, to enjoy their own culture, to profess and practise their own religion, or to use their own language.

Thus the entitlements of minority groups are the rights to enjoy their own culture, profess and practise their own faith or use their own language, either individually or in a collective capacity. It is important to note that art. 27 does not include the right to political participation. Since 1966 the discourse on minority rights has evolved considerably and the work undertaken by organizations such as the Organization for Security and Co-operation in Europe (OSCE) stresses the nature of minority participatory rights.[41] In addition, General Comments emanating from the Human Rights Committee stress a broad reading of art. 27 in terms of its inclusiveness of groups seeking classification as minorities and in terms of the rights entitlements due

---

[39] Declaration on the Rights of Persons Belonging to National or Ethnic, Religious or Linguistic Minorities, G.A. res. 47/135, annex, 47 UN GAOR Supp. (No. 49) at 210, UN Doc. A/47/49 (1993).

[40] For example, the Promise of St Louis 1250, as quoted in Thornberry (1992: 27).

[41] See generally <http://www.osce.org/>.

to members of minorities. In this sense, minority rights protection ought to be seen through the lens of the principle of non-discrimination, wherein minorities, as groups existing within a state, should be entitled to the rights available to all other groups within a state. These rights of non-discrimination are best expressed in international human rights law in the International Convention for the Elimination of All Forms of Racial Discrimination 1965, where race is interpreted broadly (see especially art. 5).

One of the issues not included in the definition and entitlements of minorities is any explicit right to identity (as highlighted in point 2 of the Opinion). While the prohibition against genocide – which seeks to physically wipe out a group based on its identity – is the strongest in human rights law,[42] and a norm of *jus cogens*, notions of cultural genocide akin to the right to an identity have not received much credence in international human rights legislation. The reference of the 'right to identity' as contained in art. 7 of the Child Rights Convention 1990 reveals a rare exception to this trend in international human rights law. However, even in that document the issue pertains to the rights of a child to have a name and nationality (Detrick 1992). Other than that the right to identity is not explicitly discussed within international human rights legal documents since issues such as identity and nationality come within the direct purview of state sovereignty and are, to that extent, heavily guarded by states as functions of their exclusive sovereignty.

The third point in Opinion No. 2 cited the joint art. 1 of the two covenants in raising the issue of self-determination as a guarantor of human rights. Article 1 states:

1.   All peoples have the right of self-determination. By virtue of that right they freely determine their political status and freely pursue their economic, social and cultural development.

2.   All peoples may, for their own ends, freely dispose of their natural wealth and resources without prejudice to any obligations arising out of international economic co-operation, based upon the principle of mutual benefit, and international law. In no case may a people be deprived of its own means of subsistence.

3.   The States Parties to the present Covenant, including those having responsibility for the administration of Non-Self-Governing and Trust Territories, shall promote the realization of the right of self-determination, and shall respect that right, in conformity with the provisions of the Charter of the United Nations.

Clearly framed in the specific context of facilitating independence from colonial rule, this article lays down the foundation for the decolonization process. Building on the

---

[42] The Genocide Convention 1950 provides the starting point, and evidence of the strength of this conviction in human rights law can also be demonstrated by the efforts of the criminal tribunals in Rwanda and Yugoslavia and the setting up of the International Criminal Court; see Schabas (2000 and 2001).

ground laid down by the two UN resolutions in 1960 (GAOR 1514 (XV) and GAOR 1541 (XV)), it seeks to empower peoples under colonial rule with the right to self-governance. Although this right has great relevance beyond the colonial discussion, it remains highly contested in this sphere (Brilmayer 1991). In practice states do not rely on this particular article in seeking to foster norms of self-governance. Rather they tend to interpret this article as referring to the one-off right of colonized entities that seek independent statehood. States fear that to allow use of the article beyond that mandate would lead to secession from within the sovereign state, thereby violating territorial sovereignty. In addition, the implication that the right could involve a choice of nationality is particularly flawed since the conferring of nationality rights comes exclusively within the domain of the relevant state authorities. Besides, the notion that the Serb populations within Bosnia-Herzegovina and Croatia be allowed the choice of Serbian nationality in a context of widespread ethnic cleansing seems highly problematic since it would violate the sovereignty of the territories of Croatia and Bosnia-Herzegovina where these minorities live and also endanger those minorities by identifying their allegiance to a different especially contested sovereign state. Finally, it has to be stressed that the question of self-determination as originally posed to the commission was not answered in its discussion of choice of nationality.

The exhortation of the commission is contained in the fourth point of the Opinion and identifies two essential features. First, that the Serb populations in Croatia and Bosnia-Herzegovina be entitled to the rights of minorities and, second, that this entitlement include access to all the fundamental freedoms and, where possible, the right to nationality of choice. These issues have already been unpacked in the preceding paragraphs although one issue that needs to be highlighted is the difference in entitlements in the rights accruing to minorities and the separate right of self-determination. International legal institutions have been extremely circumspect in linking the discourse of minority rights to that of self-determination, especially in the context of the creation of new states. The fear behind this linkage lies in the potential creation of a continuously available violent process that could only be terminated by the creation of uni-ethnic, uni-religious and uni-linguistic states. This would be against the grain of modern international law and, especially in this context, the linking of the discourse of minority rights to that of self-determination is highly problematic. Thus while discussing the entitlements of the Serbian minorities in Bosnia-Herzegovina and Croatia to assert their rights as minorities within modern international law it is important not to allow doctrinal room for access to the right to self-determination in any form, especially in the context of what was unfolding in the former Yugoslavia at the time. Thus the Opinion overall seems to argue, on the one hand, that the process of *uti possidetis juris* is applicable since what is transpiring is the 'independence' of new states that has to be accommodated within administrative frontiers, yet at the same time it engages the issue of self-determination of a group within the boundaries created by that principle, even if only to ascribe a limited right to nationality.

In delivering Opinion No. 3 on the frontiers question on 17 December 1991, the commission made the following statement:

Opinion No. 3
The Frontiers Question

1. In its Opinion No. 1 of 29th November, published on 7th December, the Committee found that 'the Socialist Federal Republic of Yugoslavia is in the process of breaking up'. Bearing in mind that the Republics of Croatia and Bosnia-Herzegovina, *inter alia*, have sought international recognition as independent states, the Committee is mindful of the fact that its answer to the question before it will necessarily be given in the context of a fluid and changing situation and must therefore be founded on the principles and rules of public international law.

2. The Committee, therefore, takes the view that once the process in the SFRY leads to the creation of one or more independent states, the issue of frontiers, in particular those of the Republics referred to in the question before it, must be resolved in accordance with the following principles:

First – All external frontiers must be respected in line with the principles stated in the United Nations Charter, in the Declaration on Principles of International Law concerning Friendly Relations and Cooperation among States in accordance with the Charter of the United Nations (General Assembly Resolution 2625 (XXV)) and in the Helsinki Final Act, a principle which also underlies Article 11 of the Vienna Convention of 23 August 1978 on the Succession of States in Respect of Treaties.

Second – The boundaries between Croatia and Serbia, between Bosnia-Herzegovina and Serbia and, possibly, other adjacent independent states may not be altered except by agreement freely arrived at.

Third – Except where otherwise agreed, the former boundaries become frontiers protected by international law. This conclusion follows from the principle of respect for the territorial status quo and, in particular, from the principle of *uti possidetis*. *Uti possidetis*, though initially applied in settling decolonisation issues in America and Africa, is today recognized as a general principle, as stated by the International Court of Justice in its Judgment of 22 December 1986 in the case between Burkina Faso and Mali (Frontier Dispute, (1986) Law Reports 554 at 565):

Nevertheless the principle is not a special rule which pertains solely to one specific system of international law. It is a general principle, which is logically connected with the phenomenon of the obtaining of independence, wherever it occurs. Its obvious purpose is to prevent the independence and stability of new states being endangered by fratricidal struggles.

Opinion No. 3 is often referred to as enunciating the so-called 'Badinter Principles' and is the subject of most controversy amongst international legal commentators. For the purposes of analysis, the Opinion can be summarized as consisting of the following principles in the determination of frontiers in the Yugoslavian context:

1   Respect for external frontiers.
2   Alteration of frontiers only by consent.
3   Transfer of former administrative boundaries into international frontiers via the doctrine of *uti possidetis*.

As Pellet, a member of the committee, points out, it laid great emphasis upon the fundamental importance that it attached to the principle in respect of frontiers existing at the moment of independence (*uti possidetis juris*). This point was not only made in Opinion No. 3 but also evoked in Opinion No. 2 when it recalled that, whatever the circumstances, 'the right to self-determination must not involve changes to existing frontiers' (Pellet 1998: 178). Nonetheless, addressing each of the issues in turn the following points need to be made. First, as regards the principles of modern international law on external frontiers, the Opinion clearly states that in international law these frontiers must be respected. In addition to the sources mentioned in the Opinion, the jurisprudence emanating from the ICJ would strongly support this assertion (see Chapter 5). The sanctity of international frontiers is a strongly framed principle of the international system as an extension of the notion of state territorial sovereignty. If this principle were not respected as one of the founding principles of the modern international system the current system of sovereign states would be compromised. The only way in which state sovereignty can be guaranteed is if the exercise of that sovereignty is contained within fixed and recognized boundaries. Failing that, weaker states would be liable to occupation and annexation by stronger states to the detriment of international legal order. As a corollary to this, where alterations are deemed necessary, these have to take place with the express consent of the parties to the alteration. This applies in the international arena for all sovereign states. The real difficulty with the 'Badinter Principles', however, lies in the commission considering that the same applies to the borders of Bosnia-Herzegovina and Croatia. Inasmuch as this is in the interests of order it can be validated. Nonetheless, to ascertain sanctity to existing administrative frontiers as international frontiers and then apply the same rules is highly problematic. This notion, as enunciated in the third principle of this Opinion, suggests that modern international law protects administrative boundaries as international frontiers almost as a matter of right. Were this to be accepted the idea expressed in the second of the principles would be seen to apply to Bosnia-Herzegovina and Croatia. However, a central flaw to this otherwise seamless argument is that the principles at stake with regard to the transfer of international status to administrative boundaries were applied strictly in the context of decolonization. In this sense the difference between decolonization and dissolution must be reiterated. The legal justification given for the third principle by the commission is the findings of the ICJ in the *Burkina Faso/Mali* case of 1986. However, that case pertained to outstanding issues after decolonization, and the two protagonists, Burkina Faso and Mali, were both successor states to colonial regimes that deemed their boundaries without any form of consent. When quoting the case the commission has been extremely selective in excluding the specific reference to decolonization contained in the judgment. The paragraph quoted from the ICJ judgment goes on to state that the purpose of the doctrine is to prevent the independence and stability of new states being endangered by fratricidal struggles

> provoked by the challenging of frontiers following the withdrawal of the administering power.[43]

The situation in Bosnia-Herzegovina and Croatia was clearly not one caused by the withdrawal of an administering power. The difference between the two situations is manifest by the essential difference emanating from a process of dissolution rather than secession. Had the commission ruled that the events unfolding in Yugoslavia amounted to those of secession then the third principle could, arguably, be considered applicable. Even then this validation would be subject to question on account of the difficulty of ascribing the Federal Presidency as an 'administering power' in the same sense as the imperial regime in the *Burkina Faso/Mali* case.[44]

The Implications of the Badinter Discourse on Issues of Territoriality

Although some authors would argue strongly that the importance of the Badinter Opinions for the treatment of territoriality is significant (Pellet 1998, Shaw 1996 and Craven 1995), this view is open to question. The main doubt that remains in reading the Opinions is the extent to which they can be considered accurate renditions and applications of international legal principles (Radan 2000, Ratner 1996). Thus, although they were significant in tackling issues of territoriality in an unfolding crisis, their potential longer term implications need to be conditioned against the backdrop of that crisis and the pressure the commission were under. In addition, due respect needs to be given to the fact that the Opinions were enunciated by a body whose mandate was 'creatively interpreted' in light of the unfolding crisis. Further, the linking of the right of self-determination with that of minority rights in a context of threatened peace and security would make the Opinions at best problematic and therefore unlikely to be accepted by state parties as being universally valid. In this context the assertion that the Opinions (especially Nos. 2 and 3) have long-term ramifications beyond the situation in Yugoslavia needs serious qualification (Pellet 1998). While the Badinter Principles reflect on issues such as the scope of the self-determination principle as applied in particular contexts, the relationship of this principle to the stability of frontiers and, finally, the general role attributable to an international arbitration body in such

---

[43] ICJ Reports (1986) 554 at 557.
[44] These issues are revisited in the final section of this chapter.

circumstances, their final value needs to be gauged against their accuracy and acceptability within modern international law.

The particular resonance of these issues can be seen in widespread increases in situations where violence is being used by groups within states seeking title and territorial rights in the creation of separate identities. This process, usually occurring within post-colonial states, is a phenomenon of which modern international law needs to be cognisant, if it is to play a role in the maintenance of international peace and security based on the principles enunciated in the UN Charter. It is in this context that the Opinions set out by the Badinter Commission are most problematic. With states gravely concerned about the possibility of intra-state conflicts caused by self-determination, it is imperative that modern international law reassess the right to self-determination and its attendant doctrine of *uti possidetis*. Should the Badinter Principles be accepted, federal states would be particularly at risk since they would appear to have ready-made grounds and territorial dimensions by which secession could proceed. These grounds would not necessarily serve the interests of the federal state since in seeking better representation by federalizing it could set in place the very basis of its own demise. This could impact on the will of these states to set up federal structures that might otherwise be considered as encouraging the effective political participation of minorities and regional groups. However, if states fear the added meaning given to internal administrative divisions, these are likely to become issues of contention rather than issues of practicality. Thus if administrative laws are given increased weight as potential international boundary regimes, the protection of minority rights could be seriously compromised.

As stated earlier, the most significant aspect of the Opinions is the issue of the 'Principles'. In this context the most significant ruling was that, 'in cases of federal units of a state gaining independence, the existing internal federal borders of such units are transformed into the international borders of the new state'. For convenience this particular segment of the ruling is hereafter referred to as the 'Badinter Principles'. In criticizing the treatment of issues in these Badinter Principles, Radan (2000: 50) argued that:

> . . . the legal arguments offered by the Badinter Commission for the Badinter Borders Principle are unsound. Furthermore . . . other justifications that have been suggested in support of the principle are without merit and . . . alternative approaches are needed on the matter of determining post-secession international borders.

His criticism of the legal grounds on which the commission relies is predicated on questions he believes ought to be asked of the commission. He identifies four main questions, namely:

1. Does it apply to the borders of new states which result from secession or dissolution or both?

2. Are they justified on the basis of the international legal principle of respect for territorial *status quo*?
3. Are they justified against *uti possidetis*?
4. Does article 5 of the Constitution of the SFRY 1974 justify the conclusion reached . . . [that the Principle applies to the fragmentation of SFRY]

(ibid. p. 51)

The analysis of these questions provides a sound basis for an examination of the legal implications and critique of the Opinions, especially Opinion No. 3. First, as regards the question of the scope of the principles in their applicability to states emanating out of processes of secession or dissolution, the text of the Opinions itself suggests that the principles are only applicable to those states that have resulted from processes of dissolution. However, as Radan argues, when the text is read in conjunction with Opinion No. 11 (16 July 1993) (Terrett 2000: 199–203), it suggests application in the context of secession since Opinion No. 11 gives the date of independence of Croatia and Slovenia as 8 October 1991. Since the 'dissolution of Yugoslavia' is said to have commenced on 29 November 1991 (see Opinion No. 11), the two states that gained independence before the dissolution had begun would have to be deemed as having done so by a process of secession (Radan 2000: 51). As Radan argues, this means that the process being considered under the Badinter Principles would have to also pertain to secession. An argument that perhaps needs to be revisited in the light of this is whether Bosnia-Herzegovina could have been considered as being created out of secession as well. Since the cut-off date for the dissolution is given as 29 November and Bosnia-Herzegovina was considered to have achieved independence only after that date, it might be appropriate to consider it as having come out of the dissolution of Yugoslavia. In terms of modern international law of territory and statehood, this raises an interesting question as to whether the process of secession and dissolution could have occurred at the same time and with regard to the same former state. Clearly on a theoretical level there is little problem with this since the first two states could have seceded and caused the subsequent dissolution of Yugoslavia. The only doubt is how modern Yugoslavia, consisting of Serbia and Montenegro, can be considered to have endured the process of dissolution and kept its international personality intact. Although this question has not gained much attention it is outside the scope of our current inquiry.

In terms of the application of the Badinter Principles outside the immediate context of Yugoslavia, the report prepared by five international legal experts examining the question of Quebec's international border post-secession from Canada is particularly informative. While the study remains hypothetical, it shows the extent to which these principles are followed. Relying heavily on the conclusion arrived at in Opinion No. 3, the Quebec Report suggested that in the event of Quebec's secession from Canada, the present provincial borders would automatically become the international frontiers of the new state. Addressing the question of whether this would be considered as transpiring in the context of secession of Quebec from Canada or from the dissolution of Canada itself the Report stated:

> [I]n the case of secession or dissolution of States, pre-existing administrative boundaries must be maintained to become the borders of the new States and cannot be altered by the threat or use of force, be it on the part of the seceding entity or the State from which it breaks off.[45]

The Canadian government, however, believes that the Badinter Principles apply only to cases of dissolution and not to secession. Thus only if the state of Quebec unilaterally seeks secession from Canada and that leads to the dissolution of the Canadian state will the borders of the new state of Quebec fall under the Badinter Principles (Radan 2000). This argument is made in direct reference to the situation that occurred in the former Yugoslavia. Admittedly, the government's stance finds little support in the Supreme Court case regarding the secession of Quebec.[46] The judgment of the Canadian court identified a few features that are salient to the current discussion on territoriality and the impact of boundaries. First and foremost, it ruled that any secession by Quebec would be illegal not only under the federal law of Canada, but also under modern international law. This would seem to contradict the Opinions of the Badinter Commission since although not deeming secession legal the commission nonetheless engaged the question to the extent of measuring its applicability to the unfolding events (Terrett 2000: 121–7). In examining the impact of this hypothetically illegal situation, the court went on to rule that although illegal, the secession could nonetheless be recognized by the international community. This is significant as it casts more doubt on the decision arrived at in the Opinions that the existence or disappearance of a state was a matter of fact. By admitting that the illegal action of secession could be made legal and acceptable by the action of recognition the Canadian Supreme Court explicitly identified the political factor in the process of creation of new states – an issue that seemed beyond the comprehension of the Badinter Commission (ibid.: 150–2). One of the implications of the Canadian decision that does mirror the Badinter findings closely is with regard to the possible frontiers of Quebec. These would seem to be the current federal structures of Quebec. In this sense the administrative border will have been transformed into an international frontier. However, the implication of this decision is affected by a number of different factors. First, if Quebec could re-negotiate its borders whilst seceding, this action would inevitably affect other Canadian provinces whose territory could be under threat from any such claim. At the other extreme, secession within the existing boundary would suggest that the Cree nation of indigenous peoples that exists within Quebec would also have to be part of the secession

---

[45] Thomas Franck et al L'integrite territoriale du Quebec dans l'hypothese de l'accession a la souverainete, Report prepared for the Quebec Department of International Relations (1992) 2.47; see also <http://www.mri.gouv.qc.ca/la_bibliotheque/territoire/integrite_plan_fr.html>.
[46] [1998] 2 SCR 217; 161 DLR (4th) 385.

from Canada since their territory would be deemed an inviolable part of the new state. The final aspect of the ruling that is pertinent to the comparison with the Badinter findings is that the court deemed that these hypothetical situations would be the result of secession and not dissolution. This increases the prospect that what could have transpired in the former Yugoslavia was an initial secession which subsequently led to dissolution. Clearly in the Canadian case it would be a gross overstatement to suggest dissolution of the Canadian state merely due to the opting out of one of its constituent federal units. Thus after considering the Report, the Canadian Supreme Court validated the Badinter Principles as applying to the hypothetical secession of Quebec even though those principles were framed in response to dissolution. Thus once again the distinction between secession and dissolution remains at the heart of the potential treatment of territory.

In a general overview of the Badinter Opinions, Radan argues two main legal principles that are open to critique. These are arguments pertaining to the principle of territorial integrity and, as identified, the doctrine of *uti possidetis*. With regard to the principles of territorial integrity, numerous sub-doctrines can be identified that recognize respect for the status quo,[47] issues pertaining to the inviolability of boundaries[48] and their stability.[49] However, it must be reiterated that while the principle of territorial integrity is a basic foundation stone of the international system of sovereign states, its application is strictly to states and it does not break down further to the territorial integrity of sub-units within a given state, even if that state happens to be federal. It is a function of territorial integrity in its relationship to state sovereignty that states are allowed to alter or modify existing boundaries within their states. This will not affect international legal principles concerning the sanctity of boundaries and, indeed, were it made to apply to internal situations it would present a gross incursion by international law into the domestic functioning of states. In addition it would politicize the drawing of administrative boundaries within states and could arguably be the precursor to future challenges of such boundaries by disenfranchised self-defined groups with vested interests. As stated simply by Radan, 'the question of stability of internal state borders is not a matter within the ambit of international law' (2000: 69). Radan also makes the related point, in tackling the issue of the doctrine of the stability of borders, that for this to be applicable, the borders would have needed to be established by treaty in the first place (ibid.: 70). However, although it is true that in a vast majority of cases colonial treaties did establish boundaries, insisting that the mere existence of such treaties is the only condition necessary and sufficient for the application of the doctrine of stability of borders would be an overstatement of the importance of colonial treaties. Such weight to colonial treaties would provide colonial

---

[47] Preference of international peace to international justice; for a criticism of this see Mazrui (1975: 12–19).
[48] See the *Temple of Prear Vihear case*, ICJ Reports (1962) 6.
[49] See the *Burkina Faso/Mali* case, ICJ Reports (1986) 554.

boundaries with even greater sanctity and would have them always prevail over boundaries that may be the result of negotiated settlement between parties not leading up to the signing of the treaty. In this context, it needs to be stressed that a treaty is merely written validation of an agreement that exists between parties. Should the parties decide to use other means to validate that agreement, whether by mutual consent, non-challenge, or internal administrative or constitutional laws which justify the location of an uncontested boundary, this would not suggest that those boundaries were any less deserving of the doctrine of the stability of borders.

Radan's argument, however, is predicated on the ruling of Judge Shahabuddeen who stated:

> The principle of stability of boundaries, as it applies to a boundary fixed by agreement, hinges on there being an agreement for the establishment of a boundary; it comes into play only after the existence of such an agreement is established and is directed to giving proper effect to the agreement. It does not operate to bring into existence a boundary agreement where there was none.[50]

This is a good indication of the importance of a boundary regime in determining the existence of an agreement between parties. Whether this needs to be in written form or in the form of a treaty is left unspecified, and thus while it is true that the doctrine of the stability of borders can only be applicable where there is an agreement, this agreement need not necessarily be in treaty form and other means of validating the agreement could be considered applicable proof. The mere presence of a treaty between two powers – colonial or otherwise – to give a boundary full legitimacy and bring it within the mechanism that protects these boundaries (namely the stability of boundaries principle) would be unsatisfactory. Clearly, even a boundary created by a despotic though non-colonial ruler would seem to have greater legitimacy if only for the fact that it was not imposed in ignorance. In addition, Radan's use of Judge Shahabudeen's Judgment seems inappropriate since it ignores the context of that particular case. In the *Libya–Chad* case, which was the matter of dispute, the primary issue the court was concerned with was whether, as Libya believed, no boundary had been agreed between the French and the predecessors to the Libyan state, since the Treaty of Friendship 1955 was not intended to fully demarcate the territory, or whether, as Chad argued, the treaty demarcating the boundary existed and the court needed to, on that basis, confirm the boundary. Thus the case was concerned with the existence and validity of a treaty and Judge Shahabudeen's statement needs to be read in that light. While it might be argued that the Arbitration Commission had the duty to examine treaties before deciding on any other basis – also referred to as the 'First duty argument'[51] – it is clear that the non-existence of a treaty does not

---

[50]   *Case concerning the teritorial dispute (Libyan Arab Jamahiriya* v. *Chad)*, ICJ Reports (1994) 6 at 45.
[51]   *Guatemala-Honduras Arbitration case* (1933) 2 *RIAA* 1307 at 1322.

mean that existing boundaries are not protected under the doctrine of stability of boundaries.

However, in the application of the doctrine of stability of borders to internal Yugoslav borders there can be little doubt that modern international law would not be the appropriate body of law to comment. This would lead to an unequal situation wherein states that were non-federal would have an advantage in being able to define themselves in whatever manner they saw fit, while such demarcation in federal states would be rife with meaning. Besides, the purpose of internal borders is quite different from that performed by international borders and in this sense modern international law would not be the theatre in which to examine the merits or otherwise of these borders.

The second international legal principle against which the Opinions can be measured is the principle of *uti possidetis*. According to Radan, the use of the Roman law principle of *uti possidetis* in international law was initially applied to 'connote a method of determining the territorial changes that occurred as a result of an armed conflict'.[52] Thus, subject to a provision in a peace treaty to the contrary, at the end of a war each state retained as its territory that which it actually possessed at the time hostilities ceased (Berriedale 1944: 622–3). As pointed out earlier, the use of *uti possidetis* in the context of border issues first arose in the early nineteenth century in the context of decolonization of Central and South America from Spanish and Portuguese rule. When applied in that context, the principle required that former colonial borders be given legitimacy as international frontiers of newly independent states (see Chapter 3). As also examined earlier, there were at the time, two versions of the *uti possidetis* principle. By *uti possidetis juris*, borders were defined according to legal rights of possession based upon legal documentation of the former colonial power at the time of independence. By *uti possidetis de facto*, however, borders were defined by territory actually possessed and administered by the former colonial unit at the time of independence, irrespective of the legal definition of former colonial borders (Neuberger 1986: 1–46).

In applying the doctrine to Yugoslavia, two main issues need to be raised. First, in the initial application of *uti possidetis* as well as subsequent applications in the decolonization process, hostilities had ceased and there were recognizable governments on each side of a contested border upon which the doctrine was considered applicable. This was clearly not the case in the dissolving Yugoslavia where different groups within the borders of the republic were seeking re-alignment of boundaries. The significance of the difference between colonial withdrawal and dissolution based upon ethnicity is also extremely relevant in this context. In the case of decolonization, power was handed over to a government-in-waiting and it was the responsibility of this government-in-waiting to protect the borders inherited internally, whilst being guaranteed external protection. However, the dissolution of the former Yugoslavia

---

[52] *Case concerning the territorial dispute (Libyan Arab Jamahiriya v. Chad)*, ICJ Reports (1994) 6 at 84 (sep. op. of Judge Ajibola).

was already accompanied by fragmentation[53] and this recital of ancient doctrine was unlikely to prevent further destruction of life and property. Thus, while in the past such a situation would be allowed to resolve itself with loss of life accompanying it, in the modern sense it was not allowed to resolve itself, but there was loss of life in any case. What made the modern approach less useful than the previous one was that the borders finally determined in Yugoslavia were validated by reliance on a doctrine that had developed in a different context with, at least initially, the consent of the parties to those conflicts.

A second issue of equal importance was that the doctrine of *uti possidetis* at the time of first application in international law did not provide clear guidance as to whether the *de facto* or *de jure* lines were sanctified (as discussed in Chapter 1). Although the Brazilians insisted on a *de facto* application, as the doctrine was codified, precedence was given to *de jure* application. This in itself is not an issue since it could be argued that the legal status of the territory ought to be given higher relevance than a situation where the territory could have been captured and administered by force. However, its relevance in the context of both post-colonial situations and the situation in the former Yugoslavia concerns that issue of the ascription to higher authority to which the *uti possidetis juris* referred. In the case of decolonization, de jure often referred to lines drawn on a map by a colonial ruler with no effort to ascertain the location of tribes and peoples. In Yugoslavia this application pertained to a reality that existed at the creation of the state of Yugoslavia by President Tito in 1963. Since then there had been considerable movement of peoples within the state and inter-marriages which had resulted in hybrid identities being created within the historical boundaries of each republic. To rely in a conflict essentially based on ethnicity on an ethnic map that existed at the birth of the state and to justify this against the doctrine of *uti possidetis* was therefore bound to be flawed.

A third basis to justify the applicability of *uti possidetis* to Yugoslavia is through the consent of the parties to the conflict (Shaw 1996: 84–7, 106–9; see also Kaikobad 1983: 134–6). However, Radan provides an interesting analysis of this issue, attacking the argument regarding fragmentation of Yugoslavia as being akin to decolonization on the claimed ground that it was consensual. The claim put forward by some authors is that the republics themselves had agreed to the use of *uti possidetis* and in this sense the Badinter Commission merely gave effect to their wishes. However, on examining this closely Radan suggests that:

> . . . the invoking of the principle was based on a statement made by a representative of the chairman of the EC Conference on Yugoslavia following a meeting which was attended by the Presidents of Serbia and Croatia and the Defence Minister of the SFRY at the Hague on 4th October 1991.

(2000: 64)

---

[53] See the *Burkina Faso/Mali case*, ICJ Reports (1986) 554.

This Hague Statement is meant to have postulated that the parties to the dispute had reached agreement to resolve it by peaceful means (Terrett 2000: 119–29). With this in mind a twin-track policy was at work – one dealing with military aspects on the ground while the other sought to clarify the political situation. It was for this particular political solution that a loose framework of three principles was agreed. These three principles pertained to:

1. Creation of a loose alliance of sovereign or independent republics.
2. Adequate arrangements for the protection of minorities and the promotion of human rights.
3. No unilateral changes to borders.

(as quoted in Radan 2000: 64)

As pointed out by Radan, the Hague Statement was made by the EC representative who chaired that particular meeting and was not, as such, a negotiated document that had been formally executed by the parties. If this were a treaty of modern international law it would not have been binding upon the parties since they did not negotiate it. In fact, the meeting at which the Hague Statement was passed was not even attended by representatives of Slovenia, Bosnia-Herzegovina, Montenegro and Macedonia (ibid.: 65). Thus, as a statement of a self-governing principle that would cover the region it was inappropriately arrived at. Most of these 'principles' were, however, contained in the Carrington Draft Convention signed by five of the republics on 18 October 1991, though Serbia refused to sign. Radan argues that it is this statement that is at the heart of the Badinter Commission's belief that the doctrine of inviolability of borders was a principle that the republics had proclaimed applicable to themselves. However, the idea that the Hague Statement was a starting point for consensus between the republics has to be refuted. For a start, if the document is taken as a whole, its legal validity could not extend beyond December 1991 since by that time as many as four of the Republics had made independent applications for international recognition to the EC. This suggests that the first principle contained in the Hague Statement was no longer considered valid by a significant cohort of the parties, enabling it as a document to be subject to invalidity under the fundamental change of circumstances rule given by art. 62 of the 1969 Vienna Convention.[54] With this central requirement defeated, the other two principles would also have to be questioned in this materially changed circumstance. While it cannot be argued that the first condition, that is a loose alliance, was a prerequisite for the other two conditions (especially since human rights norms and protection of minorities are fast achieving status as norms of *jus cogens*) the validity of the other two principles would have to be questioned in the context of the

---

[54] Article 62, Vienna Convention on the Laws Governing Treaties, 1969 states: 'A fundamental change of circumstances which has occurred with regard to those existing at the time of the conclusion of a treaty, and which was not foreseen by the Parties, may not be invoked as a ground for terminating or withdrawing from the treaty.'

first stated principle being categorically defeated. As far as the inviolability of borders is concerned, Radan concludes that 'there was no basis to argue that the Yugoslav republics had adopted the principle of *uti possidetis juris*' (ibid.).

Conclusions

Thus the Badinter Opinions, for the many reasons stated above, cannot be seen to have provided accurate treatment of the issue of territoriality in modern international law. There is an essential difference between an administering power in a colonial sense and situations such as the dissolution of a federal state such as Yugoslavia, and the manner in which the international legal principles were applied to the latter case arguably provided significant grounds for legal challenge. In addition, further extension of the doctrine of *uti possidetis* to a situation not pertaining to the withdrawal of a colonial power is dubious despite it being established as a principle of law of general scope.[55] But perhaps the most controversial treatment of international law of territory was in the manner in which the commission readily extended the doctrine of the stability of international frontiers to the internal administrative frontiers of the former Yugoslavia. While it is true that *uti possidetis* upgraded colonial frontiers into international frontiers,[56] its application in those cases was flawed and its extrapolation in this modern situation is only more problematic. Also, in terms of interpretation of modern international law, overt reliance on case law is inappropriate. The significance of case law needs to be tempered against the culture of international law itself. The fact that the discourse deals with such a diversity of issues and cultures suggests that case law cannot be binding to the same extent that it might be in domestic jurisdictions. This is the prime motivation for art. 38 of the Statute of the ICJ, which when discussing sources of modern international law ranks other sources such as treaties, international custom and general principles above case law (Akehurst 1974–5: 273). The implications of this, while not necessarily suggesting that the sources of modern international law are hierarchical, is that case law does not necessarily have as much legal force as a treaty even though it has persuasive merit. This also further substantiates the doctrine of 'first duty argument' which suggests that treaties as a codified part of international law ought to be examined first. Thus, when studying the *Burkina Faso/Mali* case it could be argued that the specificity of the judgment only applies to the dispute over that particular border and would not even apply to different borders of the same two disputants even though of great persuasive merit. When extrapolated further this suggests that the precedent-creating force of such a judgment is extremely restricted. A brief examination of arts. 38 and 59 of the ICJ Statute are worth reiterating to this effect.

---

[55] *Burkina Faso/Mali case*, ICJ Reports (1986) 554 at 565.
[56] Ibid. at 566.

Article 38 states:

1. The Court, whose function it is to decide in accordance with international law such disputes as are submitted to it, shall apply:

    (a) International conventions, whether general or particular, establishing rules expressly recognised by the contesting States;

    (b) International custom, as evidence of a general practice accepted as law;

    (c) The general principles of law recognised by civilised nations;

    (d) Subject to the provisions of Article 59, judicial decisions and the teachings of the most highly qualified publicists of the various nations, as subsidiary means for the determination of the rules of law.

2. This provision shall not prejudice the power of the Court to decide a case *ex aequo et bono*, if the parties agree thereto.

Article 38 therefore seems to make very clear that the decisions of the court will be used as a subsidiary means when being considered as a source of law. In addition, the provisions of art. 38(d) are subject to art. 59 which reads as follows:

The decision of the Court has no binding force except between the parties and in respect of that particular case.

Thus, keeping in mind these principles, the court's reliance on the *Burkina Faso/Mali* case as expressing a definitive norm of *uti possidetis* would be problematic for the following reasons:

1   The judgment in that case was only binding on the two parties to the extent of the problem first addressed to the court. It would not necessarily be binding as a principle to any other boundary that they might subsequently dispute, even though it might be of great persuasive value.

2   The parties in their *Special Compromis* address the issue of the doctrine. The significance of this fact is that rather than beginning to examine the principle as a general rule, the court was called upon by the parties to apply it to this case having already accepted its relevance by mutual consent. Thus having been called to apply it, it would be an overstatement to suggest that a general rule could flow out of these proceedings.

Thus relying on the *Burkina Faso/Mali* case to apply *uti possidetis* to the former Yugoslavia is problematic since

Nothing in the decision of the Frontier Dispute Case suggests that the principle of *uti possidetis* applies to cases of secession from internationally recognised states.

(Craven 1995: 388)

In addition, it can be stated emphatically in view of the above analysis that the tenor of the Opinions in general seems to treat the dissolution of the former Yugoslavia as a case akin to decolonization. However, as Torres Bernardez suggests:

> As a general principle of international law the *uti possidetis juris* rule is simply not concerned with the question of the definition of title to territory and boundaries in such types of succession as transfer of a territory of a State, separation from a State, dissolution of a State, [and] uniting of States.
>
> (1994: 420, 434)

In addition, the differences between secession, dissolution and decolonization are not to be underestimated and in this sense the application to one context of a rigid doctrine framed in another is highly problematic. A number of serious distinctions can be made between the process of dissolution and the situation pertaining to post-colonial countries. First, colonial countries[57] were traditionally described as being geographically removed from the 'Metropolitan State'. In this sense the withdrawal of a colonial power would leave a political vacuum unless new, albeit temporary, structures were firmly in place. Even where these structures were in place they would be relatively inexperienced in their new roles of statecraft. Second, with decolonization the process of transition of power was not always undertaken on a democratically ascertained basis. Rather, since colonialism did not allow for the grooming of appropriate successors, transition of power was made on the basis of the passage of the state machinery to the person/persons/party at the centre of the liberation struggle (Jackson 1992: 1; Grovogui 1996). In this sense there were likely to be groups within the state, usually national minorities, who felt unconsulted in the process and who might try as a result to disrupt the new fledgling state. Third, to equate the fragmentation of a federal state to the activity of decolonization merely for its impact on order would be to reduce the decolonization process to its lowest potential denominator: as a potential threat to international peace and stability. Thus, it is argued that while the break-up of Yugoslavia is in no way being classed as decolonization, to conceive of it as being similar and thereby apply the principle of *uti possidetis* would be unfair.

In addition to this, as established earlier, in Latin America and Africa the function of *uti possidetis juris* was to provide a mutually agreeable means of resolving disputes that were fundamentally different from those that arose in the context of secession of republics from the SFRY. When the principle of *uti possidetis juris* was applied in the former contexts there was no dispute that the former colonial borders would be future international borders. The principle of *uti possidetis juris* was also later applied in other arbitration processes to resolve differences between neighbouring states that

---

[57] According to ordinary usage 'colony' means a territory which a state has made legally dependent without conferring the same legal status upon the indigenous population as upon the population of its own territory; see Kunig in Wolfrum, R. *United Nations: Law, Politics and Practice* (1995: 390).

could not agree on the exact location of colonial borderlines (Shaw 1996: 98–105). However, this situation was not pertinent to the dissolution of the SFRY. The boundaries of the republics were not disputed and were clearly delineated and well documented. The disputes, rather than being about territory, in fact concerned identity. And the question posed at the time of dissolution with regard to the title of the territory was whether the possession of an identity different to the one that was in the majority was justification enough for a given territory to opt for merger with another territory in which the issue of being a minority would not arise. The ostensible justification for such a process was concern that minorities, being vulnerable because of their different and usually problematic identity in the context of the republic from which they wished to be drawn away, would be better protected by becoming part of a state in which they were not such a minority and thus the entire region of the former Yugoslavia would be reconstituted as mono-ethnic states. The danger of this approach is inherent since not all minorities are territorially based. However, in terms of the difference between cases of decolonization and the dissolution of the SFRY, the former could be classed as disputes over territory since the boundaries pre-set by colonizers were prevented from being renegotiated, while the latter was arguably a dispute over the ramifications of identity for territory. Besides, the decolonization process had largely forestalled the onset of ethnically or otherwise induced violence in policing boundaries. This did not prevent violence (notably on the India–Pakistan border where as many as a million people are estimated to have been killed in the crossing and meeting of the two main religious populations fleeing their respective countries – Mahajan 1999 and Rushdie 1980), though to a large extent it did manage to contain it.

It is also instructive that in determining the boundary issue in the SFRY, no reason as such was given for the maintenance of what have subsequently proved in some instances to be untenable boundaries, other than that the use of force to change them was unacceptable. This error of judgement was pointed out by Lord Owen, former Co-Chairman, Steering Committee of the International Conference on Former Yugoslavia:

> The refusal to make these borders negotiable greatly hampered the EC's attempt at crisis management in July and August 1991 and subsequently put all peacemaking from September 1991 onwards within a straitjacket that greatly inhibited compromises between the parties in the dispute.
>
> (Owen 1995: 33)

For Shaw, the principle of *uti possidetis* as applied by the Badinter Commission was perfectly acceptable. Shaw argued that the need to minimize threats to peace and security both internal and external, and the overarching need to provide firm territorial basis to fledgling states override criticism of the rigidity of the doctrine (1996: 111). While this argument is reflected in the ethos of the *Burkina Faso/Mali* case it could be argued that the provision of short-term order that is likely to fail in the accommodation of specific disenfranchised groups is always liable to come under threat at later stages in the life of a territorial state or, worse still, to affect the medium and longer term development of the territorial state.

In this context some of the underlying assumptions with regard to the idea of short-term order in such situations need to be questioned. The first is the assumption inherent in the application of doctrines in the interests of order in situations such as the former Yugoslavia. To suggest that application of this package of doctrines, whether the doctrine of *uti possidetis*, stability of boundaries or the inviolability of boundaries, minimized and contained the conflict would be grossly inaccurate (Owen 1995: 33). As we saw earlier in Chapter 3, even in their original application the doctrines did not contain wars over territory, which remained numerous in Latin America. Radan (2000: 68) suggests it was these wars that eventually 'resolved' the borders in Latin America and not the principle of *uti possidetis*. He extends this argument to Africa where he suggests that the Katanga crisis (1960–63) (Gerard-Libois 1966), Biafra (1967–79) (Post 1968), Eritrea (1974–93) (Gayim 1993) and the ongoing secession involving Southern Sudan from Sudan (Heraclides 1990) provide compelling evidence of the difficulty of implementing the sentiments of the 1964 Cairo Declaration on the ground. While this is valid criticism, international lawyers tend to argue that this situation is relatively constrained, in contrast to the potential havoc that could be wreaked was there no principle such as *uti possidetis*. However, while the prevalence of secessionist conflicts may be restricted to those above, the internal strife within states as groups try to re-establish themselves and renegotiate their own identities vis-à-vis the state they find themselves in has yielded much internal unrest and genocidal tendencies.[58] Also, this is independent of border conflicts (for example Somalia–Ethiopia, Nigeria–Cameroon, Ethiopia–Eritrea) and neo-colonial struggles such as that of Western Sahara. Thus there would seem to be an element of doubt at the very least in the allegation that the doctrine of *uti possidetis* provides a means for minimizing the destabilization of order. As is always the case with such analysis though, a situation where the doctrine did not exist and where borders were allowed to be negotiated by force or otherwise at times of transition such as colonial abdication is impossible to envisage.

The fact remains, however, that when arguing that the doctrine has been a positive factor in the promotion of order, further examination is required to ascertain the precise extent to which this is true. Were it proved, as argued by some, that this claim is dubiously founded (Radan 2000: 72), then it presents itself merely as another tool with which to seek maintenance of order during times of transition and not the main or most desirable one as some authors and the Badinter Commission have concluded. A more problematic claim made about the use of the package of doctrines in the SFRY was that it

> not only failed to preclude or minimise violence in the secession of Slovenia and Croatia, and later in Bosnia-Herzegovina and Macedonia, but served to prolong it.
>
> (ibid.: 71)

---

[58] Most notably in Rwanda and Burundi, see Schabas (2000).

The premise of this allegation is that the maintenance of federal boundaries as inviolable international boundaries 'where a large proportion of the population rejects them, results in the international community being required to support a war of conquest in order to maintain such borders' (Hayden 1998: 70, quoted in Radan 2000). This statement has unfortunately proved especially true in Kosovo where, using the Badinter Principles with regard to the gravity of internal boundaries, a *prima facie* case could be said to be emerging for the secession of the region from Yugoslavia on similar grounds to that used by the other republics. If a federal state can break up legally into republics with the same borders as when they were components of that federal state, why is it that autonomous regions within a non-federal state cannot be accorded similar rights? If there are reasons for this they have not been made clear enough and the reliance on boundaries and the ascription to them of such gravity is always likely to leave open disintegration along these designated lines. Were this to result, then it could be argued that the concept of *uti possidetis*, rather than supporting the need for order, sows the seeds in the medium and long run for greater disorder. That argument is supported by the fact that the enforcement of rigid borders in a situation such as the dissolution of Yugoslavia could only result in more forced expulsions as populations are compelled to realign themselves vis-à-vis new rigid international borders that have suddenly taken on greater significance than originally envisaged. The consequences of such a population transfer can be seen in the disorder that followed the transfer of Muslims and Hindus between India and Pakistan during partition. While the doctrine of *uti possidetis* could not be applied there since there was no 'federal' colonial state, this example highlights the dangers posed by the combination of redefining a formerly multinational state with regard to certain fixed factors and then requiring that the new border that comes within it will be rigid to that populations' need to realign themselves to suit the new order. This presents a classic reversal of the principle enunciated by Judge Dillard in the *Western Sahara* case regarding the fate of the people vis-à-vis that of the territory.

A second underlying assumption in the package of doctrines concerning territoriality and their modern application is that they establish 'acceptable' borders. This argument is essentially that the doctrine of *uti possidetis* is useful since its purpose is to

> minimise threats to peace and security, whether internal, regional or international, by establishing an acceptable rule of the appropriate territorial framework for the creation of new States and thus entrenching at least, territorial stability at that critical moment.
>
> (Shaw 1996: 111)

Shaw continues that since the primary need for order is recognized, the principle should be applicable beyond purely colonial contexts to break-ups of territory outside this limited situation. Without questioning whether such a principle is indeed applicable outside the colonial context, one central feature that is vital to the understanding of *uti possidetis* is that it can only create order as long as the boundaries being made unchangeable are viable or 'acceptable' in the first place. International law does allow changes to boundaries as long as the consent of the state parties can be assuaged, but the primary problem with this at a time of transition, as was seen in the Yugoslav break-up, is that it is not always possible to determine the entities of whom consent should be requested. Therefore insisting on a blanket rule about the inviolability of boundaries to prevent unrest, on the understanding that as matters settle down the boundary issue can be resolved through negotiation, proved unworkable and as a result the boundaries that were initially unacceptable came under further pressure. In addition, minority groups left within the boundaries of the republics were greatly endangered by the genocidal tendencies stirred up by a war concerning the redefinition of identities and its attendant territorial issues. Radan's criticism of the idea of 'acceptability' in terms of the boundaries is that this 'acceptability' was geared more towards the international community than the people on the ground. This sentiment is echoed in the criticism by former Tanzanian President Nyerere of the OAU's increasing emphasis on the principle of inviolability of borders during African decolonization. He argued that this principle should be given less sanctity than peace and justice in Africa (Radan 2000: 71). However, the only other dissident voices on this subject in the OAU were those of Somalia and Morocco, both of which maintained and still maintain irredentist claims to territory around them (see generally Neuberger 1986).

A third underlying assumption of the doctrine of *uti* possidetis and its application in situations such as the dissolution of former Yugoslavia stems from its inability to provide solutions to non-federal states (Radan 2000: 75). This argument, already raised above with regard to Kosovo, questions why a principle of modern international law that is considered so vital to the maintenance of international peace and stability is only applicable to federal states and provides no solutions to non-federal states which might face a secessionist movement.[59] As Radan points out, the long-term significance of Opinion No. 2 is that states are unlikely to agree to federate or decentralize their state structure since they would then run the risk of setting up the pre-conditions for future secession. This development is particularly disappointing since it further restricts the scope for the protection of minority rights within modern international law. Since in international law minorities cannot be considered a 'people' in the classical sense of the word, they are not directly entitled to the right of self-determination (Thornberry 1992: 214–18). However, they are increasingly being encouraged to seek participation within states. One of the claims made by minority rights groups in negotiations with states that fail to represent them is that they be allowed certain restricted autonomy.[60] In this way they can participate politically in the running of their own affairs within the political life of the state. The most dangerous aspect of the ramifications of the Badinter Opinions is that this process might be hindered as states realize that the

---

[59] For a general reading on actions in Kosovo, see Henkin *et al.* (1999) and also Murphy (2000).
[60] For a general overview of the Inuit in Canada, see 'Indian and Northern Affairs Canada', <http://www.inac.gc.ca/pubs/information/info.16.html>.

granting of any manner of autonomy inevitably involves definable territorial boundary limits that could potentially harm their state integrity. As a result minority groups could become locked into a doctrinal position where they cannot achieve autonomy within the state, nor can they seek secession.

A final reason for rejection of the Badinter Principles concerns the fact that internal boundaries were not construed as international boundaries (Radan 2000: 74). This argument has great merit since the function of the boundary line needs to be ultimately focused upon if its significance is to change. Within modern international law there are two specific analogies that support an argument for the re-examination of the purpose of a boundary in determining its current status. The first analogy lies in the principle of reliance on *travaux préparatoires* of treaties when seeking to examine their interpretation.[61] The underlying notion behind this principle is that to properly interpret a treaty that has been agreed, it is imperative to understand not only the words but also the aims and principles of its drafters so as to follow the letter as well as spirit of the law created. This principle could be extrapolated to suggest that if the status of a boundary was to be changed, it is imperative that those in favour of this change of status examine its primary and basic purpose before ascertaining whether the change would be appropriate. Many internal boundaries rather than demarcating territory on an ethnic basis were merely lines of convenience drawn at a specific time in history to suit a given power. Besides the essential purpose of the boundary, there is the related issue that if the boundary was not enforced as a strict division between people it was likely to be porous and as a result even if it had initially been drawn on an ethnic basis, the porosity would soon unseat this strict division.

A second principle of international law that can be brought to bear on the simple transfer of the status of a boundary is the intertemporal rule. This much abused rule, as discussed earlier (see Chapter 3), suggests that any given event or law ought to be judged against the prevailing standards at the time and should not be measured against modern standards by which it could be deemed incorrect. This rule protects the action of colonialism as occurring in a context where the conquest of overseas territory was not illegal. It is this same rule that could now be applied to suggest that the status of a boundary at formation would need to be measured against its particular function at the time of its creation rather than subjecting it to change under present conditions. There is no evidence to suggest that the Badinter Commission attempted to do this. Rather, concerned with the need to enforce order in the short-term, it merely sought to provide a modern-day basis by which the precondition of territoriality could be added to the thrust of order.

---

[61] Article 32 of the Vienna Convention on the Laws of Treaties 1969 states: 'Recourse may be had to supplementary means of interpretation, including the preparatory work of the treaty and the circumstances of its conclusion, in order to confirm the meaning resulting from the application of article 31, [interpretation of treaties] or to determine the meaning when the interpretation according to article 31: (a) leaves the meaning ambiguous or obscure; or (b) leads to a result which is manifestly absurd or unreasonable.'

As stated in the *Dubai–Sharjah arbitration*:

> One cannot attribute the same value to a boundary which has been settled under a treaty, or as a result of an arbitral or judicial proceeding, in which independent interested Parties have had full opportunity to present their arguments, as to a boundary which has been established by way of an administrative decision emanating from an authority which could have failed to take account of the Parties' views and arising from a situation of inherent inequality. In the first hypothesis, except in the case of nullity, the principles of *pacta sunt servanda* or of *res judicata* could be invoked to prevent the boundary so settled being called into question. In the second hypothesis, the boundary would have been established in the majority of cases, in the interests of the administering authority, on the basis other than legal criteria, and according to the needs of a particular political or economic context.[62]

In terms of Yugoslavia, its borders were established after the Second World War and were never intended to be anything but administrative divisions between the republics.[63] Clearly, there was a historical basis for the establishment of the republics and the autonomous regions to forge one federal state. However, had the notion of secession been factored in at the outset of the federal state, the lines might have been drawn differently (Radan 2000: 74). But as a result of the Badinter Opinions, these lines, initially drawn to facilitate decentralization and administration, took on a significance that they perhaps never deserved. Rather, the transfer of international status to these boundaries is clearly 'simplistic and inflexible' (ibid.: 75) and while the dual principles of order and protection of minority rights, both contained in the Opinions, need to be emphasized and validated, blind application of the doctrine of *uti possidetis* is clearly flawed. Application of the doctrine in its current form reduces complex questions of national allegiance and intricate layers of national identity to a simple problem of line drawing in the ostensible interest of order, while failing to recognize the potential harm that could result in the maintenance of unjust unstable order.

---

[62] *Dubai–Sharjah arbitration* (1981) 91 ILR 543 at 579.

[63] 'Iz govora Generalnog Sekretara KPJ JB Tita na osnivackom kpngresu KP Srbije', 8 May 1945, in Branko, Petranovic and Momcilo, Zecevic (eds) *Jogoslovenski Federalizam: Ideje I Stvarnost, Tematska Zbirka Dokumenta*. Drugi tom, *1943–1986* (1987): 129 and 158, as quoted in Radan (2000: 74 footnote 134).

7 The Treatment of Territory of Indigenous Peoples in International Law

Jérémie Gilbert
Candidate Ph.D., Irish Centre for Human Rights, NUI, Galway, Ireland

The history of indigenous peoples is a bloody and unfinished account of a fight to protect their lands against invaders. Since indigenous peoples' experience with international law has had, and still has, much more to do with theories of dispossession, at first glance it might seem quite ironic and paradoxical to include a chapter concerning indigenous peoples in a book dedicated to theories of acquisition in international law. Since the early developments of international law, indigenous peoples have been victims of specific interpretations of legal doctrines of acquisition of land. The making of treaties and concepts of *terra nullius* and displacement were the classical ways of dispossession, whereby indigenous territories were 'legitimately' acquired. The position of indigenous peoples in today's society is mostly a consequence of the famous doctrine of the 'three Cs', civilization, Christianization and commerce, for which international law, as the legal instrument of colonial conquest, was largely culpable. Today the position of indigenous peoples can be subsumed in one idea: they are the first inhabitants of lands they are not allowed to own or use. Their situation is an illustration of the modern development of theories concerning acquisition of land. In response to the development of anti-racist legislations and the rejection of colonialist theories, states have developed an arsenal of legal theories legitimizing acquisition of indigenous peoples' territory. In this evolution legal discourse has been an important playground for the development of theories of acquisition versus recognition and protection of fundamental rights, in which indigenous peoples' rights is a growing area.

In spite of the fact that the term 'indigenous peoples' is used in international law and generally in literature, the definition is not yet universally resolved (the term 'peoples' in international law also evades definition).[1] However, to recognize the importance of land rights within the indigenous peoples' discourse, it is vital to focus on the question of who indigenous peoples are. From a legal perspective, the

---

[1] For an informed discussion on those issues, see Makkonen (2000).

199

term 'indigenous peoples' may refer to different notions following the regional understanding of such a concept.[2] Although the UN system is elaborate,[3] there is no clear definition of the term 'indigenous peoples'. The definition proposed by Cobo in his *Study of the Discrimination against Indigenous Peoples* is usually accepted as authoritative.[4] The definition proposed is a mix between 'objective' criteria, such as 'historical continuity', and 'subjective' factors including self-definition. Three criteria seem to be fundamental to this definition. First, indigenous peoples are descendants of original inhabitants of territories since colonized by foreigners with culture, language, ancestry and occupation of land all constitutive evidence of continuity. Second, they have distinct cultures, which set them apart from the dominant society. And, third, they have a strong sense of self-identity.[5]

In this context land has to be accepted as a vital element of indigenous culture.[6] Thus, the link between land and indigenous peoples is the definitive factor that distinguishes them from other populations. To understand the basic features that make different indigenous cultures, we must understand the crucial importance of the land rights issue. The misunderstanding of indigenous peoples' relationship with their homelands by non-indigenous societies is a key factor inherent in the threat of 'western' legal systems to indigenous survival. Although this relationship is based on the need to find resources, the precise characteristic of the relationship is deeper and not restricted to the physical element.[7] In his definition, UN Special Rapporteur Cobo states:

[2] See Russel (1986) and also Declaration on the Rights of Asian Indigenous Peoples, adopted at the Asian Indigenous Peoples Pact General Assembly Meeting, Chiangmai, Thailand, 18–23 May 1993, in *APJHRL* 1 (2000) 165–8.

[3] For a review of the UN system on indigenous peoples, see HCHR, Fact Sheet No. 9 (Rev. 1), *The Rights of Indigenous Peoples*, Programme of Activities for the International Decade of the World's Indigenous Peoples (1995–2004), General Assembly Resolution 50/157 of December 1995, Annex.

[4] The Sub-Commission called it 'a reference work of definitive usefulness' and invited the Working Group to rely on it; see Sub-Commission Res. 1985/22, para. 4(a).

[5] More recently, the Special Rapporteur Erica-Irene A. Daes has defined indigenous peoples on the following criteria: priority in time, voluntary perpetuation of their cultural distinctiveness, self-identification as indigenous and experience of subjugations, marginalization, dispossession, exclusion and discrimination by the dominant society; Sub-Commission on the Promotion and Protection of Human Rights, 19 July 2000, UN Doc. E/CN.4/Sub.2/2000/10.

[6] Rouland describes the territorial issue as the 'anchorage' of the right to be different for indigenous peoples ('L'ancrage du droit a la difference: les droits territoriaux'); Rouland *et al.* (1996: 468).

[7] In most of the indigenous cultures the land is called 'Mother Earth'; 'they do not own the land but the land (the "Mother Earth") owns them and generates them as sons'; Rouland *et al.* (1996: 468).

they form a non-dominant sector of society and are determined to preserve, develop and transmit to future generations their ancestral territories.

(Cobo 1983: para. 379)

Land is inherited from descendants and 'ownership' of traditional homelands and its transmission to future generations is a vital component of indigenousness. Thus land rights have to be viewed as an expression of tribal unity and perpetuation. Pre-colonialism, the dominant feature of ownership for the majority of indigenous peoples was collective, with its source in local indigenous customary laws that were never recognized by colonial powers and, subsequently, independent states.[8] The negation of this customary law by non-indigenous legal systems is an important element in the possession of indigenous territory (see Sheleff 1999 and McNeil 2000).

While international law is the main subject of this discussion, the first place of redressal for indigenous peoples is before national courts. Native titles are usually granted by national legislation. This state practice, via the consent of state parties, transmits directly in international law. This chapter concentrates mainly on the study of the law governing indigenous (or 'aboriginal' or 'native') titles. An 'indigenous title' for this purpose is understood as a right to land given to a community that occupied the land at the time of colonization. Thus, the focus will be on states where indigenous populations represent an important part of the population and they have been dispossessed by colonial settlement. Based on these interlinked criteria, the situations in Canada, Australia and Scandinavia will be closely examined.

It needs to be stated at the outset that references to 'land' and 'territory' have been used alternatively. Indigenous claims are usually based on both notions. However, there is clear preference for recognition of territorial rather than land rights. A 'territory' refers to the totality of 'the environment of the areas which the peoples concerned occupy or otherwise use',[9] which is a broader concept than merely the land.[10]

---

[8] Recognition of such customary systems is a difficult feature for states. For example, Danish juridical expeditions to Greenland in charge of determining 'how far it was possible to introduce unity of law between Denmark and Greenland' concluded that indigenous customary law 'is not a closed system such as a modern dogmatically defined system of law. Customary law is a "living law", not written law. Data gathering must be concerned with the whole cultural context'; as quoted in Craig and Freeland (1998: 8).

[9] ILO Convention 169 is the only instrument that refers to such a distinction. Article 13 states that the 'use of the term "lands" . . . shall include the concept of territories, which covers the total environment of the areas which the peoples concerned occupy or otherwise use'; Convention Concerning Indigenous and Tribal Peoples in Independent Countries, ILO No. 169, 72, *ILO Official Bull*, 59 (1989). See also Assies (1998: 15).

[10] However, use of the plural in the expression 'rights to land' refers to the total issue of rights to land including traditional rights to enjoy fishing and/or hunting, as well as rights to the protection of the land in general. Thus, the notion of territory is mainly a reference to a right to manage land.

Nevertheless, since international law and national laws usually refer to both terms without distinction,[11] references to both concepts are necessary. However, since indigenous peoples claim the right to own land as well as rights to manage and own their natural resources, it is important to keep in mind the implications of 'territory' in understanding indigenous claims.

The issues of land, territory and resources are clearly related to the right of self-determination since the ultimate purpose of territorial rights includes the right to own and manage land with maximum liberty. While a focus on the issue of self-determination alone would not be a complete representation of the debate concerning land rights it is nonetheless important to recognize the 'shadow' that self-determination casts on a discussion about indigenous land rights.[12] In this regard, the issue of indigenous peoples' rights to land is often regarded as a question of 'internal self-determination' rather than an issue relating to international boundary disputes.[13]

Law and Indigenous Land Rights

The legal environment of the conquest of indigenous territories was one where colonial powers developed theories in favour of a right to dispossess. These doctrines of discovery and unequal treaties between indigenous peoples and invaders were used to legitimate acquisition of indigenous lands. While *terra nullius* is no longer recognized as a legal tool for acquiring indigenous peoples' lands,[14] it was historically a vital legal doctrine, justifying dispossession of indigenous peoples.

The 'Valladolid controversy' is a well-known example of the development of theories justifying the right to dispossess indigenous peoples.[15] With the 'three Cs' theory forming its main thrust, the Catholic Church is severely implicated in this dispossession.[16]

---

[11] For an example of the alternative use of the two notions, see the Draft Declaration on the Rights of Indigenous Peoples, Preamble UN Doc. E/CN.4/Sub. 2/1994/2/Add. 1 (1994).

[12] For discussions on the right to self-determination for indigenous peoples, see Aikio and Scheinin (2000) and Maivân Clech Lâm (2000).

[13] Internal self-determination is 'referring to the internal political and economic organization of a people, without necessarily affecting already existing external relations'; Stavenhagen (1994): 20).

[14] See *Western Sahara case*, ICJ Reports (1975) 12 at 16 and High Court of Australia, *Mabo v. Queensland* (1992) 175 C.L.R. 1.

[15] The 'Valladolid controversy' was a discussion between Sepulveda and Las Casas in 1550. The issue of the 'scientific' debate between those two 'scientists' was to define whether the 'Indians' of the South American colonies were some 'natural inferior human' or not. For a general review of all the legal doctrines of those times, see Rouland *et al.* (1996: ch. 3).

[16] A good example is the *Inter Caetera* bull from Pope Alexander VI which, in the name of the development of Christianity, shared the world between Portugal and Spain; see Henderson (1997).

Traditionally, the Christianization of indigenous peoples provided a doctrinal basis for non-recognition of the sacred importance of the land. As Scheinin writes:

> the essentially Christian-based approach to the practice of religion fails to address indigenous beliefs that treat the land itself as sacred, not merely a piece of property suitable for certain isolated religious practice.
>
> (Scheinin 1999: 5)

Nevertheless, fulfilment of these elaborate theories was only achieved through military domination or by fraudulent perpetration of unequal treaties (Daes 2000: 10–11). Later legal justification of indigenous dispossession was based on notions of *terra nullius* and discovery (see Chapters 1–3), interpreted in a racist manner. It is now accepted that such legal theory was merely the handmaiden of the perpetration of European political ambition,[17] and the international community has recognized these theories as blatantly racist and illegitimate,[18] though they continue to be discussed before national courts.[19] Modern state-building had direct consequences for proprietary rights of indigenous peoples. As highlighted by Makkonen:

> although the vast majority of the world's about 190 states are . . . polyethnic, most of them retain nation-statal ideas and do not formally recognize their internal diversity.
>
> (Makkonen 2000: 32)

In this process, non-recognition of indigenous peoples' rights to own land collectively is part of the process of assimilation as states seek to create a homogeneous society. In some states indigenous peoples have no right to own land irrespective of dispossession.[20] In countries where they have the right to occupy traditional lands, indigenous peoples are usually perceived as using public or national lands as a 'gift' from the government. In the British Commonwealth system though, indigenous peoples have exclusive use and occupancy of land though the respective governments are its owners. Thus even when indigenous peoples have a legal right to their lands this right is subject to the legal theory of 'the power to extinguish'. States have always had the power to extinguish if they perceive the 'need'. In this sense Special Rapporteur Daes (2000: 14, para. 40) states that the concept of aboriginal title is itself discriminatory since 'it provides only

---

[17] An illustration of such hypocritical theory was the right of white settlers in Tasmania to shoot aborigines, after whose decimation the island could factually have been 'terra nullius'.

[18] *Eastern Greenland decision*, PCIJ (1993) and the *Western Sahara case*, ICJ Reports (1975) 12.

[19] See the discussion below about the *Mabo* decision in Australia.

[20] Daes (2000: 36) states 'One of the most widespread contemporary problems is the failure of States to recognize the existence of indigenous land use, occupancy and ownership, and the failure to accord appropriate legal status and legal rights to protect this use, occupancy and ownership.'

defective, vulnerable and inferior legal status for indigenous land and resource ownership'. Thus, although *terra nullius* has been deemed racist, at present there are still legal frameworks that allow states to discriminate vis-à-vis indigenous land rights.

The right of expropriation is recognized by international law, but the power to extinguish a title is very different. Extinguishment of such indigenous titles is usually at the behest of grants of such territory to non-indigenous holders. If the indigenous right to land is 'inconsistent' with the grant given to non-indigenous holders, such a grant would 'extinguish' the indigenous right. This right to extinguish usually allows states to take land without compensation.[21] Indigenous peoples remain, in most instances, the only part of society that can be victims of the 'extinguishing' of their right to their lands. As observed by Sambo:

> . . . the ongoing implementation of state extinguishments policies constitutes a very serious threat to indigenous societies. It is another relic of colonialism. Extinguishment is used to ensure state domination of indigenous peoples and to serve their ancestral ties to their own territories.
>
> (Sambo 1993: 31)

US Supreme Court Judges echo these sentiments:

> No case in this Court has ever held that taking of Indian title or use by Congress required compensation. The American people have compassion for the descendants of those Indians who were deprived of their homes and hunting grounds by the drive of civilization. They seek to have the Indians share the benefits of our society as citizens of this nation. Generous provision has been willingly made to allow tribes to recover for wrongs, as a matter of grace, not because of legal liability.[22]

Via this decision taken in 1995 the Supreme Court recognized that the government is entitled to take Indian land without due process or compensation in direct contravention of the constitution. This decision is a direct consequence of the legal theory of 'plenary power' that allows the possibility for state control of the use of the land 'without regard for constitutional limits on governmental power that would otherwise be applicable' (Daes 2000: 16, para. 47). Thus the theory of plenary power differs marginally from the theory of extinguishments in that it requires prescribed legal procedures to be fulfilled. Nevertheless, both 'legal' theories are discriminatory and it is difficult to understand how such practices are used in states such as Canada, Australia and the USA in clear violation of basic human rights.[23] Even when land agreements

---

[21] Usually extinguishments can only be made by a governmental Act requiring 'clear and plain intention'.

[22] *Tee-Hit-Ton Indians* v. *United States*, 348 U.S. 272 (1995), quoted in Daes (2000: 15).

[23] CERD has commented on this issue, see p. 224.

are based on treaties between indigenous peoples and states, governments often deny effect to these, violating them in the absence of legal remedies (see Brownlie 1992). The Special Rapporteur on the issue of indigenous peoples and their relationship to land, highlights that

> [It] is safe to say that the attitudes, doctrines and policies developed to justify the taking of lands from indigenous peoples were and continue to be largely driven by the economic agendas of States.

(Daes 2000: 9)

Removals or relocations of indigenous peoples were often effected as practical expression of such agendas and were often justified as a solution for 'overpopulation, need for resettlement, transmigration, resources exploitation and security' (ibid.). There are many examples of forced relocation of indigenous peoples because of 'developmental' projects that include dam construction, eucalyptus tree plantations, and so on.[24] States can be deemed responsible for the threat to indigenous peoples' lands by implementing policies such as settlement programmes on indigenous lands. For instance, the current Chiapas uprising in Mexico stems from the question of land ownership and is a direct result of repeated governmental policy over the last fifty years including governmental encouragement of mass migration to the region and displacement policies towards indigenous populations (see Wilson 1998).

International Legal Regimes and the Protection of Indigenous Land Rights

Having previously been an instrument in effect putting colonialism on a legal footing, international law is shifting to give voice to the victims of a legal system based on 'western concepts'.[25] It was only during the 1970s that international human rights law rejected its assimilationist approach and started to recognize their unique existence and specific culture.[26] Modern international law seeks to protect the right of indigenous peoples to land in two ways: first, through specific instruments that especially deal with such an issue and, second, via instruments that do not specifically deal with the

---

[24] For examples of 'developmental' projects and their effects, see 'Refuge, Canada's periodical on Refugees', *Environmental Refugees* 12(1) (June 1992).

[25] The first international instrument that gave protection to indigenous peoples is the 'Covenant of the League of Nations'; art. 23 requires just treatment for native inhabitants in territories under the control of members of the League. For a chronology of international instruments relating to indigenous peoples, see Havemann (1999a: 19).

[26] International human rights law usually regarded 'indigenous peoples' as 'minorities' entitled to general minority rights protection. The first document distinguishing the two notions is the Report of the Special Rapporteur on the Problem of Discrimination against Indigenous Populations (1972).

right to land, but which give opportunities to mobilize other existing recognized rights to protect indigenous rights to land. In this regard, the interpretation of existing rights to include indigenous peoples' right to land is an important feature of existing international law. The next section explores the major instruments of international human rights law that contain these specific references to the land right issue.[27]

UN and Indigenous Peoples' Rights to Land

The UN General Assembly has proclaimed the International Decade of the World's Indigenous Peoples (1994–2004).[28] One of the purposes of this decade is the adoption of the 'Draft Declaration on the Rights of Indigenous Peoples'. This declaration, proposed by the Working Group on Indigenous Populations in 1993,[29] was rejected by the Commission on Human Rights (CHR) comprising state representatives. However, the commission is presently discussing adoption of the draft declaration[30] with amendments amenable to its members. This instrument seeks to strike:

> ... a balance between the right of indigenous peoples to be different and to control their own affairs, and their right to participate fully in the wider society.
>
> (Burger 1998: 10)

The spirit of the draft declaration is one of invitation to governments to base their relationship with indigenous communities and individuals on consent. In this regard, it deals with a wide range of issues including language rights, education, health and employment. Article 10 of the declaration, dealing with land rights, states:

> Indigenous Peoples shall not be forcibly removed from their lands or territories. No relocation shall take place without the free and informed consent of the indigenous peoples concerned and after agreement on just and fair compensation, and, where possible, with the option of return.[31]

In addition, art. 25 recognizes spiritual and material relationships of indigenous peoples with their homelands and highlights that 'land and territories' include the

---

[27] For a review of the instruments that might be applicable to indigenous peoples, see Daes (2000: Annex).

[28] See CHR, International Decade for the World's Indigenous People: Activities Undertaken Within the United Nations System in Preparation for the Decade, UN Doc. E/CN.4/1997/101. Within the UN agenda, 1993 was declared the International Year for the World's Indigenous Peoples.

[29] The preliminary text of the draft declaration was issued in 1985.

[30] The Working Group of the CHR is in charge of redrafting; see Working Group of the Commission on the Draft Declaration Report, UN Doc. E/CN.4/2002/85.

[31] Draft Declaration on the Rights of Indigenous Peoples, UN Doc. E/CN.4/Sub.2/1994/2/Add.1 (1994).

whole environment of 'lands, air, waters, coastal seas, sea-ice, flora, fauna and other resources'. Article 26 then refers to 'the right to own, develop, control and use the lands and territories . . . which they have traditionally owned or otherwise occupied or used'. States have objected to the use of the past tense and some are more in favour of the formula used by the ILO Convention that only deals with land that remains in use.[32] Where the return of land is not a possibility, indigenous peoples would have the right to just and fair compensation, as enshrined in art. 27. In general, all the articles referring to land rights also recognize collective ownership of land and invite state governments to take into account and respect indigenous traditions, customs and land tenure systems. It is important to bear in mind that this document was produced by a body of human rights experts with significant participation by indigenous representatives. The final declaration is likely to be severely restrictive, since it has to be adopted by the CHR comprising state representatives. During discussions thus far, state concern has centred on the protection of national land tenure systems, state ownership of minerals and state power to expropriate.[33] It is also important to stress that declarations are statements of purpose rather than legally binding documents. However, with the theoretical deadline for its adoption looming and with fundamental differences still remaining it is unlikely to be passed within the timeframe. In a recent debate of the Working Group for the CHR, Canada asked for an amendment to the draft stressing a distinction between 'lands' and 'territories' and clarification between 'traditional use' and 'property'[34] arguing that the wording was 'too prescriptive' with regard to conflicts of laws.[35] The Australian representatives too expressed reservations with the drafting of the declaration, whilst Guatemala called for an agreement of norms governing the concept of indigenous peoples, recognition of collective rights, self-determination and land rights before discussing the articles. Although the issue of land and resources is recognized as vital by all governments, their positions with regard to the provisions of the draft declaration vary considerably.

The first indigenous claim before an international body took place during the 1920s,[36] but the UN showed direct interest in indigenous issues only in the 1970s with the Sub-Commission on Protection of Minorities initiating a study of the problem of

---

[32] See Barsh (1996: 801). The countries concerned are Australia, Canada and the USA.

[33] On the formulation of land rights (arts. 26 and 27) only Colombia found such formulation 'acceptable in principle', whereas most of the states found it 'objectionable in parts'.

[34] For more information about the actual debate on the adoption of the draft declaration, see Indigenous Peoples' Centre for Documentation, Research and Information, <http:www.docip.org>, visited 23/04/01.

[35] Update No. 37, January/March 2001, Working Group on the Draft Declaration, Geneva, 6th session, 20 November–1 December 2000.

[36] The Iroquois Chief Deskaheh was the first indigenous 'activist' at international level, spending several months lobbying the League of the Nations in 1923.

discrimination against indigenous populations.[37] In 1982 it created the Working Group on Indigenous Populations as its subsidiary organ.[38] Since then, this working group has collected comments and suggestions concerning the draft declaration from hundreds of indigenous groups, NGOs, IGOs and governments (see Schulte-Tenckoff 1997). The first study especially dealing with land issues followed the first draft of the declaration in the 1990s. It was only in 1997 that the CHR appointed Ms Daes as Special Rapporteur 'to prepare a working paper on indigenous people and their relationship to land with a view to suggesting practical measures to address ongoing problems in that regard'. The Special Rapporteur completed her preliminary working paper in 1997 examining the facilitation of understanding of the provisions relevant to land rights contained in the draft declaration.[39] Examining state perspectives on the issues, she found that their prime objection related to the difficulty of reconciling indigenous land claims with the need for 'certainty and security' of land titles. Another difficulty was the manner in which indigenous land regimes could be integrated with the 'goal of a functional and stable nation-state'. The final working paper was submitted in 2001 even though only four states (Canada, Australia, New Zealand and Denmark) submitted comments and information, with South American and Asian states refusing to participate.

This paper is certainly the most complete work on the subject produced on behalf of the UN and more generally in international law. The report analyses the importance of the indigenous peoples' relation with their homelands and explores the contemporary problems faced by indigenous peoples in such a relationship.

ILO: The Only Binding Protection

The International Labour Organization (ILO) has adopted two Conventions on Indigenous and Tribal Peoples (Convention 107 and 169)[40] which protect the lands of indigenous peoples.[41] In this regard the ILO became active in this field long before the UN (Heintze 1993). In fact the ILO began to address indigenous peoples' issues through the rights of native workers in 1921 (the ILO was created in 1919). Its most

[37] See the series of documents prepared by Special Rapporteur Cobo between 1973 and 1984, Cobo (1983 and 1986/7).
[38] The Working Group on Indigenous Populations is composed of five members who are independent experts of the Sub-Commission.
[39] See Preliminary Working Paper prepared by Mrs. Erica-Irene Daes, UN Doc. E/CN.4/Sub.2/1997/17, 20 June 1997 and Corr. 1.
[40] The ILO adopted Convention No. 107 in 1957 and Convention No. 169 in 1989. For an overview of the ILO system, see Swepston (1998).
[41] It must be emphasized that some indigenous representatives were unhappy with the lack of consultation and have invited states not to ratify this convention; see 'Resolution of the Indigenous Peoples', Preparatory Meeting Relating to the ILO Convention Concerning Indigenous and Tribal Peoples in Independent Countries, Geneva, 28 July 1989.

significant contribution on indigenous issues was the adoption of Convention No. 169 (1989) revealing the organization as the cutting-edge for expression of indigenous concerns. This convention deals with a range of different issues and includes the land rights issue. Even though at first glance it could seem paradoxical that an organization dedicated to workers' rights has produced a convention referring to indigenous land rights, today the Convention Concerning Indigenous and Tribal Peoples in Independent Countries[42] remains the only universal binding standard on indigenous land rights. This convention recognizes the collective character of the relationship of indigenous peoples with their land, especially noting its spiritual and cultural importance.[43] At least nine of its 44 articles clearly deal with the land issue with the entire second part specifically dedicated to the right to land.[44] Article 14, in particular, contains a fundamental expression of indigenous rights to land:

> The right of ownership and possession of the peoples concerned over the lands which they traditionally occupy shall be recognised.

Use of the word 'recognize' implicitly suggests that the occupation of the land by indigenous peoples gives a right to possession that must be 'recognized' by the state. This underscores the ILO Committee of Experts statement that the convention does not necessarily require 'full title', as long as 'possession is secure'.[45] Article 14(3) invites governments to take necessary steps to identify lands which indigenous peoples traditionally occupied, guarantee effective protection of ownership and possessory rights and to take adequate procedures within domestic jurisdiction to resolve land claims. Since no reference is made to temporal limitations, these procedures could arguably also include past claims. In this context Anaya has commented that this article is:

> . . . a response to the historical processes that have afflicted indigenous peoples, processes that have trampled on their cultural attachment to ancestral lands, disregarded or minimized their legitimate property interests, and left them without adequate means of subsistence.
> (Anaya 1996: 106)

Article 16 expresses the prohibition of removal of peoples from lands and seeks creation of minimum legal standards for 'relocation'. Article 16(2) stresses the fundamental

---

[42] Convention concerning Indigenous and Tribal Peoples in Independent Countries, ILO No. 169, 72 *ILO Official Bull.* 59, 1989, see especially arts. 4 and 7.
[43] For example, art. 13(1) states 'In applying the provisions of this Part of the Convention Governments shall respect the special importance for the cultures and spiritual values of the peoples concerned of their relationship with the lands or territories, or both as applicable, which they occupy or otherwise use, and in particular the collective aspects of this relationship.'
[44] See arts. 4, 7, 13, 14, 15, 16, 17, 18 and 19.
[45] Swepston (1998: 25); see 'Observation by the Committee of Experts', 1995 (Norway) para. 17.

conditions necessary in relocation, including consent and that such relocation must only be an exceptional measure. In discussing the nature of 'necessary relocation', the conference resisted specific definition so as not to pre-empt such action.[46] Swepston (1998) suggests that the ILO has tried to set up 'a series of hurdles to be passed, with public hearings as insurance against abuse' in case of relocation. He concedes that whilst this does not always prevent abuse it marginally diminishes the risk. However, one of the most positive aspects of art. 16 is the recognition of the 'right to return' when the reason for removal ceases.

This convention is also the only legally binding international instrument that acknowledges recognition of indigenous land tenure systems and customs relating to the transmission of land that had been rejected by the forces of colonization (art. 17). A big impediment to the ILO system, however, remains the manner in which the convention is monitored. The submission of reports by states does not enable indigenous peoples to submit complaints – a fundamental flaw that weakens the effectiveness of the convention as a means of providing redress (Brölmann, Lefeber and Zieck 1993: 212).

The Proposed American Declaration on the Rights of Indigenous Peoples specifically deals with the right to land.[47] This is recognized in the preamble (para. 5):

> . . . in many indigenous cultures, traditional collective systems for control and use of land, territory and resources . . . are a necessary condition for their survival . . . and . . . the form of such control and ownership is varied and distinctive and does not necessarily coincide with the systems protected by the domestic laws of the states in which they live.

This proposed declaration highlights that ownership of traditional lands is part of the 'right to cultural integrity' of indigenous peoples. Article VII states that indigenous communities are entitled to 'restitution in respect of the property of which they have been dispossessed.'[48] According to art. XVIII 'Indigenous peoples have the right to the recognition of their property and ownership rights with respect to lands, territories and resources they have historically occupied, as well as to the use of those to which they have historically had access for their traditional activities and livelihood.' However, the document has no binding effects and remains a draft declaration. Thus, its contents are liable to change considerably before its possible adoption.

---

[46] Special Rapporteur Daes highlights that 'justification for relocations included overpopulation, need for resettlement, transmigration, resource exploitation and security'; see UN. Doc. E/CN.4/Sub.2/200/25, p. 23.

[47] 'Proposed American Declaration on the Rights of Indigenous Peoples', approved by the IACHR on 26 February 1997 at its 1333rd session, 95th Regular Session, published in Annual Report of the IACHR (1996) p. 633.

[48] Article VII, para. 2, also adds that where such restitution is 'not possible, compensation on a basis not less favourable than the standard of international law' is required.

The appropriation or degradation of indigenous peoples' homelands is a continuing threat to their survival, therefore violating basic human rights such as the right to life or physical integrity of the person. The aim of the following section is to consider whether human rights law is able to protect indigenous peoples' relationship to their homelands in the face of these consequences.

The HRC

There is no specific article dealing with indigenous peoples in the International Covenant on Civil and Political Rights (ICCPR).[49] Nevertheless the HRC, the monitoring organ of this covenant, has often dealt with indigenous issues within the framework offered to minority rights. In its General Comment on art. 27, the HRC has stated that under the exercise of cultural rights protected by art. 27 of the ICCPR:

> ... one or other aspect of the rights of individuals protected under that article – for example, to enjoy a particular culture – may consist in a way of life which is closely associated with territory and use of its resources. This may particularly be true ... of indigenous communities constituting a minority ...
> With regard to the exercise of the cultural rights protected under Article 27, the Committee observes that culture manifests itself in many forms, including a particular way of life associated with the use of land resources, especially in the case of Indigenous Peoples.[50]

Optional Protocol I to the covenant gives competence to the HRC to receive and consider communication from individuals claiming rights violation of the covenant.[51] Even though the committee does not have any implementation mechanism, its decisions are important in terms of codification and evolution of international human rights law. Article 27 of the covenant recognizes that minorities 'shall not be denied the right, in community with other members of their group, to enjoy their own culture'. *Lubicon case.* On the basis of such protection the chief of a Canadian native Indian tribe, the Lubicon Lake Band, claimed that Alberta's provincial government violated his right to enjoy his culture by expropriating part of the Band's territories to allow petrol extraction. The applicant especially emphasized that this exploration destroyed traditional hunting and trapping territory and put their livelihood and subsistence in jeopardy.[52] The federal Canadian government was concerned since it had allowed the provincial Alberta

---

[49] ICCPR (1966), G.A. Res. 2200A (XXI), 21 UN GAOR Supp. (No. 16) at 52, UN Doc. A/6316 (1966), 999 UNTS 171, entered into force 23 March 1976.
[50] HRC, 'General Comments' No. 23 (50) on art. 27, Minority Rights, 6–4, 1994, paras. 3.2 and 7.
[51] Optional Protocol of the ICCPR, G.A. Res. 2200A (XXI), 21 UN GAOR Supp. (No. 16) at 59, UN Doc. A/6316 (1966), 999 UNTS 302, entered into force, 23 March 1976, Article I.
[52] Communication n° 167/1984, Report of the HRC (A/45/40), vol. 2, annex IX A; CCPR/C/OP/2, para. 3.5.

government to expropriate the territory of the Band for the benefit of private corporate interests. The committee found that those concessions were in breach of art. 27 and condemned the government to pay some indemnity.[53]

The committee has received other similar claims.[54] In *Länsmann et al.* v. *Finland*, it stated that the right to enjoy one's culture could not be determined away from its context. This decision supports governments in allowing exploitation of natural resources or other economic activities in traditional indigenous territories, but establishes that these activities must not infringe too much upon indigenous peoples' way of life. In this case, permission to quarry and transport stones into indigenous territory was found not to be in breach of art. 27. Nevertheless, the committee stated that depending on the level of activities involved, such authorization 'may constitute a violation of the author's rights under Article 27, in particular of their right to enjoy their own culture'.[55]

Until Namibia's declaration of independence in 1990, the Rehoboth Baster community had traditionally owned and controlled their homelands. Nevertheless, Namibia's new constitution states that all property or control over property comes under the jurisdiction of the government of Namibia. The late Captain of the community and others claimed before the HRC that such legislation violated their right, as entrusted by art. 27 of the ICCPR, since the land was used by the community for grazing cattle and cattle raising was 'an essential element in the culture of the community'.[56] The committee rejected their claim of violation on the basis that the applicants failed to prove that the community relationship with their traditional land was at the base of their distinctive culture. This decision was based primarily on the fact that the authors defined their culture 'almost solely in terms of the economic activity of grazing cattle'.[57] Thus, since their claim was based on economic rather cultural grounds the protection offered by art. 27 was denied.

In *Hopu et al.* v. *France*, the committee was asked to address the claims of two indigenous Polynesians from Tahiti following a decision allowing construction of a hotel on the site of their ancestral cemetery. They alleged that the project was a violation of their right to privacy and family life.[58] The HRC stated that the covenant required broad interpretation of the term 'family' to include those comprising 'the family' as

---

[53] Communication n° 167/1984, Report of the HRC (A/45/40), vol. 2, annex IX A; CCPR/C/OP/2.

[54] See *Sara et al.* v. *Finland*, Communication No. 511/1992, UN GAOR, 52nd Sess., UN Doc. CCPR/C/58/D/511/1992; *Kitok* v. *Sweden*, Communication No. 197/1985 (1988).

[55] *I. Länsman et al.* v. *Finland*, paras. 9.6 and 9.8, Communication No. 511/1992, UN Doc. CCPR/C/52/D/511/1992 (1993).

[56] *J. G. A. Diergaardt (late Captain of the Rehoboth Baster Community) et al.* v. *Namibia*, Communication No. 760/1997, UN Doc. CCPR/C/69/D/760/1997 (6 September 2000), para. 10.6.

[57] Individual opinion of Evatt, E. and Quiroga, C. M. (concurring).

[58] *Hopu et al.* v. *France*, Communication No. 671/1995, UN GAOR, 58th Sess., UN Doc CCPR/C/58/D/671/1995.

understood in the society in question. Taking into account the specific situation, it concurred with the authors' claims that they considered their relationship to their ancestors an essential element of their identity with an important role in their family life.[59]

In conclusion, it can be stated that the HRC is sensitive to the importance of the land rights issue for indigenous peoples, even though there is no specific provision in the ICCPR. The committee has developed the idea that such protection comes under notions of rights protecting minority cultures and individual family life. This posits legal recognition that, in human rights protection, culture and family life are two important aspects of indigenous peoples' relationship with their traditional homelands.

The CERD

Article 5 of the International Convention on the Elimination of All Forms of Discrimination requires equality before law in the enjoyment of various rights, without distinction of race, colour, national or ethnic origin. This entitlement also refers to the right to own property individually and in association with others.[60] The CERD monitors compliance by state parties to the convention. General Recommendation XXIII(51) of the committee deals specifically with indigenous peoples and focuses on the right to land, clearly stating that disrespect of such a right is the basis of discrimination against indigenous peoples. Highlighting the importance of the right to restitution, it calls on state parties to recognize and protect indigenous peoples' right to own, develop, control and use communal territories. In addition, it calls upon states to take steps to return territories that were taken away without free and informed consent. Dealing with restitution it states:

> Only when this [return] is for factual reasons not possible, the right to restitution should be substituted by the right to just, fair and prompt compensation. Such compensation should as far as possible take the form of lands and territories.[61]

The monitoring mechanism under art. 9 of the convention has been occasionally successful in dealing with these issues.[62] Australia, for example, has been called on to justify the content of its legislation concerning discriminatory aspects with regard to indigenous rights to land.[63]

---

[59] *Hopu et al.* v. *France*, para. 10.3. Nevertheless, the fact that France has made a reservation on art. 27 of the ICCPR must be taken into consideration in such a solution.

[60] *International Convention for the Elimination of All Forms of Racial Discrimination*, 660 UNTS 195, reprinted in *ILM* 352 (1966), art. 5 (d)(v).

[61] CERD, General Recommendation XXIII (51) on the Rights of Indigenous Peoples, adopted at the committee's 1235th meeting, 18 August 1997, §5.

[62] For comments on this reporting procedure, see Steiner and Alston (2000: 773–8).

[63] See Reports Submitted by States Parties under art. 9 of the convention, *Twelfth periodic reports of State Parties due in 1998, Australia*, UN Doc. CERD/C/335/Add.2, 14 December 1999.

The IACHR

The Inter-American Commission on Human Rights (IACHR) has appreciated the connection between indigenous lands and indigenous survival in several cases (see Davis 1988). However, two cases are particularly good illustrations of the IACHR's position on this issue. The first case followed a petition submitted on behalf of the 'Yanomami Indians' of Brazil. They alleged that the Brazilian government had violated their rights to life and health by constructing a highway through their territory, authorizing exploitation of their territorial resources and the subsequent intrusion of outsiders carrying contagious diseases into their territory. The commission found that because the government permitted this intrusion without providing medical care, there was a violation of the American convention.[64] Following a petition on behalf of the 'Huaroni people', the IACHR examined the human rights situation in Ecuador.[65] This petition alleged that the Huaroni were under imminent threat of profound human rights violations due to planned oil exploitation activities within their traditional lands. Historically, during the colonization of Ecuador, the Huaroni were centralized in a small area on the western edge of their traditional land call the 'Oriente' – officially designated a 'protected zone'. But following the discovery of oil in the region, the land was transformed into wasteland. The claim before the commission asserted that the effects of oil development and exploitation have not only damaged the environment, but also directly impaired the Huaroni's right to physical and cultural survival as a people. Following that claim, the commission in its report highlighted the need for adequate protective measures before the damage and recommended that:

> ... the State take the measures necessary ... to restrict settlers to areas which do not infringe upon the ability of indigenous peoples to preserve their traditional culture.[66]

It is important to note, in the above cases, that the IACHR referred to specific rights, for example, the right to life and the right to health, to condemn violations of indigenous land rights. This emphasizes the lack of specific and adequate tools to protect indigenous peoples' specific relationship with their homelands.[67]

---

[64] *Yanomami Indian case*, Case 7615, IACHR 24, OEA/Ser.L/V/11.66, doc. 10 rev. 1 (1985).
[65] IACHR, 'Report on the Situation of Human Rights in Ecuador', OEA/Ser.L/V/II.96, Doc. 10 Rev. 1, Chap. IX, 24 April 1997.
[66] Ibid.: 12.
[67] A new case submitted to the court by the commission on behalf of the Mayana (Sumo) Awas Tingni Community concerns alleged violation of arts. 1 (Obligation to Respect Rights), 2 (Domestic Legal Effect), 21 (Right to Private Property) and 25 (Judicial Protection) due to the failure of the state to demarcate and officially recognize the territory of the community. This case is currently in its preliminary objections phase.

Indigenous Land Rights and State Practice: Towards Customary International Law?

Customary international law is a vital source of law that is accessible to international courts[68] and national jurisdictions. To accede to the status of international custom, a norm must fulfil two criteria. First, the *opinio juris* criteria or the belief that a norm is accepted as law and, second, evidence of general state practice.[69]

Looking at the numerous activities that come under the umbrella of the UN, namely the Working Group on Indigenous Populations, the declaration of the Indigenous Decade, the work of the World Council of Indigenous Peoples and the Draft Declaration of the Rights of Indigenous Peoples, it can be argued that there is an existing international custom relating to indigenous peoples' rights to land. In the words of Bennett and Powell:

> . . . on their own; these activities are not sufficient to constitute international custom, but, when taken in combination with state practice and the 1989 Convention on Indigenous and Tribal Peoples, they go to demonstrate a steadily broadening consensus that aboriginal title is a rule of customary international law.
>
> (1999: 64)

Anaya observes that all the different documents and instruments relating to indigenous peoples at international level express the existence of customary international law protecting indigenous peoples. Thus a large majority of the norms contained in ILO Convention No. 169 are expressions of customary international law (Anaya 1996: 49–58, 107). All the documents examined above contain specific provisions relating to land rights and thus it could be argued that recognition of the importance of the ownership of homelands could accede to customary international law. However, as noted above, one of the fundamental elements of such customary international law is to be found in state practice. This practice needs to be demonstrated in the actions of concerned states (see Malanczuk 1997: 39). Some state constitutions do make reference to indigenous peoples' rights.[70] Australia, Ecuador, Venezuela and Norway have included or are in the process of including rights to collective ownership of the land. In other countries, such rights are guaranteed by treaties.[71] National judicial

---

[68] See the Statute of the ICJ, art. 38(1), the court shall apply: 'international custom, as evidence of a general practice accepted as law'.

[69] See *North Sea continental shelf cases (Federal Republic of Germany v. Denmark; Federal Republic of Germany v. The Netherlands)*, ICJ Reports (1969) 3 at 44.

[70] See Canada, s. 35(1) of the Constitution Act 1982; Chile, art. 123; Brazil, art. 231; Panama, art. 123; Guatemala, art. 67; Peru, art. 88, Philippines, s. 22, art. II, s. 5, art. XII and s. 6, art. XIII.

[71] The USA and Norway; other states recognize such rights by local legislation, for example Ecuador, New Zealand and Venezuela.

decisions have also to be taken into consideration to appreciate the existence of customary international law. For example, Judge Brennan who sat on the *Mabo* case in Australia stated:

> It is contrary both to international standards and to the fundamental values of our common law to entrench a discriminatory rule which . . . denies [indigenous inhabitants] a right to occupy their traditional lands.[72]

This quote shows that the judge has belief, or the *opinio juris*, that there is a fundamental rule in international law, applicable domestically, which states that it is illegal and discriminatory to deny indigenous peoples the right to occupy their traditional lands.

To appreciate state practice relating to indigenous rights to land, the study of legislation and judicial decisions in Canada and Australia provides an interesting insight since both states have a long and difficult relationship with indigenous populations within their jurisdictions. Further, the land rights issues in both states are in the mainstream of domestic political agendas. Thus, the purpose of the following section is twofold: first, to provide examples of the relationship between law and the right to land for indigenous peoples and, second, to demonstrate that there is emerging customary international law concerning the importance of the land rights issue for survival of indigenous peoples.

Canada

There are approximately one million aboriginal peoples in Canada,[73] descendants of the first inhabitants of North America who arrived some 12 000 years ago (Elliott 1997). Canada has a long history of dialogue with aboriginal peoples. While this dialogue was not always based on a respect for aboriginal cultures, aboriginal peoples have sometimes recognized the British Crown and have exchanged their lands for protection by the Crown. Even though, as elsewhere, there was a large process of assimilation, ethnocentricity and colonial politics, the Crown tried to recognize aboriginal peoples' customs and laws in relation to their lands. Indeed, legislation concerning native peoples has been part of the federal remit since 1867. This legislative and executive relationship can be classified into three different periods of time (ibid.: 19–22). The first period was based on the 1763 Royal Proclamation. During that time for aboriginal rights to be acknowledged they were submitted to formal governmental recognition. Thus, land rights were dependent on legislative or executive recognition, which provided legal justification for the reservations. The second phase of legal relationships between Canada and aboriginal peoples involved the 'occupancy and

---

[72] High Court of Australia, *Mabo* v. *Queensland* (1992) 175 C.L.R. 1 at 29.
[73] In the Canadian legal system the term 'aboriginal peoples' is used. Such a notion refers to the same group as indigenous peoples in international law.

use approach'. This approach was based on recognition of aboriginal occupancy and use of land by the common law system after the European invasion. The third phase is characterized by 'the land and societies approach'. In terms of the evolution of legislative and judicial approaches to indigenous land rights, this period from 1973–96 was crucial to the establishment of the theory dealing with aboriginal land rights in Canada.

The case of *Guerin v. R.*[74] suggested that aboriginal titles did not depend only on a royal proclamation, but derived from common law recognition of aboriginal occupancy and use of the land prior to European settlement. In this regard, *Calder*,[75] the decision that recognized aboriginal rights as *sui generis* rights, is at the 'foundation' of the movement to rethink the relation between Canada and aborigines (Asch 1999). However, on the issue of the extinguishments of native titles, the court said, in a split decision (4 : 3) that such rights could be extinguished by general rather than specific legislation.

The repatriation of the Canadian constitution from London to Ottawa in 1982 offered aborigines an opportunity to claim more legal recognition. This resulted in s. 35(1) of the Constitution Act 1982 that states that 'existing aboriginal and treaty rights of the aboriginal peoples of Canada are hereby recognised and affirmed'.[76] This section of the constitutional act transfers aboriginal rights from common to constitutional law. Prior to this Act, the Canadian parliament had the power to 'extinguish' natives' rights and titles, a possibility aborted by s. 35(1) of the 1982 Act. While it is still possible to extinguish native rights this can only be fulfilled with the consent of aboriginal peoples. Nevertheless even though the Act states that aboriginal rights are constitutionally protected, it does not discuss any substantive content of those rights.

The *Sparrow* case[77] was the first in which the Supreme Court was invited to examine the contents of s. 35(1). In this decision the Supreme Court interpreted the meaning of 'existing aboriginal rights' as stated in the Constitution Act as rights that existed when the Act was passed. However, it added that 'existing aboriginal rights must be interpreted flexibly so as to permit their evolution over time'. The court added that such a position suggests that those rights are 'affirmed in a contemporary form rather than in their primeval simplicity and vigour'. This position rejected a 'frozen rights' approach as incompatible with the meaning of s. 35. In fact, this means that Canada offers constitutional protection not only to practices and customs of aboriginal cultures that pre-dated the arrival of European colonizers but also to contemporary expression of such cultures.[78] The judgment also established how the rights protected by s. 35(1)

---

[74] *Guerin v. R.*, 2 SCR (1984) 335.

[75] *Calder et al.* v. *Attorney-General of British Columbia* (1973) 34 DLR (3d) 145.

[76] Section 35(3) adds: 'For greater certainty, in subsection 1 "treaty rights" includes rights that now exist by way of land claim agreements that may be so acquired.'

[77] *R.* v. *Sparrow* (1990) 70 DLR (4th) 289 (SCC).

[78] Such affirmation closed the debate on the question of the impact of the French law governing property in Québec; see *R* v. *Côté*, 3 SRC (1996) 139–98.

could be extinguished. In this decision the court ruled that aboriginal rights are 'not absolute'. Thus if the government decided there is need to infringe upon such rights and if this is justified by needs of society, it can infringe on those constitutionally recognized rights. The Supreme Court has set up a strict test for such extinguishments. For the court, s. 35 provides 'unextinguished aboriginal rights with constitutional protection against legislative infringement' (McNeil 1997a: 1–8). Thus, the government would have to prove it has valid grounds to extinguish and that it has a valid legislative objective respecting the fiduciary duty of the Crown regarding aboriginal peoples.[79] This judgment is part of the theory of the 'fiduciary duty' of the government to allow aboriginal peoples to use unoccupied land until it is required for alternative use. To appreciate if the government had 'plain and clear intention' to extinguish the aboriginal right, the judicial system applies a two-part test. The first part of the test is based on an assessment of whether legislation would infringe existing aboriginal rights and whether such infringement was reasonable. Second, it would determine whether the infringement is justifiable on any grounds.

Another legal episode, from a lower court of British Columbia to the Supreme Court of Canada, concerned the sale of ten salmon for 50 Canadian dollars contrary to state legislation by Ms Van Der Peet.[80] The claimant argued that such trade should be recognized as an expression of traditional cultural practice of her tribe, and claimed protection under s. 35(1).[81] The debate was whether her right to fish was protected under the rights of aboriginal peoples. Thus, the fundamental issue for the judges was to address the question: '[H]ow should the Aboriginal rights recognised and affirmed by s. 35(1) of the *Constitution Act, 1982* be defined?'[82] In answer the judgment stated that the rights:

> . . . are best understood as, first, *the means by which the Constitution recognises the fact that prior to the arrival of Europeans in North America the land was already occupied by distinctive aboriginal societies* and as, second, the means by which that prior occupation is reconciled with the assertion of Crown sovereignty over Canadian territory.[83]

Ultimately the Supreme Court clarified that aboriginal rights are based on two notions: first, that of original occupation prior to European settlement and, second, on cultural

---

[79] The fiduciary obligation refers to the duty of consultation that the Crown has when indigenous rights are involved in a decision. See Chief Justice Lamer: 'There is always a duty of consultation. Whether the aboriginal group has been consulted is relevant to determining whether the infringement of aboriginal title is justified', *Delgamuukw* v. *British Columbia*, 3 SCR (1997), 1010, 1081 DLR at 265.

[80] *R.* v. *Van Der Peet*, 2 SCR (1996) 507.

[81] Van Der Peet must be read with the five others decisions issued in 1996 relating to similar subject; see *R.* v. *Gladstone*, 21 August 1996; *R.* v. *NTC Smokehouse*, 21 August 1996; *R.* v. *Adams*, 3 October 1996; *R.* v. *Côté*, 3 October 1996.

[82] *R.* v. *Van Der Peet*, 2 SCR (1996) 507 at 299.

[83] *R.* v. *Van Der Peet*, 2 SCR (1996) 507 at 309–10 (emphasis added).

and traditional practices. This decision also emphasized that the purpose of s. 35(1) is 'to reconcile prior occupancy of land by aboriginal peoples with the Crown assertion of sovereignty'. Therefore, it could be argued that the court acknowledged the occupation of the land by the aborigines as falling under the protection of the constitution.

The court further established a test to determine how to prove the existence of aboriginal rights. This test can be summarized thus: 'in order to be an aboriginal right an activity must be an element of a practice, custom or tradition integral to the distinctive culture of the aboriginal group claiming the right'.[84] Even though this test was framed in the context of a traditional right to fish, it must be understood that the right to land is an inherent element of aboriginal rights.[85] This extension of the principle to land rights returned to the agenda of the Supreme Court in the following year with complementary legal interpretation of constitutional protection in its decision in *Delgamuukw* v. *British Columbia*.[86] This decision followed the claim of the 'Gitksan and Wet'suwet'en peoples' of unextinguished title over their traditional territories in British Columbia. The judgment highlighted the legal importance within the Canadian system of the collective right to land for indigenous peoples.[87] The court defined this title as that of 'exclusive use and occupation of land, including mineral rights and non-traditional uses of land' (Ülgen 2000: 148). The determination of the existence of a right to land is very different from the test set up for other aboriginal rights. The regime requires three conditions to be met for the establishment of aboriginal title. First, that the land must have been occupied prior to the assertion of state sovereignty to such land. Second, that occupation of the land be continuous though '[t]his requirement does not demand an "unbroken chain of continuity" but "substantial maintenance of the connection" between the people and the land' (Assembly of the First Nations 2000: 580, quoting the Delgamuukw case). Third, that at the time of the assertion of sovereignty by the Crown, the occupation must have been exclusive. The Assembly of First Nations in Canada has highlighted that exclusivity does not refer to the absence of other groups on the land, but rather 'the intention and capacity to retain exclusive control' (ibid., citing McNeil 1989: 580). In discussing use and development of such land the court stated:

> If occupation is established with reference to the use of the land as a hunting ground, then the group that successfully claims aboriginal title to that land may not use it in such a fashion as to destroy its value for such a use (e.g. by strip mining it). Similarly, if a group claims a special bond with the land because of its ceremonial or cultural significance, it may

---

[84] For an interpretation of the meaning of such a test, see Dick (1999).

[85] Chief Justice Lamer stated that 'Aboriginal title is the aspect of Aboriginal rights related specifically to Aborginal claims to land' (1996, 4 CNLR 177).

[86] *Delgamuukw* v. *British Columbia*, 3 SRC (1997) 1010.

[87] Ibid. at 1082.

not use the land in such a way as to destroy that relationship (e.g. by developing it in such a way that the bond is destroyed, perhaps by turning it into a parking lot).[88]

Such a position must be seen as a consequence of the development of general concerns for the conservation of the natural environment in Canada. The Assembly of the First Nations has endorsed this 'underlying rationale' since 'conservation concerns are consistent with indigenous values and beliefs and ultimately benefit indigenous peoples'. Even though this decision recognized aboriginal titles as being protected by the constitution the case also provided the court with an opportunity to complete the theory of the power to 'extinguish' or 'adjust' aboriginals' titles. While in the *Sparrow* decision the court decided that in case of extinguishments, the government has to show 'clear and plain intention', in *Delgamuukw* the court specified that the legislation that could infringe aboriginal title must be based on the development of agriculture, forestry, mining and hydro-electric power, the general economic development of the interior, protection of the environment or endangered species, the building of infrastructures and the settlement of foreign populations to support those aims.[89] Thus, in determining legality of extinguishment of aboriginal title, the judicial power is required to assess whether the infringement has been minimal enough, whether fair compensation has been paid and, finally, whether concerned aboriginal groups were consulted before the final decision.[90]

Thus, the Canadian system highlights three major issues regarding indigenous peoples' rights to land.[91] First, that indigenous rights are inalienable and can only be surrendered by the Crown. Second, that indigenous titles arise from occupation of land prior to arrival of other settlers and not from any legal recognition (they are *sui generis* act). Thus aboriginal peoples have 'historical sovereignty' over their traditional lands, the proof of which is based on historical or physical occupation, and continuity and exclusivity of the occupation. Third, indigenous titles are collective and land cannot be used in a manner 'irreconcilable with the nature of the attachment to the land which forms the basis of the group's claim to aboriginal title'.[92] The Canadian example shows that in the last ten years the principle of cultural relativism concerning ownership of land has had to be recognized. As Asch points out, it is important to realize that only a few years ago the exercise of governmental power on the land was 'unmitigated', while 'the current theory of Aboriginal rights seeks to balance the supremacy of State power with respect for cultural difference' (1999: 428–46).

---

[88] *Delgamuukw* v. *British Columbia*, 3 SRC (1997) 1010 at para. 129.
[89] Ibid. at para. 165 (Lamer CJ).
[90] Ibid. at paras. 167–9.
[91] Canada also offers indigenous peoples the possibility of governance of their territories in Nunavut, see p. 226.
[92] *Delgamuukw* v. *British Columbia*, 3 SRC (1997) 1010.

Australia

Australia provides an example of one of the most amazing contemporary disputes between legislature and judiciary powers with regard to land rights. This debate centres on a definition concerning the rights of 'native title'[93] holders against those of non-indigenous persons to use the land for their own interests. In this debate, the two major issues were, first, whether the annexation of territories by the government had extinguished native titles and, second, to establish precisely whose rights should be given priority – aboriginal peoples already on the land, or the incoming colonizers who were granted titles to use the land. Another focus of Australian legislation on this issue lies in the fundamental link between anti-racist legislations and land right issues for indigenous peoples. During colonial times, rules were based on the idea that white settlers had 'freehold title' over land. As a result, aborigines had no legal right to own land. However, the post-colonial period was equally turbulent due to the policy of resettlement of aborigines in reservations. In legal terms aborigines had no rights – not even the right to be part of a treaty. That could be explained by the fact that in Australia jurisdiction relating to indigenous issues was subject to provincial law while in Canada and the USA such jurisdiction was federal (see Bartlett 1999).[94] Following a referendum that gave the federal government concurrent jurisdiction over aboriginal issues, the first recognized right arose in 1970 with constitutional acknowledgement that the federal government could only acquire land on a basis of 'just term'. Judicial action based on this principle was brought before a court to invalidate the grant of mining rights on traditional lands. In the decision in *Milirrpum v. Nabalaco Pty Ltd* the court stated that the 'doctrine of communal native title' was neither part of Australian law nor part of any common law system.[94] This decision meant that valid title to land must have been granted by the Crown in direct consequence of the doctrine of *terra nullius*.[96] Under this doctrine, the Crown acquired all the land in Australia. Thus to be recognized as the owner of a land specific recognition of this ownership was required from the Crown which was impossible in view of aborigines' customs and traditions concerning land ownership.

---

[93] The term 'native title' describes interests and rights of indigenous inhabitants to land, whether communal, group or individual, possessed under the traditional laws acknowledged by, and traditional customs observed by, the indigenous inhabitants – National Indigenous Working Group Fact Sheet – Native Title.

[94] Only in 1967 did the federal government obtain concurrent jurisdiction with the states concerning aboriginal peoples.

[95] This decision was mainly based on the decision of the British Columbia Court of Appeal in *Calder* that rejected the concept of native title at common law. However, eight months after that decision, the Supreme Court of Canada overruled the decision of the British Columbia Court of Appeal.

[96] In a decision of 1889, *Cooper v. Stuart*, it was ruled that Australia had not been 'conquered' but 'settled'; 14 App. Cas. 286 (1889).

The *Mabo 1* decision followed a claim of the Meriam People against the State of Queensland, which proclaimed that some of the islands vested by the Crown, where the Meriam peoples used to live, were 'free from all other rights, interests and claims of any kind whatsoever'.[97] In this decision, the High Court decided that the Act established by the State of Queensland did not comply with the Racial Discrimination Act 1975[98] as such legislation denied the principle of equality before the law of the Meriam people. This first decision was a pre-revolutionary link wherein discrimination and right to own land was clearly made, but the court did not determine if aborigines had rights over land. The better-known *Mabo* decision came in 1992 and was the first recognition of native title (on an anti-discrimination ground). In the first instance, the decision recognized the existence of native title in common law. One of the consequences of this acknowledgment was that until explicit appropriation by the Crown, native title endured. Second, if native title was subject to extinguishments, such a procedure, if completed after 1975, had to comply with equality before the law as enacted by the Racial Discrimination Act. The existence of native title itself is based on two factors, 'exclusive occupation' of the land, and the content of the title as given by customary aboriginal laws (McNeil 2000 and 1997b: 117). Thus, native titles are distinguished from statutory land rights which:

> . . . flow from the Crown under legislation, similar to freehold and leaseholds titles. Native Title is not a grant created through legislation . . . [but] . . . comes from indigenous law and custom which pre-exists the Crown.[99]

This decision is famous for its legal rejection of the principle of *terra nullius* which was deemed outdated, inappropriate and discriminatory. Nevertheless, titles acquired by white settlers during the period when *terra nullius* was law were still considered valid. Such rejection thus had no effect in relation to the past (Bartlett 1999: 413), but the importance of this decision was to specify that indigenous rights do not disappear in case of settlement. As every legal 'revolution' carries some clauses of attenuation, the court specified that native title 'is a form of permissive occupancy at the will of the crown', thus extinguishments do not require specific compensation when carried out in the interest or the will of the nation.

Following the *Mabo* decision there was an important debate in Australia. Even though this decision was not perfect recognition of the right to own land for aborigines, public reaction was governed by the impression that aboriginal rights were overprotected by it. This reaction was mainly orchestrated by mining companies and others business interests.[100] The legal result of such 'unfounded

---

[97] Queensland Coast Islands Declaratory Act 1985.
[98] This Act is the implementation of the ICERD in Australian law.
[99] National Indigenous Working Group Fact Sheet – Native Title.
[100] For an illustration of such an orchestration by mining companies, see Australian Mining Industry Council, Advertisement, *West Australia* 14 August 1993 – a campaign that asked 'Is

fear'[101] was the passage of a new bill before parliament, namely the Native Title Act 1993, which recognized immunity for freehold and other titles from native title claims. Where other titles were threatened by the existence of native title, the Act recognized the legitimacy of all the Crown grants made before 1 January 1994. This Act also specified that if dispossession had taken place before 1975, aborigines were not allowed to claim title to their traditional land. It further stated that pastoral grants of mining interests suspended native title until the mining interest expired. The Act also recognized a right to negotiate over development on native title lands.[102] When allowing exploitation on native land, the government was required to notify native title holders, and an agreement made in 'good faith' had to be elaborated between the parties.[103]

In *Wik People* v. *State of Queensland*[104] the High Court was invited to resolve the crucial question of the relationship between the right of pastoral leases and native title.[105] The people of Cape York claimed ownership of their traditional land which was controlled by pastoral leases. Thus the issue was to define whether such grants of pastoral title were able to extinguish native title. This question was of immense importance since 42 per cent of all Australian land is held under pastoral leases. The majority of the court decided that the grant of pastoral leases under the Queensland Land Acts 1910 and 1962 did not 'necessarily extinguish all incidents of Aboriginal title'. This decision went beyond simply defining the relationship between native titles and pastoral leases and aspired for equality of status between any title over the land and native titles.[106] Therefore, native title fell in the same category as every other title and, as a result of this decision, when the Crown wished to confiscate land owned by aborigines it was no longer a question of extinguishment but rather a general

---

this really one Australia for all Australians? . . . The Australian Mining Industry is not opposed to Aborigines being granted titles . . . But we believe all Australians should have the same rights over these titles'; as quoted in Bartlett (1999: 417).

[101] This expression was used by Hill (1995: 306) to describe that overreaction – 'Unfounded fear of "Aborigines claiming your backyard as traditional lands" spread among the general public'.

[102] 'The statutory right to negotiate provisions of the Native Title Act provide a process to deal with compulsory acquisition of lands for the benefit of a third party. It applies to resource development and land use affecting native title. It strikes a balance between the rights and interests of native title holders and those resources developers'; National Indigenous Working Group on Native Title, Fact Sheets.

[103] Native Title Act, ss. 26–44.

[104] *Wik People* v. *State of Queensland*, 141 ALR (1969) 129.

[105] 'A pastoral lease gives the lease-holder the right to use the land for pastoral purposes, including raising livestock and developing infrastructure necessary for pastoralism – fence, yards, bores, accommodation, etc.'; National Indigenous Working Group on Native Title, Fact Sheets.

[106] Pastoral leases were a Crown grant.

question of expropriation.[107] The relationship between pastoral leases and native title is governed by the theory of 'co-existence'. Thus grants of pastoral leases were not considered to have extinguished native titles nor are they considered to have effected expropriation of such titles. However, the Court also defined that leaseholder rights prevailed over native title in cases of 'inconsistency'. Some commentators have highlighted that a direct consequence of the *Wik* decision is 'that where a subsisting native title right is inconsistent with another interest validly granted by the Crown, the other interest will prevail over native title to the extent of the inconsistency' (Dick 1999: 68). Thus native title is considered inferior to other grants if inconsistent with those grants. To determine the inconsistency, the test set up in *Wik* is based on whether the native title can be exercised without altering the grant. If alterations are created, the native title has to be considered legally extinguished. However, this decision left both communities, the aboriginal as well as the non-indigenous community, unsatisfied and as a result the issue of co-existence remained unresolved.

The government proposed a 'Ten Point Plan' for adoption by parliament, most of which was adopted under the Native Title Amendment Act 1998. The principal provisions of this amendment are the validation of acts or grants made between 1994 and 1998 (confirmation of past extinguishments), removal of rights to negotiate over acquisition of native title in cities and removal of the government obligation to negotiate in 'good faith'. The amendment also includes a list of grants that extinguish native titles permanently (freehold, commercial leases, exclusive agricultural/pastoral leases, residential leases) (Schiveley 2000: 427). The Act also expands the rights of pastoralist leaseholders by diversification of activities allowed (cultivation, fishing, forestry, aquaculture, off-farm activities, and so on).[108] Even though, the amendment includes a reference to the application of anti-discriminatory legislation, in 1999 the CERD observed that some of the provisions of the Act 'extinguish or impair the exercise of indigenous title rights and interests and discriminate against native title holders'.[109] The CERD also noted:

> . . . in particular, four specific provisions that discriminate against indigenous title holders under the newly amended Act. These include the Act's 'validation' provisions; the 'confirmation of extinguishment' provisions; the primary production upgrade provisions; and the restrictions concerning the right of indigenous title holders to negotiate non-indigenous land uses.[110]

---

[107] One of the legal consequences of such an evolution is that the Crown needs to show 'clear and plain legislative intention' to expropriate and such measure must be based on a just compensation.

[108] For a complete understanding of the content and the validity of this amendment, see Triggs (1999: 372).

[109] CERD, Findings on the Native Title Amendment Act 1998 (Cth), UN Doc. ERD/C/54/Misc.40/Rev.2 (18 March 1999), para. 21. CERD expressed concern over the compatibility of the amended Native Title Act 1993 . . . with Australia's international obligations under the ICERD.

[110] CERD expressed concern over the compatibility of the amended Act with arts. 1(4), 2 and 5 of the convention, in particular, that the principle of non-discrimination applies to the 'right to own property alone as well as in association with others'.

Thus the CERD found that the amended Native Title Act was in breach of the convention since it appeared 'to discriminate on the basis of race to the significant detriment of indigenous peoples and thus to breach the Racial Discrimination Convention and international law in other respects'.[111]

The judicial debate concerning native titles is most evolved in Canada and Australia where significant developments with regard to adoption of legislation have taken place during the past two decades. While judicial settlement seems too insufficient, it remains extravagant to ask a court to determine the structure of the negotiation between aboriginals and settlers – to determine the structure of future relationships and what is ultimately required to resolve these issues (Schiveley 2000: 11). The establishment of political dialogue and negotiation before litigation in court is certainly preferable in resolution of land issues; moreover it leaves the courts as a last resort if negotiations fail. Thus, even though legislative innovations during recent decades are important, the evolution of political dialogue between indigenous representatives and governments on land rights merits deeper attention. To protect their specific relationship with the land, indigenous peoples are sometimes given a degree of governmental representation but this can vary significantly. In Scandinavia, for example, the Sami have a representative parliament that can invite national parliaments to take cognisance of indigenous issues. In other countries, indigenous peoples' rights to land are recognized via a degree of autonomy with regard to the management of territory. For example, in Greenland and Canada, the Inuit have access to a more developed system of self-governance.[112]

The Sami[113] peoples, formerly, the inhabitants of Lapland, are divided between the boundaries of Norway, Sweden, Finland and Russia.[114] Nowadays, in their relationship with the governments of Norway, Sweden and Finland, their situation is almost similar; in these three countries they have political expression within the 'Sami parliaments' which are advisory bodies to national parliaments and propose legislation regarding

---

[111]   On the validity of the amended Act with regard to the Convention on the Elimination of All Forms of Discrimination, see Triggs (1999).

[112]   For a general overview concerning the current situation of the Inuit, see 'Indian and Northern Affairs Canada', *Inuit in Canada*, <http://www.inac.gc.ca/pubs/information/info.16.html>. See also <http://www.innu.ca> or <http://www.nunanet.com/~jtagak/resources/> (consulted 27/08/01).

[113]   There are several appellations for the Sami, they call themselves 'Saemi', 'Sápmi', or 'Saa'm'. In the literature the terms 'Sámi', 'Saami' or 'Same' are also often used; see Craig and Freeland (1998). The Sami were referred to as Lapps but after many years of campaigning by Sami representatives this term, considered derogatory, was changed.

[114]   The Sami population is estimated to be roughly between 75 000 and 100 000, between 40 000 and 60 000 are in Norway, 20 000 in Sweden, 6500 in Finland and the rest in Russia. As there is no representative Sami parliament in Russia, these comments only apply to Norway, Sweden and Finland.

Sami issues.[115] However, it is important to note that the Sami parliament does not have any role on the issue of ownership rights. In this regard, the Sami experience in Scandinavia highlights that granting a certain degree of political representation before, or without, domestically recognizing rights to land is illusory. Even though it is very important that indigenous peoples have political voice within their states, the land rights issue is of such importance that today in all these countries the political situation is frozen by the lack of development on this crucial issue.

The Inuit live in four areas: Canada, Alaska, Russia and Greenland (see Nuttall 1994).[116] In 1992, in Northern Canada an 'Aboriginal-governed territory' called Nunavut was created after 15 years of negotiation between the government and the Inuit of the Northwest Territories.[117] The Canadian federal parliament has delegated territorial powers to the public government of Nunavut. Via art. 19 of the agreement between Canada and the Tungavik Federation of Nunavut, lands within the new territory are established as 'Inuit-owned'. Such ownership is seen as a way of providing and promoting economic self-sufficiency. The title is owned collectively and vested in the Nunavut government. Thus the situation in Nunavut presents a good example of the manner in which states can deal with indigenous peoples' rights to title to territory.

Conclusions

The argument often made in discussing issues of the rights of indigenous peoples to title to territory is that preference should be given to political discussion rather than judicial litigation.[118] However, while general rules cannot be inferred from the Inuit example it does reveal a model of a viable land management strategy within a demarcated territory without threatening the fundamental unity of the state. As Special Rapporteur Cobo has stated:

> Diversity is not, in itself, contrary to unity, any more than uniformity itself necessarily produces the desired unity.
>
> (Cobo 1983: 54, para. 402)

---

[115] The Sami have always tried to maintain a relationship between the Sami populations in the different countries. The Sami Council is an NGO that represents all Sami (it has NGO status within the ECOSOC system). Since 1986 they have a common flag and a national anthem. The first Sami parliament was created in Finland in 1973, the second in Norway (1989) and the third in Sweden (1993).

[116] The political situation of Greenland is still evolving, with access to independence in the near future; see <http://www.gh.gl/>.

[117] Administrative difficulties delayed the official separation to April 1999.

[118] Such political dialogue is also a sign of the end of the 'paternalist' approaches of most western societies; approaches that were racist and destructive for indigenous societies via the notion of guardianship in issues governing land rights.

International law as regards land rights of indigenous peoples is underdeveloped in comparison to national laws. The ILO Convention remains the only legally binding instrument specifically addressing this issue. Even though general protection is afforded by human rights law, this is only a protection by default. The national legislations of Canada, Australia, Finland, Norway and Sweden all point towards an evolving body of international customary law. In these countries national legislation has evolved because of international pressure. In all the case law studied explicit references to international law were made and such case law was of crucial importance for the evolution of national legislation. Even though international law regarding indigenous land rights is not strong, state practice reveals that judges have the belief (*opinio juris*) that a change in their national legislation dealing with land rights is necessary as regards indigenous peoples. Therefore, international customary law as both practice and *opinio juris* seems to exist in the international arena. Since the land rights issue is a primary issue for indigenous peoples there remains great scope for the evolution of international norms in this respect. Triggs (1999) summarizes four salient points pertaining to existing international law regarding the indigenous land rights issue. Building on this, national legislations and international law could be said to have evolved in four main directions:

1   Recognition and protection of the relationship between indigenous peoples and land as indicated by joint arts. 1(1) and 1(3) of the 1966 Human Rights Covenants.
2   Indigenous peoples have 'some rights to own land in association with others and to inherit that land', as provided by the principle of non-discrimination under ICERD.[119]
3   Indigenous peoples have a right 'not to be discriminated against on the basis of race and to have the benefit of law to ensure substantive equality' as given by art. 1 of ICERD.
4   Law has to clearly stipulate that 'where a government acts in relation to indigenous title it is bound to ensure participation in the decision through full and bona fide consultation with, and in some instances, through the consent of, the indigenous peoples concerned and to provide full compensation where their rights are adversely affected'.[120]

Nevertheless, it is important to keep in mind that even when such rights are theoretically recognized by national legislations, their practical implementation is always very different. In the words of Moses, the Grand Chief of the Grand Council of Crees:

---

[119] For text and references of those instruments, see E/CN.4/Sub.2/2000/25, Annex.
[120] This discussion was central to debates at the World Conference Against Racism, Racial Discrimination, Xenophobia and Related Intolerance, Durban, September 2001. This conference might be another forum for indigenous land claims. See <http://www.un.org/rights/racism/>.

Under this system, and as exemplified by Canada, it is the aboriginal peoples who must attempt to claim back from the state the lands we have lived on for thousands of years. And it is the state which determines the validity and extent of the claim and its final resolution. The baseline or starting-point in this process is total dispossession. The onus is upon the indigenous peoples to prove their indigenous ancestry, their original possession, and the extent of the use of their lands and territories. It is the state that makes judgement, and it is the state that is the ultimate beneficiary. Finally, in perhaps the most confounded and convoluted contradiction of all, the indigenous peoples must surrender to the state their aboriginal title in order to have title to their meagre remainder confirmed through treaty by the state. The alleged objective is to provide the state with some guarantees of 'finality' and 'certainty'.

(Moses 2000: 167)

In the future it is clearly essential to recognize the importance of the land rights issue for indigenous peoples. If there is no progress on this issue, international law will be unable to offer adequate protection, thus rendering previous declarations of concern expressed by the international community as empty rhetoric. It is clear that such development must be carried out in the face of a 'global market' that commercially values indigenous lands and seeks acquisition of territories where natural wealth is concentrated. Thus there is a real threat of increase in the claims of states, multinational companies and indigenous peoples for ownership of these territories. In this potential battle indigenous peoples in their precarious position are particularly poorly protected. As stated by Rapporteur Daes, 'the gradual deterioration of indigenous societies can be traced to non-recognition of the profound relationship that indigenous peoples have to their lands, territories and resources, as well as the lack of recognition of other fundamental human rights' (Daes 2000: 3).

8 Conclusion

One of the preconditions inherent in the definition of a state in modern international law is that it will have a defined territory.[1] This single concept is enshrined as one of the main conditions concomitant to statehood and is given by the Montevideo Convention 1933.[2] For most sovereign states this condition is apparent enough, yet the process of colonization has rendered the notion of territory in some entities extremely problematic.[3] Modern international law has been slow to address these notions of territoriality since it is framed from a particular perspective that has not been forced to consider these kinds of issues.[4] Rather, in seeking to address the growing spate of violence induced by conflict over territory it has invoked legal notions that were first developed during the Roman era. Roman property regimes and their resultant principles, notably *uti possidetis juris*, have been applied and reapplied in different contexts to become the problematic bedrock of the treatment of territory within modern international law.[5]

The work undertaken in this book involved the questioning and critical analysis of some of the basic underlying assumptions inherent in the transmission of the doctrine to modern situations. For this purpose it started by setting out the manner in which the doctrines of *uti possidetis* have come to be interpreted in modern international law. This initial chapter laid down the basis against which the intertemporal development of the law was then examined. However, as has been established, the actual treatment of *uti possidetis juris* in contemporary international law is far removed from its original development as an interim mechanism available to the praetor under Roman private law. Chapter 2 examined these contextual nuances of the norm vis-à-vis its original application within Roman jurisprudence in a bid to assess its relevance towards transposition into international jurisprudence by classical jurists such as Gentilli and Vattel. Initially applied as an equitable principle that informed the rulings of the Roman

---

[1] For a treatment of territory in international law, see Jennings and Watt (1992: 563–718).

[2] Article 1, Montevideo Convention 1933 states: 'The State as a person of international law should possess the following qualifications: (a) a permanent population; (b) a defined territory; (c) government; and (d) capacity to enter into relations with other states.'

[3] As can be seen in liberation movements in countries such as India, Nigeria, Sudan, Indonesia and the Philippines.

[4] For the impact of western notions, see Mazrui (1975).

[5] For a general reading on *uti possidetis*, see Ratner (1996), Shaw (1996) and Castellino and Allen (2000).

praetor in disputes between individuals over a possession, it assumed that the possessor of a disputed property would be considered its owner in the interim while the claimant had to demonstrate his[6] case against them. However, when transmitted into international law this basic principle was called upon to justify the boundaries left in Latin America by the Spanish and Portuguese as they were defeated in the face of the Creole liberation action.[7] In the interests of order the Creoles decided that the doctrine of *uti possidetis* would be most appropriate. They interpreted this doctrine to mean 'as you possess so you possess' and when applied to the unfolding decolonization of Latin America it was considered to validate the boundaries left behind by the colonial powers, which the new incumbents to power decided by concensus not to challenge. The result was that former administrative boundaries within the Spanish Empire were transformed into international frontiers with the same technical sanctity afforded them that was bestowed upon historical negotiations of territory between sovereigns in Europe. The guarantee of these boundaries benefited the Creoles for a number of reasons, most of which could be attributed to the maintenance of order in a period of transition. Attendant to the use of the doctrine of *uti possidetis* in this context was the development of another important and extremely vital concept. This concept was that of *terra nullius* and the resonance of it pertained to the acquisition of territory. International law, as it had developed at the time, was clear that only unoccupied territory could be legally acquired (Jennings and Watt 1992: 567). All other acquisition of territory would need to take place via other means existing within international law, such as cession or treaties of accession. This doctrine was essentially set up to prevent wide-scale acquisition of the territory of one state by another – which would be to the detriment of international order. While the colonization of America had already taken place in contravention of this prevailing principle, past actions were prevented from being judged against the contemporary standard by use of the rule of intertemporal law. This rule is vital to the dynamics of international law since it deems that all actions need to be judged in the strict temporal context in which they occurred, so as to prevent the retrospective application of more modern ideas to activities that took place before their development. The prime aim is to prevent the finding of past injustices against the vagaries of legal evolution. Thus while the colonization of the Americas was beyond the scope of international law, the Creoles, in seeking to ensure that Latin America would never be the victim of further European colonization, sought to rein in the principle of *terra nullius* by declaring that there was no such territory in Latin America. By this statement they inferred that all territory in the continent came within sovereign jurisdiction of an existing power. These concepts were sanctified in numerous treaties

---

[6] In Roman law women did not have any rights to property due to their status in society as 'minors'.

[7] For a general reading on the contribution of Latin America to international law, see Alvarez (1909) and Woolsey (1931).

and were even included in the Monroe Doctrine of 1823.[8] However, the use of this terminology by the Creoles was essentially flawed since in claiming the territory without the acquiescence of the native peoples of Latin America they had implied acceptance of it as *terra nullius* before their own arrival and therefore capable of their own occupation.[9] Nonetheless, in sanctifying interpretation of the doctrines of *terra nullius* and *uti possidetis* and seeking to crystallize them within international law with reference to regional custom, it could be argued that the doctrines themselves came to signify a particular meaning relevant to Spanish decolonization. These events took place towards the middle and latter stages of the nineteenth century and, it could be argued, reflected the standards developing in international law against notions of conquest, occupation and colonization of international territory.

Despite these developments, further colonization did take place. Unable to turn west to colonize, the imperial powers of Europe competed against each other in seizing territories elsewhere (see Pakenham 1991). The worst affected was the continent of Africa where in a frenetic swoop towards the end of the nineteenth century, the European powers began the process of carving out and demarcating territory between themselves armed with the philosophy of the 'three Cs' – civilization, Christianity and commerce.[10] Chapter 4 analysed the process by which this philosophy was accompanied by various international legal developments wherein the powers sought to agree between themselves and justify their action by recourse to various principles of public international law. This process was largely achieved by means of 'treaties' of dubious validity in international law, with spurious and sometimes fraudulent entitlements (Touval 1969). Nonetheless since the powers themselves remained the ultimate gatekeepers of international law the process remained skewed in their favour. However, with decolonization gaining steam in the face of the self-determination movements of the UN era, these colonies gradually began to unravel (see Sureda 1973). The situation was now similar to that faced by the Spanish in the face of Creole action, and once again the response was dictated by the need to preserve order. The process of division of territory in Africa had been informed in most instances by nothing more than a desire to restrict the influence of a rival's jurisdiction and rarely pertained to naturally occurring fault lines, nor to tribal or traditional custom.[11] As a

---

[8] For general reading on the Monroe Doctrine, see Hughes (1923) and Jessup (1935).

[9] For the significance of *terra nullius* in international law, see Jennings and Watt (1992: 564).

[10] For more information, see Gann and Duignan (1969–75) Vol. 1 and Flint (1988).

[11] In the words of Lord Salisbury: 'We [the colonial powers] have engaged . . . in drawing lines upon maps where no white man's feet have ever trod; we have been giving away mountains and rivers and lakes to each other, but we have only been hindered by the small impediment that we never knew exactly where those mountains and rivers and lakes were'; as cited by Judge Ajibola, *Case concerning the territorial dispute (Libyan Arab Jamahiriya v. Chad)*, ICJ Reports (1994) 6 at 53.

result, African administrative territories that 'belonged' to the various powers seldom corresponded to pre-colonial dimensions of past kingdoms or tribal lands. In the negotiations that took place between two or more European powers over territory that they did not know or understand, they cut across all kinds of traditional divides.[12] When it was time to decolonize the same principles that informed the Spanish withdrawal in Latin America were called upon and thus, via the principle of *uti possidetis*, these random and problematic administrative boundaries took on the sanctity of international frontiers. While this was, in most instances, conducive to peace, security and order in the short-run, it proved extremely difficult to sustain. As a result, a spate of violent renegotiations began, starting with the actions in Katanga and Biafra. The Organization of African Unity, the regional body, was extremely concerned by these threats to statehood and adopted the strongest terms by which to protect the territorial sovereignty of states.[13]

Problems concerning territoriality and its allocation persist, as can be seen in the numerous cases brought before the International Court of Justice as states seek delimitation of boundaries that pertain to historical allegiances against the weight of rigid and alien principles such as *uti possidetis*. Eight of these cases have been reviewed in the fifth chapter of this book to analyse the extent to which states recognize and comply with the doctrine of *uti possidetis* and also to examine the means by which they seek to justify their positions against this doctrine. The pleadings to these cases are rich material for the presentation of alternative histories of these territories, which reveal various intricacies that remain unaccommodated within the rigid treatment of territory in international law. Also included in various cases are the pronouncements of the jurists of the ICJ and their analysis of the doctrines and the manner of their application in the different contexts. One of the major problems with this particular regime of redressal is that it remains closed to non-state actors. Yet it is non-state actors who are in the forefront of the renegotiation of territorial rights. Modern international law has come a long way since its acceptance of the discourse as being purely one that governed relations between states. Indeed non-state actors have an increasing role to play within international society, whether in the form of international NGOs,[14] pressure groups[15] or national liberation movements.[16] Yet the ICJ in its current

---

[12] See the Libyan pleadings in the *Libya–Chad case*, ICJ Reports (1994) 6, Libyan Written Pleadings at p. 88 para. 4.46.

[13] Resolution 16(1) of the OAU Assembly of Heads of State and Government at Cairo in July 1964. This provided that 'all Member States pledge themselves to respect the borders existing on their achievement of national independence'; cited in Brownlie (1971: 360–1).

[14] For example, Amnesty International and Human Rights Watch play a significant role in the perpetration and monitoring of worldwide human rights standards.

[15] For example, child rights NGOs have been allowed to participate in the discussions of the Committee for the Rights of the Child.

[16] The Palestinian Liberation Organization was granted observer status in the UN General Assembly on 22 November 1974; see General Assembly Resolution 3237 (XXIX).

format is unable to accommodate the interests of these groups even if they represent those most affected by the doctrinal injustices of the past. In addition, the mechanism of the ICJ, structured as it is to adjudicate disputes *between* states, fails to provide remedies in *intra*-state conflicts over territory. The last two chapters of this book have focused on two such contemporary situations within states, where issues of the title to territory were raised and required clarification.

The first situation examined concerned the break-up of the former Yugoslavia. This conflict dominated international attention for much of the 1990s and initially began as a movement within the state of Yugoslavia by which different groups within the federal state sought to protect and strengthen their position in the face of growing ethnic identification. However, this process was overtaken by events that unfolded at a frenetic pace. As a result the body set up by the European Commission Committee on Yugoslavia to draw up a new constitution that would accommodate the different peoples of the state within a new structure was forced to 'creatively interpret' its own role (Terrett 2000). Thus the Badinter Arbitration Commission that had been set up to negotiate with different powers in the disintegrating state in a bid to agree on a constitution that would benefit and protect the rights of the different peoples was forced instead to rule on issues of territoriality within modern international law. This change of role was essentially brought about by the speed of events that ruled out the possibility of accommodation within the state and instead saw the creation of new states from the six republics. Once again order was threatened, and the commission responded by professing the doctrines of *uti possidetis* in seeking to sanctify administrative boundaries within the former Yugoslavia. This process was accompanied by numerous problems, partly a result of the changing role of the commission itself, but the opinions of the commission, nevertheless, present a modern interpretation of the doctrines governing the treatment of territory in international law.

The second contemporary situation examined focused on the intricacies of the treatment of territory in a completely different setting. While studying different territories and different eras, it is easy to ignore, as has been done in the creation and sustenance of the sovereign state, indigenous peoples who have lived largely uninterrupted in particular territories. These peoples, sometimes oblivious to systems that are developing around them, are suddenly required to conform to alien systems for their possession of their land to be recognized internationally. In addition, more often than not, their right to the land that sustains them has been overridden by the propagation of settlers and settlements that contradict their ethos and render them bereft of the basic rights that they have been exercising for centuries. Modern international law and its accompanying principles have been unable to penetrate this area of law since it has traditionally come within the strict purview of the mandate of the sovereign state, even if that mandate was not necessarily achieved taking into account the rights of these indigenous peoples. Thus, the situation in many states with indigenous peoples is more akin to the issues concerning Creole action in Spanish America than the classical vision of self-determination that is synonymous with the romantic notions of decolonization in the UN era.[17] Even in that particular era, the rights of indigenous peoples and other peoples who were in a non-dominant position within the transfer of power were rendered voiceless. Thus the final chapter sought to examine the issues concerning indigenous peoples through the lens of different instruments of international and national law. In this sense the book has sought to present a chronological analysis of the issues that have shaped doctrines governing territoriality in international law and to examine them against the growing norms of human rights and entitlements within modern international law.

One of the most important purposes of this exercise concerns the analysis of the issue of the intertemporal rule. Past injustices such as colonization are usually protected from intense scrutiny by modern international law through this rule. The rule itself needs to be commended since it would clearly be unjust to seek to project a more progressive notion of law and its underpinning morality onto the actions of the past in a bid to seek culpability. This would violate basic legal entitlements against retrospection in contradistinction to revisionist notions. While the validity of revisionist notions is being questioned in other forums, it is not the purpose of this book to question the rule itself. Rather the purpose of this book is to demonstrate the extent to which the rule is incoherently and often inappropriately applied to situations governing the treatment of territory in modern international law. If it is argued that the actions of the imperial powers in annexing territories in Africa in the late nineteenth century are beyond culpability since they ought to be subject to the intertemporal rule, then the temporal context of that time bears examination. It is in this quest that the decolonization in Latin America provides the appropriate temporal context. By analysing and discussing notions that concerned not only territoriality but also the manner of conquests of colonies it could be argued that the tone had been set, in customary international law at least, for the development and further solidification of norms of international law against wanton conquests and annexation of territory. Although the norms had developed to this extent and were considered appropriate in Latin America, they were nonetheless either held to be invalid or disregarded on purpose in the colonization of Africa. Indeed the situation was compounded by blatant violation of the norms governing the signing of 'treaties' as European powers sought to challenge each other in a bid to accumulate colonies in the continent. Further, in decolonizing these territories the need for 'international' order was considered so sacrosanct that it overruled the history and geography of the post-colonial entities. Rather than accommodating and negotiating with the diverse peoples that came within the rigidly defined territories, the simplistic decision was taken to maintain colonial boundaries, an action that was bound to have longer term implications. This action, while nearly universally accepted by western-trained state leaders in Africa, failed to accommodate non-state actors who sought to gain legitimacy by seeking statehood themselves. The result has been numerous so-called conflicts of 'post-modern

---

[17] For notions of classical and romantic self-determination, see Koskenniemi (1994: 249–51).

tribalism' (Franck 1993: 3) as attempts are made to reformulate artificial colonial boundaries (of significance for only fifty years or less) along more historical lines.

While the application of the doctrine of *uti possidetis*, which solidifies the sanctity of colonial boundaries, does allow change in the face of consent, it is important to stress that this consent is required between existing sovereign states. Non-state actors have no explicit right to demand territorial adjustment even though the right to self-determination is enshrined as the first and foremost right in the two international covenants of 1966 that are the blueprint for the human rights regime. Thus existing states have sought to minimize the impact of the right of self-determination by declaring it as a right that only exists in an 'internal' guise. While notions of international order are to be cherished, the offer of autonomous regimes to groups that fail to see why they should exist within an externally defined unit for the sake of the historical convenience of a colonial power remains difficult to resolve. The fact that this historical convenience is in some cases further perpetrated by neo-colonists who fail to represent the inhabitants of a given territory serves only to aggravate the situation. This can often result in aggrieved and unrepresented peoples within a state seeking secession and in bid to access the international right to self-determination these groups attempt to pierce the veil of domestic sovereignty and internationalize their conflicts with their respective state governments.

Thus in summarizing the propositions of this book the following points can be made.

1   International law governing territoriality is premised on private law notions that emanate from Roman property regimes attributable to *jus civile* and *jus gentium*. These notions were applicable to the treatment of immovables when disputes arose between two or more parties with regard to possession of a given property. Accordingly the praetor ruled on interdictory proceedings wherein interim possession of the property would be given to the existing possessor while the claim of the aspirant was examined.

2   The Creole action in Latin America sought to apply this concept to sanctify boundaries inherited from colonial regimes in a bid to prevent the disintegration of these units. It was felt that such disintegration would hamper immediate development. In seeking clarification of these terms in international regional custom, the Creoles sought to codify other principles of international law too. One of these is the notion of arbitration to settle disputes, which has had some resonance in the determination of title to territory. The other concept that has been more important from the perspective of this examination of principles in international law is the consolidation of the denial of the notion of *terra nullius*.

3   It could be argued that the Creole action and subsequent continent-wide discussions and treaties emanating from the New World with regard to the treatment of territory

were an indication of existing customary international law. In this context it needs to be stressed that the Creoles were not the first to discuss the notions of the occupation of territory. The laws governing the acquisition of territory had already been in place prior to the Creole action. This action merely strengthened norms such as *terra nullius* and refocused them within the remit of international law.

4   In annexing territories in Africa, the imperial powers sought to justify their action by recourse to domestic laws as well as international legal principles. However, the principles in acquisition of territory were selectively applied and, as a result, even though an international conference such as the Berlin West Africa Conference of 1884–5 took place, the competitive nature of the quest prevented any real crystallization of consensus on issues governing the treatment of colonial territory. As a result, the acquisition of territory in Africa became an adversarial exercise wherein one power sought to outdo its rivals in making territorial claims. These claims were based on notional occupation and spurious 'treaties' that defeated principles of international law at the time.

5   The argument that the actions of the colonial powers in Africa are beyond reproach within international law is justified by application of the intertemporal rule. This rule of law states that actions of a given era must only be judged against the standards prevailing in that era and not by modern more progressive standards. It is argued that the standards prevailing at the time of the 'Scramble for Africa' could be viewed comprehensively under the guise of the legal tenets expressed in treaties signed in Latin America; and they clearly reveal the extent to which the laws governing treatment of territory had already developed. Therefore in wilfully choosing to disregard these laws, the colonial powers ought not to be able to claim refuge under the intertemporal rule.

6   The International Court of Justice has reiterated the importance of order in delivering its judgments. In this context it has validated the doctrine of *uti possidetis* and applied it in various cases, using as the 'critical date', the departure of the colonial power. Yet in doing so, it has admitted that the maintenance of these regimes is based on uncertain colonial legal regimes and that there is a revisionist quality about the doctrine itself. In the course of different pleadings, the court does seem to reveal a strong western bias which treats territory as a possession belonging to a sovereign even where that possession could not be justified as being *de jure* at that time. The court is also extremely restricted in the number of cases it can try based on the acceptance of its jurisdiction and the fact that non-state parties cannot access it. The recent proliferation of cases might suggest a change in the attitudes of state parties towards the court but this remains difficult to justify at this stage.

7   The Badinter Opinions, especially the so-called 'Badinter Principles', are instructive on the development, application and dangers of modern notions of territoriality.

Commissioned to work with disputants in Yugoslavia in a bid to create a multi-ethnic constitution, the Badinter Commission's work quickly exceeded its mandate. Nonetheless, being the prime legal organ in place during the conflict, it was asked for its opinions on various matters. While the Opinions are ridden with difficulties, some scholars have backed the expression of the Badinter Principles. These principles support the sanctity of boundaries and their inviolability. There is also explicit support for the doctrine of *uti possidetis* in the Opinions even though it had hitherto only been used in the context of decolonization. The rigidity of the boundary regime in the former Yugoslavia, where the sanctity of boundaries was held irrespective of ethnic fault lines that were still in the process of being negotiated, led to numerous conflicts that continue to remain a threat to longer term order, even if in the short-term the threat appears to have been alleviated.

8   The people with the best claim to territory remain those of indigenous origin. Not having had to claim territory in the manner that is inherent in settled cultures, their failure to assert this right was taken by the settlers as proof that the territory they inhabited was *terra nullius,* and on those territories regimes were built that excluded their original owners. This was either justified on the basis that the peoples were not socially and politically organized enough to dispel the notion of *terra nullius* and thereby save themselves from occupation, or assuaged by the signing of unequal treaties that would be of dubious value in modern international law. These indigenous peoples have tried to seek redress through international mechanisms for the protection of minority rights, but their claims are particularly different because of the thrust of the territorial element that is contained in them. While this claim might be seen as evidence that they now subscribe to similar notions of territoriality as the settled communities upon the lands, in most cases it is in fact simply a call to be able to claim in the settled sense, the territory that was traversed by their forefathers; the rights to which have been lost in obscure legal regimes to which they did not subscribe.

Modern international law as a discourse is premised upon notions of justice and order. While it is imperative that a legal regime protect the interests of order, to do so at the cost of justice suggests the interplay of political elements. While it is impossible to separate the legal from the political it is important to stress that the legal may contain an inherent political element. If this assertion can be accepted, it also suggests that the doctrines that have been rigidly interpreted as strict laws should be examined against the different contexts in which they have been developed and subsequently applied. To apply a concept that was incorrectly transposed from the obscure confines of Roman private law governing a dispute over immovable property to sanctify colonial boundaries is problematic in itself. To alter the doctrine to suggest a new rigidity strictly applicable to colonial situations is to aggravate the grievance. However, this now largely flexible and broad doctrine has been applied to non-colonial situations by the Badinter Commission in its Opinions on the disintegration of Yugoslavia. What is particularly problematic about this application is the manner in which the commission accepted it as a universally accepted rule that was to govern every situation in which new entities would come to power. Selectively quoting from the *Burkina Faso/Mali* case, it ignored the basic premise that the doctrine was applicable only in the post-colonial context. Meanwhile, the negotiation for land rights by indigenous peoples continues unabated, with sporadic progress due to the territorial nature of the sovereign state. Modern international law is largely helpless in assisting this cause and thus despite pronouncements regarding the right to self-determination and non-governance by foreign domination, the discourse is unable to penetrate the facade of domestic sovereignty that governs these causes. This has severely hampered the treatment of land rights and, as a result, they remain open to the vagrancies of particular state policies whether through the misapplication of the right as in the 'land reform' movements in Zimbabwe or in the continued denial of land rights to indigenous peoples worldwide.

Bibliography

Aikio, P. and Scheinin, M. (eds) (2000) *Operationalizing the Right of Indigenous Peoples to Self-Determination*, Institute for Human Rights, Åbo Akademi University, Turku/Åbo

Akehurst, M. (1974–5) 'The Hierarchy of Sources in International Law', *BYIL* 47: 273

Aleinikoff, T. A. and Klusmeyer, D. (eds) (2000) *From Migrants to Citizens: Membership in a Changing World*, Washington: Brookings Institute Press

Alexandrowicz, C. H. (1971) 'The Juridical Expression of the Sacred Trust of Civilization', *AJIL* 65(1): 149–59

Alexandrowicz, C. H. (1973a) 'The Partition of Africa by Treaty' in Ingham K. (ed.) *Foreign Relations of African States*, London: Butterworth

Alexandrowicz, C. H. (1973b) *The European-African Confrontation*, Leiden: A. W. Sijthoff

Alexandrowicz, C. H. (1975) 'The Role of Treaties in the European–African Confrontation in the Nineteenth Century' in Mensah-Brown, A. K. (ed.) *African International Legal History*, New York: UN Institute: 27–68

Alfredsson, G. and De Zayas, A. (1993) 'Minority Rights: Protection by the United Nations', *Human Rights Law Journal* 14(1–2) (26 February): 1

Ali, S. S. (1997) 'Conceptual Foundations of Human Rights: A Comparative Perspective', *EPL* 3(2): 261–82

Allott, A. (1973) 'The Changing Legal Status of Boundaries in Africa: A Diachronic View' in Ingham, K. (ed.) *Foreign Relations of African States*, London: Butterworth: 111–28

Allott, A. (1975) 'Boundaries in Africa: A Legal and Historical Survey' in Mensah-Brown, A. K. (ed.) *African International Legal History*, New York: UN Institute: 69–86

Alvarez, A. (1909) 'Latin America and International Law', *AJIL* 3(2): 269–353

Ames J. B. (1913) *Lectures on Legal History*, Cambridge, Mass.: Harvard University Press

Anaya, S. J. (1996) *Indigenous Peoples in International Law*, New York: Oxford University Press

Anderson, B. (1993) *Imagined Communities: Reflections on the Origin and Spread of Nationalism*, Ithaca: Cornell University Press

Andrews, J. A. (1978) 'The Concept of Statehood and the Acquisition of Territory in the Nineteenth Century', *LQR* 94: 408–27

Anene, J. C. (1966) *Southern Nigeria in Transition*, Cambridge: Cambridge University Press

Anene, J. C. (1970) *International Boundaries of Nigeria 1885–1960*, London: Longman

Antunes, N. S. M. (1999) 'The Eritrea–Yemen Arbitration: First Stage – The Law of Title to Territory Re-Averred', *ICLQ* 48: 362–86

Armstrong, D. (1998) 'Globalisation and the Social State', *Review of International Studies* 24: 461–78

Asch, M. (1999) 'From Calder to Van Der Peet, Aboriginal Rights and Canadian Law, 1973–96' in Havemann, P. (ed.) *Indigenous Peoples' Rights in Australia, Canada, and New Zealand*, Auckland: Oxford University Press: 428–46

Asiwaju, A. I. (ed.) (1985) *Partitioned Africans*, London: Hurst & Co

Assembly of the First Nations (2000) 'The *Amicus Curiae* Brief of the Assembly of First Nations', *HRQ* 22: 580

Assies, W. (1999) 'Indigenous Peoples and Reform of the State in Latin America' in Assies, W. and Van Der Haar, G. (eds) *The Challenge of Diversity: Indigenous Peoples and Reform of the State in Latin America*, Amsterdam: Thela Thesis: 15

Assies, W. J. and Hoekema, A. J. (eds) (1994) *Indigenous Peoples' Experiences with Self-government*, Copenhagen: University of Amsterdam

Axelson, E. (1967) *Portugal and the Scramble for Africa*, Johannesburg: Witwaterstrand University Press

Baker, R. S. and Dodd, W. E. (eds) (1925–7) *The Public Papers of Woodrow Wilson*, New York: Harper

Baldwin, D. (1997) 'The Concept of Security', *Review of International Studies* 23: 5–26

Baldwin, S. E. (1907) 'The International Congresses and Conferences of the Last Century as Forces Working Towards the Solidarity of the World', *AJIL* 1(3): 808–29

Ballantine, H. (1918–19) 'Title by Adverse Possession', *HLR* 32: 135–59

Barbour, K. M. and Prothero, R. M. (1961) *Essays in African Populations*, London: Routledge

Barkin, J. S. and Cronin, B. (1994) 'The State and the Nation: Changing Norms and the Rules of Sovereignty in International Relations', *IO* 48(1): 107–30

Barnett, M. N. (1995) 'Sovereignty, Nationalism and Regional Order in the Arab States System', *IO* 49(3) (Summer): 479–510

Barry, B. (1998) 'The Limits of Cultural Politics', *Review of International Studies* 24: 307–19

Barsh, R. L. (1996) 'Indigenous Peoples and the UN Commission on Human Rights: A Case of Immovable Object and Irresistible Force', *HRQ* 18(4): 797–827

Bartlett, R. H. (1999) 'Native Title in Australia: Denial, Recognition and Dispossession' in Havemann, P. (ed.) *Indigenous Peoples Rights in Australia, Canada and New Zealand*, Auckland: Oxford University Press: 408–27

Bartos, T. (1997) '*Uti Possidetis: Quo Vadis?*', *AYIL* 18: 37

Bekker, P. H. F. (1998) *Commentaries on World Court Decisions (1987–1996)*, The Hague: Martinus Nijhoff

Bennett, T. W. and Powell, C. H. (1999) 'Aboriginal Title in South Africa Revisited, South African Journal on Human Rights' 15: 449–85

Bernandez, S. T. (1994) 'The "Uti Possidetis Juris Principle" in Historical Perspective' in Kondrad, Gunther *et al.* (eds) *Volkerrecht Zwischen Normativem Anspruch und Politischer Realitat Festschrift fur Karl Zemanek zum 65 Geburtstag* (International Law between Normative Claims and Political Reality: Essays in Honour of Karl Zemank's 65th Birthday), Berlin: Dunker & Humboldt: 417–40

Berriedale, K. A. (1944) *Wheaton's International Law*, vol. 2 *War*, 7th edn, London: Stevens and Sons Ltd.

Birds, P. and McLeod, G. (1987) *Institutes of Justinian*, Ithaca, NY: Cornell University Press

Boggs, S. W. (1980) *International Boundaries: A Study of Boundary Functions and Problems*, New York: Columbia University Press

Bolintineanu, A. (1974) 'Expression of Consent to be Bound by a Treaty in the Light of Vienna Convention 1969', *AJIL* 68(4): 672–86

Borkowski, A. (1994) *Textbook on Roman Law*, 2nd edn, London: Blackstone Press

Bothe, M., Kurzidem, T., and Schmidt, C. (eds) (1993) *Amazonia and Siberia: Legal Aspects of the Preservation of the Environment and Development in the Last Open Spaces*, London: Graham & Trotman Ltd.

Bouchez, L. J. (1963) 'The Fixing of Boundaries in International Boundary Rivers', *ICLQ* 12 (July): 789–817

Bovill, E. (1968) *The Golden Trade of the Moors*, 2nd edn, London: Oxford University Press

Boyle, J. (ed.) (1994) *Critical Legal Studies*, Aldershot: Dartmouth

Brading, D. A. (1983) *Classical Republicanism and Creole Patriotism: Simon Bolivar (1783–1830) and the Spanish Revolution*, Cambridge: Cambridge University Press

Brenner, N. (1999) 'Beyond State-Centrism? Space, Territoriality and Geographical Scale in Globalisation Studies', *Theory and Society* 28: 39–78

Brierley, J. L. (1963) *The Law of Nations*, Oxford: Clarendon Press

Briggs, H. W. (1954) 'The Proposed European Political Community [Editorial Comment]', *AJIL* 48(1): 110–22

Brilmayer, L. (1991) 'Secession and Self-determination: A Territorial Interpretation', *YJIL* 16: 177–202

Brittain, V. (1999) 'Colonialism and the Predatory State in the Congo', *New Left Review*, no. 236, (July/August): 133–44

Brölmann, C., Lefeber, R. and Zieck, M. (eds) (1993) *Peoples and Minorities in International Law*, The Hague: Nijhoff

Brooks, R. L. (ed.) (1999) *When Sorry Isn't Enough: The Controversy over Apologies and Reparations for Human Injustice*, New York: New York University Press

Brown, J. S. (1927) 'The Gradual and Progressive Codification of International Law', *AJIL* 21(3): 417–50

Brownlie, I. (1963) *International Law and the Use of Force by States*, Oxford: Clarendon Press

Brownlie, I. (1971) *Basic Documents on African Affairs*, Oxford: Clarendon Press

Brownlie, I. (1979) *African Boundaries: Encyclopaedia*, London: Hurst & Co.

Brownlie, I. (1982) 'Recognition in Theory and Practice', 53 *BYIL* 197 (D&M, 3rd edn, 160–3)

Brownlie, I. (1992) *Treaties and Indigenous Peoples*, Oxford: Clarendon Press

Brownlie, I. (1998) *Principles of Public International Law*, 5th edn, Oxford: Oxford University Press

Buchanan, A. (1997) 'Self-determination, Secession and the Rule of Law' in McKim, R. and McMahan, J. (eds) *The Morality of Nationalism*, Oxford: Oxford University Press

Buchheit, L. C. (1978) *Secession: The Legitimacy of Self-determination*, New Haven, Conn.: Yale University Press

Buchheit, L. C. (1979–80) 'The Logic of Secession', *YLJ* 89: 802–24

Buckland, W. W. (1925) *A Manual of Roman Private Law*, Cambridge: Cambridge University Press

Buckland, W. W. (1963) *A Textbook of Roman Law from Augustus to Justinian*, 3rd edn, Cambridge: Cambridge University Press

Buckland, W. W. and McNair, A. (1952) *Roman Law and Common Law – A Comparison in Outline*, 2nd edn, Cambridge: Cambridge University Press

Buckland, W. W. and McNair, A. D. (1980) *Roman Law and Common Law: A Comparison Outline*, Cambridge: Cambridge University Press

Bull, H. (1995) *The Anarchical Society: A Study of Order in World Politics*, 2nd edn, New York: Columbia University Press

Bull, H., Kingsbury, B. and Roberts A., (eds) (1990) *Hugo Grotius and International Relations*, Oxford: Clarendon Press

Burger, J. (1998) 'Indigenous Peoples and the United Nations' in Price, C. (ed.) *Human Rights of Indigenous Peoples*, Ardsley, New York: Transnational Publishers: 10–48

Burke, E. (1972) 'The Image of the Moroccan State in French Ethnological Literature' in Gellner, E. and Micand, C. (eds) *Arabs and Berbers: From Tribe to Nation in North Africa*, London: Duckworth: 177–204

Burkeholder, M. A. and Johnson, L. L. (1998) *Colonial Latin America*, 3rd edn, New York: Oxford University Press

Butler, J. (ed.) (1964) *Boston University Papers on African History*, Boston, Mass.: Boston University Press

Camilleri, J. and Falk, R. (eds) (1992) *The End of Sovereignty? The Politics of a Shrinking and Fragmenting World*, Aldershot: Edward Elgar

Cassese, A. (1995) *Self-determination of Peoples: A Legal Reappraisal*, Cambridge: Cambridge University Press

Castellino, J. (1999a) 'Liberty, Fraternity and Equality: The Dubious Fruits of "National Self-determination" in International Law', *TLJ* 1(1): 1–32

Castellino, J. (1999b) 'Order and Secession: National Minorities and Self-determination', *International Journal of Minority and Group Rights* 6(4) (Autumn): 389–416

Castellino, J. (1999c) 'Territory and Identity in International Law: The Struggle for Self-determination in the Western Sahara', *MJIS* 28(3): 523–51

Castellino, J. (2000a) *International Law and Self-determination*, The Hague and London: Martinus Nijhoff

Castellino, J. (2000b) 'The Secession of Bangladesh in International Law: Setting New Standards?', *AYIL* 8: 83–104

Castellino, J. (2000c) 'The Saharawis and the Stratification of the Western Saharan Self' in Tierney, S. (ed.) *Accommodating National Identity: New Directions in National and International Law*, The Hague: Kluwer Law International: 257–84

Castellino, J. and Allen, S. (2000) 'The Doctrine of *Uti Possidetis* and Post-Colonial National Identity', *GYIL* 43: 205–26

Catholic Association for International Peace (History Committee) (1934) *The Catholic Church and Peace Efforts*, Washington, DC: Catholic Association for International Peace

Chadwick, E. (1996) *Self-determination, Terrorism and the International Humanitarian Law of Armed Conflict*, The Hague and London: Martinus Nijhoff

Chang, K. (1972) 'The UN and Decolonisation: The Case of Southern Yemen', *IO* 26(1): 37–61

Chase, P. (1995) 'Conflict in the Crimea: An Examination of Ethnic Conflict under the Contemporary Model of Sovereignty', *CJTL* 34: 219–39

Cheney, H. C. (1947) *International Law Chiefly as Interpreted and Applied by the United States*, 2nd edn

Chime, S. (1969) 'The Organization of African Unity and African Boundaries', in Widstrand, C. G. (ed.) *African Boundary Problems*, Uppsala: Scandinavian Institute of African Studies, pp. 65–78

Chopra, J. (1994) *United Nations Determination of the Western Saharan Self*, Oslo: Norsk Utenriks Politisk Institut

Clarke, R. F. (1907) 'A Permanent Tribunal of International Arbitration: Its Necessity and Value', *AJIL* 1(2): 342–408

Clarke, S. (1979) *Invasion of Zululand 1879*, Johannesburg: Brenthurst Press

Cobo, J. R. M. (1983) Special Rapporteur between 1973 and 1984, UN Sub-Commission on Prevention of Discrimination and Protection of Minorities, *Study of the Problem of Discrimination Against Indigenous Peoples, Final Report* (last part), UN Doc. E/CN.4/Sub.2/1983/21/Add.8

Cobo, J. R. M. (1986/7) Special Rapporteur between 1973 and 1984, UN Sub-Commission on Prevention of Discrimination and Protection of Minorities, *Study of the Problem of Discrimination Against Indigenous Peoples*, UN Doc. E/CN.4/Sub.2/1986/7 & Adds. 1–4

Collins, R. O. (1962) *The Southern Sudan 1883–1889: A Struggle for Control*, New Haven, Conn.: Yale University Press

Connolly, W. E. (1991) *Identity/Difference: Democratic Negotiations of Political Paradox*, Ithaca: Cornell University Press

Conrad, J. (1902) *Heart of Darkness*, Garden City: Doubleday, Page & Co.

Constantinou, C. (1998) 'Before the Summit: Representations of Sovereignty on the Himalayas', *MJIS* 27: 23–53

Coolidge, C. (1926) 'In the Matter of the Arbitration between the Republic of Peru and the Republic of Chile with Respect to the Unfulfilled Provisions of the Treaty of Peace of October 20, 1883' [Judicial Decisions], *AJIL* 20: 614–19

Craig, D. and Freeland, S. (1998) *Indigenous Governance by the Inuit of Greenland and the Sámi of Scandinavia*, Indigenous Law Resources, Reconciliation and Social Justice Library, Australian Research Council, Discussion Paper 8

Craven, M. (1995) 'The European Community Arbitration Commission on Yugoslavia', *BYIL* 66: 333–413

Crawford, J. (1979) *The Creation of States in International Law*, Oxford: Clarendon Press

Cross, M. (1978) 'Colonialism and Ethnicity: A Theory and Comparative Case Study', *ERS* 1(1) (January): 37–59

Crowe, S. E. (1942) *Berlin West-African Conference*, London: Longmans Green

Cukwurah, A. O. (1967) *The Settlement of Boundary Disputes in International Law*, Manchester: Manchester University Press

Curzon, G. N. C. (1908) *Frontiers*, Oxford: Clarendon Press

Daes, Erica-Irena A. (2000) Special Rapporteur, UN Sub-Commission on the Promotion and Protection of Human Rights, *Final Working Paper*, UN Doc. E/CN.4/Sub.2/2000/25, 30 June 2000

Davidson, B. (1992) *The Black Man's Burden: Africa and the Curse of the Nation-State*, New York: Times Books

Davis, M. C. (1996) 'Towards Modern Concepts of Sovereignty and Statehood' in Henckaerts, J. M. (ed.) *The International Status of Taiwan in the New World Order*, The Hague: Kluwer Law International

Davis, S. H. (1988) *Land Rights and Indigenous Peoples: The Role of the Inter-American Commission on Human Rights*, Cambridge: Cambridge University Press

Detrick, S. (1992) The United Nations Convention on the Rights of the Child: A Guide to the *Travaux préparatoires*, Dordrecht: Martinus Nijhoff Publishers

Deutsch, K. (1966) *Nationalism and Social Communication*, Cambridge, Mass.: MIT Press

Deutsch, K. and Foltz, W. (1963) *Nation Building*, New York: Atherton Press

De Vissher, C. (1968) *Theory and Reality in Public International Law*, Princeton, NJ: Princeton University Press

Dick, D. (1999) 'Comprehending the Genius of the Common Law – Native Title in

Australia and Canada compared post-Delgammuukw', *Australian Journal of Human Rights* 5(1)

Dike, K. O. (1929) *Documents Diplomatique Français (1871–1914)*, First Series, Paris

Dike, K. O. (1956) *Trade and Politics in the Niger Delta 1830–1885*, Oxford: Clarendon Press

Dixon, W. J. (1994) 'Democracy and the Peaceful Settlement of International Conflict', *APSR* 88 (March): 14–32

Dragadze, T. (1996) 'Self-determination in the Former Soviet Union and Eastern Europe', *ERS* 19(2) (April)

Dugard, J. (1972) 'Namibia, Southwest Africa: The Courts Opinion, South Africa's Response and Prospects for the Future', *CJTL* 11: 14

Dugard, J. (1987) *Recognition and the United Nations*, Cambridge: Grotius

Dugard, J. (1992) *Recognition in International Law*, Cambridge: Grotius

Dugard, J. (1996) '1966 and all that: South West Africa and East Timor', *Afr.JIL* 8: 549

Dugdale, E. (ed.) (1928–31) *German Diplomatic Documents, 1871–1914*, 94 vols.

Elias, T. O. (1974) *The Modern Law of Treaties*, New York: Ocean Press

Elias, T. O. (1980) 'The Doctrine of Intertemporal Law', *AJIL* 74 (2) (April): 285–307, and 'Correction', *AJIL* 74(4): 916

Elliott, D. W. (1997) *Law and Aboriginal Peoples in Canada*, Canadian Legal Studies Series, 3rd edn, North York, Ont.: Captus Press

Ellis, A. (1986) *Ethics and International Relations*, Manchester: Manchester University Press

Emerson, R. (1960) *From Empire to Nations: The Rise to Self Assertion of Asian and African Peoples*, Cambridge, Mass.: Harvard University Press

Emerson, R. (1971) 'Self-determination', *AJIL* 65: 459–75

Eulau, H. H. F. (1941) 'Theories of Federalism under the Holy Roman Empire', *APSR* 35(4): 643–64

Evans, M. D. (1995) 'Case Concerning the Territorial Dispute (Libyan Arab Jamahiriya/ Chad)', *ICLQ* 44: 683–90

Fage, J. D. (1995) *A History of Africa*, 3rd edn, London: Routledge

Fauchille, P. (1921–6) *Traite de Droit International Public*, vol. 1, Paris: Rousseau

Fenwick, C. G. (1939) 'The Monroe Doctrine and the Declaration of Lima', *AJIL* 33(2): 257–68

Fenwick, C. G. (1942) 'The Third Meeting of Ministers of Foreign Affairs at Rio de Janeiro', *AJIL* 36(2): 169–203

Fisch, J. (1988) 'Africa as *Terra Nullius*: The Berlin Conference and International Law' in Forster, S., Mommsen, W. J. and Robinson, R. (eds) *Bismarck, Europe, and Africa*, Oxford: Oxford University Press: 347–75

Fisher, F. C. (1933) 'The Arbitration of the Guatemala–Honduran Boundary Dispute', *AJIL* 27(3) (July): 403–27

Flint, J. E. (1960) *Sir George Goldie and the Making of Nigeria*, London: Oxford University Press

Flint, J. E. (1969) 'Nigeria: The Colonial Experience from 1880–1914' in Gann, L. H. and Duignan, P. (eds) *Colonialism in Africa 1870–1960*, vol. 1, Cambridge: Cambridge University Press: 220–60

Flint, J. E. (1988) 'Chartered Companies and the Transition from Informal Sway to Colonial Rule in Africa' in Forster, S., Mommsen, W. J. and Robinson, R. (eds) *Bismarck, Europe, and Africa*, Oxford: Oxford University Press: 69–83

Forde, S. (1998) 'Hugo Grotius on Ethics and War', *APSR* 92(3) (September): 639–48

Forsberg, T. (ed.) (1995) *Contested Territory: Border Disputes at the Edge of the Former Soviet Empire*, Aldershot: Edward Edgar

Forster, S., Mommsen, W. J. and Robinson, R. (eds) (1988) *Bismarck, Europe, and Africa*, Oxford: Oxford University Press

Franck, T. M. (1976) 'The Stealing of the Sahara', *AJIL* 70: 694–721

Franck, T. M. (1983) '*Dulce et Decorum Est*: The Strategic Role of Legal Principles in the Falklands War [Editorial Comment]', *AJIL* 77(1): 109–24

Franck, T. M. (1992) 'The Emerging Right to Democratic Governance', *AJIL* 86(1) (January): 46–91

Franck, T. M. (1993) 'Post-modern Tribalism and the Right to Secession' in Brölmann, C., Lefeber, R. and Zieck, M. (eds) *Peoples and Minorities in International Law*, The Hague: Nijhoff

Franck, T. M. (1996) 'Clan and Super Clan: Loyalty, Identity and Community in Law and Practice', *AJIL* 90(3), 359–83

Gaius (1988) *Institutes*, ed. Gordon, W. M. and Robinson, O. F., London: Duckworth

Galbraith, J. S. (1974) *Crown and Charter: The Early Years of the British South Africa Company*, Berkeley: University of California Press

Gamberale, C. (1995) 'National Identities and Citizenship in the European Union', *EPL* 1: 629

Gann, L. H. and Duignan, P. (1977a) *The Rulers of German Africa 1884–1914*, Stanford, Calif.: Stanford University Press

Gann, L. H. and Duignan, P. (1977b) *The Rulers of Belgian Africa 1884–1914*, Princeton, NJ: Princeton University Press

Gann, L. H. and Duignan, P. (1978a) *The Rulers of British Africa 1879–1914*, London: Croom Helm

Gann, L. H. and Duignan, P. (1978b) *African Proconsuls: European Governors in Africa*, New York: Free Press

Gann, L. H. and Duignan, P. (eds) (1978) *Colonialism in Africa 1870–1960*, Cambridge: Cambridge University Press

Gavin, R. J. and Betley, J. A. (eds) (1973) *The Scramble For Africa*, Nigeria: Ibadan University Press

Gayim, E. (1993) *The Eritrean Question: The Conflict between the Right of Self-determination and the Interests of the States*, Uppsala: Iustus Forlag

Gayim, E. (1995) 'The Eritrean Question: Self-determination and State Interests', *GYIL* 38: 439

Gellner, E. (1972) *Arabs and Berbers: From Tribe to Nation in North Africa*, London: Duckworth

Gentilis, A. (1877) *De Jure Belli*, Oxford

Gerard-Libois, G. J. (1966) *The Katanga Secession*, Madison, Wisc: University of Wisconsin Press

Gifford, P. and Louis, W. R. (eds) (1967) *Britain and Germany in Africa: Imperial Rivalry and Colonial Rule*, New Haven, Conn.: Yale University Press

Gifford, P. and Louis, W. R. (eds) (1971) *France And Britain in Africa: Imperial Rivalry and Colonial Rule*, New Haven, Conn. and London: Yale University Press

Gleny, M. (1999) *The Balkans 1804–1999: Nationalism, War and the Great Powers*, London: Granta Books

Goebel, J. (1927) *The Struggle for the Falklands Islands*, New Haven, Conn. and London: Yale University Press

Goldie, L. F. E. (1963) 'The Critical Date', *ICLQ* 12: 1251–84

Gordon, Scott (1999) *Controlling the State: Constitutionalism from Ancient Athens to Today*, Cambridge, Mass.: Harvard University Press

Gordon, W. M. and Robinson, O. F. (1988) *Institutes of Gaius*, Ithaca, NY: Cornell University Press

Gross, Hanns (1975) *Empire and Sovereignty: A History of the Public Law Literature in the Holy Roman Empire, 1599–1804*, Chicago: University of Chicago Press

Gross, L. (1948) 'The Peace of Westphalia, 1648–1948', *AJIL* 42(1): 20–41

Grotius, H. (1853) *De Pacis Juris Bella*, Cambridge

Grotius, H. (1951) *Mare Liberum*, New York: Carnegie Endowment for International Peace

Grovogui, S. (1996) *Sovereigns, Quasi-Sovereigns and Africans: Race and Self-determination in International Law*, Minneapolis: University of Minnesota Press

Hall, D. H. (1948) *Mandates, Dependencies and Trusteeship*, London: Stevens & Sons

Hall, W. E. (1894) *A Treatise on the Foreign Powers and Jurisdiction of the Crown*, Oxford

Hall, W. E. (1924) *A Treatise on International Law*, 8th edn, Oxford: Clarendon Press

Halperin, M., Scheffer, D. and Small, P. (1992) *Self-Determination in a New World Order*, Tcherkes: BEKO

Hannum, H. (1980) *Autonomy, Sovereignty and Self-determination: The Accommodation of Conflicting Rights*, Philadelphia: University of Pennsylvania Press

Hannum, H. (1993) 'Rethinking Self-determination', *Va.J.Int'l* 34: 1

Hargreaves, J. D. (1974) *West Africa Partitioned*, vol. I, London: Macmillan

Hargreaves, J. D. (1985) 'The Making of the Boundaries: Focus on West Africa' in Asiwaju, A. I. (ed.) *Partitioned Africans*, London: Hurst & Co.: 19–27

Hargreaves, J. D. (1988) 'The Berlin Conference, West African Boundaries, and the Eventual Partition' in Foster, S., Mommsen, W. J. and Robinson, R. (eds) *Bismarck, Europe, and Africa*, Oxford: Oxford University Press: 313–20

Harris, D. J. (1998) *Cases and Materials in International Law*, London: Sweet & Maxwell

Harris, D. and Livingstone, S. (eds) (1998) *The Inter-American System of Human Rights*, Oxford: Clarendon Press

Havemann, P. (1999a) 'Twentieth-Century Public International Law and Indigenous Peoples' in Havemann, P. (ed.) *Indigenous Peoples' Rights in Australia, Canada, and New Zealand*, Auckland: Oxford University Press: 19

Havemann, P. (ed.) (1999b) *Indigenous Peoples' Rights in Australia, Canada, and New Zealand*, Auckland: Oxford University Press

Hayden, Robery M. (1999) *Blueprints for a House Divided: The Constitutional Logic of the Yugoslav Conflict*, Ann Arbour Michigan: Michigan University Press

Hayton, R. (1956) 'The "American" Antarctic', *AJIL* 50(3) (July): 583–610

Hayward, J. (1991) *After the French Revolution: Six Critiques of Democracy and Nationalism*, New York: University Press

Hazlehurst, K. M. (ed.) (1995) *Legal Pluralism and the Colonial Legacy: Indigenous Experiences of Justice in Canada, Australia and New Zealand*, Aldershot: Avebury; Brookfield, Vt.: Ashgate

Heintze, H. J. (1993) 'The Protection of Indigenous Peoples under the ILO Convention' in Bothe, M., Kurzidem, T. and Schmidt, C. (eds) *Amazonia and Siberia: Legal Aspects of the Preservation of the Environment and Development in the Last Open Spaces*, London: Graham Trotman: 310–27

Helleiner, J. (1995) 'Gypsies, Celts and Tinkers: Colonial Antecedents of Anti-Traveller Racism in Ireland', *ERS* 18(3) (July): 532–54

Henderson, J. (Sákéj) Youngblood (1997) *The MÍkmaw Concordat*, Halifax: Fernwood Publishing

Henkin, L. (1999) 'Kosovo and the Law of "Humanitarian Intervention" [Editorial Comment]', *AJIL* 93(4): 824–28

Henkin, L., Wedgewood, R., Charney, J. I., Chinkin, C. M., Falk, R. A., Franck, T. M. and Reisman, W. M. (1999) 'Kosovo Intervention [Editorial Comment]', *AJIL* 93(4): 824–62

Heraclides, A. (1990) 'Secessionist Minorities and External Involvement', *IO* 44(3): 341–78

Heraclides, A. (1991) *The Politics of Self-determination and Minorities*, London: Cass

Herbst, J. (1989) 'The Creation and Maintenance of National Boundaries in Africa', *IO* 43: 673–92

Herbst, J. (1992) 'Challenges to Africa's Boundaries in the New World Order', *JIA* 46: 17–30

Hershey, A. S. (1911) 'The History of International Relations During Antiquity and the Middle Ages', *AJIL* 5(4): 901–33

Hertslet, E. (1909) *The Map of Africa by Treaty*, vols. I–III, London: HMSO; 3rd edn reprinted by Frank Cass & Co. 1967

Heydte, F. A. F. von der (1935) 'Discovery, Symbolic Annexation and Virtual Effectiveness in International Law', *AJIL* 29(3): 448–71

Higgins, R. (1983) 'Judge Dillard and Self-determination', *Va.J.Int'l* 23: 387–94
Higgins, R. (1990) 'Grotius and the Development of International Law During the United Nations Period' in Bull, H., Kingsbury, B. and Roberts, A. (eds) *Hugo Grotius and International Relations*, Oxford: Clarendon Press
Hill, R. P. (1995) 'Blackfellas and Whitefellas: Aboriginal Land Rights, The Mabo decision, and the Meaning of Land', *HRQ* 17(2): 303–22
Hille, S. (1995) 'Mutual Recognition of Croatia and Serbia (+ Montenegro)', *EJIL* 6 (4)
Hinsley, F. H. (1986) *Sovereignty*, Cambridge: Cambridge University Press
Hobson, J. A. (1902) *Imperialism: A Study*, London: Unwin Hyman
Hoebel, E. A. (1973) *The Law of Primitive Man*, New York: Atherton Press
Holdich, T. H. (1916) *Political Frontiers and Boundary Making*, London: Macmillan
Hugh, T. (1997) *The Slave Trade: The History of the Atlantic Slave Trade 1440–1870*, London: Picador
Hughes, C. E. (1923) 'Observations on the Monroe Doctrine', *AJIL* 17(4): 611–28
Hunt, A. (1986) 'The Theory of Critical Legal Studies', *OJLS* 6: 1–45
Hunt, A. (1993) *Explorations in Law and Society*, London: Routledge
Hurd, I. (1999) 'Legitimacy and Authority in International Politics', *IO* 53 (Spring): 397–408
Husserl, G. (1939) 'The Political Community Versus the Nation', *Ethics* 49(2) (January): 127–47
ILO (1953) *Indigenous Peoples*, Geneva: ILO
Jackson, R. (1992) 'Juridical Statehood in Sub-Saharan Africa', *JIA* 46(1): 1–16
Jennings, R. Y. (1962) *The Acquisition of Territory in International Law*, Manchester: Manchester University Press; New York: Oceana Publications
Jennings, R. and Watt, A. W. (1992) *Oppenheim's International Law*, 9th edn, Harlow, Essex: Longman
Jessup, P. C. (1928) 'The Palmas Island Arbitration', *AJIL* 22(4): 735–52
Jessup, P. C. (1935) 'The Generalisation of the Munroe Doctrine', *AJIL* 29(1): 105–9
Johnson, D. H. N. (1950) 'Acquisitive Prescription in International Law', *BYIL* 27: 332–54
Johnson, D. H. N. (1955) 'Consolidation as a Root of Title in International Law', *CLJ*: 215–25
Jolliffe, J. (1978) *East Timor: Nationalism and Colonialism*, St Lucia: University of Queensland Press
Jolowicz, H. F. (1957) *Roman Foundations of Modern Law*, Oxford: Clarendon Press
Jolowicz, H. F. and Nicholas, B. (1972) *Historical Introduction to the Study of Roman Law*, Cambridge: Cambridge University Press
Justinian (1985) *Digest*, text by Mommsen, T. and Krueger, P.; trans. Watson, A., Philadelphia: University of Pennsylvania Press
Justinian (1987) *Institutes*, ed. Birks, P. and McLeod, G., London: Duckworth

Kaikobad, K. H. (1983) 'Some Observations on the Doctrine of Continuity and Finality of Boundaries', *BYIL* 49: 119–41

Kapil, R. (1966) 'On the Conflict Potential of Inherited Boundaries in Africa', *WP* 18: 656–73

Keller, A. S., Lissitzyn, O. J. and Mann, F. J. (1938) *Creation of Rights of Sovereignty Through Symbolic Acts 1400–1800*, New York: Columbia University Press

Kolodziej, E. (2000) *Great Powers and Genocide Lessons from Rwanda*, Illinois: Program in Arms Control, Disarmament and International Security: Occasional Paper

Korff, S. A. (1924) 'An Introduction to the History of International Law', *AJIL* 18(2): 246–59

Koskenniemi, M. (1994) 'National Self-determination Today: Problems of Legal Theory and Practice', *ICLQ* 43(2): 241–69

Kunig, Phillip (1995) 'Decolonisation' in Wolfrum, R. (ed.) *United Nations: Law, Politics and Practice*, revised English edn, Dordrecht: Nijhoff: 390

Kunz, J. L. (1946) 'Guatemala v Great Britain: in Re Belice', *AJIL* 40(2): 383–90

Langenhove, F. van (1954) *The Question of Aborigines Before the United Nations*, Brussels: Royal Colonial Institute of Belgium, Social & Political Section

Lapidoth, R. (1992) 'Sovereignty in Transition', *JIA* 45: 325–66

Lauterpacht, H. (1970) *Private Law Sources and Analogies of International Law*, Hamden, Conn.: Archon

Legum, C. (1965) *Pan Africanism*, London: Pall Mall Press

Leiven, D. (1999) 'Dilemmas of Empire 1850–1918: Power, Territory, Identity', *JCH* 34: 163–200

Lenoir, J. L. (1942) 'The Monroe Doctrine and International Law: 1933–1941', *JP* 4(1): 47–67

Lindley, M. F. (1926) *The Acquisition and Government of Backward Territory in International Law*, New York: Negro Universities Press

Lissitzyn, O. J. (1967) 'Treaties and Changed Circumstances (*Rebus Sic Stantibus*)', *AJIL* 61(4): 895–922

Louis, W. R. (1971) 'The Berlin Congo Conference' in Gifford, P. and Louis, W. R. (eds) *France and Britain in Africa*, New Haven, Conn. and London: Yale University Press: 210–14

Lucas, C. P. (1922) *The Partition and Colonisation of Africa*, Oxford: Clarendon Press

Lugard, F. J. D. (1893) *The Rise of an East African Empire*, vol. 2

McCoubrey, H. and White, N. (1992) *International Law and Armed Conflict*, Aldershot: Dartmouth

McEwen, A. C. (1971) *International Boundaries of East Africa*, Oxford: Clarendon Press

MacGibbon, I. C. (1953) 'Some Observations on the Part of Protest in International Law', *BYIL* 30: 293–319

MacGibbon, I. C. (1957a) 'The Scope of Acquiescence in International Law', *BYIL* 31: 143–86

MacGibbon, I. C. (1957b) 'Customary International Law and Acquiescence', *BYIL* 33: 115–45

McGoldrick, D. (1991) *The Human Rights Committee: Practice and Procedures of Law Making at the UN*

Mackenzie, J. (1983) *The Partition of Africa 1880–1900*, London: Methuen

McNair, A. D. (1961) *The Law of Treaties*, Oxford: Clarendon Press

McNeil, K. (1997a) 'Aboriginal Rights in Canada in 1996: An Overview of the decisions of the Supreme Court of Canada', *ILB* 17 4(2)

McNeil, K. (1997b) 'Aboriginal Title and Aboriginal Rights: What's the Connection?', *Alb.LR* 36: 117

McNeil, K. (2000) *The Relevance of Traditional Laws and Customs to the Existence and Content of Native Title at Common Law*, Sasketchewan: Native Law Centre

Mahajan, S. (1999) *Independence and Partition: The Erosion of Colonial Power in India*, New Delhi: Sage Publications

Maier, G. (1969) 'The Boundary Dispute between Ecuador and Peru', *AJIL* 63(1): 28–46

Maine, H. S. (1894) *Ancient Law*, 15th edn, London: John Murray

Maivân Clech Lâm (2000) *At the Edge of the State: Indigenous Peoples and Self-Determination*, New York: Transnational Publishers

Makkonen, T. (2000) *Identity, Difference and Otherness: The Concepts of 'Peoples', 'Indigenous People' and 'Minority' in International Law*, Publications of the Faculty of Law, University of Helsinki, The Erik Castrén Institute of International Law and Human Rights, Research Reports 7/2000

Malanczuk, P. (1997) *Akehurst's Modern Introduction to International Law*, 7th edn, London, New York: Routledge

Manger, W. (1928) 'The Pan American Union at the Sixth International Conference of American States', *AJIL* 22(4): 764–75

Mazrui, A. (1967) *Towards a Pax Africana: A Study of Ideology and Ambition*, London: Weidenfeld & Nicolson

Mazrui, A. (1975) *Cultural Forces in World Politics*, London: Currey

Mommsen, T. and Kruger, P. (1985) *The Digest of Justinian*, trans. A. Watson, Philadelphia: University of Pennsylvania Press

Moore, J. B. (1944) 'Memorandum on *Uti Possidetis:* Costa Rica–Panama Arbitration 1911' in *The Collected Works of John Bassett Moore* Vol. 3: 328

Morris, H. F. (1972) 'Protection or Annexation? Some Constitutional Anomalies of Colonial Rule' in Morris, H. F. and Read, J. R. (eds) *Indirect Rule and the Search for Justice: Essays in East African Legal History*, Oxford: Clarendon Press: 41–70

Morris, H. F. and Read, J. R. (eds) (1972) *Indirect Rule and the Search for Justice: Essays in East African Legal History*, Oxford: Clarendon Press

Moses, T. (2000) 'The Right of Self-Determination and Its Significance to the Survival of Indigenous Peoples' in Aikio, P. and Scheinin, M. (eds) *Operationalising the Right of Indigenous Peoples to Self-Determination*, Institute for Human Rights, Åbo Akademi University, Turku/Åbo: 167

Muirhead, J. (1916) *Historical Introduction to the Private Law of Rome*, London: A & C Black

Muller, A. S., Raic, D. and Thuranszky, J. M. (eds) (1997) *The ICJ: Its Future Role After Fifty Years*, The Hague: M. Nijhoff

Murdoch, H. (1993) *A Dictionary of Irish Law*, 2nd edn, Dublin: Topaz

Murphy, R. (2000) 'Kosovo: Reflections on the Legal Aspects of the Conflict and its Outcome', *ISIA* 11: 7–30

Murphy, S. D. (1999) 'Democratic Legitimacy and the Recognition of States and Governments', *ICLQ* 48: 545–84

Mwa Bawele, M. (1988) 'Afro-European Relations in the Western Congo Basin 1884–5' in Forster, S., Mommsen, W. J. and Robinson, R. (eds) *Bismarck, Europe, and Africa*, Oxford: Oxford University Press: 469–89

Naldi, G. J. (1987) 'The Case Concerning the Frontier Dispute (*Burkina Faso/Republic of Mali*): *Uti Possidetis* in an African Perspective', *ICLQ* 36: 893–903

Neuberger, B. (1986) *National Self-Determination in Postcolonial Africa*, Boulder, Colo.: L. Rienner

News and Notes (1908) 'The First Pan-American Scientific Congress', *APSR* 2(3): 441–3

Nicholas, B. (1962) *An Introduction to Roman Law*, Oxford: Clarendon Press

Nugent, P. and Asiwaju, A. I. (eds) (1996) *African Boundaries: Barriers, Conduits and Opportunities*, London: Pinter

Nuttall, M. (1994) 'Greenland: Emergence of an Inuit Homeland' in Minority Rights Group (ed.), *Polar Peoples – Self-determination and Development*, London: Minority Rights Publications: 1–28

Oppenheim, L. F. L. (1992) *International Law*, 9th edn, Harlow: Longman

Osnitskaya, G. A. (1962) 'Colonialist Concepts of Equal and Unequal Subjects of International Law in the Theory and Practice of Imperialist States', *SYIL*: 49–63

Owen, D. (1995) *Balkan Odyssey*, London: Harvest Books

Pakenham, T. (1991) *The Scramble for Africa*, London: Abacus

Pastor, B. B. (1992) *The Armature of Conquest: Spanish Accounts of the Discovery of America 1492–1589*, trans. from Spanish by Longstreth, Stanford, Calif.: Stanford University Press

Pellet, A. (1992) 'The Opinions of the Badinter Arbitration Committee: A Second Breath for the Self-determination of Peoples', *EJIL* 3(1): 178–85

Phillimore, R. J. (1879) *Commentaries upon International Law*, vol. 1, 3rd edn, London: Lon&C

Phillipson, C. (1911) *The International Law and Custom of Ancient Greece and Rome*, vol. 1, London: Macmillan

Picon-Salas, M. (1962) *A Cultural History of Spanish America from Conquest to Independence*, Berkeley: California University Press

Pollock, F. and Maitland, W. M. (1898) *History of English Law before the Time of Edward I*, Vol. 2, 2nd edn, Cambridge: Cambridge University Press

Post, M. (1968) 'Is there a Case for Biafra?', *Int. Aff.* 44: 42–67

Price Cohen, Cynthia (ed.) (1998) *Human Rights of Indigenous Peoples*, London: Transnational Publishers

Pufendorf, S. (1710) *Of the Law of Nature and Nations*, Oxford

Quane, H. (1998) 'The UN and the Evolving Right to Self-determination', *ICLQ* 47: 537–72

Rabl, K. (1973) Das Selbstbestimmungsrecht der Völker – Geschichtliche Grunlagen und Umriss der gegenwärtigen Bedeutung (The Peoples' Right of Self-determination – Historical Foundations and Outline of Contemporary Relevance), Koln: Böhlau Verlag

Radan, P. (1994) 'Secession and Self Determination: The Case of Slovenia and Croatia', *Aus.JIL* 48: 183

Radan, P. (2000) 'Post-succession International Orders: A Critical Analysis of the Workings of the Badinter Commission', *MULR* 24: 50–76

Ragazzi, M. (1992) 'Conference on Yugoslavia Arbitration Commission: Introductory Note', *ILM* 31: 1488

Ratner, S. (1996) 'Drawing a Better Line: *Uti Possidetis* and the Borders of New States', *AJIL* 90(4): 590–624

Reeves, S. (1944) 'International Boundaries', *AJIL* 38 (4): 533–45

Rigo-Sureda, A. (1973) *The Evolution of the Right to Self Determination: A Study of the United Nations Practice*, Leiden: Sijhoff

Roberts-Wray, K. (1966) *Commonwealth and Colonial Law*, London: Stevens & Sons

Root, E. (1914) 'The Real Monroe Doctrine', *AJIL* 8(3): 427–42

Rosenne, S. (1995) *The World Court: What it is and How it Works*, 5th edn, The Hague: M. Nijhoff

Rouland, N., Pierré-Caps, S. and Poumarède, J. (1996) *Droit des minorités et des Peuples Autochtones*, Paris: Presse Universitaire de France

Rushdie, S. (1980) *Midnight's Children*, New York: Knopf

Russel, L. B. (1986) 'Current Development: Indigenous Peoples: An Emerging Object of International Law', *AJIL* 80: 369

Rutherford, G. W. (1926) 'Spheres of Influence: An Aspect of Semi-Suzerainty', *AJIL* 20(2): 300–25

Sambo, D. (1993) 'Indigenous Peoples and International Standard-Setting Processes, Are State Courts Listening?', *TLCP* 3: 31

Saxena, J. N. (1978) *Self Determination: From Biafra to Bangladesh*, Delhi: University of Delhi

Schabas, W. A. (2000) *Genocide in International Law: The Crime of Crimes*, Cambridge: Cambridge University Press

Schabas, W. A. (2001) *Introduction to the International Criminal Court*, Cambridge: Cambridge University Press

Scheinin, M. (1999) 'The Right to Enjoy a Distinct Culture: Indigenous and Competing Uses of Land' in Orlin, T., Rosas, A. and Scheinin, M. (eds) *The Jurisprudence of Human Rights Law: A Comparative Interpretative Approach*, Institute for Human Rights, Åbo Akademi University, Turku/Åbo

Scheinin, M., Orlin, T. and Rosas, A. (eds) (1999) *The Jurisprudence of Human Rights Law: A Comparative Interpretative Approach*, Institute for Human Rights, Åbo Akademi University, Turku/Åbo

Schiveley, G. R. (2000) 'Negotiation and Native Title: Why Common Law Courts Are Not Proper Fora for Determining Native Land Title Issues', *VJTL* 33: 427

Schulte-Tenckoff, I. (1997) *La Question des Peuples Autochtones*, Brulyant, Paris: L.G.D.J.

Schwarzenberger, G. (1957) 'Title to Territory: Response to a Challenge', *AJIL* 51(2): 308–24

Schwarzenberger, G. (1962) *The Frontiers of International Law*, London: Stevens & Sons

Schwarzenberger, G. (1968) *International Law*, vol. 1, London: Stevens & Son

Shahenn, S. (1956) *The Communist (Bolshevik) Theory of National Self Determination: Its Historical Evolution up to the October Revolution*, The Hague: W. Van Hoeve

Shaw, M. N. (1986) *Title to Territory in Africa*, Oxford: Clarendon Press

Shaw, M. N. (1996) 'The Heritage of States: The Principle of *Uti Possidetis Juris* Today', *BYIL* 67: 75–154

Shaw, M. N. (1997a) *International Law*, 4th edn, Cambridge: Cambridge University Press

Shaw, M. N. (1997b) 'Peoples, Territorialism and Boundaries', *EJIL* 8(3): 478–507

Shelef, L. (1999) *The Future of Tradition, Customary Law, Common Law and Legal Pluralism*, London, Portland: Frank Cass

Sherman, G. E. (1918) '*Jus Gentium* and International Law', *AJIL* 12(1): 56–63

Sherman, G. E. (1921) 'The Nature and Sources of International Law', *AJIL* 15(3): 349–60

Simma *et al.* (eds) (1994) *The Charter of the United Nations Charter – A Commentary*, Oxford: Oxford University Press

Sinclair, I. (1984) *The Vienna Convention on the Law of Treaties*, 2nd edn, Manchester: Manchester University Press

Sinclair, J. D. (1996) *The Law of Marriage*, vol. 1, Cape Town: Juta & Co.

Staruschenko, G. (1965) *The Principle of National Self Determination in Soviet Foreign Policy*, Moscow: Foreign Languages Publishing House

Stavenhagen, R. (1994) 'Indigenous Rights: Some Conceptual Problems', in Assies, W. J. and Hoekema, A. J. (eds) *Indigenous Peoples' Experiences with Self-Government*, Copenhagen: University of Amsterdam: 20

Stead, W. T. (ed.) (1902) *The Last Will and Testament of Cecil J. Rhodes*, London: 'Review of Reviews Office'

Stein, P. (1999) *Roman Law in European History*, Cambridge: Cambridge University Press

Steiner, H. J. and Alston, P. (2000) *International Human Rights In Context: Law, Politics, Morals*, Oxford: Oxford University Press: 773–8

Stojanovic, S. (1996) 'The Destruction of Yugoslavia', *FJIL* 19: 337

Stuyt, A. M. (1972) *Survey of International Arbitrations 1794–1970*, Leiden: Sijthoff

Sullivan, J. L. (1988) *ETA and Basque Nationalism: The Fight for Euskadi 1890–1986*, London: Routledge

Sureda, R. (1973) *The Evolution of the Right to Self-determination: A Study of the United Nations Practice*, Leiden: Sijthoff

Suzuki, E. (1976) 'Self-Determination and World Public Order: A Community Response to Territorial Separation', *Va.J.Int'l* 16: 779–862

Swepston, L. (1998) 'The ILO Indigenous and Tribal Peoples Convention (No. 169): Eight years after Adoption' in Price, C. (ed.) *Human Rights of Indigenous Peoples*, London: Transnational Publishers: 17–36

Talalayev, A. N. and Boyarshinov, V. G. (1961) 'Unequal Treaties: A Mode of Prolonging the Colonial Dependence of the New States in Asia and Africa', *SYIL*: 156–70

Terrett, S. (2000) *The Dissolution of Yugoslavia and the Badinter Arbitration Commission*, Aldershot, UK: Ashgate

Thomas, J. A. C. (1976) *Textbook on Roman Law*, London: North-Holland

Thornberry, P. (1989) 'Self-determination, Minorities, Human Rights: A Review of International Instruments', *ICLQ* 38: 867–89

Thornberry, P. (1991) *International Law and the Rights of Minorities*, Oxford: Clarendon Press

Thornberry, P. (1992) *The Rights of Minorities*, Oxford: Clarendon Press

Thornberry, P. (1994) 'The Democratic or Internal Aspect of Self-determination' in Tomuschat, C. (ed.) *Modern Law of Self-determination*, The Hague: Martinus Nijhoff: 101–38, Oxford: Clarendon Press

Thruston, A. B. (1900) *African Incidents*, London: John Murray

Tierney, S. (ed.) (2000) *Accommodating National Identity: New Directions in National and International Law*, The Hague: Martinus Nijhoff

Tilly, C. (1975) 'Revolutions' in Greenstein, F.I. and Polsby, N.W. (eds) *Handbook of Political Science*, Addison: Wesley

Tilly, C. (1993) *European Revolutions 1492–1992*, Oxford: Blackwell Press

Tomuschat, C. (ed.) (1994) *Modern Law of Self-determination*, The Hague: Martinus Nijhoff

Touval, S. (1966) 'Africa's Frontiers – Reactions to a Colonial Legacy', *IA* 42: 641

Touval, S. (1969) 'The Sources of *Status Quo* and Irrendentist Policies' in Widstrand, C. G. (ed.) *African Boundary Problems*, Uppsala: Scandinavian Institute of African Studies: 101–18

Touval, S. (1972) *The Boundary Politics of Independent Africa*, Cambridge: Harvard University Press

Trifunovska, S. (ed.) (1994) *Yugoslavia Through Documents: From Creation to Dissolution*, Dordrecht; Boston: Martinus Nijhoff Publishers

Triggs, G. (1999) 'Australia's Indigenous Peoples and International Law: Validity of the Native Title Amendment Act 1998 (CTH)', *MULR* 23: 372

Tronvoll, K. (1999) 'Borders of Violence – Boundaries of Identity: Demarcating the Eritrean Nation-State', *ERS* 22: 1037–60

Ülgen, Ö. (2000) 'Aboriginal Title in Canada: Recognition and Reconciliation', *NILR* XLVII (2): 148

Umozurike, U. O. (1979) *International Law and Colonialism in Africa*, Nigeria: Nwamife Publishers

Uzoigwe, G. N. (1976) 'Spheres of Influence and the Doctrine of Hinterland in the Partition of Africa', *Afr.JIL* 3: 183–203

Vallat, F. (1974) First Report on Succession of States in Respect of Treaties, UN DOC. A/CN/.4/278 & Adds 1–6 reprinted in *Year Book of International Law Commission*, vol. 2

Verzijl, J. H. W. (1955) 'Western European Influence on the Foundations of International Law', *IR* : 137–46

Waldock, C. H. G. (1948) 'Disputed Sovereignty in the Falkland Island Dependencies', *BYIL* 25: 311–53

Weller, M. (1992) 'The International Response to the Dissolution of the Federal Republic of Socialist Yugoslavia', *AJIL* 86(3), 569–607

Wessling, H. L. (1996) *Divide and Rule: The Partition of Africa 1880–1914*, London: Praeger

Westlake, J. (1910) *International Law*, vol. 1, Cambridge: Cambridge University Press

Whelan, A. (1994) 'Wilsonian Self-Determination and the Versailles Settlement', *ICLQ* 43: 99–115

Williams, B. (1921) *Cecil Rhodes*, London: Constable

Wilson, R. J. (1998) 'Environmental, Economic, Social, and Cultural Rights of the Indigenous Peoples of Chiapas, Mexico' in Price, C. (ed.) *Human Rights of Indigenous Peoples*, London: Transnational Publishers: 201–34

Woolsey, L. H. (1931) 'Boundary Disputes in Latin America', *AJIL* 25(2): 324–33

Woronoff, J. (1970) *Organising African Unity*, NJ: Scarecrow Press

Wright, Q. (1919) 'The Constitutionality of Treaties', *AJIL* 13(2): 242–66

Wright, Q. (1962) 'The Goa Incident', *AJIL* 56(3): 617–32

Yearbook of the International Law Commission (1974) vol. 2: 196–208

Zoon, I. (2001) *On the Margins: Roma and Public Services in Romania, Bulgaria and Macedonia*, New York: Open Society Institute

Index

260   *Title to Territory in International Law*

Canada 216–20
definition 199–200
and international law 215–16, 233–4
and *terra nullius* 237
UN bodies concerned with 215
Valladolid controversy 202–3
indigenous territories, law 202–5
interdictory proceedings
and possession 38–9
and *vindicatio* 39
International Covenants (1966) 1, 27
international law
autonomy 24
customary
and acquisitory treaties 107–10
and boundaries 114–15
and human rights 172
indigenous land rights 205–14, 227–8
and indigenous peoples 215–16, 233–4
and minorities 176–7
and order 24, 237
origins 8, 31
principles 7
uti possidetis 8, 10–11, 23–4, 229–31
development 13–20
and Yugoslavia 165
international relations, Roman concept 32–3
international society
and Africa 96–8
goals 9
Hedley Bull on 9
meaning 1
international system, *jus gentium* as basis of 33
intertemporal rule 234–5, 236
Inuit, indigenous land rights 226

jus civile
and *jus gentium* 33–9, 41, 55
and legal personality 40
and ownership 34
and the praetor 36
and *uti possidetis* 9, 13–14
jus gentium
as basis of international system 33
Gaius on 39

and Grotius 30, 33
and *jus civile* 33–9, 41, 55
and *jus naturale* 39–40
modern
from *res nullius* 43–4, 54
and Roman property law 42–55, 235
and states 96
and *Pax Romana* 33
private
and foreign nationals 42
Justinian on 42
public and private 29
Roman concept 31–2
theoretical origins 30–3
jus naturale 29, 31
and *jus gentium* 39–40
and territorial acquisition 43
jus praetorium 36
Justinian, on private *jus gentium* 42

Kosovo
sovereignty 27
and *uti possidetis* 20

land
and indigenous peoples 200–1
right to 4, 203–5
territory, distinction 201–2, 207
see also indigenous land rights; territory
Latin America
arbitration 80–4
boundary disputes resolution 63–6, 71, 73–6
confederacy 67, 68
conflict resolution 67, 69, 72–3, 80–4
congresses
Lima (1826) 69
Panama (1847) 68
ethnic diversity 59, 82
and European expansion 67
independence
legal basis 61–2, 230–1, 235
role of Creoles 59–63
sovereignty assertion 67
Spanish withdrawal 7, 11
and *terra nullius* 15, 58, 64–5, 66–74, 77–9, 82–3, 89, 230, 235–6